W9-CIR-303

3 2044 128 578 259

Democracy in Motion

The Kettering Foundation is a nonprofit operating foundation rooted in the American tradition of cooperative research. Established in 1927 by inventor Charles F. Kettering, the foundation is a 501(c)(3) organization that does not make grants but engages in joint research with others. The interpretations and conclusions in this book represent the views of the authors. They do not necessarily reflect the views of the Charles F. Kettering Foundation, its directors, or its officers.

WITHDRAWN

Democracy in Motion

Evaluating the Practice and Impact of Deliberative Civic Engagement

EDITED BY
TINA NABATCHI
JOHN GASTIL
G. MICHAEL WEIKSNER
MATT LEIGHNINGER

OXFORD
UNIVERSITY PRESS

RECEIVED

NOV 26 2012

'ARVARD KENNEDY SCHOOL LIBRAF'

OXFORD
UNIVERSITY PRESS

Oxford University Press is a department of the University of Oxford.
It furthers the University's objective of excellence in research,
scholarship, and education by publishing worldwide.

Oxford   New York
Auckland   Cape Town   Dar es Salaam   Hong Kong   Karachi
Kuala Lumpur   Madrid   Melbourne   Mexico City   Nairobi
New Delhi   Shanghai   Taipei   Toronto

With offices in
Argentina   Austria   Brazil   Chile   Czech Republic   France   Greece
Guatemala   Hungary   Italy   Japan   Poland   Portugal   Singapore
South Korea   Switzerland   Thailand   Turkey   Ukraine   Vietnam

Oxford is a registered trade mark of Oxford University Press in the UK and certain other countries.

Published in the United States of America by Oxford University Press
198 Madison Avenue, New York, NY 10016

© Oxford University Press 2012

All rights reserved. No part of this publication may be reproduced,
stored in a retrieval system, or transmitted, in any form or by any means, without
the prior permission in writing of Oxford University Press, or as expressly
permitted by law, by license, or under terms agreed with the appropriate
reproduction rights organization. Inquiries concerning reproduction outside the
scope of the above should be sent to the Rights Department, Oxford University Press,
at the address above.

You must not circulate this work in any other form and you must impose this
same condition on any acquirer.

Library of Congress Cataloging-in-Publication Data
Democracy in motion : evaluating the practice and impact of deliberative civic
engagement / edited by John Gastil ... [et al.].
     p.   cm.
Includes bibliographical references and index.
ISBN 978-0-19-989926-5 (hardback : alk. paper)—ISBN 978-0-19-989928-9 (pbk. : alk. paper)
1. Political participation. 2. Deliberative democracy. 3. Decision making—Citizen participation.
4. Political planning—Citizen participation. I. Gastil, John.
JF799.D442   2012
323'.042—dc23   2012006947

1 3 5 7 9 8 6 4 2

Printed in the United States of America
on acid-free paper

CONTENTS

ACKNOWLEDGMENTS

The editors would like to thank the Deliberative Democracy Consortium (DDC) and all of the participants at the 2007 DDC Annual Meeting held in Bethesda, Maryland. Their hard work helped identify the questions addressed in this book. We would also like to thank Jason Gilmore, Jessica Prue, and Kyle Doran for their editorial assistance. Finally, we would like to thank the researchers and practitioners listed below, who were instrumental in assisting the chapter authors and editors:

Thomas Bryer: Assistant Professor, University of Central Florida; Director, Center for Public and Nonprofit Management

Kiran Cunningham: Professor of Anthropology and Faculty Fellow with the Arcus Center for Social Justice Leadership, Kalamazoo College

Jacquie Dale: Partner, Founding President, and CEO, One World Inc.; board member of the Canadian Community for Dialogue and Deliberation (C2D2)

John Dedrick: Vice President and Program Director, Charles F. Kettering Foundation

Cynthia Farrar: Research Scholar, Institution for Social and Policy Studies, Yale University

Will Friedman: President, Public Agenda

Joe Goldman: Investment Director at Omidyar Network; formerly Vice President of Citizen Engagement, America*Speaks*

Sandy Heierbacher: Director and Co-Founder, National Coalition for Dialogue and Deliberation (NCDD)

Gail Leftwich Kitch: Chief Operating Office, The Voter Participation Center; formerly Executive Director, By the People, MacNeil/Lehrer Productions

Peter Muhlberger: Director, Center for Communications Research, Texas Tech University

Francesca Polletta: Professor of Sociology, University of California, Irvine

Gloria Rubio-Cortés: President, National Civic League

David Michael Ryfe: Associate Professor of Journalism and Senior Scholar, Reynolds School of Journalism, University of Nevada Reno

Patrick L. Scully: President, Clearview Consulting LLC; Director, Participedia.net

Lars Hasselblad Torres: Innovation Prize Advisor to USAID's Grand Challenges for Development; formerly with the Massachusetts Institute of Technology Global Challenge, and founding researcher for the Democracy Lab for Innovation and Research at America*Speaks*

Mark E. Warren: Harold and Dorrie Merilees Chair for the Study of Democracy, Department of Political Science, University of British Columbia

Miriam Wyman: Principal Consultant, Miriam Wyman & Associates; Coordinating Committee, Alberta Climate Change Dialogue; Co-Founder, Canadian Community for Dialogue and Deliberation (C2D2)

ABOUT THE EDITORS

John Gastil (PhD, University of Wisconsin-Madison, 1994) is a professor in the Department of Communication Arts and Sciences at Penn State University. His books include *The Jury and Democracy* (Oxford, 2010), *The Group in Society* (Sage, 2010), *Political Communication and Deliberation* (Sage, 2008), *By Popular Demand* (University of California, 2000), *Democracy in Small Groups* (New Society Publishers, 1993), and a volume co-edited with Peter Levine, *The Deliberative Democracy Handbook* (Jossey-Bass, 2005). His current projects examine the 2010–2012 Oregon Citizens' Initiative Reviews and the 2009 Australian Citizens' Parliament. John lives in State College, Pennsylvania, with his muse, Cindy Simmons, and their effervescent standard poodle, Toby.

Matt Leighninger is the executive director of the Deliberative Democracy Consortium (DDC), an alliance of the major organizations and leading scholars working in the field of deliberation and public engagement. The DDC represents more than fifty foundations, nonprofit organizations, and universities, collaborating to support research activities and advance democratic practice, in North America and around the world. Over the last eighteen years, Matt has worked with public engagement efforts in over 100 communities, in forty states and four Canadian provinces. Matt is also a senior associate for Everyday Democracy and serves on the boards of E-Democracy.Org, the National School Public Relations Association, and The Democracy Imperative. He has advised a number of foundations and has worked with government agencies and national associations on their public engagement strategies. He has written for numerous publications such as *The Christian Science Monitor*, *The National Civic Review*, *Public Management*, *School Administrator*, and *Nation's Cities Weekly*. His first book, *The Next Form of Democracy: How Expert Rule Is Giving Way to Shared Governance—and Why Politics Will Never Be the Same* (Vanderbilt University Press, 2006), traces the recent shifts in the relationship between citizens and government, and examines how these trends are reshaping our democracy. Matt lives in Hamilton, Ontario, with his wife Pamela Swett and their three children.

Tina Nabatchi (PhD, Indiana University-Bloomington, 2007) is an assistant professor of public administration and international affairs at the Maxwell School of Citizenship and Public Affairs, Syracuse University. Her research focuses on citizen participation, collaborative governance, and conflict resolution. She has published her work in numerous journals such as *Public Administration Review, Journal of Public Administration Research and Theory, American Review of Public Administration, National Civic Review, Conflict Resolution Quarterly,* and the *International Journal of Conflict Management,* as well as in several edited books. Her current research examines the relationships between participatory process design and outcomes. Tina lives in Syracuse, New York, with her cat, Orcus, and travels as often as possible.

G. Michael Weiksner (PhD, Stanford University, 2010) is CEO of TipOrSkip. com and a trustee of e-thePeople.org. He is a student of new patterns of persuasion in online social networks. Based on his research, he founded Tip or Skip, an addictive digital shopping experience. At e-thePeople, he launched an electronic clearinghouse for high-quality election information that partners with media sites and nonprofits like CBS and the League of Women Voters to inform tens of millions of voters. Michael lives outside of New York City with his wife Maria and their four children.

ABOUT THE AUTHORS

Gregory Barrett works for the United Nations Department of Economic and Social Affairs. He previously worked as a researcher on a variety of projects about inequality, social policy, and social accountability. He holds an MSc from the London School of Economics and Political Science.

Laura W. Black (PhD, University of Washington) is an assistant professor in the School of Communication Studies at Ohio University. She studies public deliberation, dialogue, and conflict in small groups and is specifically interested in how personal storytelling functions in public forums. Her research on public meetings, juries, and online communities has appeared in *Communication Theory, Human Communication Research, Journal of Public Deliberation, Small Group Research, Political Communication*, and several edited books.

Reid Chandler is an undergraduate at Stanford University, studying architectural design. He is affiliated with the Stanford Symbolic Systems Program.

Vera Schattan P. Coelho has a PhD in social science. She is the research director of the Brazilian Centre of Analysis and Planning (Cebrap), an interdisciplinary research center located in São Paulo, Brazil, where she also serves as the coordinator of the Citizenship and Development Group. Her interests center on the processes of democratization and development taking place in Brazil and other countries. She has led various comparative studies in the areas of new forms of citizen involvement, deliberation, and consultation to improve social policies and democracy. She is author of numerous articles on health policy, pension reform, and participatory governance, and is editor of *Pension Reform in Latin America* (FGV, 2003), *Participation and Deliberation in Contemporary Brazil* (with Marcos Nobre, 34 Letras 2004), *Spaces for Change?* (with Andrea Cornwall, Zed Books, 2007), and *Mobilizing for Democracy* (with Bettina von Lieres, Zed Books, 2010).

Loren Collingwood is a PhD candidate in political science at the University of Washington. Collingwood's research has appeared in *Political Research Quarterly, American Politics Research, Presidential Studies Quarterly,* and the *Journal of Information Technology and Politics.* Collingwood is a fellow at the Center for American Politics and Public Policy (CAPPP) and the Washington Institute for the Study of Ethnicity, Race, and Sexuality (WISER).

Todd Davies is associate director of the Symbolic Systems Program at Stanford University. He worked as a computer scientist in the Artificial Intelligence Center at SRI International before obtaining a PhD in cognitive psychology at Stanford in 1995. He is the lead designer of Deme, a social Web content management system, and is the co-editor, with Seeta Pena Gangadharan, of *Online Deliberation: Design, Research, and Practice* (CSLI Publications/University of Chicago Press, 2009).

Meghan Kelly recently earned her law degree and master of public administration (MPA) degree from the University of Washington. Her research interests include civic engagement in immigrant communities and the efficacy of self-help legal orientation programs for detained immigrants facing deportation. Her thesis examined the service delivery model of a Los Angeles-based nonprofit that works with noncitizens facing the immigration consequences of criminal activity. She currently practices immigration law, with a focus on serving detained populations.

Bo Kinney recently earned master of public administration (MPA) and master of library and information science (MLIS) degrees at the University of Washington. He is a librarian in the Special Collections department at the Seattle Public Library and is the author of "The Internet, Public Libraries, and the Digital Divide," published in the July 2010 issue of *Public Library Quarterly* and a co-author of the University of Washington/Gates Foundation/IMLS report, *Opportunity for All: How the American Public Benefits from Internet Access at U.S. Libraries.*

Katie Knobloch is an assistant professor and the associate director of the Center for Public Deliberation in the Department of Communication Studies at Colorado State University. She received her PhD from the Department of Communication at the University of Washington. Her research interests include deliberation, civic identity, democratic theory, and civic education. Her current work focuses on evaluating deliberative public events and the impact of deliberative participation on democratic norms.

Heather Pincock is an assistant professor of conflict management in the Department of Political Science and International Affairs at Kennesaw State University. She received her PhD from the Department of Political Science at the Maxwell School of Citizenship and Public Affairs at Syracuse University. Her current research examines the educative effects of deliberation and seeks to bridge the gaps between normative and empirical approaches to the study of deliberative democracy.

Justin Reedy is a doctoral candidate in the Department of Communication at the University of Washington. He studies political communication and group behavior, with a focus on how groups of people make political and civic decisions. His research on political discussion and conversation, media use, and public opinion has appeared in *Political Psychology, University of Colorado Law Review, George Washington Law Review,* and the *Handbook of Internet Politics.*

David Michael Ryfe is an associate professor in the Reynolds School of Journalism, University of Nevada Reno. He has published widely in many areas of political communication, including the practice of deliberative democracy. His current work involves an ethnographic study of newsrooms in major metropolitan American daily newspapers.

Alice Siu is the associate director of the Center for Deliberative Democracy at Stanford University. Alice received her PhD from the Department of Communication at Stanford University, with focus in political communication, deliberative democracy, and public opinion. She received her BA degrees in economics and public policy and MA degree in political science from Stanford University. Alice's research interests in deliberation include what happens inside deliberation, including examining the effects of socioeconomic status in deliberation, the quality of deliberation, and the quality of arguments in deliberation. In addition, her work on deliberative polling in China has been published in *The Search for Deliberative Democracy in China* (Palgrave Macmillan), *Governance Reform under Real-Word Conditions: Citizens, Stakeholders, and Voice* (World Bank), and "Deliberative Democracy in an Unlikely Place: Deliberative Polling in China" (*British Journal of Political Science*).

Brittany Stalsburg is a PhD candidate in political science at Rutgers University. Her research interests include gender and racial stereotypes, candidate self-presentation, and voter evaluation. Brittany's dissertation examines how being a parent matters differently for men and women political candidates. Her research has won numerous awards including the New York Chapter of the American Association for Public Opinion Research (NYAAPOR) Best Paper Award and the Carrie Chapman Catt Prize. In addition to her academic work, she is also a consultant for the Service Women's Action Network (SWAN) in New York City.

Dragan Stanisevski is an assistant professor of public administration and political science at Mississippi State University. His research focuses on issues of multiculturalism and diversity in public administration and public policy, administrative and political theories, theories of democratic governance, and public budgeting and finance. His work has appeared in *Administration & Society*, *Administrative Theory & Praxis*, *Critical Policy Studies*, and *International Journal of Organization Theory and Behavior*.

Miriam Wyman is principal of Miriam Wyman & Associates, a Toronto-based consulting firm specializing in the design and implementation of participatory processes. She has had the good fortune to work at local, national, and international levels to promote dialogue and deliberation in practice and in policy. She has been a member of the Steering Committee of the Deliberative Democracy Consortium (www.deliberative-democracy.net), and the Citizens and Governance Programme Team of the Commonwealth Foundation (www.commonwealthfoundation.com), as well as the Minister's Advisory Committee on Democratic Renewal in the Ontario Office of the Attorney General. She currently facilitates the Citizens Council of the Ontario Ministry of Health and Long Term Care. She holds a master's degree in environmental education, with a special interest in women, health and environment.

EDITORIAL ASSISTANTS

Kyle Doran recently earned a master of public administration (MPA) degree at the Maxwell School of Citizenship and Public Affairs at Syracuse University, where he worked as a graduate assistant for Tina Nabatchi. He also holds bachelor of arts degrees in English and government and law from Lafayette College.

Jason Gilmore is a doctoral candidate in communication at the University of Washington, where he worked for John Gastil. He holds a master of social science and a bachelor of arts degree in international studies from the University of Colorado.

Jessica Prue recently earned a master of public administration (MPA) degree from the Maxwell School of Citizenship and Public Affairs at Syracuse University, where she worked as a graduate assistant for Tina Nabatchi. She also holds a bachelor of science degree in applied economics and management from Cornell University. She currently works for a nonprofit organization in San Francisco.

Democracy in Motion

PART ONE

OVERVIEW

An Introduction to Deliberative Civic Engagement

TINA NABATCHI

The paramount political question today is how spaces can be created in which citizens can discover their capacity to respond to or generate change.

—Hal Saunders, *International Institute for Sustained Dialogue*

Growing numbers of scholars, practitioners, politicians, and civic reformers recognize the power of deliberative civic engagement. In these official or quasi-official processes, lay citizens, often in concert with policy makers and stakeholders, devise solutions to public problems through democratic discussion.[1] Though the principles of public deliberation trace back to the founding documents of the United States, and even to ancient Greece, modern expressions of this ideal have appeared in new constitutions, civic reform programs, and the resolutions of transnational movements and organizations, such as the United Nations Millennium Declaration.

In the past ten years, interest in deliberative civic engagement has grown tremendously (see Chapter 2). Since the mid-1990s, dozens of organizations around the world have committed themselves to understanding and institutionalizing various public deliberation processes and programs. Meanwhile, colleges and universities have established research institutions to study the theory and practice of deliberative civic engagement.[2] This has resulted in thousands of publications, from books and monographs, to primers and research articles, and to project reports and case studies. The field has developed its own peer-reviewed periodical, the *Journal of Public Deliberation*, but deliberative scholarship spans a variety of academic disciplines, from anthropology to engineering and from political science to medicine.

Despite growing interest in deliberative civic engagement, serious debate continues about its benefits and limitations. Disagreement occurs not only among advocates and critics but also among scholars and practitioners who support such work. Some of this stems from different views of where, when, why, and how deliberation should be used. Such divergence of opinion partly reflects a problem in the study of deliberation. Despite a wealth of practice, thinking, and research, work on deliberative civic engagement remains fragmented. It is as if the puzzle pieces have been dumped and scattered on a table, with the box lid showing the picture thrown away.

The fragmentation of work about deliberative civic engagement has at least four causes. First, the research comes from an unusually wide range of academic fields, such as political science, public administration, public policy, anthropology, communication, sociology, conflict resolution, law, urban planning, environmental science, and many others. Second, the work suffers from an "academic-practitioner divide." That is, the lines of communication between scholars and practitioners have been historically weak and have become stronger only recently. Some theoretical work does not adequately take into account the knowledge generated by practice, and many deliberative events lack a research component, or even a reliable empirical evaluation. In short, the disciplines seldom talk with each other, and researchers and practitioners do not always work in concert.

A third issue further complicates the situation: The processes and designs of deliberative civic engagement vary widely across many salient dimensions, including the participants in deliberation, the way participants exchange information and make decisions, the link between the deliberations and policy or public action, and the point of connection to the policy process.[3] Though it is beyond the scope of this chapter to consider all the different deliberative designs, for purposes of illustration, simply consider that deliberative civic engagement processes differ in these ways:

- *Purpose.* Some processes are designed principally to explore an issue and generate understanding (e.g., Conversation Cafés, Wisdom Circles, and Open Space), whereas other processes are designed to resolve conflicts, foster healing, and improve group relations (e.g., Sustained or Intergroup Dialogues, Compassionate Listening, and Public Conversations Project dialogues), foster collaborative action (e.g., Future Searches and Appreciative Inquiry), or help make decisions on policy issues (e.g., National Issues Forums, Deliberative Polling, Citizen Choicework, and 21st Century Town Meetings).[4]
- *Convener.* Some processes are convened by an individual group or organization or by a consortium of interested groups and organizations. Others are convened by one or more administrative officials representing one or more government agencies. Still others are convened by one or more elected officials.

- *Deliberative Methodology.* Some deliberative processes have official names and may even be trademarked; however, many other processes do not use branded methodologies at all or use hybrids thereof. Most operate by the same general principles, but the events convened under the deliberative flag range from short discussions to intimate dialogues to complex multi-stage decision-making processes (see Chapter 2).
- *Locus of Action.* Some processes are conducted with intended actions and outcomes within an organization or social network, whereas others seek actions and outcomes for a neighborhood or community, a municipality, state, or nation. Some even occur at the international level.
- *Connection to Policy Process.* Some processes are designed with explicit links to policy and decision makers. Others have no such connection and instead seek to engender changes in individual attitudes or behavior or to spur collective action.

This tremendous diversity of deliberative civic engagement processes means that practitioners and researchers sometimes struggle to know and understand what works when, where, why, and how. It remains a challenge to draw theoretical and empirical connections from specific design features to concrete outcomes.

Finally, it is important to understand that deliberative civic engagement is taking place around the world, from America to Zimbabwe, at all levels of government, and across the public, private, and nonprofit or nongovernmental spheres. Keeping track of all these deliberative processes and outcomes (even for the same type of process, let alone different processes) would be a daunting and time-consuming challenge for even the most tireless and well-staffed research team.[5]

If nothing else, it should be clear that work in public deliberation is historic and current, inherently multi- and inter-disciplinary, oriented toward both theory and practice, incredibly diverse, and international in scope. This makes it all but impossible for those interested in deliberative civic engagement to read, process, synthesize, comprehend, and use the full literature, let alone access the accumulated body of practical knowledge as yet unpublished. Prompted by our desire to put the puzzle together and understand the big picture of deliberative civic engagement, this edited volume represents an effort to systematically and comprehensively compile what we know about the subject. Such work is particularly important now because deliberative civic engagement processes, when properly understood and implemented, can help address effectively the most complex social, political, and economic challenges of our time.

The problem of fragmentation and the need for synthesizing knowledge emerged as a clear concern at the 2007 Deliberative Democracy Consortium

(DDC) conference in Bethesda, Maryland, where scholars and practitioners from around the world gathered in what was itself a deliberative event. Participants questioned what we currently know from published scholarly work and less well circulated project reports, and attendees confessed difficulty accessing— let alone absorbing—the full body of extant knowledge about deliberative civic engagement.

We collected and examined the notes from the two-day conference and distilled a list of the "big questions" of public deliberation. We then circulated this list among expert practitioners and academics, and eventually reached a broad consensus. Teams of graduate students, researchers, and practitioners conducted a guided scan of the literature across disciplines, geographic boundaries, and deliberative processes to integrate the current research and answer these big questions. Our goal was to create a concise, yet comprehensive, summary of what we know, how we know it, and what remains to be learned.

This book is the result of that effort. More than a simple summary of research, it represents the most comprehensive assessment of deliberative civic engagement available, and each chapter makes substantial contributions to our scholarly and practical understanding of deliberation. In doing so, it significantly enhances current scholarship, and it suggests possibilities for more and better evaluations of deliberative civic engagement in the future.

Democracy in Motion will help civic reformers and public officials think through design issues and articulate desired outcomes, thus enabling them to garner more support for public deliberation. By identifying what remains to be learned about public deliberation, the book may inspire practitioners and public officials to connect with scholars to conduct research and evaluations of their efforts, as has occurred in the city-academy partnership embodied in the Edmonton Centre for Public Involvement.

Deliberative Civic Engagement

Before discussing the chapters and the "big question" each addresses, we back up one step to define deliberative civic engagement and examine its goals and potential outcomes.

To explain what we mean by *deliberative civic engagement*, we find it useful to break the term into two components. First, *deliberative* refers to a process characterized by *deliberation*, or the thoughtful and reasoned consideration of information, views, experiences, and ideas among a group of individuals. (For more discussion about communication during deliberation, see Chapter 4.) Though individuals often "deliberate" internally about an issue of personal concern, deliberation within the context of this book refers to a particular type of communication among groups, wherein people "carefully examine a problem and arrive at a well-reasoned solution after a period of inclusive, respectful consideration of diverse points of view."[6]

More specifically, deliberation requires that a diverse group of participants take part in an open and accessible process of reasoned discussion during which they "reflect carefully on a matter, [weigh] the strengths and weaknesses of alternative solutions to a problem [and] aim to arrive at a decision or judgment based on not only facts and data but also values, emotions, and other less technical considerations."[7] To qualify as a democratic social process, deliberation must also ensure that all participants receive an adequate opportunity to speak, fulfill an obligation to listen attentively and consider carefully the contributions of other participants, and treat each other with respect.[8]

Second, *civic engagement* "means working to make a difference in the civic life of our communities and developing the combination of knowledge, skills, values, and motivation to make that difference. It means promoting the quality of life in a community, through both political and nonpolitical processes."[9] Civic engagement can happen in many places and take different forms—from individual volunteering to voting, and from identifying community problems to taking collective action, among others. At the heart of civic engagement lies the belief that "a morally and civically responsible individual recognizes himself or herself as a member of a larger social fabric and therefore considers social problems to be at least partly his or her own; such an individual is willing to see the moral and civic dimensions of issues, to make and justify informed moral and civic judgments, and to take action when appropriate."[10] In short, civic engagement involves forging connections "among citizens, issues, institutions, and the political system. It implies voice and agency, a feeling of power and effectiveness, with real opportunities to have a say. It implies active participation, with real opportunities to make a difference."[11]

When these terms are joined, *deliberative civic engagement* denotes processes that enable citizens, civic leaders, and government officials to come together in public spaces where they can engage in constructive, informed, and decisive dialogue about important public issues. A public, private, nonprofit, or nongovernmental organization can organize such processes, all of which aim to foster respectful communication among a diverse group of citizens, public officials, civic leaders, and others. Each process engages one or more public issues, with the ultimate goal of participants either understanding or directly addressing those common concerns. Deliberative civic engagement can take place face-to-face or online (see Chapter 6), and considerable thought must be given to the recruitment of participants (see Chapters 3 and 5).

Deliberative civic engagement is but one of many forms of *public participation,* an even broader term that encompasses various ways of involving citizens not just in formal institutions but also in the broader process of democratic self-governance. This includes events, meetings, and processes that are far less structured and do not use deliberation as the primary means of communication.[12]

Complicating matters further, scholars and practitioners use many other related terms to capture the ideas of deliberative civic engagement. These concepts overlap and are often used synonymously. For the sake of comparison, I offer the following definitions:

- *Group or intergroup dialogue* is a facilitated group experience that provides people with a safe and structured opportunity to explore attitudes about divisive social issues.[13]
- *Public dialogue* is another kind of talk, distinguished from deliberation because it focuses more on mutual understanding and has less emphasis on analytic rigor and decision making.[14]
- *Public deliberation* is a particular kind of talk done by the public about public issues that involves rigorous problem analysis with an eye toward finding agreeable high-quality solutions.[15]
- *Democratic deliberation* is public deliberation with more explicit requirements for egalitarian social relations and democratic decision making.[16]
- *Deliberative democracy* is a particular model of democracy in which public deliberation is embedded in institutions, norms, and practices.[17]
- *Discursive democracy* is closely related to deliberative democracy, but emphasizes the character of discourse (how we talk and with whom) at all levels in a society, as well as the flow of argument and reason through larger social processes, rather than focusing on the design of particular deliberative arrangements.[18]

In spite of their technical and procedural differences, all of these approaches can fit under the deliberative civic engagement umbrella because they share a common denominator—respectful and rigorous communication about public problems. Because all of these approaches center on such talk, they entail processes that generally proceed through—or at least contribute to—the following (often iterative) steps:[19]

1. The creation of a solid information base about the nature of the problem at hand, often beginning with storytelling and the sharing of personal experiences;
2. The identification, weighing, and prioritization of the key values at stake in an issue;
3. The identification of a broad range of potential solutions to the problem;
4. The weighing of the pros, cons, and trade-offs of the solutions through the systematic application of relevant knowledge and values to each alternative;

5. The arrival at the best decision(s) possible in light of what was learned through deliberation (if in a decision-making body), or the arrival at independent judgment(s) (if not in a decision-making body).[20] This is sometimes followed by an action planning process that allows participants to decide how they can help implement the ideas and recommendations they have generated.

Advocates for deliberative civic engagement generally deploy two broad rationales.[21] Many point to the *intrinsic* value of democracy and assert that deliberation and civic participation are ends in themselves and should be judged as such regardless of their other potential benefits. Numerous scholars look to the work of German social theorist Jürgen Habermas as the theoretical source of moral (i.e., "normative") arguments for deliberation. Habermas calls for the extension of participation and inclusion in democracy through deliberation as a remedy for the power inequalities present in communication among and between decision makers and the public.[22] In this view, deliberative civic engagement is an end that stands apart—and should be judged separately—from other benefits such processes might produce.

Beyond the intrinsic benefits of deliberative civic engagement, scholars and practitioners also point to its *instrumental* benefits for individuals, communities, government institutions, and the broader processes of governance and policymaking. For the individuals who take part, deliberative civic engagement may have many benefits, particularly civic educational effects (see Chapter 7).[23] Advocates assert that deliberation can help cultivate skills such as rhetorical expression, eloquence, empathy, courtesy, imagination, and reasoning ability. Through the active and reflective exchange of ideas and perspectives, participants can help clarify, understand, and refine their own positions on public issues. Even if their preferences do not change, deliberation can foster greater mutual understanding or at least tolerance among persons with divergent views. Because people deliberating together often think beyond their own self-interest, the experience can yield greater empathy for the wider community. Moreover, deliberative civic engagement is expected to improve participants' civic skills and dispositions, particularly in terms of political efficacy, sophistication, interest, trust, and public-spiritedness.[24]

Advocates also assert that deliberative civic engagement can help build the capacity of communities (whether they be geographic, political, social, or defined in some other way) to understand and address the most important issues they face (see Chapter 8). Deliberative civic engagement is purported to build a sense of community, thereby supporting the commitment and ability to solve problems through increased access to resources of all types. Moreover, such engagement is believed to cultivate leadership, increase organizational development, promote community organizing, and foster collaboration.

Finally, advocates argue that public deliberation results in better policy decisions (see Chapter 9), which can help improve government institutions and the quality of governance.[25] Because deliberation deemphasizes the aggregation of interests and crude bargaining among preestablished preferences, it can reveal private information, lessen or overcome the impacts of bounded rationality, force the public justification of private demands, and increase policy consensus.[26] This can give effective voice to weaker political groups and opinion minorities, break cycles of political inequality, improve the justice of decisions, legitimize the ultimate choice, and yield superior decisions.[27] The generation of legitimate outcomes may also lead to longer-term support of policy implementation and generally improve the effectiveness of public action.[28]

Not all scholars agree that public deliberation has such benefits, and Chapter 11 addresses the strongest critiques. On a practical note, some critics point to the high transaction costs for participants in deliberative forums and suggest that these costs may outweigh any potential benefits. For citizens, such costs may include time, money (e.g., lost wages or child or elder care costs), and the forgoing of preferable activities.[29] For government officials and decision makers, the most notable costs include money and time[30] and the ability to broker policy compromises and satisfy diverse demands.[31] Some critics assert that public deliberation can increase citizens' frustration and sense of powerlessness,[32] and other critics raise the possibility of co-optation by more powerful groups or interests.[33] It is important to note, however, that part of the reason that advocates and critics of deliberation do not see eye-to-eye is because they often employ mismatched definitions. That is, many critics are not examining the kinds of deliberative civic engagement processes that advocates support. Consequently, evaluation efforts have been able to shed little light on these (and other) issues (see Chapters 10 and 12). Nevertheless, these debates, and the questions they raise, are the inspiration for this volume.

Overview of the Book

Each chapter addresses a "big question" about deliberative civic engagement. The chapter authors, aided by researcher and practitioner support teams, reviewed both published and unpublished writings across disciplines, settings, locations, and processes to assess what we know, how we know it, and what we do not yet know about these big questions.

Part I is a primer for the rest of the book. It provides a broad overview of deliberative civic engagement and prepares readers for what comes in later chapters. In Chapter 2, "Mapping Deliberative Civic Engagement: Pictures from a (R)evolution," Matt Leighninger examines the questions, *What organizations are doing work related to deliberative civic engagement and what type of work are they doing?* Specifically, Leighninger contextualizes the theory and practice of deliberative civic engagement and explores the "what, who, when, why, and where" of this work. He asserts that growing interest in deliberative civic engagement is driven by a confluence of forces: the new political, social, and economic conditions facing public leaders and managers; shifts in the expectations and capacities of ordinary people; and the realization that the old ways of dealing with public problems no longer work. In short, deliberative civic engagement provides a potential solution to the varied and complex problems and challenges faced today. In his attempt to "map the field," Leighninger finds a patchwork of experiments and adaptations. These have some emergent general principles but no clear imprint of central planning or leadership. Rather than treating deliberative civic engagement as a "new idea" for the betterment of society, he argues that we should think of it as part of the ongoing development and evolution of democracy.

Part II introduces the reader to process and design questions central to deliberative civic engagement. In Chapter 3, "The Participation and Recruitment Challenge," David Michael Ryfe and Brittany Stalsburg examine the question, *Who participates in deliberative civic engagement initiatives?* They concede that we know little about this question given the dearth of research in this area, but they root through a vast body of scholarship about participation in other political and civic activities, such as voluntarism, social movements, and voting. They find that public participation increases when, from the perspective of the individual, its material and symbolic costs are lowered, and/or its benefits are increased. The authors identify a number of factors that influence participation, including socioeconomic status, education, ideological intensity, and membership in various social networks. Finally, they examine several recruitment strategies that may enable organizers to assemble a broad and diverse group of participants in deliberative civic engagement events.

In Chapter 4, "How People Communicate during Deliberative Events," Laura Black explores the question, *What do we know about how people actually communicate during deliberative civic engagement events?* Black finds that surprisingly little research has been done to systematically examine the discursive practices of citizens as they communicate with one another in a deliberative forum; rather, most scholarly literature tends to offer theoretical models of ideal public deliberation or empirical assessments about the effects of participation in such events. She argues that a better understanding of how people actually communicate during deliberative civic engagement events can improve both practice and research. To that end, Black reviews the observations of deliberative scholars and practitioners about communication during deliberation, and she describes the key features that characterize deliberative practice as it occurs in some of the more prominent types of events. The bulk of the chapter provides a review of the research that investigates communication during deliberative civic engagement and explores the extent to which research findings connect with the scholarly conceptions of deliberation. She concludes by discussing implications for deliberative research and practice.

In Chapter 5, "Deliberation in Multicultural Societies: Addressing Inequality, Exclusion, and Marginalization," Alice Siu and Dragan Stanisevski address the questions, *How can we foster greater inclusion of culturally diverse participants in intercultural deliberative civic engagement? And how can we enable deliberative civic engagement across cultural differences?* To that end, their chapter provides insights into the deliberative experiences of diverse participants and the effectiveness of various strategies used to alleviate inequalities, marginalization, and other obstacles in deliberative processes, such as the mandatory inclusion of diverse groups, providing adequate information to participants, using moderators, adhering to standards of deliberative reciprocity, using alternative modes of communication, and providing opportunity for consensual and concurrent decision making. Though citizens rarely remain color-blind, objective, or impartial, Siu and Stanisevski suggest that by using these and other strategies, citizens can transcend racial or other cultural divisions to discover mutual respect, or even common ground.

Chapter 6, "Online Deliberation Design: Choices, Criteria, and Evidence," rounds out Part II of the book. In it Todd Davies and Reid Chandler explore the questions, *How do we design deliberative e-democracy forums in the light of both available and prospective information/communication technologies? And how does online deliberative civic engagement differ from face-to-face deliberative civic engagement in terms of both process and outcomes?* They assert that the evolution of information and communication technologies provides alternatives for public interaction and information exchange. In turn, this generates new opportunities and choices for the creation of online deliberative civic engagement processes. In the first half of the chapter, Davies and Chandler discuss several categories of design decisions that organizers of an online deliberative forum must address. In the second half of the chapter, the authors review empirical findings related to each dimension. They find that although there is a large volume of literature suggesting guidelines for online deliberative designs, there is too little research that connects these design choices to outcomes. Nevertheless, they glean from the available theory and research important lessons for designers of online engagement.

Part III examines another set of issues integral to deliberative civic engagement—the impacts, outcomes, and evaluation of such processes. In Chapter 7, "Does Deliberation Make Better Citizens?" Heather Pincock seeks to answer the question, *What are the educative effects of deliberation on participants?* She begins by articulating a central truth about democracy: Conflict is an essential and regular feature of democratic life, and citizens need civic skills and dispositions to effectively cope with and address controversies. Pincock notes that participatory and deliberative democrats have long made claims about the educative potential of participation, and specifically deliberative participation. Pincock then discusses the educative assumptions embedded in participatory and deliberative theory, noting that "better citizen" claims have received relatively limited analytical attention, despite the fact that such claims form a recurring normative justification for using such processes. Next, she examines the empirical literature for evidence that deliberation makes better citizens. She finds support for the educative effects of deliberation, but also notes that research is limited both by the way it conceptualizes educative effects and by the empirical contexts in which it tends to focus. As a result, neither are the skeptics convinced nor the advocates vindicated in claims about the educative effects of deliberation.

In Chapter 8, "Deliberation's Contribution to Community Capacity Building," Bo Kinney explores the question, *How does deliberative civic engagement contribute to community capacity building?* He asserts that one justification for the greater use of deliberative civic engagement is that it can help remedy the declining health of communities by, among other things, fostering and strengthening civic infrastructure, social capital, and the general ability of communities to address effectively the problems they face. He notes, however, that "community building" and "community capacity" are conceptually fuzzy and challenging to operationalize, making it difficult to evaluate the community-level impacts of deliberative civic engagement. To address this problem, Kinney introduces the Community Capacity Building framework,[34] which breaks down the notion of community capacity into several more manageable (and observable) elements. He then reviews the relevant empirical literature about the elements in this framework, finding that although evidence supports the claim that deliberation enhances community capacity, there is a significant lack of systematic research on *how* this happens. Nevertheless, Kinney asserts that the Community Capacity Building framework provides a useful operationalization of community capacity, and offers a starting point for future research on this issue.

In Chapter 9, "Assessing the Policy Impacts of Deliberative Civic Engagement: Comparing Engagement in the Health Policy Processes of Brazil and Canada," Gregory Barrett, Miriam Wyman, and Vera Schattan Coehlo address the questions, *What is the relationship between deliberation and the public policy process? And what is the impact of deliberative civic engagement on policy making?* These authors look to a growing number of recent studies that explore how deliberative civic engagement experiments improve the inputs and outcomes of both policy-making processes and policies themselves. The authors begin with a conceptual discussion about the link between deliberation and policy processes. They examine the role citizen participation can play in policy making, outline its presumed policy impacts, and summarize the challenges and difficulties associated with assessing such impacts. Next, the authors present examples from across a spectrum of deliberative civic engagement processes and policy areas, followed by two in-depth case studies of deliberative public involvement in the health policy processes of Brazil (with a focus on local health councils addressing local problems) and Canada (with a focus on a national consultation concerning a policy response to an ethical problem). Though the cases are quite different in context, both shed light on the kinds of policy proposals generated by deliberative civic engagement, as well as the degree to which such proposals are incorporated into final policy decisions. They then turn to questions regarding the legitimacy of these cases by comparing the features of the participants involved, the dynamics of decision making, and the nature of the issues under discussion. The authors conclude by discussing potential trade-offs between giving the lay public greater say in policy versus maintaining high standards of technical input and formal political representation.

Part III ends with Chapter 10, "Evaluating Deliberative Public Events and Projects," in which John Gastil, Katie Knobloch, and Meghan Kelly explore the question, *What research designs and evaluation methods are used to assess the processes and outcomes of deliberative projects and programs?* With growing numbers of agencies and organizations turning to deliberative civic engagement, evaluation methods must be taken more seriously. The systematic and comprehensive evaluation of different deliberative processes requires overcoming a disagreement about appropriate research methods. Accordingly, the authors assert that to improve our understanding of the strengths, weaknesses, and varied impacts of deliberative civic engagement projects, the field must begin to evaluate more carefully the design, processes, and outcomes of such activities. To that end, Gastil, Knobloch, and Kelly first review the purposes and pitfalls of evaluation to clarify why and how it should be done. Next, they look to theory, research, and practice to identify and propose a set of four general evaluation categories (each with specific sub-elements), including design integrity, democratic deliberation and judgment, influence, and long-term effects. The authors suggest measurement approaches for each criterion that can be combined to produce robust evaluations with any size research budget.

Part IV, the final section of the book, contains two chapters that draw together the work in the previous sections and look to the future. In Chapter 11, "Listening and Responding to Criticisms of Deliberative Civic Engagement," Loren Collingwood and Justin Reedy address the questions, *What are the critics' views on deliberative civic engagement, and given what we know, what, if any, are the most persuasive counterarguments?* Looking to the previous chapters in the volume, Collingwood and Reedy note that deliberative civic engagement can have advantages over some other systems of governance, such as deeper involvement by citizens, thoughtful and reasoned debate of issues, respect for diverse viewpoints, and stronger policy decisions that have greater democratic legitimacy, among others. Despite these benefits, however, several criticisms are leveled against such processes. In particular, Collingwood and Reedy discuss two sets of related issues. First, they address numerous theoretical concerns about deliberative civic engagement, including citizen motivation and aptitude, idealism, deliberation as reason-based argumentation, and cognition and open-mindedness. Next, they discuss several practical concerns, including models of deliberation, the ability to represent diverse viewpoints, public policy outcomes, and individual benefits from deliberation. For each set of criticisms, they discuss not only the literature supporting those concerns, but also the theoretical and empirical rebuttals. In doing so, they identify areas where additional clarification and research are needed. When taken as a whole, this chapter provides a wider perspective on the potential drawbacks of deliberative civic engagement, as well as its prospective advantages in producing effective, legitimate policy, and helping citizens become better connected to governance.

The book concludes with Chapter 12, "Advancing the Theory and Practice of Deliberative Civic Engagement: A Secular Hymnal." In this last chapter, this volume's editors address two final questions, *How should the findings in the previous chapters influence the practice and study of deliberative civic engagement? And what should be the agenda for the future?* The editors begin by drawing together the main findings, themes, and observations about the big questions of deliberative civic engagement addressed throughout the book. Next, they critically examine some nagging uncertainties about deliberative civic engagement and discuss unresolved questions implicit in the previous chapters. Finally, they suggest how scholars, practitioners, and others can advance the practice and study of deliberative civic engagement.

I began this introduction by noting the growing interest in deliberative civic engagement around the world. As should now be apparent, scholarly and practical knowledge about this form of engagement needs to catch up with the pace of civic experimentation. Those who wish to expand and refine deliberative processes in coming years can do so effectively only by pooling their collective experience and academic knowledge. That goal animates *Democracy in Motion*, and the editors of this volume hope that each of the following chapters offers insight about how to infuse modern democracy with more diverse voices, more engaged citizens, and more deliberative politics.

Notes

1. This definition is adapted from Gastil (2008).
2. American scholars and politicians have also called for widespread governmental changes to institutionalize deliberation in national politics. For example, Ackerman and Fishkin (2004) proposed Deliberation Day, a new national holiday for each presidential election year when citizens throughout the country would deliberate in public spaces about issues that divide the candidates. Similarly, Leib (2004) proposed an institutional design to embed the practice of deliberation in the United States by integrating a "popular" branch of government into the existing federal structure. Similarly, former presidential candidate John Edwards called for the creation of "Citizen Congresses" through which millions of Americans nationwide would periodically participate in deliberations about critical policy issues. More recently, President Barack Obama issued the Open Government Memorandum, which calls for more public participation, collaboration, and transparency in federal policy making.
3. Bingham, Nabatchi, and O'Leary (2005); Fung (2006).
4. See National Coalition for Dialogue and Deliberation (2008) for a framework explaining different goals for dialogue and deliberation processes.
5. www.participedia.net is a project aimed at cataloguing these different events and processes, but it remains in an early stage of development.
6. Gastil (2008: 8); see also Burkhalter, Gastil, and Kelshaw (2002). On "deliberation within," see Goodin (2003).
7. Gastil (2005: 164).
8. Gastil (2008: 9–10).
9. Ehrlich (2000: vi).
10. Ehrlich (2000: xxvi).
11. McCoy and Scully (2002: 118).
12. Creighton (2005).
13. Pearce and Littlejohn (1997).
14. Bojer, Roehl, Knuth, and Magner (2008).
15. Mathews (1994); see also Gastil and Levine (2005).
16. Gastil (2008).
17. Gutmann and Thompson (2004). It is important to note that many advocates use deliberative civic engagement and deliberative democracy synonymously, arguing that they want to "embed" or institutionalize such practices in the work of government, thus changing the institutions of governance. For a discussion within the realm of public administration, see Nabatchi (2010a).
18. Dryzek (1990).
19. These steps can be traced back to philosopher John Dewey's model of reasoning in *How We Think* (1910).
20. Gastil (2008: 9). Sometimes people are focused on a single decision or judgment. Other times, they have several decisions or judgments to make, or they are making decisions or judgments about personal attitudes, behaviors, and actions.
21. See Nabatchi (2010a).
22. Habermas (1975, 1984).
23. See, for example, Elster (1998), Mansbridge (1995), and Pateman (1970).
24. Luskin and Fishkin (2003).
25. See, for example, Elster (1998), Gutmann and Thompson (1996, 2004), and Young (2000).
26. Elster (1998).
27. Elster (1998); Fung (2003, 2005); Gutmann and Thompson (1996, 2004).
28. Fung (2005).

29. Rydin and Pennington (2000).
30. Irvin and Stansbury (2004).
31. Sunstein (2003).
32. See, for example, Hibbing and Theiss-Morse (2002).
33. See, for example, Arnstein (1969) and Young (2003).
34. Chaskin, Brown, Venkatesh, and Vidal (2001).

Mapping Deliberative Civic Engagement

Pictures from a (R)evolution

MATT LEIGHNINGER

What drove me to try structured, planned public engagement was my
awful experience with unstructured, unplanned public engagement.
—John Nalbandian, *University of Kansas, and former mayor of
Lawrence, Kansas*

It is easy to miss or misunderstand the growth of deliberative civic engagement.
Some of its advocates treat it merely as a hoped-for outcome, a perpetual vision
of the future rather than something that is happening in the here-and-now.
Others are so caught up in the "trees" they are familiar with—various models,
organizations, or subsets of the field—that they have no sense of the forest. Still
others are betrayed by the fuzzy language of the civic sphere; they know only
one term (*public engagement, deliberative democracy*, or *citizen participation*), and
they fail to see parallels between their own work and efforts carried out under
different labels.

In fact, deliberative civic engagement is proliferating dramatically. This
growth is driven by the new political conditions facing leaders and managers,
and by shifts in the expectations and capacities of ordinary people.[1] In many situations, the old ways of dealing with public problems no longer work, and deliberative processes emerge as a potential solution. Because these problems and
challenges are so varied, the practice of deliberative civic engagement is diverse
and diffuse, and it deviates from theorists' visions. The result is a patchwork of
experiments and adaptations, with some emergent general principles but no
clear imprint of central planning or leadership. Rather than treating deliberative
civic engagement as a "new idea" for the betterment of society,[2] we should think
of it as part of the ongoing development of democracy. It is at least one prominent
response to the factors shaping that evolution.[3]

This chapter contextualizes the theory and practice of deliberative civic engagement by asking and answering the questions, *What organizations are doing work related to deliberative civic engagement and what type of work are they doing?* Specifically, this chapter provides a broad overview of the what, who, when, why, and where of this work. Though the amount of empirical research on these questions still lags far behind the practice, much can be learned from the conferences, activities, and connections fostered by the Deliberative Democracy Consortium and other key networks in the field.[4]

What Do We Mean by *Deliberative Civic Engagement*?

Unwieldy terms like *deliberative civic engagement* are among the main reasons that such practices continue to fly under the radar.[5] Among academics, deliberative democracy is a relatively well-known idea, and labels like public *engagement, participation,* and *involvement* have some currency among practitioners and (to some extent) public officials. But none of these terms appears to resonate with everyday citizens, and such jargon rarely appears in front-page discussions of politics or policy. Deliberative civic engagement may be moving forward, but it is not a movement.[6]

In practice, successful deliberative civic engagement initiatives tend to have four key characteristics:

1. They assemble a large and diverse "critical mass" of citizens (or in some cases, a smaller, demographically representative set of people intended to serve as a proxy for the larger population).
2. They involve those citizens in structured, facilitated small-group discussions, punctuated by large forums for amplifying shared conclusions and moving from talk to action. These have traditionally been face-to-face meetings, but increasingly they are being held online, or online tools are being used to inform and complement face-to-face discussions.
3. They give participants in these meetings the opportunity to compare values and experiences, and to consider a range of policy options and relevant arguments and information. This is the deliberative heart of the work, allowing a diverse group of people to decide together what they think should be done about a shared concern.
4. These activities aim to produce tangible actions and outcomes. Some efforts focus on applying citizen input to policy and planning decisions, whereas others seek change within organizations and institutions or in public attitudes and behaviors.[7]

The original visions of deliberative democracy put forward by German social theorist Jürgen Habermas and others principally concerned how citizens might communicate with one another.[8] And yet here too, the reality has diverged somewhat from the vision: These discussions typically feature personal experiences, storytelling, passion, and conflict, in addition to fully formed and "reasoned" arguments.[9] Deliberative civic engagement proves emotional, cathartic, and complex as much as it can be rational, an insight that many modern theorists acknowledge.[10]

As noted in the introductory chapter, deliberative civic engagement overlaps many other commonly used terms, such as *public engagement, democratic governance, citizen participation, participatory democracy, civic engagement, public involvement, citizen-centered work, public work,* and *public deliberation.*[11] The advocates, practitioners, researchers, and local leaders who use these terms rarely define them clearly, yet when one examines the projects and initiatives they uphold as illustrations of what they mean, the same four characteristics listed previously usually appear.

Meanwhile, many civic innovators are local leaders who do not identify with any of these terms; they are often simply unaware of them, let alone the larger fields of practice. In their attempts to engage citizens in more productive ways, they essentially reinvent the wheel, and the four listed characteristics represent the wheel they usually reinvent.[12]

Finally, as the practice of community organizing diversified and evolved over the last thirty years, these four characteristics became increasingly apparent in that work.[13] Some observers would even flip this script to argue that deliberative civic engagement grew out of community organizing. Regardless of who claims credit for the terms and philosophies, it is important to give expediency its due. Community organizers, just like other local leaders, have found that in some situations, projects following these four principles help them accomplish their goals.

Having emphasized the similarities across variously named civic practices, one particular point of divergence warrants emphasis. Some projects aim to mobilize a diverse, broadly representative "critical mass" of participants, whereas others use random digit dialing (and other techniques borrowed from opinion polling) to assemble a smaller, more representative sample of citizens (see Chapter 3).[14]

Critical mass projects work toward several goals: influencing public officials by involving large numbers of voters; maximizing the possibility of nongovernmental action by bringing more problem solvers to the table; and providing the individual benefits of deliberative civic engagement to the widest possible number of people. They also reflect the idea that no one should be turned away from participating in public life.

Random sample projects assume that when ordinary people deliberate, they provide policy input uniquely valuable to public officials. The notion of "representativeness" is sacrosanct in these efforts; random-sample advocates worry that projects open to all comers may dilute or diminish the voices of those people generally less likely to participate, or less likely to have their own pre-set agenda. Though these two types of projects have often occurred in isolation from one another, there is growing agreement within the field that each has strengths and weaknesses. Thus, critical mass and random sample approaches should be considered complementary components of broader strategies.[15]

Who Are the Deliberative Democrats?

Though the number of people who use terms like *deliberative civic engagement* may be small, the number of people initiating, organizing, facilitating, or researching such engagement is much larger, more heterogeneous, and on the rise. The biggest subset of this group consists of the leaders and managers who initiate (and in many cases organize and facilitate) these projects. They are sometimes assisted by a second subset—practitioners working either as solo consultants, in nonprofit organizations, or in a growing number of for-profit consulting firms that have added deliberative democracy to their portfolio.[16] Academic researchers, who sometimes provide technical assistance and project leadership in addition to their traditional role of research/evaluation, make up the third subset.

There have been hundreds and perhaps thousands of these efforts launched in the last twenty years.[17] The vast majority have been local efforts initiated by local leaders. These leaders include mayors, city council members, city managers, employees of community foundations, human relations commissioners, nonprofit directors, planners, leaders of interfaith groups, policy practitioners, community organizers, school superintendents and school board members, school communications officers, police chiefs, librarians, youth program directors, members of the League of Women Voters, neighborhood association presidents, real estate agents, employees of university Cooperative Extension services, active recent retirees, and policy advocates. Some of these people bring the perspective of grassroots organizations and citizen groups that try to affect government and policy making from the bottom up, while others are government officials and other decision makers who want to reach citizens from the top down.[18]

Though less numerous than their local counterparts, some leaders and managers at the state and federal level have initiated deliberative civic engagement efforts. They include managers within federal agencies, particularly the

Environmental Protection Agency (EPA) and the Centers for Disease Control and Prevention (CDC), as well as people working for national issue-focused nonprofit organizations. Recent examples include the CDC's National Conversation on Chemical Exposures, the Community Action for a Renewed Environment program of the EPA, and the Citizen's Initiative Review, which the Oregon state legislature established as part of its electoral process in 2009.[19]

These local, state, and federal leaders often work with deliberation practitioners (or to use Will Friedman's term, *democratic entrepreneurs*) typically based in small nonprofit organizations.[20] These practitioners come to the work from a range of professional backgrounds, having started out as planners, public administrators, organizational development consultants, pollsters, psychiatrists or therapists, human rights activists, journalists, experts in race and race relations, mediators, community organizers, political theorists, or social workers. Their academic backgrounds are equally diverse. A survey of practitioners conducted by Caroline Lee and Francesca Polletta found that respondents had earned degrees in public administration, education, conflict resolution, public participation, communications, business, law, urban planning, social work, and psychology. In fact, the most common response to this question on the survey was "Other."[21]

While most of these practitioners have coalesced around the four defining principles listed in the previous section, there is a great deal of variation in how they actually work with clients/communities. Three of the most active and well-known practitioner organizations, the Kettering Foundation, Everyday Democracy, and the Orton Family Foundation, are operating foundations that provide free or low-cost technical assistance to deliberative projects. Other organizations are national nonprofits that attract grants from national and local foundations to support their work in communities. This list includes America*Speaks*, Public Agenda, the National Civic League, Viewpoint Learning, and the Center for Deliberative Democracy, among others. The majority, however, are either solo consultants or staff members of very small for-profit or nonprofit organizations. There is a strong ethic of "open source" knowledge in the field; most practitioners are quite willing to share their discussion materials, process designs, and other details about their methodologies, though some operate with proprietary designs or even place service marks or trademarks on their particular processes.

Within academia, deliberative democrats can be found in a wide range of disciplines, and they have formed whole new deliberation-focused subdisciplines. In a 2007 study, Martin Carcasson found clusters of these researchers (with relevant subfields in parentheses):

- Political science (rhetoric and public affairs, democratic theory, normative theory, local/state politics);

- Public policy (civic culture);
- Public administration (democratic governance, collaborative decision making, public participation);
- Sociology (critical/cultural studies, diversity studies, community organizing);
- Urban planning;
- Natural resources (multi-stakeholder dispute resolution, environmental communication, negotiation, conflict resolution);
- Communication (small-group and organizational communication, conflict resolution, intercultural communication, rhetorical studies, political communication);
- Education (civic education, adult education, deliberative pedagogy, experiential learning, service learning);
- Philosophy (ethics, public reason, public sphere, argumentation, epistemology, judgment);
- Information technology (online deliberation, deliberation and new media);
- Journalism (public or civic journalism, media studies); and
- Law (public law, mediation, legal rhetoric).[22]

Meanwhile, centers and institutes that focus on some aspect of deliberative civic engagement have emerged on a number of campuses. The Center for Public Deliberation (Colorado State), the Institute for Civic Discourse and Democracy (Kansas State), the Center for Democratic Deliberation (Penn State), the Center for Deliberative Democracy (Stanford), and the Centre for Citizenship and Public Policy (Western Sydney) are just a few examples.

When Does Deliberative Civic Engagement Happen?

Though this work points toward new systems of government or governance, thus far it is more accurate to say that deliberative civic engagement has been realized mainly as a temporary practice, a phenomenon experienced by citizens, public officials, and other leaders within the confines of a single issue over a short period of time. There are some examples where democratic principles have been more or less embedded in the routines of public decision making and problem solving for a particular community, but these are rare cases. With an eye toward exceptional deliberative institutions, such as the jury system in the United States or participatory budgeting in Brazil, researchers and practitioners are focused on the question of how to achieve and sustain "embeddedness."[23]

Some cities also have permanent citizen structures, such as neighborhood councils or community boards that receive some support from local government and have some official or semi-official role in local decision making. The most prominent examples are in larger cities such as Los Angeles, California; Portland, Oregon; Minneapolis, Minnesota; and Dayton, Ohio, although there are similar systems in smaller places like Cupertino, California. In most cases, these were set up as representative bodies rather than democratic, participatory ones; they could be considered neighborhood-level city councils. This has been their greatest weakness, since they have many of the same dysfunctions of city councils, but with less authority and fewer resources.[24] Recognizing these limitations, some local leaders try to infuse deliberative democratic principles and strategies in the way that neighborhood councils function.

This interest in combining the successful tactics of temporary projects with the staying power of permanent structures is a critical strategic question that concerns future efforts. It is appropriate, therefore, to consider what kinds of situations provoke people to organize deliberative civic initiatives or structures.

Some of these efforts are inspired by concerns or frustrations with the policy-making process. In one of the most common scenarios, local officials and other leaders face a policy decision they know will be unpopular no matter what they decide. This is particularly evident in California, where the state's budget crisis has led scores of local governments to involve citizens in discussions of whether and how to raise revenues or cut public services.[25] School redistricting, school closings, and land use decisions about landfills, highways, shopping malls, and other potentially unpopular building projects also fall into this category. Sometimes the initiative is launched only after public officials have caused a furor by trying to make the decision themselves. For example, Philadelphia Mayor Michael Nutter launched "The City Budget: Tight Times, Tough Choices" after his initial list of proposed budget cuts proved wildly unpopular with Philadelphia residents.[26]

In other policy-making situations, decision-making bodies have become so deadlocked that putting the question before the public seems the only way to break the impasse. Among the relatively rare examples of statewide deliberative civic engagement projects, stalemate in the state legislature has been a common motivator. Two early cases, "Balancing Justice in Oklahoma" (1996) and "Oregon Health Solutions" (1988), helped lawmakers move past deadlocks on corrections reform and health reform, respectively.[27] Similarly California Speaks (2007) engaged citizens in discussions of health care reform in the state, and a New Hampshire project called "What's at Stake" (2010) allowed people to weigh in on the state's controversial policy decision on legalized gambling.[28]

The deliberative projects that emerge from concerns with policy making are not always led by public officials. Sometimes they begin when an advocacy organization, a set of political activists, or some other nongovernmental group decides that they are not making sufficient progress toward their policy goals and chooses public deliberation in lieu of traditional advocacy. Instead of continuing to push their agenda through lobbying, the media, or other established avenues within the political arena, these advocates are essentially trying to change the arena by bringing a larger number and wider array of people into the debate, and thus creating a deliberative environment where people can decide for themselves what they think should be done. Sociologist David Ryfe refers to these deliberation advocates, who may be politically powerful but are not quite powerful enough to achieve their aims, as the "oppressed fraction of the oppressing class."[29] Though the path to policy influence may seem more difficult for efforts initiated outside government, these initiatives actually have a good track record of success—the participation of large numbers of voters in a project seems to be a more significant factor than whether the project was initiated by government.[30]

In other situations, deliberative civic engagement happens because the public problem being confronted clearly requires individual actions, behavioral changes, or small-group efforts on a large scale. Hundreds of deliberative projects have been organized around issues of race and diversity, which have individual, organizational, and policy dimensions.[31] Crime is another problem that requires action at a range of levels, from safety-conscious behavior to neighborhood watch groups to decisions made about policing. Within the realm of education, some deliberative projects are inspired by surveys showing the effects of increased parent involvement on the academic success of their children.[32]

Finally, some of these initiatives take place in situations where there has been an acknowledged, structural shift in political power. Sometimes this is due to demographic changes, and sometimes to political ones (e.g., when a city council elects to move from a ward-based system to at-large voting). Recognizing the concerns about how such a shift affects "representativeness" and equity in the political system, and fearing a backlash from voters, leaders on both sides of the debate may turn to a neighborhood council system, or a temporary involvement effort, to try to redress the balance. The best-known example of this phenomenon is Los Angeles. After neighborhoods in the San Fernando Valley attempted to secede from the rest of the city, the city council created a system of neighborhood councils and a Department of Neighborhood Empowerment.[33]

What Motivates Deliberative Democrats?

Compiling these varied answers to the question of *when* deliberative civic engagement happens can help us better understand *why* it happens. This is especially true of the local leaders who have been the most common initiators of these projects.

As noted earlier, when they decide to engage the public, leaders usually seek to address immediate political perils or seize emerging opportunities. There are many other perfectly valid reasons for local leaders to support public deliberation (e.g., gathering information, promoting citizenship, generating buy-in, and so on) and many local leaders cite such goals.[34] But in themselves, these are usually insufficient to trigger democracy-building efforts. The prospect of achieving a key policy goal, or avoiding the voter backlash that can arise from an unpopular decision, is a more powerful motivator.

While this mind-set of local leaders may seem pragmatic, it is often imbued with a great deal of emotion. Most have had painful, scarring experiences in public hearings, town hall meetings, and other poorly planned interactions with citizens over contentious issues.[35] A study of California public managers conducted by communication scholars Barnett and Kim Pearce concluded that "everyone involved in this study had personal experience with—or could relate to descriptions of—instances of the public-acting-badly and civic engagement-gone-wrong. These experiences were personally painful and often degraded the quality of decision-making and policy implementation."[36] The quote from a former mayor that opens this chapter expresses a similar sentiment.[37]

Most state and federal managers have been more removed from these kinds of painful public encounters, and involving citizens may not seem as potent a strategy for dealing with the political perils and opportunities they face. That said, the state and federal agencies that have experimented the most with deliberative civic engagement are those who make local decisions and have the highest exposure to the public (e.g., environmental agencies, including the EPA and the US Forest Service). However, because citizen activists have been taking a more persistent role even in federal policy-making processes, the same rational and emotional motivations that have been felt by local officials are becoming more evident among their state and federal counterparts.[38] The failure of the "town hall meetings" held by members of Congress on health care reform in the summer of 2009 was one of the most visible examples of this shift.[39]

The second subset of deliberative democrats, the deliberation practitioners or "democratic entrepreneurs," have some of the same motivations. Some practitioners came to this work through an interest in interpersonal dynamics—a desire to resolve conflicts, mediate disputes, and achieve greater understanding and cooperation among people of different views and backgrounds. The orientation of these practitioners is one reason for the field's growing sensitivity to cultural differences, commitment to neutral facilitation techniques, and reliance on small-group discussion formats. These practitioners helped introduce the belief that when discussing a public problem, it is important for people to share the experiences and stories that inform their policy opinions and explain their passion for the issue.[40]

Other practitioners seem to be motivated mainly by their interest in advancing political causes. Though deliberation has, at times, been initiated by politically conservative governments, the vast majority of deliberation practitioners describe themselves as being on the left side of the political spectrum.[41] They see deliberative processes as the best hope for making progress on their core issues, such as poverty, racial justice, education, environmental protection, and social justice. They have turned away from traditional advocacy, deciding that if ordinary citizens have a chance to compare experiences, learn the facts, and consider a range of policy options, they will arrive at progressive solutions. Some of these practitioners are particularly focused on engaging traditionally marginalized populations and amplifying their voices in the policy-making process. These individuals may be responsible for infusing deliberative civic engagement with community organizing tactics, such as proactive, network-based recruitment of citizen participants.

A third primary motivation for practitioners is one they share with many of the deliberative democrats in academia—an interest in reforming or transforming democratic structures and institutions.[42] The core assumption is that current systems of government are inequitable, inefficient, or disempowering and that modern citizens are capable of taking on more meaningful roles in governance.[43] The researchers and practitioners who focus on democratic reform seek to build permanent citizen-centered structures, such as neighborhood councils, and other innovations in governance.

Among these different motivations for conducting deliberative civic engagement, financial considerations appear irrelevant. On a National League of Cities survey, local officials were asked to list the main barriers to engaging the public in more deliberative, meaningful ways; they put "lack of funding" last on the list, after barriers such as "lack of training."[44] Another study found that the average budget for a deliberative project was $6,000, and the median cost was zero.[45]

Where Is Deliberative Civic Engagement Happening?

People new to this work often assume that it is limited to certain regions and political contexts—that it mostly occurs in the United States, Canada, and Western Europe. In fact, mapping deliberative civic engagement is a global project. Remarkably similar initiatives have emerged, without any connection to one another, in completely different cultures on opposite sides of the world—from numerous innovations in Australia to local initiatives in Kerala, India.[46] There are even instances of successful deliberative projects occurring in countries that (at least at the national level) are not considered to be democratic at all; recent examples include the Wenling City Deliberative Poll in China and the Abuja Town Hall Meetings in Nigeria.[47]

Within the United States, it is possible to discern differences among deliberative projects based on the kinds of issues being addressed. The budget crisis in California, for example, inspired a wave of participatory budgeting efforts in that state, though the financial challenges now being encountered by local governments all over the country may mean that California is simply a bit ahead of the curve. Initiatives on race and diversity were particularly prominent in the Midwest during the 1990s, as cities in that part of the country came to grips with the legacy of segregation caused by the Great Migration a generation before.[48] Though the particular issues may differ and spawn further differences in how projects get organized, the basic principles of deliberative civic engagement vary little across the United States.

Meanwhile, the emergence of deliberative civic engagement in the Global South is a story that is starting to receive broader attention. Scholars and practitioners are studying and promoting the work of ward committees in South Africa, citizen-driven state and local development planning in India, participatory budgeting in Brazil, and "co-production" by citizens and government in the construction of water systems in the Philippines.[49] As development researchers John Gaventa and Nick Benequista argue, "It is no longer time for the U.S. or Europe to pretend to be the guardians or promoters of democracy for other nations."[50]

There is a strong tradition in these newer democracies of citizens rolling up their sleeves and adding their own effort and ingenuity to public problem solving. This impulse mirrors the US efforts that mobilize citizen action on priorities like racial justice, crime prevention, and education.[51] In fact, there may be greater similarities between deliberative civic engagement initiatives in the United States and the Global South than between the United States and Western Europe, where government is generally viewed as the sole public problem solver. Even in Canada, where there is a much stronger tradition of governments soliciting input from citizens than in the United States, the resulting "consultations" often fail to tap the full potential of people and organizations outside government.

Mapping the Field of Deliberative Civic Engagement

The professional infrastructure for deliberative civic engagement is difficult to map. This is due partly to the limitations of the field's inconsistent terminology— a result of its development outside the boundaries of any single profession or academic discipline. In addition, many deliberative democracy initiatives are "homegrown" and disconnected from any of the established groups or experts in the field. Thus, any list of the main organizations will likely prove incomplete.

Nevertheless, several networks have worked to build this infrastructure and help deliberative democrats recognize and articulate the common principles and strategies in their work. Such networks include these:

- The Deliberative Democracy Consortium (DDC)—an alliance of practitioners and researchers representing more than fifty organizations and universities, all of whom share an interest in deliberation and democratic governance. More a think tank than a membership organization, the DDC develops publications, builds connections between different fields, and convenes meetings targeted at particular issues and areas for collaboration.[52]
- The International Association for Public Participation (IAP2)—a network of practitioners that has particularly strong representation in the United States, Canada, and Australia. Many of its members are planners and development specialists who have used democratic principles to involve citizens in land use and development decisions.[53]
- The National Coalition for Dialogue and Deliberation (NCDD)—a network of over 1,300 organizations and individuals. NCDD convenes practitioners in many fields related to deliberation and democratic governance. The NCDD Web site offers a comprehensive assortment of thousands of tools, best practices, and links related to participatory democracy, public engagement, collaborative action, and conflict resolution. The NCDD listserv reaches over 20,000 people.[54]
- LogoLink—a network of democracy practitioners in the Global South, mainly from civil society organizations, research institutions, and governments, all working to deepen democracy through greater citizen participation in local governance. LogoLink encourages learning from field-based innovations and expressions of democracy that contribute to social justice.[55]

In addition to these networks, many other professional associations play an increasingly important role in the field. In the United States, groups like the National League of Cities, International City/County Management Association, League of Women Voters of the USA, National School Boards Association, National School Public Relations Association, American Association of School Administrators, American Planning Association, and Grassroots Grantmakers are responding to their members' interest in (and experimentation with) deliberative civic engagement. Each of these associations provides training and seminars for their members on how to engage citizens in more deliberative and meaningful ways. Each upholds particularly successful examples through awards programs and more informal kinds of recognition, and some provide technical assistance to members who are trying to initiate new projects.

Delineating the professional infrastructure of deliberative civic engagement is further challenged because there are many different "named" models and methodologies for deliberative civic engagement, and the models are often confused with the organizations that promote them. The most widely used processes have been adapted in many different ways, as local leaders (or sometimes the "owners" of the models) adjust the approach to fit the specific needs of a community or issue. While some groups identify themselves with a particular model (or models), others do not. Furthermore, there are a few models, like World Cafe and Open Space Technology, that are not closely associated with any single organization. Because the models tend to have more similarities than differences, the rest of this section is structured as an alphabetical list of key organizations doing work in the area of deliberative civic engagement. Table 2.1 lists and describes some of the main organizations in the field of deliberative civic engagement; the descriptions were contributed by the groups themselves.

(R)evolutionizing Democracy

Deliberative civic engagement proliferated so rapidly that it may seem as though it sprang, fully formed, from the minds of academic visionaries. Indeed, the development of this new form of politics could be taken as evidence that ideas matter, that leaders and managers can seize abstract concepts and make them real.

A closer look reveals that its growth has been more of a geographically dispersed evolution than an organized revolution. Its development has been motivated more by practical concerns than theoretical ones. Many of the people who have implemented and improved deliberative processes did not know that there was an idea out there to be seized, and others saw that the initial theoretical visions needed substantial and continual modification to work effectively. Above all, these initiatives were (and continue to be) developed in reaction to pressing political and economic conditions.

As this work moves forward, practitioners, researchers, and leaders will have to continue negotiating this tension between inspiring visions and pressing realities. The practice of deliberative civic engagement needs substantial improvement, and this book contains many ideas for new enhancements and innovations. For deliberative advances to take hold, the people advocating them will have to understand the political conditions affecting leaders and managers and frame their recommendations with these contexts in mind.

Meanwhile, leaders, managers, and practitioners need opportunities to think outside the box of their individual, immediate public involvement needs. A more holistic, yet pragmatic, discussion needs to take place, where all kinds of people

Table 2.1 **Organizations in the Field of Deliberative Civic Engagement**

Organization	Type	Description
AmericaSpeaks	Nonprofit	AmericaSpeaks is a nonprofit organization with the mission of providing citizens with a greater voice on the most important issues that impact their lives. Since its founding in 1995, AmericaSpeaks has engaged more than 150,000 citizens on important issues, like the federal budget deficit, the recovery of New Orleans after Hurricane Katrina, health care reform in California, economic development in Northeast Ohio, and creating the municipal budget in Washington, DC. AmericaSpeaks' 21st Century Town Meetings engage groups of 50–10,000 citizens at a time to shape policy making and planning. The organization seeks to reflect the actual demographic diversity of the community in its meetings by developing highly customized recruitment strategies that combine grassroots organizing, organizational partnerships, and sophisticated media campaigns.
Ascentum	For-profit	Ascentum fosters local democracy by helping entire communities come together to work through tough issues and answer questions that matter to them. Using a complementary mix of online and face-to-face tools, Ascentum allows foundations to foster dialogue across whole communities, including a broad range of interested and affected citizens, as well as local stakeholders. Ascentum's unique process is supported by its innovative, dialoguecircles.com platform—a suite of face-to-face and online tools to support deliberative democracy.

Center for Deliberative Democracy	Academic Center	The Center for Deliberative Democracy (CDD), housed in the Department of Communication at Stanford University, is devoted to research about democracy and public opinion obtained through Deliberative Polling. Numerous Deliberative Polls have been conducted in the United States, Britain, Australia, Denmark, Italy, Hungary, Bulgaria, China, Northern Ireland, and other countries. The CDD has tackled a variety of issues, including health care, education, national security, housing, the economy, and candidate selection. In October 2007, the CDD and its European collaborators conducted the first European-wide Deliberative Poll with more than 360 randomly selected citizens from all 27 member states and discussions conducted in 23 languages. In February 2008, the CDD helped supervise and plan the third Deliberative Poll in Zeguo Township, Wenling City, China. In this project, the deliberations focused on the entire town budget, and the local People's Congress observed the process to consider budget adjustments based on the results of the Deliberative Poll.
e-democracy.org	Nonprofit	Launched as the world's first election information Web site in 1994, today E-democracy.org focuses on hosting local online Issues Forums. E-democracy provides a service-club-like infrastructure for local volunteers (and partners) using a shared, low-cost technology base and, more important, a universal set of civility rules and facilitation guides that help communities succeed with online engagement.
Everyday Democracy	Operating Foundation	Everyday Democracy (formerly the Study Circles Resource Center) helps local communities find ways for all kinds of people to think, talk, and work together to solve problems. Everyday Democracy helps communities pay particular attention to how racism and ethnic differences affect the problems they address. Since its founding in 1989, Everyday Democracy has worked with more than 550 communities across the United States on issues including racial equity, poverty, diversity, immigration, police-community relations, education, neighborhoods, youth issues, and growth and sprawl. Everyday Democracy is the primary project of The Paul J. Aicher Foundation, a national, nonpartisan, nonprofit operating foundation.

(continued)

Table 2.1 (*continued*)

Organization	Type	Description
Harwood Institute for Public Innovation	Nonprofit	For more than 20 years, the Harwood Institute for Public Innovation has been researching, developing, and innovating practical approaches for changing the negative conditions in society that often prevent neighborhoods and communities from making progress. The Harwood Institute has recently shifted its work to focus on diffusing and sharing our ideas, tools, and frameworks so that people can make them their own, and accelerate their efforts to create hope and change.
International Institute for Sustained Dialogue	Nonprofit	The International Institute for Sustained Dialogue (IISD) designs and conducts dialogues in international conflicts and in peacebuilding (for example, with Americans and Russians; among participants from the civil war in Tajikistan; between democratic reformers from the Muslim Arab heartland, Western Europe, and the United States; on national reconciliation with Iraqis). IISD aspires to take Sustained Dialogue into corporations, organizations, and communities and to develop other partnerships. It is home to the Sustained Dialogue Campus Network, an autonomous program within the Institute.
Jefferson Center	Nonprofit	The Jefferson Center pioneered the use of the Citizens' Jury process in the United States, starting in 1974. The use of randomly selected citizens to participate in a deliberative method is at the heart of the Citizens' Jury process and it is now internationally recognized.
Kettering Foundation	Operating Foundation	The Kettering Foundation, established in 1927 by inventor Charles F. Kettering, is a nonprofit operating foundation that does not make grants but engages in joint research with others. Kettering's primary research question is, what does it take to make democracy work as it should? Kettering's research is distinctive because it is conducted from the perspective of citizens and focuses on what people can do collectively to address problems affecting their lives, their communities, and their nation. The foundation seeks to identify and address the challenges to making democracy work as it should through interrelated program areas that focus on citizens, communities and institutions. The foundation collaborates with an extensive network of community groups, professional associations, researchers, scholars, and citizens around the world.

Keystone Center	Nonprofit	The Keystone Center brings together public, private, and civic sector leaders to confront critical environment, energy, and public health problems. In conjunction with working on issues in the policy domain, the Keystone Center also uses its educational programs to arm the next generation of leaders with the 21st Century intellectual and social skills they will require to solve the problems they will face.
National Charrette Institute	Nonprofit	The National Charrette Institute (NCI) is a nonprofit organization that advances the fields of community planning and public involvement through research, publications, and facilitation. NCI increases local capacity for communities to work collaboratively to implement innovative, smart growth solutions for land-use planning and development. NCI provides solutions for what is often the weak link in the chain—the point of communication and decision making between public and private entities such as community members and local governments.
National Civic League	Nonprofit	The National Civic League (NCL) is a nonprofit, nonpartisan, membership organization headquartered in Denver, Colorado. It is dedicated to strengthening democracy by increasing people's capacity to build and fully participate in healthy and prosperous communities. Embracing and promoting diversity and inclusiveness are among NCL's core values. NCL fosters innovative community building and political reform, assists local governments, and recognizes cross-sector collaborative community achievement. NCL accomplishes its mission through technical assistance, training, publishing, research, and two awards programs: the MetLife Foundation Ambassadors In Education Awards, recognizing educators who connect school and community, and the All-America City Awards, which for 60 years has recognized neighborhoods, villages, cities, counties, and regions for outstanding civic accomplishments, collaboration, inclusion, and innovation. NCL offers technical assistance to towns, cities, counties, government agencies, and organizations through its Community Services (CS) program, which works with communities all over the country employing a "visioning/strategic planning" approach to goal setting, problem solving, and capacity building.

(*continued*)

Table 2.1 (continued)

Organization	Type	Description
National Issues Forums	Network	The National Issues Forums (NIF) is a nonpartisan, nationwide network whose participants include an array of civic educational and professional groups, organizations, and individuals that promote public deliberation in communities across the country. NIF is rooted in the simple notion that people need to come together to reason and talk—to deliberate about common problems. Each year major issues of concern are identified by the NIF network. Issue guides are prepared to provide an overview of the problem and alternative approaches to dealing with it and to help those attending the forums frame the deliberation. Forums, sponsored by schools, civic groups, and other organizations in many communities, offer citizens the opportunity to jointly deliberate about difficult issues and consider common ground for action. Issue guides are available through the NIF Institute.
Orton Family Foundation	Operating Foundation	The Orton Family Foundation has worked since 1995 to develop new tools and processes to better engage citizens and help small cities and towns plan their development futures. This work includes the creation of CommunityViz, an innovative GIS planning software, development of community video and place-based education programs, and most recently the launch of its "heart and soul community planning" initiative, which brings story gathering, value mapping, scenario planning, and other high-tech and low-tech tools to provide citizens a stronger, better informed voice, and more effective involvement and leadership in steering the change of their communities.
Public Agenda	Nonprofit	Public Agenda, a nonprofit, nonpartisan organization, brings more than 30 years of experience in engaging the public in productive and meaningful dialogue and deliberation, conducting qualitative and quantitative public opinion studies, and producing high quality citizen education materials. Since its beginning in 1975, Public Agenda has been a pioneer in the practice of public engagement, with hands-on experience in hundreds of communities and on dozens of tough issues. In addition to Community Conversations, Public Agenda employs leadership dialogues, multisession stakeholder dialogue groups, focus groups, online strategies, and other methods.

Right Question Project	Nonprofit	The Right Question Project (RQP) has worked with hundreds of programs and agencies in communities all around the country for 17 years developing, implementing, and refining an educational strategy to make it possible for more people in low-income communities to participate effectively in democracy on all levels. The RQP Strategy builds the skills of all people, no matter their educational, income, or literacy level, to focus on key decisions, ask strategic questions, expect and require accountable decision making, and participate effectively in decisions that affect them. RQP's work focuses on making it possible for people in low-income communities to acquire skills to participate more effectively in decisions made on a "micro" level across all fields, such as at their children's schools, the welfare office, the job training program, the Medicaid-funded health care center, and other basic services.
Viewpoint Learning	Nonprofit	Viewpoint Learning has applied its innovative dialogue-based methods to a wide range of issues, including health care, education, the federal debt, foreign policy, land use, housing, local budgeting, aging, and environmental sustainability. Founders Daniel Yankelovich and Dr. Steven Rosell have more than 80 years of combined experience in public opinion research, dialogue, and governance issues. Viewpoint Learning builds upon Yankelovich's groundbreaking work on highly sophisticated polls and focus groups and the in-depth issues forums of the Kettering Foundation and Public Agenda, as well as on Rosell's work on scenarios, group and societal learning, and learning-based approaches to governance.

who care about their community can take stock of the challenges and opportunities they face. By assembling the pictures of their own local democratic (r)evolution, communities will have a better sense of where they want to take it next. Mike Huggins, city manager of Eau Claire, Wisconsin, and a veteran democratic innovator, put it best: "The relationship between government, formal institutions, and citizens in community governance is changing dramatically. The question is to what extent you want to impact that."[56]

Notes

1. Numerous studies and surveys have charted citizens' changing attitudes toward authority and the erosion of their trust in government. Daniel Yankelovich, who inspired many people to rethink their views about citizenship with his 1991 book, *Coming to Public Judgment*, now argues, "In recent years, the public's willingness to accept the authority of experts and elites has sharply declined. The public does not want to scrap representative democracy and move wholesale towards radical populism, but there will be no return to the earlier habits of deference to authority and elites" (Yankelovich and Friedman 2011b: 23). One of the recurrent findings in the annual Civic Health Index is "overwhelming support for laws and policies that would support greater citizen engagement" (National Conference on Citizenship 2008, www.civicyouth.org/PopUps/08_pr_civic_index.pdf).
2. Klein (2010).
3. Skidmore and Bound (2008); Leighninger (2006, 2009a); Levine and Torres (2008).
4. The author has served as executive director of the Deliberative Democracy Consortium since 2006. This chapter draws on those experiences, in addition to empirical evidence such as the survey work conducted by Lee and Polletta (2009); see also Lee (2011).
5. Thomas and Leighninger (2010).
6. For a sociological analysis of this not-quite-movement, see Ryfe (2007).
7. For other variations on these principles, see Involve (2008) and NCDD (2010).
8. Habermas (1984).
9. Walsh (2007); Black (2008, 2009); Lee (2007); Polletta (2008); Polletta and Lee (2006); Ryfe (2006); Morrell (2010).
10. See, for example, Mansbridge, Hartz-Karp, Amengual, and Gastil (2006); Pearce and Littlejohn (1997).
11. Thomas and Leighninger (2010); Lee and Polletta (2009); Lee (2011).
12. Some processes, such as the Deliberative Poll (Fishkin 2009c) and Citizens' Jury (Crosby and Nethercutt 2005), grew directly out of political philosophy. Nonetheless, these are exceptions. Even the widely acclaimed British Columbia Citizens' Assembly—one of the more groundbreaking instances of modern deliberative democracy—emerged directly from local ideas and policy goals. Though by the time it got under way, its organizers were welcoming advice from Jim Fishkin, Ned Crosby, and others who had worked on deliberative democracy for years, it did not initially draw on their experience. For more discussion, see Warren and Pearse (2008).
13. Leighninger (2010a); Smock (2004); Traynor (2002).
14. Gastil (2000, 2008); Gastil and Levine (2005); Fishkin (2009c); Yankelovich and Friedman (2011a).
15. For an example of an effort blending such approaches, see Carson and Hartz-Karp (2005).
16. Lee and Polletta (2009); Lee (2011).
17. Leighninger (2006). An international team of scholars and practitioners has begun archiving these activities on www.participedia.net.
18. Leighninger (2006).

19. See www.atsdr.cdc.gov/nationalconversation, www.epa.gov/care, and www.healthyde-mocracyoregon.org.
20. Friedman (2006).
21. Lee and Polletta (2009); Lee (2011).
22. Carcasson (2008).
23. Fung and Fagotto (2009).
24. Berry, Portney, and Thomson (1993); Leistner and Alarcon (2009); Leighninger (2009b); Fung and Fagotto (2009).
25. Marois and Amsler (2008).
26. See http://phillyist.com/2009/02/20/itemize_me_last_chance_for_citizen.php.
27. Leighninger (2006).
28. Personal conversation with Alison Kadlec, January 2011.
29. From a 2007 personal communication from David Ryfe. For related ideas in print, see Ryfe (2007).
30. Fung and Fagotto (2009); Leighninger (2006).
31. Walsh (2007).
32. Bridgeport, Connecticut, is an especially good example; see Friedman, Kadlec, and Burbank (2007). Many deliberative projects on school issues were inspired by David Mathews' *Is There a Public for the Public Schools?* (1997).
33. Some critics argue that the experiment, while ambitious, was never fully deliberative or participatory, and that the state's legal framework for open meetings caused additional complications—for example, see Greene (2004). For a more comprehensive assessment, see Cooper, Musso, and Kitsuse (2002), Cooper and Kathi (2005), Kathi and Cooper (2008), and Musso, Weare, Bryer, and Cooper (2011).
34. Mann and Barnes (2010).
35. For a discussion of state and federal legislators' views on participation, see Nabatchi and Farrar (2011).
36. Pearce and Pearce (2010).
37. Leighninger (2010c).
38. Leighninger (2009a).
39. Levine (2010).
40. Pearce and Littlejohn (1997). On the influence of small group models on public discussion, see the final chapter of Gastil (2010).
41. See Lee and Polletta (2009), Lee (2011), and Ryfe (2007). The British Columbia Citizens' Assembly came from a politically conservative party (Warren and Pearse 2008), and the Oregon Citizens' Initiative Review was passed with bipartisan support in the state legislature.
42. This orientation can seem both radical and practical—radical if you consider our political institutions to be static and entrenched, practical if you assume that politics and political institutions are constantly evolving, and that they sometimes undergo dramatic changes in relatively short periods of time. See Morone (1992) and Sirianni and Friedland (2001).
43. For a discussion, see Nabatchi (2010a) and Leighninger (2006).
44. Mann and Barnes (2010).
45. Lee and Polletta (2009); Lee (2011).
46. Briggs (2008); Gaventa and Barrett (2010); Spink, Hossain, and Best (2009).
47. See www.vitalizing-democracy.org.
48. Walsh (2007).
49. Spink, Hossain, and Best (2009).
50. Gaventa and Benequista (2009).
51. See Peterson (2009) for a noteworthy example in Hawaii.
52. www.deliberative-democracy.net.
53. www.iap2.org.
54. http://ncdd.org/.
55. www.logolink.org.
56. Leighninger (2010c).

PART TWO

PROCESS AND DESIGN

3

The Participation and Recruitment Challenge

DAVID MICHAEL RYFE AND BRITTANY STALSBURG

It isn't practical to engage citizens in every public decision or problem—nor would citizens want to be engaged in everything. But if
you're not engaging them proactively and intensively in at least some
decisions, you're probably not doing enough.
—Robin Beltramini, *city council member, Troy, Michigan*[1]

A great deal of research has been dedicated to testing whether "deliberation
makes better citizens," as Heather Pincock puts it in Chapter 7 of this volume.
Researchers have sought, for instance, to discover whether participation in deliberation results in greater open-mindedness and whether it increases the perceived legitimacy of political decisions. In part inspired by a larger literature in
political theory on representation,[2] some thought also has been given to the
question of representation in deliberative activities, with attention focused on
whether the legitimacy of a deliberative group hinges on how well it represents a
broader constituency (see Chapter 5).[3] Such work on representation has been
especially influential among scholars and practitioners thinking through recruitment strategies for deliberative civic engagement initiatives.[4]

Comparatively less attention, however, has been devoted to a question that is
in many respects no less central, *Who participates in deliberative civic engagement
initiatives?* After all, deliberative civic engagement cannot have an effect or generate legitimacy if people do not actually participate in the activity. Yet, as political scientist Michael Neblo and his co-authors report, "Given the recent
proliferation of applied deliberative forums and research on them, surprisingly
little work has focused on who is willing to participate."[5]

Though significant variation exists among different kinds of civic and political engagement, researchers have found that an underlying logic shapes all
forms of public participation: Participation goes up when, from the perspective

of the individual, its material and symbolic costs are lowered and/or its benefits are increased. This logic suggests that unless practitioners take corrective measures of some kind, participation of all varieties will be skewed in favor of those with higher socioeconomic status (SES) and formal education. As we show later, a significant volume of scholarship has demonstrated these connections for politics in general, and a recent study of informal political talk suggests it also applies to deliberative civic engagement.[6]

Though there are broad similarities in terms of who participates in varieties of political and civic activities, different factors mitigate the impact of SES and education on different kinds of participation. For instance, studies have shown that ideological intensity may increase the likelihood that people with lower SES and education will join social movements. In contrast, ideological intensity seems to be less influential than proximity to particular sorts of social networks on rates of voluntarism. These differences translate into slightly different populations for different sorts of participation. In the case of deliberative participation, membership in civic and political organizations plays a critical role in mitigating the impact of SES and educational attainment.[7] This explains why many deliberation practitioners have adopted recruitment strategies that rely heavily on local networks.

Even with relatively little research on the specific question of who deliberates, there remains much to discuss. As we review the relevant literature, our goal is to set the scene for further exploration of a subject that most agree is of decisive importance for the future of deliberative civic engagement. We begin with a brief discussion of why participation matters—that is, why deliberative theorists and practitioners care about who participates. We then review the literature on public participation and compare its findings to the research on participation in deliberative civic engagement initiatives.

Why Participation Matters

From the 1970s to the late 1990s, the study of deliberation remained a relatively small subfield of political theory. At the time, the notion that citizens ought to have robust, substantive opportunities to deliberate in politics was not conventional wisdom. In fact, public participation of any kind has been a minor theme in examinations of liberal democratic politics since the 1920s.[8] The great bulk of empirical research on politics, which depicted citizens as rationally ignorant and politically apathetic, seemed to justify this neglect.[9] Beginning in the 1970s, however, theorists and researchers alike began to question this wisdom.[10] They worried about the thinning of civic life,[11] the decline of traditional voluntary organizations,[12] and the growing distrust between citizens and public officials.[13] In response, they began to articulate variations on what political theorist Benjamin Barber called "strong democracy," in which politics centers on and flows from the active participation of citizens.[14]

Many scholars argued specifically for a deliberative form of public participation, and lacking (or failing to recognize) examples of real-world deliberative civic engagement, they turned to normative arguments to justify their views and claims.[15] In essence, the arguments in favor of deliberation focused on its intrinsic value and the proposition that it fosters democratic, and specifically liberal democratic, values.[16] For instance, in its classic formulation, deliberation honors the assumption that individuals are rational agents capable of formulating and articulating their interests. Deliberation also embraces the ideals of equality and inclusivity—the idea that every person in a community should have a voice in any public discussion that affects his or her life. Finally, deliberation encourages mutual respect, or at least tolerance. When exposed to alternative views, theorists argue, people are more likely to understand and empathize with those who espouse them.

Since deliberation manifests these and other core democratic values, it became a natural benchmark for the relative health of a democratic polity. More deliberation would mean more democracy. This notion stood in contrast to the conventional wisdom of the time, which proposed nearly the opposite. As Walter Lippmann put it, the "masses cannot be counted upon to apprehend regularly and promptly the reality of things."[17] Thus, as Mark Button and David Ryfe have argued, it was perhaps revolutionary to assert that the "essential meaning of democracy [is the ability of] free and equal citizens . . . [to] participate in a shared public life and to shape decisions that affect their lives."[18]

Over time, the deliberative ideal won adherents, and deliberative civic engagement began to flower in the United States and elsewhere around the world.[19] (For a discussion of deliberative civic engagement initiatives, see Chapter 2.) Not surprisingly, as deliberative events spread, empirical researchers set about testing the claims of deliberative theorists.[20] Meanwhile, more pragmatic arguments emerged to justify citizen participation in deliberative exercises. Researchers found that deliberation increased citizens' political knowledge and the robustness of their opinions and that it improved citizens' perceptions about the legitimacy of democratic processes.[21] Additionally, a large body of work discovered that when individuals are confronted by a greater diversity of ideas, either in the context of their own social networks or in face-to-face discussions with strangers, they tend to become more open-minded, learn more from others, and engage in a deeper consideration of issues—in short, deliberation was shown to create "better citizens" (see Chapter 7).[22] Of course, other researchers contested these claims, and the debate between advocates and critics has been extensive and at times fierce (see Chapter 11).[23] To date, however, this conversation has largely ignored the central question of *who* deliberates.

As we acknowledged at the outset of this chapter, we do not know the answer to this question. Though it has grown considerably in recent years, the literature on deliberative civic engagement is skewed in at least two ways: It tends to focus on particular initiatives, events, or programs, and it devotes too much attention to debating the theoretical benefits of deliberation.

As a way forward, it seems intuitively sensible to suppose that deliberation is, in many respects, similar to other kinds of public participation. Much like voting, deliberation is oriented toward political decision making. Like voluntarism, participation in deliberative exercises represents for many people a kind of "giving back" to the community. And, as with social movements, people often turn to deliberation out of frustration with traditional forms of politics. This is not to say that deliberation is identical to these other activities, only that it fits under the broad umbrella of civic and political participation. The next section provides a brief overview of the broader literature on public participation.

Who Participates

To begin this discussion, it is important to understand how researchers have approached the question of public participation. Much of this research builds on assumptions first articulated by Anthony Downs in *An Economic Theory of Democracy*.[24] In particular, this research assumes that commitment to public participation takes the form of a rational cost-benefit calculation: People commit to participation when they perceive the costs (for example, time, money, attention, or energy) to be low and the benefits relative to those costs to be high.[25] However, this simple answer does not identify the variables that lower costs and/or increase the benefits of participation. We turn our attention now to those.

Demographic Factors

Generations of scholars have investigated this issue and discovered numerous variables that trigger or inhibit participation in particular contexts. We focus on three variables that have been shown repeatedly to correlate strongly with public participation of all kinds: formal education, socioeconomic status, and proximity to social networks.

First, numerous studies have shown that education is a "universal solvent" for public participation. As political scientist Philip Converse wrote,

> Whether one is dealing with cognitive matters such as level of factual information about politics or conceptual sophistication in its assessment; or such motivational matters as degree of attention paid to politics

and emotional involvement in political affairs; or questions of actual behavior, such as engagement in any of a variety of political activities from party work to voter turnout itself: education is everywhere the universal solvent, and the relationship is always in the same direction.[26]

Why is education so important? One common explanation is that education reduces the cognitive and material expenses of participation.[27] For instance, education increases the cognitive skills of individuals, thus facilitating learning. It provides people with skills that make information retrieval and processing easier, and enhances civic skills that allow people to efficiently translate their interests into words and actions. Finally, in developing a fuller sense of their connection to civic and public affairs, education appears to increase the gratification people get from participating in public life. Education, in short, is a "universal solvent" because it bears so directly on the costs and benefits of public participation.

Second, socioeconomic status (SES) also predicts participation. In fact, SES is so predictive of participation in political affairs that political scientists Sidney Verba and Norman Nie place it at the center of their "standard model" of political participation. "According to this model," they write, "the social status of an individual . . . determines to a large extent how much he participates."[28] Why? Much like education, higher levels of SES are correlated strongly with the possession of the sorts of human capital that make participation easy, or at least easier, relative to individuals with lower SES. High SES is also linked to a greater sense of civic duty on the part of individuals. This sense of duty increases the emotional rewards associated with civic and political participation, making it more likely that people are willing to get involved.

Finally, proximity to social networks populated by other highly participative individuals is also routinely associated with participation.[29] Social networks have been found to interact with education and SES to form what political scientist Hahrie Han terms a "pathway to commitment" in public participation.[30] The logic is that education and SES increase the likelihood that individuals will come into contact with and develop social networks, which in turn reduces the costs of participation.[31] For example, a lawyer working for a corporate law firm has a greater likelihood of being invited to a political fund-raiser than a service worker simply because of proximity to people who hold such fund-raisers. Essentially, people tend to frequent the social networks of other people like themselves, so those more inclined to participate are socially networked to those who also possess the capacity and willingness to participate. In this context, a simple invitation is all that is necessary to catalyze participation.

Thus, it is important to consider the differential influence of the workplace (where social networks are often developed) on the political and civic participation of men versus women. As political scientist Nancy Burns and her colleagues report, "Because women are less likely than men to be in the workforce and because, even if employed full time, women are less likely to hold jobs that develop civic skills, gender differences in workforce experiences figure prominently in explaining gender differences in political activity."[32] The same logic often holds for social categories besides gender.

Psychological Factors

The literature cited thus far deals mostly with participation in standard political activities such as voting, but research on social movement participation and voluntarism tells much the same story. For example, a sociological study on recruitment to "high-risk activism" found that people who affiliate themselves with social movements exhibit "biographical availability," defined as the "absence of personal constraints that may increase the costs and risks of movement participation, such as full-time employment, marriage, and family responsibilities."[33] At different moments in their lives, people will have varying degrees of economic and social freedom. The less constrained they are at a given moment, the more likely they will be willing to participate. The same is true for participation in voluntary associations.

Sociologists David Knoke and Randall Thomson were the first to recognize that "an individual's position in the family cycle affects his or her involvement in voluntary associations."[34] People with young children, for example, are much less likely to participate in voluntary associations than single adults or married adults with older children. More recent research extends this insight to argue that participation in voluntary associations is inherently cyclical, and that "role shifts associated with transitions to marriage and parenthood influence joining and leaving rates of voluntary associations."[35] The logic of this argument is simple: Transitions in family roles invite individuals to reassess their involvement with voluntary groups in the context of changing familial obligations.

Social psychologists have also identified a number of internal factors that lower the costs of public participation, including a craving for mental stimulation, a sense of personal and political self-confidence, and openness toward conflict. These factors tend to correlate with the external factors already identified (education, SES, and social networks), but they are worth mentioning, if only to offer a more complete picture of the typical participative citizen.

A first psychological factor associated with participation is what has been called a "need for cognition."[36] People who have this quality enjoy thinking through difficult problems and are more likely than others to organize, elaborate, and evaluate information to which they are exposed. Rather than seeing situations involving complex information as cognitively costly, these people are likely to enjoy themselves when challenged in this way. Since many opportunities to engage in civic and political life involve nettlesome issues, it is easy to understand how and why the need for cognition is positively associated with such participation. Simply put, a strong need for cognition lowers perceived costs and increases perceived benefits.

A high sense of personal efficacy represents a second psychological variable associated with participation. Personal efficacy refers to one's confidence—that one can master tasks and situations.[37] Many studies have shown that personal efficacy is connected to political efficacy, defined as the "feeling that individual political action does have, or can have, an impact upon the political process,"[38] and, by extension, to an individual's willingness to participate in public activities.[39] For instance, one study found that people who exhibit high levels of personal efficacy are more likely to feel responsible for solving the problem of global warming, and that this sense of responsibility leads them to participate more often (relative to those with lower levels of personal efficacy) in collective activities aimed at solving that problem.[40] Moreover, the relationship between personal efficacy and participation represents something of a virtuous cycle: When people participate, they gain civic skills, which in turn enhances their sense of personal efficacy, which leads them to participate more, and so forth.[41]

A final psychological factor associated with an individual's willingness to participate concerns one's openness toward conflict.[42] People who are more "conflict avoidant" are less likely to participate in activities in which they may encounter people whose opinions differ from their own, such as protests, campaign support activities, and interpersonal discussions of politics.[43] In part, this means that social heterogeneity potentially dampens participation.[44] (For a discussion of diversity in deliberative civic engagement, see Chapter 5.) People with a disposition toward conflict-avoidance are likely to see heterogeneity as prohibitively raising the cost of participation because of the potential for increased conflict.

Ideological Intensity

To summarize, those people with more material, symbolic, and cognitive resources are more likely to participate. Because this finding has been replicated so many times, it now represents a conventional wisdom within the literature.[45] Assuming that this is true, what are we to make of the curious fact that many resource-poor individuals also participate in public life?[46] In attending to this question, researchers have concluded that personal commitment to and ideological intensity toward public issues may also lessen the impact of SES and education as predictors of participation and override cost-benefit calculations especially for resource-poor individuals.[47]

As Han writes, "People have children they care about . . . parents who are aging, or neighbors they want to get to know. These [sorts of] personal concerns generate emotional arousal and, sometimes, direct behavior toward political action."[48]

Some of these personal concerns may be instrumental. A small business owner, for example, may get involved in finding solutions to local crime out of a personal interest in not being robbed. But personal concerns can be expressive as well. Some people explain their involvement as a matter of civic duty: they simply feel obligated to participate when they see a problem that needs to be solved. Others get involved to meet people, have something to do, or simply to learn new things. In his study of political activists, Nathan Teske confirms that many people become motivated to participate precisely because of these sorts of concerns. His research shows "how some of the most profoundly held moral concerns . . . can be very much about oneself, about what kind of person one is, about who one is as an individual, and about how one chooses to live one's life."[49]

Government policies may also mitigate the impact of social and economic inequalities on participation in several ways.[50] For instance, public policies may create incentives to mobilize, as when policies associated with the welfare state catalyze American senior citizens to become involved on these issues.[51] Public policy may also provide opportunities for citizens to gain civic skills, and in so doing reduce the costs of participation.[52] Alternatively, public policy may directly subsidize participation. The Community Action Programs of the 1960s, for instance, provided African American activists with offices, supplies, and meeting spaces.[53] Public policy may also shape citizens' experiences with government in ways that facilitate participation. For example, studies have shown that the responsiveness of the federal Social Security Disability Insurance program has fostered continued involvement with the program. In contrast, other studies have shown that the Federal Aid to Families with Dependent Children program has been less responsive, and thus oriented its recipients away from further public participation.[54]

Finally, civic organizations like churches, unions, and other volunteer groups may mobilize their communities, thus reducing the costs of participation.[55] Such mobilization is fostered in several ways: Training can increase the civic skills of organizational members; providing an infrastructure for participation (e.g., places to meet, phone banks, and the like) can ease the costs of participation; and setting expectations and engaging in motivational talk can increase the perceived benefits of this work. Above all, these organizations and associations create and maintain a network of trusting relationships through which recruitment messages can circulate.

Recruiting Participants for Deliberative Events

Of course, practitioners of public deliberation know well that unless they are proactive, participation is likely to be skewed in predictable ways.[56] Thus, it is worth examining the strategies practitioners use to broaden their participant base. In general, deliberative civic engagement practitioners pursue one of four recruitment strategies: election, random sampling, purposive or "targeted" sampling, and self-selection.[57]

The first recruitment strategy is election, wherein citizens vote for deliberative participants. Although rarely implemented in the United States, this strategy is fairly common in other countries.[58] For example, the Municipal Health Council of São Paulo, Brazil, elects Councilors every two years, and by law, organizations from civil society are guaranteed half of these seats (see Chapter 9).[59] As long as all citizens have an equal opportunity to vote and to be elected, this strategy can be a democratic solution to participant recruitment. Organized in the wrong way, however, it can reproduce social inequalities by allowing individuals with more money, skills, and time to dominate. Moreover, it has the obvious drawback that the majority may stifle minority views.

Random selection is a second strategy. As the name implies, event planners use this strategy to select a random group of participants by lot from the universe of people who might participate.[60] The process of inviting usually occurs through random digit dialing, but sometimes practitioners send a "warm-up letter" to a random sample of listed numbers followed by phone calls. Multiple calls are made to increase the response rate, and additional targeted calls are sometimes made to ensure the participation of individuals from traditionally underrepresented groups. As an incentive to participate, practitioners who use this strategy sometimes offer to pay participants. Two deliberative civic engagement formats—Deliberative Polling and Citizens Juries—rely on this strategy to populate their events. The American jury system, which some deliberative theorists describe as a natural deliberative body, also uses this method.[61]

Random selection mitigates the force of SES and education, but it is not a panacea. It is not clear, for instance, that random selection ensures representativeness; individuals who are selected to participate must also agree to participate. Evidence suggests that even when personally contacted and paid, individuals from the lower end of the SES spectrum are less likely to attend. Deliberative Poll conveners James Fishkin and Cynthia Farrar report, for instance, that despite their best efforts, the people who attended one of their deliberative events were older, more likely to have telephone landlines, better educated, more willing to talk to pollsters, more politically active, and predominantly English-speaking.[62] The process of ensuring a random sample, particularly if it is intended to be representative, is also time-consuming and poses significant logistical dilemmas, such as transportation, accommodation, correspondence, and so on. These can become so pronounced that relatively few deliberative events attempt—and succeed—to bring together large random samples of individuals.

Purposive sampling is a third strategy practitioners use to cobble together a diverse set of participants at their events. This method can take a variety of forms. One is the "stakeholder model," which involves inviting participants from a variety of organizations in the community. These people are assumed to "represent" others in their organization and to bring alternative voices into the discussion. Another variant of purposive sampling is a "targeted recruitment" strategy, in which the organizers make the deliberative events open to anyone in the community, but then focus their recruitment time and energy on the types of people they believe are affected by the issue being discussed and less likely to attend on their own initiative. Factors such as race, gender, age, geographic region, and income are usually considered. To reach these populations, practitioners map the informal and formal networks in relevant communities and reach out to various kinds of network leaders. The goal is to ensure that recruitment messages are transmitted by people who are already trusted and influential members of the communities.

This "targeted recruitment" approach may be the most common tactic employed by deliberative practitioners.[63] For example, America*Speaks* regularly uses this strategy, as it did to convene a 21st Century Town Meeting in New Orleans.[64] Using census data, America*Speaks* organizers gather information about the demographic composition of the community and then reach out to community leaders, gain endorsements from trusted sources, and partner with local media to bring together a group that matches, as closely as possible, the demographic composition of the community. This allows America*Speaks* to claim that participants at their events represent the broader community. In the New Orleans case, these methods were especially successful in reaching low-income African Americans who were displaced by Hurricane Katrina. Like America*Speaks'* events, most targeted recruitment strategies use a combination of grassroots organizing and media campaigning to ensure that all stakeholders are represented in a discussion.

Finally, when not using these three strategies, event planners rely on self-selection. This strategy can look more like a nonstrategy in that it allows any interested person to participate. Conveners simply alert citizens of the date, time, and location of the event and wait to see who shows up. Since anyone can participate, self-selection often produces a snowball sample, meaning that individuals recruit others in their social networks; consequently, the deliberative group usually becomes fairly homogenous.[65] For example, the National Issues Forums (NIFs) often use self-selection for their events. News of upcoming NIFs are posted at libraries, schools, and other public locations, and people voluntarily choose to attend. Not surprisingly, NIFs tend to be populated by individuals who fit the profile of highly participative citizens.

Though self-selection is sometimes used because deliberative event planners are constrained by costs, time, and resources, it can be an intentional choice. Some groups require self-selection for deliberative forums because the issues under discussion are contentious or sensitive. The idea is that for such issues, participants have to be willing and eager to talk to achieve the goal of the forum.[66] Moreover, practitioners sometimes argue that self-selection is preferable because it brings in the most dedicated citizens who are motivated to complete their assigned tasks.[67] Thus, although it often serves as a default strategy, self-selection can be especially useful in certain contexts.

Who Shows Up in the Absence of Active Recruitment

Our final section returns to the initial question of who participates, with reference to those deliberative opportunities that do *not* involve intensive recruitment. In this context, it is useful to consider here the findings of a landmark study by the research team of Lawrence Jacobs, Fay Lomax Cook, and Michael Delli Carpini. Their survey on "discursive" political participation sheds some light on the potential of the recruitment strategies we have enumerated.[68] They surveyed 1,501 randomly selected respondents from the general US population, plus an additional 500 individuals (in technical jargon, an "over-sample") who reported attending a meeting to discuss a public issue in the past year. In their larger survey, they found 756 cases of "face-to-face deliberation," defined as "attend[ing] a formal or informal [organized] meeting in the past year to discuss a local, national, or international issue." Given the costs of participating in such events, Jacobs and his colleagues call this proportion "impressive" and argue that it might have been even higher if those who said they had not attended such a meeting had simply been invited to do so.

Other research supports this conclusion. In an essay titled, "Who Wants to Deliberate?" Michael Neblo and colleagues report results from survey and experimental data which suggest that, under the right conditions, a majority of Americans (over 60 percent) would be willing to engage in deliberative exercises if given the opportunity.[69] Of course, a body of research also exists claiming the exact opposite—most of the time, most people are generally not inclined to deliberate.[70]

The question before us, however, is not how many, but rather *which kinds* of people are more likely to attend meetings to discuss public issues. On this question, the results of the discursive participation survey tend to support the conventional view. Of "face-to-face deliberators"—those who reported participation in a formal or informal meeting—53 percent had at least some college education (39 percent had a college or postgraduate degree), and 51 percent had a family income around $50,000–$75,000 per year. These percentages were much higher than in the population as a whole. For instance, while only 9 percent of the whole sample had a postgraduate degree, twice that proportion of face-to-face participants had attained that level of education. Of respondents who indicated that they *never* talk about public issues, over 70 percent had a high school degree or less, and a similar percentage had a family income of less than $50,000 per year. Thus, the authors conclude that these disparities show education and income represent the most "consistent types of variation" in attendance at public meetings.[71]

Of course, it is difficult to make firm conclusions based upon a single survey. But other research indirectly supports this finding.[72] Research on communication within juries, for instance, shows that higher-status individuals speak more, make more suggestions, and are perceived by other jurists as being more accurate in their comments.[73] Similarly, research in psychology demonstrates that perceptions of an individual's expertise or competence are an important determinant of influence within a group.[74] Although such research is within the context of juries and other small group environments, it is broadly in line with the findings in the discursive participation survey and buttresses the criticism that political participation of all forms tends to be dominated by wealthier and more educated individuals.[75]

That said, Jacobs and his co-authors also find that inequalities in participation can be mitigated by social capital (measured in terms of organizational membership, religious attendance, and length of residence in the community) and to a lesser extent by political capital (measured in terms of political efficacy, political trust, social trust, political knowledge, political interest, political attention, and political tolerance).[76] In particular, they find that organizational membership strongly shapes participation: People who belong to organizations are more likely to have participated in a public meeting in the past year. Based on this finding, Jacobs and his colleagues argue for an expanded SES model that takes into account the conditionality of deliberative participation. They conclude that "social and economic status bias discursive participation," but that "opportunities created by community organizations and other factors" may mitigate the impact of these inequalities.[77] This connection between organizational membership and participation suggests that deliberative practitioners who use network-based "targeted recruitment" strategies seem to have found an approach that enhances participant diversity while limiting cost.

Moving Forward

What we do not know about participation in deliberative civic engagement far outweighs what we do know. Indeed, the question of who deliberates represents one of the most significant gaps in our understanding of deliberative practice. It is therefore a wide open and rich area for future research. What questions ought to guide this research?

The first is simply to ask whether the conclusions reached in the discursive participation survey apply to more carefully designed forms of deliberative civic engagement. This task might be accomplished in one of two ways. First, researchers might simply replicate the discursive survey and add questions that delve more deeply into the differences and similarities between ordinary political events and ones that feature the more advanced recruitment tactics we have discussed. Such work will provide a better sense of whether and how much deliberative civic engagement skews toward wealthier and more educated individuals. Of course, the costs associated with conducting a random, representative survey of a national population is an obstacle to such research.

Another approach—collecting better participation data at the hundreds of deliberative events sponsored every year across the country—addresses this concern. Given that these events are already under way, the inclusion of a short questionnaire would add little additional cost. It would require only that an enterprising researcher handle the logistics of distributing the questionnaires and gathering the data. Of course, the results of such a study would be less generalizable than a national survey. Moreover, given the many ways in which they differ, straight comparisons across deliberative civic engagement events would not be possible. Still, such work would have value; at the very least, it would provide a check on national survey data.

Second, more research is needed on the role of social and political capital in mitigating the impact of SES and educational inequalities. Although organizational memberships reduce inequalities, we do not yet know if this finding holds across contexts and circumstances. We also do not know if particular variables, like religious attendance or political knowledge, are more important in some contexts than others. It might be the case, for instance, that religious attendance is a stronger predictor of deliberative participation only when discussions are explicitly values-oriented. Or perhaps political knowledge is a stronger predictor of participation in policy-oriented events, but less so in more social or values-based conversations. Finally, we have little sense of the links across different variables. When it comes to deliberative participation, is education linked to political knowledge but not so much to SES? Or is social trust linked to length of residence in a community, and are these two variables linked to educational level? Do these links vary by deliberative context? Without knowing how variables relate to one another, our picture of the deliberative citizen will remain murky at best.

Recent work by political communication scholar Diana Mutz suggests a third and final avenue for future research. Using survey data, Mutz shows that people are more likely to participate in political activities when their social networks are homogeneous, and less likely to deliberate when their social networks are heterogeneous. As she puts it, "within any individual, enthusiastic participation rarely coexists with ongoing exposure to diverse political viewpoints and careful consideration of the political alternatives. Deliberation and participation, in other words, do not go hand in hand."[78] If true, Mutz's findings directly contradict a central tenet of deliberative theory, namely, that deliberation is a building block of participatory democracy.[79] Indeed, it suggests the exact opposite conclusion—that deliberative participation may be antagonistic to conventional political participation.

That being said, many other studies challenge this conclusion. For example, research shows that jury deliberators are more likely to vote,[80] that participants in Deliberative Polls often become more politically active,[81] and that online deliberation participants became more engaged in other community activities than nonparticipants.[82] Moreover, some research contradicts the link found by Mutz between heterogeneity of social networks and participation, instead showing that the diversity of an individual's social network actually increases the chances of participation in deliberation because people who have more heterogeneous networks are more accustomed to conflict and disagreement, and therefore have fewer qualms about participating in activities that require assessing divergent viewpoints.[83] Still other research has sought to qualify Mutz's claim, noting that individual psychological differences, such as ideological strength, or the presence/absence of emotions like aversion and anxiety, may create different links between deliberation and political participation.[84]

Given the importance of the issue of who deliberates, the inconclusiveness of the debate and empirical research is frustrating. Moving forward, the discovery of whether (and under what conditions) deliberation inhibits or promotes other forms of political participation is a vital task for the field.

Notes

1. Quoted in Mann and Leighninger (2011).
2. For reviews, see Shapiro (2010) and Urbinati (2006).
3. Mansbridge (1999c); Mendelberg (2002); Young (2000).
4. Callenbach, Phillips, and Sutherland (2008); Carson and Martin (1999); Leib (2004); Warren and Pearse (2008).
5. Neblo, Esterling, Kennedy, Lazer, and Sokhey (2010: 567).
6. Jacobs, Cook, and Delli Carpini (2009).
7. Jacobs, Cook, and Delli Carpini (2009).
8. Barber (1984); Bobbio (1987); MacPherson (1977).
9. Downs (1957); Olson (1965).
10. Pateman (1970); Dahl (1989).
11. Bellah, Madsen, Sullivan and Swidler (1984, 1989).
12. Putnam (2000); Skocpol and Fiorina (1999).

13. Hibbing and Theiss-Morse (1995); Nye, Zelikow and King (1997).
14. Barber (1984).
15. See, for example, Bessette (1997), Dryzek (1990), Elster (1998), and Gutmann and Thompson (1996).
16. For reviews, see Chambers (2003) and Freeman (2000). For a discussion of the rationales behind deliberative civic engagement in public administration, see Nabatchi (2010a).
17. Lippmann (1955: 24–25); see also Schumpeter (1950).
18. Button and Ryfe (2005: 30).
19. Gastil and Levine (2005); Sirianni and Friedland (2001); Leighninger (2006).
20. For reviews, see Delli Carpini, Cook and Jacobs (2004), Mendelberg (2002), and Ryfe (2005).
21. For a review of the empirical literature on these and other issues, see Delli Carpini, Cook, and Jacobs (2004) and Ryfe (2005).
22. Gastil, Deess, Weiser, and Simmons (2010); Gastil (2008); Melville, Willingham, and Dedrick (2005).
23. Huckfeldt and Sprague (1995); Knoke (1990); Krassa (1990); Leighley (1990, 2001); McLeod, Scheufele, Moy, Horowitz, Holbert, Zhang, Zubric, and Zubric (1999); Moscovici (1976, 1980); Mutz (2002a, 2002b); Nemeth (1986); Nemeth and Kwan (1985); Turner (1991); Walsh (2004).
24. Downs (1957).
25. Fiorina (2003); Leighley (2001); Rosenstone and Hansen (1993); Schuessler (2000).
26. Converse (1972: 324).
27. Nie, Junn, and Stehlik-Barry (1996: 4).
28. Verba and Nie (1972: 13).
29. Burns, Schlozman, and Verba (2001); Schlozman, Verba, and Brady (1994); Verba, Schlozman, and Brady (1995).
30. Han (2009).
31. Clary, Snyder, and Stukas (1996); Cutler and Danigelis (1986); Woodard (1987).
32. Burns, Schlozman, and Verba (2001: 360–361).
33. McAdam (1986: 70).
34. Knoke and Thomson (1977: 48); for reviews of this literature, see Knoke (1986) and Smith (1994).
35. Rotolo (2000: 1136).
36. Cacioppo and Petty (1982); Cacioppo, Petty, Feinstein, and Jarvis (1996); Cohen (1957); Cohen, Stotland, and Wolfe (1955).
37. Bandura (1997).
38. Campbell, Gurin, and Miller (1954: 187).
39. Vecchione and Caprara (2009).
40. Kellstedt, Zahran, and Vedlitz (2008).
41. See, for example, Finkel (1985) and Pateman (1970).
42. See, for example, Ulbig and Funk (1999).
43. Hayes, Scheufele, and Huge (2006).
44. Alesina and La Ferrara (2000); Mutz (2002a, 2006); Costa and Kahn (2003); Hill and Leighley (1999).
45. Jacobs and Skocpol (2005).
46. Lichterman (2005); Sundeen (1992); Warren (2001); Wilson and Janoski (1995); Wilson and Musick (1997, 1998).
47. Bartels (2008); Frank (2004); Patterson (2002).
48. Han (2009: 39).
49. Teske (1997: 96).
50. For a discussion, see Mettler and Soss (2004).
51. Campbell (2003).
52. Fung (2004).

53. Marston (1993).
54. Kumlin (2002); Lawless and Fox (2001).
55. Verba and Nie (1972).
56. Carr and Halvorsen (2001).
57. Davies, Blackstock, and Rauschmayer (2005); see also Fung (2003).
58. Leib (2004); O'Leary (2006).
59. For more on Brazil's participatory processes, see Coelho, Pozzoni, and Montoya (2005).
60. Burnheim (1985); Carson and Martin (1999); Sutherland (2008).
61. Gastil, Deess, Weiser, and Simmons (2010).
62. Fishkin and Farrar (2005).
63. Lee and Polletta (2009); Lee (2011); Leighninger (2006).
64. Lukensmeyer, Goldman, and Bingham (2005).
65. Conway (2000); Nie, Junn, and Stehlik-Barry (1996).
66. Ryfe (2002).
67. Personal conversation with Taylor Willingham, co-founder and director of Texas Forums.
68. Jacobs, Cook, and Delli Carpini (2009).
69. Neblo, Esterling, Kennedy, Lazer, and Sokhey (2010).
70. Eliasoph (1998); Hibbing and Theiss-Morse (2002); Posner (2004).
71. Jacobs and Skocpol (2005: 48).
72. Mendelberg (2002).
73. Hastie, Penrod, and Pennington (1983); Strodtbeck, James, and Hawkins (1957).
74. Bottger (1984); Kirchler and Davis (1986); Ridgeway (1981, 1987).
75. Mansbridge (1983); Sanders (1997); Young (2000).
76. Jacobs, Cook, and Delli Carpini (2009).
77. Jacobs and Skocpol (2005: 63).
78. Mutz (2006: 133).
79. Fishkin (1995); Katz (1994).
80. Gastil, Deess, Weiser, and Simmons (2010).
81. Fishkin (1995).
82. Price and Capella (2002).
83. McLeod, Scheufele, Moy, Horowitz, Holbert, Zhang, Zubric, and Zubric (1999).
84. MacKuen, Wolak, Keele, and Marcus (2010); Wojcieszak, Baek, and Delli Carpini (2010).

4

How People Communicate during Deliberative Events

LAURA W. BLACK

> I just wanted to blurt out that participating in this process has been the closest I have felt to being a part of a democratic process in my life. Though I have to admit that voting and jury duty are also pretty amazing and more direct. But still, this dialog, and all the participation— this is an important element of democracy, and it's an amazing feeling to be a part of it. It's also been really inspiring to see so many insightful comments from different people.
>
> —*Participant in Listening to the City online forum*

Participants in deliberative events routinely report excitement or even wonder at what they and their fellow citizens can accomplish together. For participants like the one quoted at the beginning of the chapter, it feels "inspiring" and "amazing" to be "part of a democratic process" by discussing issues and hearing "insightful comments from different people." Such reflections, however, raise questions. What is the character of the comments that participants find so inspiring? Were the discussions actually insightful, and how were such insights received? More generally, how do citizens talk with one another when given the opportunity and necessary tools to deliberate about public issues? This chapter addresses these issues by responding to a single focal question, *What do we know about how people actually communicate during deliberative civic engagement events?*

In the past twenty years, theories of democracy have taken a "deliberative turn,"[1] as scholars embrace a vision of democracy that centers on citizen discussions of public issues. During this time, deliberation has enjoyed growing popularity. Hundreds of organizations around the world have taken a deliberative approach to public problems.[2] (For an in-depth discussion, see Chapter 2.) In the United States, national and state-level events have been convened by well-known organizations, such as America*Speaks*, the Kettering Foundation, and the Center for Deliberative Polling, among many others. Many successful deliberative civic

events have also been convened in other countries, or even among multiple nations. Some of the best known of these events include participatory budgeting
meetings in Brazil,[3] the recent Australian Citizens' Parliament,[4] and Deliberative
Polls that have been held a variety of countries including Australia, Poland, Italy,
Ireland, Hungary, China, Denmark, and across the European Union.[5]

Still other deliberative events occur at a local level and are organized and
hosted by members of the community in which the event is held. Some of these
local events in the United States are aided by materials from national organizations such as Everyday Democracy. However, many are conducted by for-profit
planning and engineering firms or run by local agencies without guidance from
any outside group. Moreover, many localized environmental public forums have
been conducted as required by environmental legislation. Deliberative scholars
have studied many aspects of these local and national-level events, resulting in a
large body of scholarly work on deliberative civic engagement generally, and deliberative democracy specifically.[6]

Despite prolific scholarship in deliberative theory and great amounts of time,
energy, and resources devoted to running deliberative forums, surprisingly little
research has been done to systematically examine the actual discursive practices
of citizens as they deliberate.[7] Much of the scholarly literature offers theoretical
models of public deliberation that are seen as ideals groups might strive toward
but are likely never to fully achieve.[8] Moreover, the bulk of academic research on
deliberation tends to measure the *effects* of participating in these events,[9] often
without fully investigating what actually occurs when forum participants communicate with one another.

Critics and proponents of deliberation have raised concerns about this
research gap. As scholars Mark Button and Kevin Mattson argue:

> Democratic theory often generates models of deliberation which are
> then used as critical yardsticks against which political practices are
> nearly always found wanting. The deductive application of philosophic
> first principles through a fixed and often narrow definition of delibera-
> tion effectively shuts scholars off from existing political realities by sug-
> gesting that they have nothing to learn from actual political processes.
> A great deal of work has tried to define what scholars mean by delibera-
> tion. Not enough has been said about how deliberation actually works
> among citizens in localized contexts.[10]

This statement was written over a decade ago. Since that time, a modest body of
work has taken up the challenge of documenting and describing how participants in deliberative forums actually communicate when they are given the opportunity to deliberate. However, more work remains to be done. Such research

could aid those who design and host deliberative forums by describing the communication patterns they might expect to see and offering suggestions on how to facilitate productive deliberative discussion. A better understanding of how people communicate during deliberative civic events can also show where further study is needed and suggest particular aspects of participants' communication that might be more, or less, helpful for furthering deliberative ideals.

This chapter reviews the observations of deliberative scholars and practitioners about how people communicate during deliberation. I begin with a brief synopsis of some of the scholarly work that aims to define "deliberation." I then describe the key features that characterize deliberative practice as it occurs in some of the more prominent types of deliberative events. In the bulk of the chapter, I review the research on how people talk during deliberative events and explore the extent to which research findings connect with the scholarly conceptions of deliberation. I conclude with a summary and discussion of implications for deliberative research and practice.

Defining Deliberation

As other chapters in this book explain, many deliberative theorists base their conceptions on models of democracy such as those proposed by political scientist Robert Dahl, who provides ideal standards that bodies wishing to be democratic can use as criteria against which to measure themselves. In an ideal democracy, Dahl argues, citizens should have "adequate and equal" opportunities to participate in the democratic process, equal voting rights, and the ability to decide the topics to be put forth to the group. Democratic groups should also be inclusive of all citizens and promote citizens' "enlightened understanding" of public issues, including adequate information and understanding of their interests.[11] Deliberative theorists take these principles of democracy and place them in the context of communication.[12] For example, communication scholar John Gastil and his colleagues conceptualize deliberation in small groups as "(a) a process that involves the careful weighing of information and views, (b) an egalitarian process with adequate speaking opportunities and attentive listening by participants, and (c) dialogue that bridges differences among participants' diverse ways of speaking and knowing."[13]

Another way to think of this definition is to conceptually distinguish two distinct aspects of deliberation that occur simultaneously.[14] One aspect is an analytic process, which involves group members talking together in ways that allow them to develop a shared information base, clarify the key values at stake, identify and weigh the pros and cons of possible solutions, and make the best decision possible. The second process necessary in deliberation is the social interaction that develops quasi-democratic relationships among participants. This social process involves participants having equal and adequate opportunities to speak, demonstrating mutual comprehension and consideration of others' views, and communicating respect of the group members and their perspectives. The theoretical commitments to both analytic and social dimensions that are embedded in deliberative democracy serve as the anchor for deliberative events described in this chapter.

What Are Deliberative Events?

The growth of scholarship on democratic deliberation has coincided with the emergence of modest deliberative civic initiatives and proposals for even more far-reaching political reforms that foreground deliberative discussion among citizens.[15] Deliberative forums usually have specific goals. For instance, some aim to give officials a sense of what the public would think about a topic if the citizens all sat down and talked about it together,[16] and others hope to provide voters more information about multiple aspects of important issues.[17] Additionally, forum organizers have goals for the participants. The hope is that participating in deliberative discussion will not only to improve citizen knowledge of public issues but could also inspire individuals to get involved and take political action, such as volunteering, participating in small action groups, or influencing policy change.[18]

As the second chapter in this book attests, there are many types of deliberative forums in practice around the world. Many deliberative events occur at a local level, focus on community-level issues, and are organized by a wide range of local organizations. Other deliberative events are designed and/or hosted by larger organizations. Some examples of the better-known deliberative events are National Issues Forums, 21st Century Town Meetings, Study Circle Programs, Citizen Juries, and Deliberative Polls.[19] Despite their differences, each of these forums has three shared characteristics: They showcase interaction among participants, manifest characteristics of deliberative discussion, and are focused on public issues and public goods. (For more discussion on these and other issues, see Chapters 1 and 2.)

Features of Deliberative Civic Engagement Events

First, deliberative civic engagement forums provide attendees with an opportunity to interact with each other, usually in small groups. Unlike public hearings and other forms of public participation where citizens predominantly listen to experts and have very little opportunity to speak, deliberative events are premised on the idea that participants need to communicate with one another to think together about the issue at stake. For many forums, participants spend the bulk of their time talking together in groups of eight to twelve people. With the advent of interactive new media, many deliberative events are incorporating interactive technology to augment or replace face-to-face meetings (see Chapter 6 for a discussion about designing online deliberative civic engagement).[20] There is a great deal of variety in the types of media used and the process designs, but the bulk of these events use new media in ways that promote interaction among citizen participants.

Another defining feature of deliberative civic engagement is that such events provide some means to help the participants engage in a type of conversation that roughly corresponds with the tenets of deliberative theory. In other words, participants are not only given the opportunity to interact, but they are also provided with tools to help guide their communication toward the deliberative ideal. This guidance is provided through the incorporation of issue booklets or expert presenters, which provide comprehensive information about the issue being discussed, and the use of moderators or facilitators to guide group discussion.[21] Forum organizers and facilitators expend considerable effort designing the forums, creating ground rules with the participants, and thoughtfully managing the process of discussion. Through these efforts to structure the event and facilitate the communication process, moderators help guide the group's interaction to be in line with the analytic and social aspects of deliberative theory.

The final defining feature of deliberative civic engagement is that such forums are framed in public terms. One aspect of the public nature of deliberative forums is that the topic of the discussion is some kind of public concern or problematic situation.[22] Deliberative events are also public in two other ways. The participants themselves are often taken to represent "the public" as either a microcosm or a critical mass of people whose voices can represent the perspective of the broader civic group (see Chapters 3 and 5). Moreover, deliberative forums are public in the sense that most have some kind of connection to public officials or other experts. In addition to having public officials present to provide information, deliberative events often put the experts into a new role of listening to and taking responsibility to act on recommendations from deliberative participants.[23] Although the link to policy is not always present (and almost never guaranteed), many organizers of deliberative events make efforts to connect the forum outcomes to some kind of public action (see Chapter 9).

In sum, deliberative civic engagement events are public participation efforts that engage citizens in deliberative conversation with one another, often in the hope of informing public practice. The research reviewed later in this chapter examines the communication that occurs among participants during deliberative civic events. Research shows that there is evidence of both the analytic and social aspects of deliberation, yet there are also communication patterns that do not fit well into our current models of deliberative theory, and there is a great deal about participants' communication that we do not know.

Analysis and Decision Making

The analytic aspect of deliberation involves *creating a shared information base, clarifying values, identifying options, weighing pros and cons of possible solutions,* and *making decisions.* To what extent are these characteristics of deliberative discussion evident in the communication that occurs among participants of deliberative forums? Although only a handful of studies directly assess the communication that occurs in deliberative civic engagement, many provide evidence that participants engage in some degree of analytic communication. This section reviews that research and highlights the types of communication behaviors that are commonly found in deliberative groups.

Stating Opinions and Arguments

One predominant form of communication that occurs in deliberative events is argument. Several studies note that deliberative civic engagement participants often express their opinions about the issues being discussed and provide arguments to support their positions. For example, Jennifer Stromer-Galley's content analysis of online discussions in the Virtual Agora project[24] shows that 55 percent of the statements made by participants fell into the category of "reasoned opinion." This category includes making opinion statements, such as "I'm for K-8, because I think it solves the problems we face," and expressions of agreement or disagreement with other participants.[25] Similarly, in their examination of online discussions that occurred during the Electronic Dialogue Project, political communication scholars Vincent Price and Joseph Cappella note that about half of the statements made by participants were categorized as "arguments" for or against a proposed solution.[26]

These studies of online discussions provide direct evidence about the communication that occurs in deliberative forums because researchers systematically examined what people said during the group discussions. This kind of direct observation is much easier to perform for online forums—where contributions to the conversation are typed or otherwise recorded and easily available for analysis—than it is for forums that involve face-to-face meetings.

Another way that researchers investigate aspects of the communication itself is to ask participants for retrospective accounts of their experiences. Some research of face-to-face deliberative forums uses post-forum questionnaires and shows that deliberative participants believe their discussions included opinion statements and arguments. For example, a study of the 1996 National Issues Convention (NIC) notes that "almost 94 percent of the participants agreed that the important aspects of each issue were covered in the group discussions."[27] A recent study of over 700 citizens who had engaged in deliberative events found that participants described their experiences as "consistently grounded in the use of balanced information and fairly moderated reason-giving."[28]

The opinion statements and arguments made by participants during deliberative events can help them identify options and weigh the pros and cons of the proposed solutions. The studies cited previously do not provide an indication of the *quality* of the opinions and arguments made, or how systematically and rigorously participants weighed the pros and cons of the options provided. Yet roughly half the statements in the forums cited in these studies provided some kind of opinion statement or argument, and this could be encouraging to deliberative scholars, since it suggests that reasoned discussion occurred.

Citing Sources and Telling Stories

There are also indications that deliberative participants work to create a shared information base by providing evidence to support their statements. Sometimes participants use examples from the mass media or documents provided by the forum organizers as sources for their arguments. In online groups, members can post links to news stories or other information sources.[29] Other times they draw on statements made by other members of their discussion group.[30] But several studies have noted that the most common evidence that participants draw on to support their claims are personal stories.[31] For example, in his study of five National Issues Forums, communication scholar David Ryfe notes,

> What I find in my analysis is simply stated: when deliberating, participants in small group forums tell stories. They tell stories about themselves, their families, and their friends. They tell stories about events in the news, people at work, and casual acquaintances. Sometimes, they use other modes of talk: they argue, debate, or lecture. But the clear pattern is that they prefer to tell stories.[32]

Participants' stories provide examples of their experiences that are relevant to the issues being discussed and can also help group members build their own arguments or attempt to discredit or cast doubt on a proposal that they oppose.[33] Stories not only act as evidence for an argument but also can help participants make the implications of political issues more real and evident in their everyday lives.[34] Participants can then use stories to show connections between seemingly disparate positions by demonstrating how aspects of each proposal are reflected in people's everyday lives.[35] Moreover, stories can help participants in deliberative forums elicit help from other deliberators in identifying their own preferences[36] or even critique and resist the assumptions underlying claims from expert sources.[37] In these ways, stories can help deliberative groups build an information base, critically analyze information, and further their problem analysis and decision making.

Disagreement and Questions

As we might expect, when forum participants state opinions, make arguments, and provide evidence, they also sometimes disagree with each other.[38] The presence of different perspectives is central to deliberative theory,[39] and disagreements can be a useful way for these different perspectives to come to light. Disagreements can also help participants understand the trade-offs required for any one solution to be workable. In deliberative civic engagement, disagreement can be quite animated as participants engage in debate about proposals and challenge one another's arguments with counterexamples. Although deliberation varies from formal debate, the kind of analysis that comes from rigorous debate is important in deliberative events[40] and disagreement can influence how participants evaluate their experiences in deliberative forums.[41]

Recent research shows that deliberative groups engage in both agreement and disagreement.[42] For example, a national survey by political scientist Lawrence Jacobs and colleagues found that public forums strike a good balance between agreeing and disagreeing among participants. Although most of the survey respondents noted that "agreement" was the goal of the deliberative forum they participated in, they also noted that disagreement was common and that facilitators helped groups to air these differences. According to the retrospective accounts of forum participants, Jacobs and his colleagues found that "face-to-face deliberation does not appear to rely persistently on stereotyped arm twisting by a dogged advocate. Instead, public talk in face-to-face meetings tends to rely on raising differences and allowing the discussion of those differences to convince people, with some encouragement by facilitators."[43]

Yet, other research indicates that such disagreement is infrequent, and participants are sometimes reluctant to engage in overt conflict with each other. For example, Ryfe's study of National Issues Forums found that participants often engaged in disagreement indirectly, through telling stories, rather than directly challenging one another's opinions.[44] In a study of online deliberative groups, sociologists Francesca Polletta and John Lee found that telling personal stories was a way for group members to disagree with fellow deliberators without seeming antagonistic. But there was a downside: Participants were unwilling to tell personal stories during discussions that they saw as technical or policy focused.[45] Moreover, Tom Smith's study of the NIC reports that participants sometimes supported their arguments with facts that were incorrect or inaccurate, but those facts were usually not challenged or corrected by other participants.[46] Such self-correction by fellow citizens, along with external critique by policy advocates and neutral witnesses, was also an effective feature of the Oregon Citizens' Initiative Review, which used a more intensive week-long deliberative process to evaluate statewide ballot measures.[47] That said, if a reluctance to challenge others emerges during public forums, it can inhibit deliberation by fostering a superficial analysis of the proposals under discussion.

One study of a series of deliberative meetings in Seattle, Washington, found that participants challenged one another and engaged in disagreement through "raising questions."[48] Participants asked "factual questions" (such as, "What is the rate structure [in this proposal]?") when they wanted something to be clarified, but they "raised questions" to indicate that some issue needed further discussion. Such questions functioned not only to put or keep an issue on the table for further discussion but also to reinitiate conversation about a topic that, in the participant's opinion, might have been passed over too quickly. Although only a handful of studies has explicitly examined conflict during deliberative forums, it seems that people often engage in disagreement indirectly—through raising questions and telling stories—rather than through spirited and rigorous debate of the issues.

Exploring Key Values

One component of the analytic side of deliberation is that participants should articulate the key values at stake for the issue. Very few studies have directly investigated whether or how participants in deliberative forums explore their key values. Smith's study of the NIC group discussions notes that people asked questions related to the values of various proposals that were on the table,[49] but it is unclear from his report how thoroughly the group articulated and worked through these values in their conversations. At the aforementioned Oregon Citizens' Initiative Review, researchers identified values-consideration as the lowest-rated deliberative feature of two separate citizen panel discussions on important policy issues.[50]

Although understanding the key values at stake is important, it is often more difficult for people to talk about their values than it is to talk about positions and opinions. Typically, values are expressed subtly rather than articulated as the topic of conversation itself. Because of this subtlety, values expressed in deliberative forums may be most evident in the *way* people talk about their positions and reasons.

One way that people can express their core values is through telling stories. For example, Heather Walmsley's ethnographic study of deliberative events in British Columbia explains how participants told stories about their experiences, other people, and events from the news that demonstrated their own ethical concerns about biomedical issues.[51] Similarly, in the study of National Issues Forums cited earlier, David Ryfe provides an example using a story that one participant told during a discussion about the Internet. This participant says:

> I have been on the Internet for at least six years because my husband and I own a computer business. I've always been very excited by the potential of it, but I have to say that for about the last year and a half I have been just confounded by all the obscene material that flashes unsolicited on the screen. I go online at night when my fam—when my two young daughters and my husband are sitting in the family room, and I've had advertising banners with video clips with sex acts pop up. I feel that I'm being invaded in my home. We need to police this, or we need to have some kind of control.[52]

On the one hand, it is evident that this story is used to provide support for her argumentative position advocating more regulation of the Internet. However, what may be less obvious is that her story also displays her value on the importance of family, privacy, and having control over what occurs in her own home.

Facilitators of deliberative events may pick up on the key values expressed in stories such as this one and explicitly bring them into the discussion to help inform analysis. This kind of discussion about values is crucial to organizations that foster dialogue about controversial moral issues (such as the Public Conversations Project), and is built into their protocols for moderators.[53] Some deliberative civic engagement events emphasize value-oriented discussions, particularly as a way to link stories of personal experience to the larger policy issues on the table for discussion. This commitment to working through values can be seen in many of the community-level programs using Study Circles guides or other locally grown approaches to deliberation. For example, political scientist Katherine Cramer Walsh's research describes how community-level dialogues about race centered on discussion of the values held by community members and forum participants.[54] These values came out in personal stories, but then were also the focus of explicit discussion throughout the conversation.

However, value-oriented discussion is often not quite as explicit in deliberative forums that center on what National Issues Forum organizers call "choice work." Some forums use "dilemma activities" or scenarios designed to help participants walk through how different decisions might play out and what core values would be implicated in these decisions.[55] Yet, not much research has investigated the communication that occurs in these scenarios, so we know very little about how deliberative participants communicate their values during these forums. More research could be done to explore the ways in which people talk about their values in deliberative events and the extent to which these values are important in shaping their analysis and decisions.

Summary

The evidence we have from studies that directly examine the communication occurring during deliberative forums indicates that participants seem to take the analytic task seriously. They *create a shared information base* by drawing on the materials provided, the mass media, their personal experiences, and the statements made during the discussion. They *identify options* by stating their opinions and providing arguments for their preferred position. At times they disagree with each other, and they raise questions to further the discussion of the issues. They even seem to *weigh pros and cons* of different solutions to help them *make good decisions*. However, very little research has investigated whether or how participants *clarify the key values* at stake in their discussions. Moreover, some research indicates that participants are often uncomfortable engaging directly in conflict, and tend not to challenge the truthfulness of one another's facts, even when the facts are incorrect.

Because very few studies directly investigate conflict in deliberative forums, we really do not know much about how people manage their disagreements during deliberative events. Yet, if the tendency to avoid confrontation noted by some research holds true, it could limit participants' ability to adequately perform the analytic tasks posed by deliberation. Such a tendency may also indicate the importance of deliberation's social aspects. Even if deliberative groups are able to engage in analytic problem solving, the conversations are not living up to deliberative scholars' and practitioners' hopes unless those conversations can also embody aspects of democratic social relationships.

Building and Sustaining Social Relationships

Deliberative theory is not limited to the analytic aspects of group discussion. Ideal models of deliberation also provide some guidance about the social process and relationships that are created and maintained through group members' communication. In deliberative discussion, participants ought to have *equal and adequate opportunities to speak, understand and fully consider* each other's views, and *communicate respect* for their fellow group members.

Equality

Critics note that there are considerable barriers to equality in deliberative discussions because of group members' social status differences and the ways in which conversational norms privilege ways of speaking that are more comfortable for some social groups than others (see Chapters 5 and 11).[56] Deliberation scholars and practitioners advocate equality as centrally important in public discussions, but there is no consensus on how to assess such equality. It is rare for all group members to have exactly equivalent numbers of speaking turns or to speak the same number of words or to hold the floor for the exact same amount of time. And even so, trying to measure "equality" by counting the minutes or words or speaking turns taken by each member does not adequately address what deliberative scholars mean. More important in deliberation events is that all participants *feel* they had the same opportunity to speak and that they were able to say what they wanted to say. For some, that might take five minutes, whereas for others it would take twenty, and for still others it might require no time at all if someone else had already expressed their view earlier in the discussion.

Take, for example, Smith's study of the NIC conversations. He found that participation in this event was widespread (approximately 80 percent of the participants said something during the conversations), but not balanced (all conversations studied had some participants who were much more active than others). At the same time, 99 percent of the respondents agreed with the questionnaire item "the group leader provided the opportunity for everyone to participate in the discussion."[57] In online forums, to take another example, equality can be harder to measure if discussions are asynchronous and it is easy for many group members to "lurk" by reading comments without posting their own contributions. Although everyone has equal opportunity to speak, by virtue of the online forum design, considerable differences remain in the levels of participation.[58]

Perhaps the most noteworthy efforts to promote equality in deliberative conversations come from trained facilitators who moderate the discussions. These moderators receive extensive training on how to help participants engage in discussion that involves both well-informed analysis and respectful listening by giving equal and adequate consideration of diverse viewpoints.[59] Good facilitators are important in deliberative events because they monitor the conversational flow to make sure everyone has been given the opportunity to speak and that groups are following the norms of deliberative discussion as much as possible. Facilitators can also help frame how group members respond to others' comments by summarizing key points, asking clarifying questions, thanking group members for participating, and reminding the group of the interaction guidelines they agreed to for the conversation.[60] A recent survey of citizens who had engaged in deliberative forums indicates that most participants found their facilitator to be successful at "making sure that everyone's opinion was heard" during the event.[61]

Facilitation is not unproblematic, however. In a case study of deliberative meetings, Caitlin Wills Toker raises questions about facilitators' positions of authority in the group. She observed that facilitators were able to take more speaking time than they should (thus not promoting equality) and use the language of the "deliberative framework" to unfairly define which topics were important. This framing discouraged participants from voicing concerns that seemed disconnected to the framework provided but may still have been relevant to the issues.[62]

Another study, which examined public deliberation in New York after 9/11, describes how facilitators guided participants away from analyzing and responding to one another's arguments and toward "the round-robin non-participatory style" because the topic was so volatile that equal participation was of primary importance.[63] In the case of the New York discussions, the control exerted by facilitators seemed to be appropriate and helpful for deliberation, rather than coercive. Yet both studies indicate the power and responsibility facilitators have to both promote equality and to foster the other social aspects of deliberative discussion such as consideration and respect.

Consideration and Comprehension

Two more elements of deliberation's social aspect are that participants fully consider each other's views and that they make efforts to understand one another. According to several studies, participants in deliberative event express and are exposed to a range of diverse opinions in their conversation and report that they find themselves reflecting on and appreciating perspectives and opinions that are different from their own.[64] For example, Polletta's study of the deliberations following 9/11 found that participants gave more credence to perspectives voiced by other group members simply because the speaker was right there in front of them. The personal co-presence that accompanies face-to-face deliberation helped group members consider other people's perspectives more than they might have if they had heard the same information from a more distant source. In other studies, participants report feeling that their opinions were really listened to and that they made efforts to listen to others.

To consider fully another's point of view, participants need to make efforts to understand each other. Studies of online forums have shown that discussion posts tend to build on the topics introduced by other participants and demonstrate a basic level of comprehension among the participants.[65] Clearly, it is good to know that participants can have topical coherence and that the speakers demonstrate that they understand each other on a basic level, but this does not tell us how much comprehension is occurring for the quieter members of deliberative forums. Moreover, Thomas Webler and Seth Tuler's case study of a Citizens' Advisory Council provides an example of the difficulties that can arise when stakeholders from different groups use terminology and language choices not shared by the group. One participant in their study reported,

> I think, in many instances, people in a certain profession, whether it is medicine or education or logging, there is a certain terminology that goes with that profession. And many times people, when they are trying to explain or get a point across, they talk over people who are not familiar. . . . And that does happen when you go to meetings. There are people there— environmental people, industrial people, wildlife people—and all of a sudden they are putting an X up and someone else is seeing a Y there.[66]

The stakeholders' language choices and the varied meanings of terminology used can make it difficult for participants in deliberative civic engagement to fully understand each other. Forum organizers and facilitators can be useful in this regard by introducing shared terminology, asking participants to define their terms, and monitoring group members' nonverbal behavior to gauge how well they understand one another and when they are confused. The move toward a shared understanding of the issue is important for deliberative groups, and more research is needed to help us understand exactly how group members and facilitators go about building that understanding.

Respect

The final social aspect of deliberation requires that participants demonstrate respect for one another. Although respect is difficult to measure, it is also an important part of what scholars and practitioners notice about the discussion during deliberative events. In a sense, respect is the cornerstone of deliberation's social aspects; without it, group members would scarcely be motivated to listen to each other, consider one another's views, or give everyone equal opportunity to participate.

The good news is that several case studies observe respectful discussions. Polletta notes that the participants she interviewed after the post-9/11 deliberations "appreciated that their table-mates had been 'respectful;' that discussion had been 'calm,' that people didn't 'rant,' that 'there was no shouting and everyone heard us.' They referred frequently to the fact that they liked their table-mates, and that their group had, as one put it, 'clicked.'"[67] Similarly, participants in the NIC commented about the respect in the forum. A moderator noted that she was impressed with the "respect and cooperation" in the group. One participant commented, "I thought it would be screaming and yelling, but it wasn't," and another said, "It was great to be able to say what you think in a group of people without getting into a bar fight."[68]

Although these comments are encouraging because they seem to indicate that participants find their conversations to be respectful, there is still a great deal about respect that we do not understand. For instance, these retrospective accounts seem to define respectful interaction by what it is not (i.e., screaming, yelling, ranting) rather than by describing what it is. Although it is very good news that participants feel respected during deliberative events, that the extant research does not provide a good description of *how that respect is communicated* during the forum is troubling. Most of our measures of respect come from post-event surveys rather than the analysis of the conversation itself, so we have only a limited understanding of what respectful communication looks like, and how (and to what extent) it occurs, in deliberative events.

Communicating beyond "Deliberation"

The studies reviewed here also demonstrate that participants in deliberative forums sometimes communicate in ways that do not easily fit into the model of deliberative communication provided by academics. Two other general observations are that participants express a wide range of emotions, some of which are seen as quite valuable by facilitators, and that they make statements about their identities that can bear on the deliberative process. The categories of emotional expression and identity are relevant to how communication unfolds during deliberative events, as well as to many of the concerns articulated by deliberative theorists. Yet they have not been fully integrated into normative models provided by deliberative theory. Their occurrence in deliberative forums indicates the need for more detailed study and may also indicate the usefulness of revisiting aspects of deliberative theory.

Emotional Expression

As described earlier, the traditional deliberative models emphasize "reason giving" as the primary form of deliberative discourse, and more recent scholars have argued that emotional expression and personal experience are also important in deliberative discussion. Yet the role that "emotion" plays in deliberation is not very clear. Despite this theoretical dispute, it is not surprising that participants in deliberative civic engagement events express emotions and evaluate certain emotions as helping or hindering their discussion.

An influential article by political scientists Simon Thompson and Paul Hoggett noted that the emotional dynamics of deliberative groups are very real, and some of these dynamics threaten the group's ability to deliberate well.[69] For example, it is easy for groups to become factionalized or engage in emotional dynamics that intimidate certain group members and create unequal opportunity for participation. The authors argue that forum organizers, moderators, facilitators, and members of deliberative groups should become aware of the emotional dynamics to help groups avoid these negative dynamics and encourage emotional dynamics that facilitate productive deliberation. The aforementioned national survey found that most respondents did *not* indicate that they felt emotions such as anger or anxiety during public forums they attended,[70] but a study of actual criminal and civil jurors found that the overwhelming majority had emotional experiences during the course of their deliberation, with most of those experiencing conflicting emotions ranging from civic pride (at serving as a juror) to sadness (about a victim) and frustration (with the process).[71] Thus, the possibility of potentially damaging emotional dynamics should be considered.

Only a handful of studies explicitly examine emotional expression in deliberative groups. One communicative use of emotion that has been observed in a few studies is humor. Political scientist Jane Mansbridge and her colleagues asked experienced facilitators to observe recordings of deliberative groups and note when "good" and "bad" moments occurred.[72] The deliberative practitioners who watched videotaped forum discussions indicated humor as being important to help build the social atmosphere of trust among participants. Communication scholar Rebecca Townsend's ethnographic study of a New England town meeting describes how participants' inside jokes helped them establish a shared frame of reference for their work.[73] Similarly, Smith noted that many of the statements in the NIC groups he observed were humorous and that those statements seemed to be appreciated by other group members.[74] These findings hint that humor could be part of the relational aspect of deliberation, as it is in the more general field of group communication, but so far humor has not received much attention in deliberative theory.

The facilitators in Mansbridge's study also noted that some other aspects of emotional expression were important, with a significant distinction being made between "positive" and "negative" emotion. Emotional expressions such as humor could be positive by furthering the social atmosphere, and other emotional expressions could help further the participants' ability to complete the task by allowing participants to show the "depth" of the problem or "passion" about the issue. This second function of emotion is somewhat consistent with claims made by feminist scholars who advocate testimony, emotional expression, and storytelling as important parts of deliberation.[75] These studies also indicate the need for further research that examines how emotionality is expressed in deliberative civic engagement forums and what influence emotional expression has on the analytic tasks and social relationships inherent in a deliberative process.

Identity Statements

Another communicative phenomenon that has been noticed by a few deliberative scholars is the way people identify themselves during their discussions. Many deliberative scholars postulate that participating in deliberation can enhance one's sense of identity as a citizen,[76] and the few studies that have noticed identity statements during deliberative events pose some interesting questions for how identity ought to factor into deliberative theory and practice.

One way that group members express identity is to note that they are speaking "for" the public in some way. Polletta observes that participants in the post-9/11 forums viewed themselves as representative of the public and were proud of the "diversity" in the group, even though they were not randomly selected to participate based on a demographically representative sample. Nonetheless, the participants articulated a sense of collective identification as public representatives.

In contrast, participants could identify themselves as members of specific social groups and provide arguments that serve their own best interest rather than sharing a common concern for their collective identity. For example, a study of deliberative decision making in Sweden found that participants sometimes perform their identities as "concerned parents" through their argumentative statements.[77] This study offers only a glimpse into the actual communication occurring in public forums, but it poses questions about how these identity performances are accomplished and what difference they might make for the quality of the deliberative discussion.

In their study of the 1996 NIC discussions, political communication scholars Rod Hart and Sharon Jarvis note that the participants used "us" and "we" during their discussions to refer to a wide range of identification targets (for example, "us" could refer to the American people, a participant's family, members of the NIC discussion group, or a number of other groups). Their study finds that the pattern developed from these plural first-person pronouns can provide a glimpse into the cultural identity of Americans.[78] In the equally individualistic cultural context, a study of the Australian Citizens' Parliament found that identity expressions of "us Australians" did more than express mutual affection; it also served to raise consciousness of the need to address the distinct political concerns of Aboriginal Australians, who were explicitly included in the collective "we."[79]

A few studies have noted that identity statements are evident in people's personal stories and the responses given during deliberative events. Ryfe notes that stories told during a National Issues Forum discussion can help participants take on what he calls the "deliberative posture" necessary for deliberative discussion.[80] In my study of an online forum following the post-9/11 deliberative events, I find that the way people use the words "us" and "we" can be important for how they identify with one another and manage their disagreements during deliberation.[81] For example, when people told stories that used "inclusive" pronouns (referring to social groups that included their fellow group members), they demonstrated a connection with other group members that helped them manage their disagreement in a collegial and collaborative way. In contrast, using "exclusive" pronouns highlighted the speaker's own social identity, but placed the speaker in contrast with other members of the deliberative group. These exclusive identity categories tended to put the other deliberative group members into a group of "them" or "you," rather than "us," which emphasized an adversarial conflict management approach that furthered divisiveness in the group.

Finally, a brief write-up comparing face-to-face and online forums using the National Issues Forum format found that participants use more "I" statements and "we" statements in the online forum.[82] The authors posit that there may be something about the online format that prompts people to use more identity statements, which is an argument also made in a study of the Virtual Agora Project.[83] A fuller examination of how deliberative group members present, negotiate, and manage their identities through their discussions could be particularly important for forums dealing with cultural, rather than policy, issues[84] and for the movement toward understanding the role of dialogue in the deliberative process.[85]

Conclusion

The studies reviewed for this chapter provide a relatively positive assessment of the quality of communication that occurs in public events designed to promote citizen deliberation. The available research indicates that when citizens are gathered together in deliberative forums and given appropriate structure and guidance, they engage in conversation that generally embodies the analytic and social aspects of deliberative civic engagement. Participants state opinions, exchange arguments, provide sources for their opinions, raise questions, and disagree with one another. They recognize the importance of equality, feel that the facilitators are generally fair, consider each other's views, and observe, and appreciate, that their conversations are respectful.

Nonetheless, sometimes the information participants exchange is incorrect, or their disagreements remain too vague, or their opinions are poorly formed. Sometimes group members use confusing language or feel that facilitators unfairly manipulate the conversations. Also, full equality is hard to gauge when people participate at different levels or unconsciously defer to social norms that privilege certain social groups more than others. Moreover, issues of emotion and identity seem relevant in deliberative events, yet it is unclear how these are communicated and what role they play in discussions. In addition, personal storytelling seems to be common, and important, in deliberative events, and yet it is only beginning to be adequately recognized by theorists and researchers.

Very few studies provide detailed descriptions and depictions of the actual communication that occurs in deliberative civic engagement events, so claims offered in this chapter need to be taken cautiously. It would be useful to have more research that investigates aspects of how people communicate in deliberative events. Specifically, studies could explore some of deliberation's social dimensions such as comprehension and respect, to see how these are communicated and what happens when they do not occur. Research on analytic dimensions could include issues of argumentation and persuasion, conflict management, and the role of personal experience. Moreover, research is needed to understand how people communicate about their values and the ways in which they go about prioritizing the key values of the community at stake for the issues.

Given that much of the research cited here was done in the United States, there is still a great deal we do not know about how people communicate in deliberative events in other countries. It would be useful to know how communication styles vary across different groups and how those differences affect deliberation in different cultural settings. Finally, as computer-mediated communication becomes a common means of citizen engagement and deliberation, it would be useful to have more research comparing how the communication in online forums relates to what we know about deliberative discussion in more traditional face-to-face events. Such investigations could help further deliberative theory and provide practitioners with a sense of best practices and an assessment of how well their programs are meeting the aims of deliberative civic engagement.

These findings also provide a challenge for deliberative scholars to think differently about our research. If we truly want to understand the communication processes that occur in deliberative events and get a sense about why the communication matters, we need to start asking different research questions. In addition to asking how well people deliberate according to ideals put forth by deliberative theory, we should do more to approach research from another direction. That is, more studies need to address descriptive questions such as "What are people doing when they come together to deliberate?" "What does deliberation look and sound like in particular localized contexts?" and "What does deliberation mean to people who design, facilitate, and participate in these events?" Such an inductive approach to understanding communication practices and meanings not only holds practical implications for forum design and implementation but also can extend, critique, and develop deliberative theory. Although this call for descriptive research in deliberation has been made before,[86] and a handful of deliberative scholars have taken up this challenge,[87] I argue that we still have a long way to go.

In conclusion, regardless of how well the actual communicative practices of forum participants fit with theoretical models, what is happening in deliberative forums is innovative, promising, and exciting. Deliberative practice engages citizens in public life and uses the insights generated by ordinary citizens' conversations to build better communities and address public problems. What happens in deliberative events is vastly different from politics as usual, and participants often report being pleasantly surprised by their experiences in these events. Deliberative ideals are just that—*ideals*. The actual practice of deliberative discussion will always come up somewhat short, albeit by varying degrees. When we look at what is happening in deliberative civic forums, however, and compare that with other types of public participation (or with the hopes and expectations of forum designers and participants), we see much success. Though more research is needed, the results thus far affirm a great deal of deliberative civic engagement's promise.

Notes

1. Dryzek (2000).
2. Ryfe (2002) makes this claim in his review of deliberative organizations, and some examples of organizations that employ aspects of deliberation can be found through the Deliberative Democracy Consortium (http://www.deliberative-democracy.net/) and the National Coalition for Dialogue and Deliberation (http://www.thataway.org/).
3. Coelho, Pozzoni, and Montoya (2005).
4. Dryzek (2009); Hartz-Karp and Carson (2009).
5. Fishkin (2009c); Fishkin and Farrar (2005). Also see the Center for Deliberative Democracy's Web site (http://cdd.stanford.edu/).
6. Delli Carpini, Cook, and Jacobs (2004) offer an excellent review of the empirical research on deliberation. Some more recent work can be found in the *Journal of Public Deliberation* (http://services.bepress.com/jpd/).
7. This observation is made by many deliberative scholars, including Black, Burkhalter, Gastil, and Stromer-Galley (2010), Button and Mattson (1999), and Ryfe (2006).
8. Gastil (2000).
9. Muhlberger's (2006) review of the deliberation literature and Black, Burkhalter, Gastil, and Stromer-Galley's (2010) chapter about methods for studying deliberation provide many examples of such studies. Also see Chapter 10 in this volume.
10. Button and Mattson (1999: 610).
11. Dahl (1989: 109–116).
12. See, for example, Habermas (1984, 1987, 1996b) and Cohen ([1989] 1997a, [1996] 1997b).
13. Burkhalter, Gastil, and Kelshaw (2002: 21). This definition is similar to one offered by Guttman (2007).

14. This argument is developed fully in Gastil (2008) and Gastil and Black (2008).
15. See, for example, Ackerman and Fishkin (2002), Chambers (2003), Crosby (1995), Crosby and Nethercut (2005), Delli Carpini, Cook, and Jacobs (2004), Fishkin and Luskin (1999), Gastil (2000), Gastil and Levine (2005), Lukensmeyer, Goldman, and Brigham (2005), and Ryfe (2005).
16. This phrase comes from Jim Fishkin (1991), the creator of Deliberative Polling.
17. Gastil and Knobloch (2010).
18. See, for example, studies by Cappella, Price, and Nir (2002), Gastil and Dillard (1999a, 1999b), Gastil, Deess, Weiser, and Simmons (2010), Price and Capella (2002), and Warren (1992).
19. Specific information on the organizations hosting these deliberative events can be found at their Web sites: National Issues Forums (http://nifi.org/), 21st Century Town Meetings (http://americaspeaks.org/), Study Circles (http://www.everyday-democracy.org/), Citizen Juries (http://www.jefferson-center.org/), and Deliberative Polls (http://cdd.stanford.edu/).
20. Some well-known events that use computer-mediated technology include 21st Century Town Meetings, the Virtual Agora Project (Muhlberger 2005a), e-the People (Weiksner 2005), and the Electronic Dialogue Project (Cappella, Price, and Nir 2002; Price and Cappella 2002). See Davies and Gangadharan (2009) for a comprehensive review of online forums and design choices.
21. Jacobs, Cook, and Delli Carpini's (2009) survey of people who had participated in deliberative events indicate that 83 percent of the people stated that their forum had a facilitator.
22. Guttman (2007).
23. See Hendriks (2005b).
24. Stromer-Galley (2007).
25. Stromer-Galley (2007: 10).
26. Price and Cappella (2002).
27. Smith (1999: 46).
28. Jacobs, Cook, and Delli Carpini (2009: 75). This study is discussed in detail in Chapter 2 of this volume.
29. Polletta, Chen, and Anderson (2009).
30. Stromer-Galley (2007: 15).
31. Both Stromer-Galley (2007) and Smith (1999) make this claim. Other work about storytelling in deliberation includes Black (2008, 2009), Polletta (2008), Polletta and Lee (2006), Ryfe (2006), and Walmsley (2009).
32. Ryfe (2006: 73).
33. See Black (2009), Polletta (2008), Polletta and Lee (2006), and Walsh (2007).
34. Black (2008); Walsh (2007).
35. Black (2008); Walsh (2007).
36. Polletta and Lee (2006).
37. Walmsley (2009).
38. Black (2009); Smith (1999); Stromer-Galley (2007).
39. Barber (1984); Bohman (2007); Gutmann and Thompson (1996); Wyatt, Katz, and Kim (2000).
40. See Walsh (2007) on the importance of debate in deliberation.
41. Stromer-Galley and Muhlberger (2009).
42. Stromer-Galley and Muhlberger's (2009) investigation of online deliberative groups found that group members expressed both agreement and disagreement. Agreement was expressed more often (about three times for every two statements of disagreement), but both were common.
43. Jacobs, Cook, and Delli Carpini (2009: 77).
44. Ryfe (2006). Stromer-Galley (2007) noted that disagreement occurred in only 5 percent of the "thought units" present in the discussion. See also Walsh (2007).
45. Polletta and Lee (2006).

46. Smith (1999: 48).
47. Gastil and Knobloch (2010).
48. Leighter and Black (2010).
49. Smith (1999: 49). More generally, see Black (2008).
50. Gastil and Knobloch (2010).
51. Walmsley (2009).
52. Ryfe (2006: 78).
53. See Public Conversations Project's Web site for more information (http://publicconversationsproject.org).
54. Walsh (2007).
55. See Hartz-Karp (2005); Gutmann (2007: 421).
56. Fraser (1992); Karpowitz and Mansbridge (2005a); Rushdon (2007); Sanders (1997).
57. Smith (1999: 44–45).
58. Stromer-Galley (2007).
59. For examples, see moderator training information provided by NIF (http://nifi.org/forums/organize.aspx) and AmericaSpeaks (http://americaspeaks.org/index.cfm?fuseaction=Page.viewPage&;pageId=550). See also Gastil (2000: 116–117) for a description of the moderators' role during National Issues Forums.
60. See Gastil and Levine (2005), Mansbridge, Hartz-Karp, Amengual, and Gastil (2006), Matthews and McAfee (2003), and Ryfe (2006) on the importance of facilitators for deliberative events.
61. Jacobs, Cook, and Delli Carpini (2009: 77).
62. Toker (2005).
63. Polletta (2008).
64. Polletta (2008); Smith (1999); Webler and Tuler (2000).
65. Stromer-Galley (2007) makes this observation about the conversations that occurred during the Virtual Agora Project. Black, Welser, DeGroot, and Cosley (2008) report a similar finding about the policy-making discussions on Wikipedia.
66. Webler and Tuler (2000: 584).
67. Polletta (2008: 7).
68. Smith (1999: 46).
69. Thompson and Hoggett (2001).
70. Jacobs, Cook, and Delli Carpini (2009: 78).
71. Gastil, Deess, Weiser, and Simmons (2010: 83–88).
72. Mansbridge, Hartz-Karp, Amengual, and Gastil (2006).
73. Townsend (2009).
74. Smith (1999).
75. Fraser (1992); Sanders (1997); Young (1996).
76. Citizen identity is mentioned by Burkhalter, Gastil and Kelshaw (2002) as a part of model of deliberation, and linked to the concept of "pro-social reasoning" by Muhlberger (2007). Gastil, Black, Deess, and Leighter (2008) also tested the relationship between deliberation and civic identity in their study of jurors.
77. Svensson (2008).
78. Hart and Jarvis (1999).
79. Hartz-Karp, Anderson, Gastil, and Felicetti (2010).
80. Ryfe (2006).
81. Black (2008); Black (2009).
82. Dudley, Morse, and Armstrong (2008).
83. Muhlberger (2007).
84. See Levine, Fung, and Gastil (2005).
85. See Black (2008), Kelshaw (2007), Levine, Fung, and Gastil (2005), and Pearce and Littlejohn (1997); see also the National Coalition for Dialogue and Deliberation (http://www.thataway.org).

86. For instance, by Button and Mattson (1999), whose call is presented in the beginning of this chapter.

87. Deliberative scholars such as Katherine Cramer Walsh (2007), David Ryfe (2006), Jay Leighter (2007), Leighter and Black (2010), Rebecca Townsend (2009), and Heather Walmsley (2009) provide excellent examples of research that investigates localized deliberative practices by using ethnographic research methods.

5

Deliberation in Multicultural Societies

Addressing Inequality, Exclusion, and Marginalization

ALICE SIU AND DRAGAN STANISEVSKI

Princeton: "Well he's Trekkie Monster, and you're Kate Monster . . .
Are you two related?"
Kate Monster: "What?! Princeton, I'm surprised at you! I find that
racist! . . . No, not all Monsters are related . . . "
Both (signing): "Everyone's a little bit racist, sometimes . . . . Doesn't
mean we go around committing hate crimes. . . . No one's really color
blind . . . "[1]

> —*Excerpts from the song "Everyone's a Little Bit Racist" in the Tony
> Award-winning musical, Avenue Q.*

In the musical *Avenue Q*, Kate Monster dreams of opening a school exclusively
for monsters, a move that Princeton initially finds racist. This dilemma, so well
illustrated in the play, stresses one of the crucial issues for facilitating deliberation in culturally diverse democracies: How do we reconcile the individual freedom of association, often with like-minded voices, with the perceived necessity
of communicating across cultural differences?[2] One cannot assume the feasibility of genuine intercultural deliberation and dialogue because significant challenges await those who seek to bridge divisions among the incommensurable
cultural narratives that often ground citizens' views.[3]

Avenue Q wittily points out how people are treated differently because of gender, race, education, and other socioeconomic classifications. If people are not
really color-blind (or gender-blind or class-blind) on the street, in the neighborhood, and in the workplace, how can they be color-blind in deliberative civic
engagement events with strangers?

In this chapter, we argue that although it is often possible to transcend racial or
other cultural divisions even in situations of seemingly intractable intercultural
conflicts, citizens rarely remain color-blind, objective, or impartial.[4] Thus, we assert that deliberative civic engagement processes are most effective when they

encourage participants to bring up questions of race and difference and create a safe space for addressing those issues candidly and productively. Helping participants recognize and deal with difference, rather than expecting them to be blind to it, may be essential for the broader social inclusion of marginalized voices and tolerance of diverse views in intercultural deliberative civic engagement.

We focus on two crucial questions pertinent to deliberative civic engagement in culturally diverse societies, *How can we foster greater inclusion of diverse participants in intercultural deliberative civic engagement? And how can we enable deliberative civic engagement across cultural differences?* We aim to provide insight into the experiences of diverse deliberative participants, and we assess the effectiveness of various strategies used to alleviate inequalities, marginalization, and other obstacles to deliberation. In addressing these questions, we distinguish between external and internal exclusion.[5] We also discuss how diverse people experience deliberative civic engagement and whether current strategies effectively address inequality, marginalization, and other similar challenges. Finally, we present and consider alternative strategies for addressing these issues, such as the mandatory inclusion of diverse groups, providing adequate information to participants, using moderators, adhering to standards of deliberative reciprocity, the inclusion of alternative modes of communication, and providing opportunity for consensual and concurrent decision making. We conclude with a brief discussion about areas for future research.

Exclusion and Marginalization in Deliberative Civic Engagement

Proponents of deliberative civic engagement argue that during deliberation people carefully weigh arguments, listen to competing viewpoints, and emerge with considered, reasoned opinions.[6] Theorists also assert that deliberation increases civic engagement and political interest and creates a more participatory citizenry (see Chapter 7).[7] In *Considerations on Representative Government*, nineteenth-century British philosopher and civil servant John Stuart Mill discusses the importance of political participation. He emphasizes the need for an environment conducive to deliberation or, in his words, a "school of public spirit."[8] Specifically, Mill argues that every citizen should

> weigh interests not his own; to be guided, in case of conflicting claims, by another rule than his private partialities; to apply, at every turn, principles and maxims which have for their reason of existence the general good; and he usually finds associated with him in the same work minds more familiarized than his own with these ideas and operations, whose

study it will be to supply reason to his understanding, and stimulation to his feeling for the general good. . . . Where this school of public spirit does not exist, scarcely any sense is entertained that private persons, in no eminent social situation, owe any duties to society, except to obey the laws and submit to the government. There is no unselfish sentiment of identification with the public.[9]

In these "schools of public spirit," Mill argues, every citizen, "from those who have done nothing in their lives but drive a quill or sell goods over a counter," would be given the opportunity to enlighten his or her fellow citizens with personal stories, experiences, and opinions.[10] He stresses the importance of providing such deliberative atmospheres, so that average citizens can participate in the political process. In these deliberative environments, people from varying socioeconomic backgrounds would gather in one place to share their thoughts and opinions, and in doing so, become more open-minded and empathic toward others in their communities.

This normative vision of deliberative civic engagement has not only been criticized by opponents (see Chapter 11)[11] but has also been qualified by deliberative theorists themselves.[12] Even social theorists and historians as far back as Alexis de Tocqueville, writing in the nineteenth century, have observed the tendency of the majority suppressing the minority in participatory forms of democracy.[13] Critics therefore argue that the full and equal participation ideal of deliberative democracy cannot be achieved in the presence of social inequalities, cultural divisions, and uneven distribution of power.[14] Furthermore, they suggest that deliberation could do more harm than good not only to the participants, but also to democracy; societal inequalities are inevitably brought into deliberative settings and could exasperate intercultural conflicts and further marginalize minority voices. Thus, critics argue, participants from marginalized communities, if included in a deliberation, would not be treated fairly and would not be able to participate as equals.

Though inclusion and equality are normative ideals in both democracy and deliberative civic engagement, some degree of exclusion and marginalization is likely even in pluralist democracies. Iris Marion Young, a University of Chicago professor until her death in 2006, argued that the almost inevitable struggle for resources and uneven distribution of power perpetuates the exclusion of marginalized voices in public deliberations.[15] In her typology, Young distinguished between external and internal exclusion. External exclusion refers to the many ways in which individuals and groups are purposely or inadvertently left out of public deliberations. Typical forms of external exclusion include back-door brokering and lobbying, inaccessibility of deliberative fora, and the ability of economically or socially powerful actors to exercise political domination, such as media influence, political influence through campaign finances, and economic intimidation of the local citizenry.[16]

Others also emphasize external exclusion as a serious obstacle to achieving the normative ideal of equal and open deliberation in the public sphere. In particular, many social and political theorists have criticized conceptions of the public sphere that follow those of German scholar Jürgen Habermas, who defines it as "the sphere of private people coming together as a public."[17] Nancy Fraser questions the legitimacy of the public sphere as a place where culture is debated and agreements are built in the form of public opinions through use of critical-rational argumentation.[18] She argues that the public sphere is incapable of bracketing societal inequalities, and people cannot deliberate "as if" they are social equals.[19] Similarly, Jane Mansbridge argues that the bracketing of societal inequalities would benefit dominant groups and disadvantage minority groups, and that deliberation could legitimate domination over minority groups.[20] Habermas himself recognizes that the advent of mass advertising, commercialization of media, bureaucratization of society, and increasing influence of special-interest associations and corporate businesses transform the public in modern societies from a culture-debating to a culture-consuming public.[21]

In contrast, internal exclusion concerns the ways that participants in deliberative engagement lack the ability to influence the thinking of other participants.[22] In theory, Young writes, "the deliberative model of democracy is a form of practical reason," whereby "participants arrive at a decision not by determining what preferences have greatest numerical support, but by determining which proposals the collective agrees are supported by the best reasons."[23] In practice, however, even if deliberation is inclusive of every affected person, there remains a difference in how participants are treated because of people's inability to strip themselves of their political and social statuses and deliberate as equals.[24] By not acknowledging differences and "by restricting their concept of democratic discussion narrowly to critical argument," Young writes, "most theorists of deliberative democracy assume a culturally biased conception" of deliberation "that tends to silence or devalue some people or groups."[25]

Proponents of this "difference critique" argue that people of different social and economic classes are treated differently on a daily basis—men and women, whites and blacks, and more and less educated people are not treated as equals.[26] On the issue of gender, for example, men may not treat women as equals, and women may not feel that they can participate equally in deliberations.[27] Moreover, proponents of the difference critique argue that men and women deliberate differently—men are generally more "assertive," while women are generally more "tentative" and accommodating.[28] This difference in deliberation styles can lead to male domination of deliberation and be detrimental to participants. In particular, less privileged groups tend to use stories to make their arguments and share their opinions.[29] (For more on the use of stories in deliberation, see Chapter 4.) In a rigidly structured democratic discussion setting, people from less privileged classes may not be comfortable sharing their personal stories. Even if such stories are shared, the people from more privileged social classes may not understand the purpose or meaning of such stories. Again, this might lead to participation bias favoring advantaged groups. Such outcomes contradict the normative ideal of deliberative civic engagement, and in the long run, they could prove detrimental to democracy.

Evidence from the Field

Given this brief theoretical background on exclusion and marginalization in deliberative civic engagement, it is now useful to look at the empirical evidence. We first present research that supports the difference critique, then we review studies that do not.

Evidence for the Difference Critique

Jury and mock jury studies have found evidence of persistent social influence within group discussions. Though there are differences between jury deliberations and deliberative civic engagement, this literature helps us understand the dynamics of difference that can predominate in public discussions of public issues.[30]

In a comprehensive review of the literature, psychologist Reid Hastie and a team of jury scholars examined juror performance based on demographic differences.[31] They not only found that men contributed significantly more than women, but also that men and women contributed to deliberations in significantly different ways.[32] For example, men referenced and disputed facts and discussed organizational matters significantly more often than women. Women contributed more statements related to verdicts and what were categorized as "irrelevant" topics.[33] In addition, those with higher occupational status contributed more than their counterparts. Likewise, jurors with more formal education contributed more often than did less educated jurors, with the number of statements increasing steadily with education level. More educated jurors were also more vocal about legal and factual issues and generated a greater variety of statements for the jury to consider. The authors of the study also found, however, that juries of more highly educated individuals did not generate many more facts or produce better decisions. This is not surprising given other research showing that the quality of remarks, not their quantity, drive jury decision making.[34]

Other studies also find that men, regardless of occupational level, participate more in juries than women.[35] Research has found that men who are proprietors or clerical workers contribute the most to jury deliberations, while the
contribution rates of female proprietors and clerical workers are closer to
those of male skilled and unskilled laborers. Female skilled and unskilled laborers contributed the least. The relationship between participation levels and
income differences were similar to the findings for education and occupation,
likely because education and occupation are highly correlated with income.[36]
Furthermore, research shows that selected jury forepersons are usually male[37]
and likely to be from higher occupation levels and have the highest levels of
participation.[38]

In short, the evidence from jury studies demonstrates that males, more highly
educated participants, higher-income participants, and those with higher occupation levels tend to participate more and have a greater presence in deliberations. This picture of deliberation in jury studies captures exactly the concerns of
critics who worry about external and internal exclusion—that the deliberative
process does not provide equal opportunity for all participants but instead is
dominated by the more privileged.

Evidence against the Difference Critique

There are limited studies examining what actually happens during deliberation, and only a few of these have called the difference critique into question.
For example, researchers studied the survey responses of over 3,000 jurors in
local courthouses to examine the relationship between demographic variables
and jurors' satisfaction with their experience at the courthouse.[39] No single
demographic variable consistently predicted jurors' satisfaction, contrary to
the expectation that underrepresented groups might have had a less rewarding
jury experience. That said, the imbalance of jury composition with respect to
gender also predicted jurors' satisfaction: Jurors were more satisfied with
majority-female or majority-male jury compositions than with evenly mixed
juries.

Research that analyzes transcripts of deliberation also finds mixed evidence
of participatory dominance by privileged groups. In one study that examined
two deliberative polls, no evidence of inequality of participation by gender was
found.[40] However, such equality of participation is not as clear for other demographic variables. For example, income was found to be a significant predictor of
participation, with higher-income persons participating more than lower-
income persons. In terms of race, the results are mixed. On some measures in
one poll, whites did indeed participate significantly more than nonwhites. But in
another poll, whites contributed significantly *less* than nonwhites across all three

indicators. This research found similarly mixed evidence for participation differences and education. Thus, participatory dominance by more privileged individuals is not as clear as some would think.

An empirical study of deliberative civic engagement in an AmericaSpeaks 21st Century Town Meeting in North Carolina provides additional evidence about these issues.[41] Prior to the deliberative event, minorities and women had lower perceptions of political self-confidence (a.k.a. internal political efficacy) than did whites and men. Proponents of the difference critique would expect this finding and suggest that low perceptions of political efficacy can influence the deliberative process by potentially making it less equitable. However, after minorities participated in the deliberative event, their perceptions of internal efficacy increased in a statistically significant way.[42] Thus, the study indicates that deliberative engagement can positively affect minority perceptions of their own internal political efficacy, and suggests that although deliberative civic engagement exists in a world of inequitable conditions, the process can indeed help ameliorate some inequalities. It is important to note, however, that the format of the 21st Century Town Meeting is more open to participants sharing their experiences and surfacing issues of difference than are legal juries and other deliberative formats, and this aspect of process design may help explain the different effects on participants. For this reason, it is important to examine how various strategies in deliberative civic engagement can be used to help address inequalities and marginalization.

Strategies to Address Inequalities and Marginalization

Although there is tremendous variety in deliberative civic engagement methods (see Chapters 1 and 2 for more discussion), researchers and practitioners have identified several strategies that may help address inequality, exclusion, and marginalization. Rather than providing an exhaustive list, we present and discuss some of the most common strategies.

Mandatory Inclusion

Equal representation of diverse cultural groups can help ensure that external exclusion resulting from various socioeconomic and political inequalities is minimized in deliberative processes. One strategy for ensuring equal representation is the mandatory inclusion of diverse social groups. However, it is not enough to simply announce a process as being open to all and expect the room to represent all segments of the wider society.[43] Rather, for mandatory inclusion to work, organizers of deliberative events must consider the structural barriers that prevent or discourage members from lower socioeconomic classes or marginalized groups from fully participating in deliberative processes. They must also use various recruitment techniques for ensuring representativeness in deliberative forums. (For more discussion about recruitment strategies, see Chapter 3.)

James Fishkin, a political theorist and communication scholar who pioneered the Deliberative Poll, proposes that selecting random, representative samples from the broader population is one way of mandating representativeness in deliberative forums.[44] When participants are not randomly selected yet still are expected to represent specific constituencies with whom they maintain an active connection, mandatory inclusion of minority groups could be facilitated with other special representation techniques, such as the use of quotas, proportional representation, reserved seats, and overrepresentation in case of fairly small cultural groups to ensure that their voices are adequately heard.[45] For example, a study of Indian panchayats (village councils) indicates that the use of quotas for women—especially when combined with new training opportunities and participatory support networks—was crucial in opening the discursive space and removing some of the barriers for more equal participation of women in these settings.[46] In some cases, providing payments and other incentives for participation in deliberative events could also be a method to increase the level of social inclusion and diversity of deliberative forums.[47]

By far the most common tactic used by deliberation practitioners is the practice of proactive, network-based recruitment for meetings that are open to the public.[48] In this approach, organizers map the different networks found in a community, reach out to leaders within those networks, and pay special attention to populations that seem less likely to attend. In most cases, practitioners work hardest to recruit people of color, people from low-income households, and political conservatives, under the assumption that these groups will be among the least likely to attend. It is difficult to assess the effectiveness of this approach, partly because it has been used so often and there are both successes and failures to report.[49] Some recent evaluations of public deliberations suggest that this form of recruitment is effective with most demographic groups, with the exception of participation by Hispanics.[50]

These are critical considerations because the perception that the deliberative body is representative of the community is one factor that could enhance political efficacy among participants.[51] This notion is consistent with long-standing arguments made by classical theorists like Alexis de Tocqueville and John Stuart Mill, who point to the importance of wide-ranging inclusion for social validation of political processes.[52] Enhancing the perceptions of political efficacy among a broad spectrum of citizens is not just a matter of social justice; it is also essential for legitimizing the political process of public deliberation, and it could be crucial for successful implementation of deliberative agreements in practice.[53]

Information

The information and knowledge levels of participants in deliberative civic engagement vary considerably, especially when engaging diverse participants. In general, it is fair to assume that the public will not be completely informed about politics and specific policy issues; thus, it is important that all participants have access to the same consistent and balanced information and materials when they gather for deliberative civic engagement.[54] Access to such information may help overcome the issues associated with exclusion and marginalization by better preparing all participants to deliberate.

Deliberative Polling and the Citizens' Jury are two (among many) examples of deliberative civic engagement processes that provide participants with briefing materials in an effort to ensure that they are equipped with the necessary information to deliberate effectively.[55] In the case of Deliberative Polls, stakeholder and/or advisory groups are formed to create and review balanced, accurate, and comprehensive briefing materials, which are provided to participants before deliberation begins.[56] In addition, the Deliberative Polling process has plenary sessions during the event, where all participants attend and ask experts questions developed in the small group discussions. These plenary sessions are moderated, and panelists adhere to strict time limits; thus, the plenary sessions are more like a conversation or dialogue between the participants and the panelists than a lecture or seminar. Research about the Deliberative Polling process shows that the combination of balanced briefing materials, small group discussions, and plenary sessions generates significant knowledge gains for participants.[57]

The Jefferson Center's Citizens' Jury method is an intensive five-day deliberative process in which a small group of individuals, usually eighteen to twenty-four people, come together to learn, deliberate, and provide informed recommendations to officials. Research shows that Citizens' Jury participants become more informed, often offer innovative recommendations, and have very positive reactions to the process.[58] For example, one juror said she "learned a great deal this week and have seen how I can make changes in my own life . . . regarding this issue."[59] Another juror said she "would strongly recommend a Citizens' Jury project on any topic that would greatly impact our society when you would want to get a true cross-representation of what the 'common man' thinks once he is educated on a subject."[60]

In short, balanced background information about the discussion topics provides participants with the facts necessary to counter misinformation and make an informed decision. Moreover, they give participants access to differing opinions so they can better weigh all sides of an argument and engage in reasoned discussion. Such information may help overcome some cognitive barriers and reduce the difficulties of exclusion and marginalization in deliberative civic engagement.

Moderators

Using forum moderators or discussion facilitators to balance the contributions of all participants is another strategy for overcoming exclusion and marginalization in deliberative civic engagement.[61] Moderators are typically volunteers who undergo at least a day of training during which they learn about the importance of neutrality and participation, among other skills. In terms of neutrality, moderators are to remain unbiased during deliberations. Their primary task is to facilitate the group discussions; they are not eligible to participate in the deliberations. As a neutral presence in the room, moderators are asked to ensure that participants discuss competing arguments. If a group is generally in agreement, moderators are asked to have groups consider the opposing side and think through the opposition's arguments. In terms of participation, moderators are trained to ensure that more talkative members do not dominate the discussions and less talkative members have opportunities to voice their opinions. Given these important roles, the presence of a neutral moderator to enforce discussion rules can help ensure participation parity in deliberation, thereby reducing the impacts of exclusion and marginalization.[62] Political scientist Katherine Cramer Walsh, for one, has found ample evidence to support this thesis, though she suggests that "neutrality" may not be the most essential trait of successful facilitation, or at least a misleading way of characterizing the stance of a good moderator: "What is needed is not so much neutrality as fairness woven with a good dose of provocativeness."[63]

In short, the presence of impartial moderators is important in umpiring the deliberative process and maintaining equal opportunity for the involvement of all participants. This does not mean, however, that deliberation practitioners expect complete impartiality and objectiveness from participants. It is, in fact, the impartiality—or as Walsh would put it, the combination of fairness and provocation—of the facilitators that allows participants to surface and examine their own biases, passions, and policy opinions, for the purpose of finding common ground with others.

Deliberative Reciprocity

American political theorists Amy Gutmann and Dennis Thompson suggest that impartiality may be an inappropriate demand in pluralist societies because it requires citizens to suppress or disregard their partial perspectives and individual preferences when thinking about policies and laws. Therefore, they recommend using deliberative reciprocity, which sets standards for practices of mutual respect, where citizens continue to hold competing views, but provide each other equal recognition of differences in the process of justification of their reasons to others.[64] Reciprocity goes beyond mere reason giving, holding that "citizens owe one another [substantive] justifications for the mutually binding laws and public policies they collectively enact."[65]

It is difficult to measure deliberative reciprocity precisely. One possible measure is participants' willingness to fully answer and respond to questions by other debaters. Using this measure, one study of the parliamentary budget committees of France, Sweden, and the United Kingdom, as well as in the European Parliament, found that the willingness to engage in mutually respectful deliberations was unexpectedly high and stable over time in these bodies (more than a third of questions were classified by the author as fully answered based on principles of deliberative reciprocity).[66] While parliamentary budget committees are not akin to deliberative civic engagement, this research does offer one potential measure for deliberative reciprocity.

Two notions related to reciprocity are the concepts of mutual culture recognition[67] and tolerance for cultural diversity.[68] Although there are various perspectives on the politics of culture recognition and cultural tolerance,[69] theorists in these schools of thought generally agree about the necessity of public acknowledgment and recognition of difference in the public sphere. Cultural tolerance and mutual recognition include requirements for pluralist openness and willingness to listen to diverse perspectives, even those with which one might adamantly disagree.[70] Two separate case studies of Macedonia explain the relative success in practice of a nation that has constitutionally mandated the values of mutual recognition and deliberative reciprocity in intercultural dialogues.[71]

Given that the disparity in power relationships is likely unavoidable in practice, deliberative reciprocity is always an ideal that is never fully achievable in the absolute sense.[72] For this reason, public policy scholar Archon Fung argues that it is important to understand deliberative reciprocity and deliberative activism not as mutually exclusive absolutes but as relationally interdependent concepts.[73] He suggests that an ethic of deliberation permits civil disobedience in situations where the power holders refuse to abide by the principles of deliberative reciprocity. Moreover, the extent of permissible deviation from deliberative norms increases as the adversity of political circumstances increases. The twenty-one-day Harvard sit-in in 2001, in which students and workers occupied the administrative offices of Harvard University demanding "living wages," is an example in which civil disobedience should be permitted.[74] As a result of the sit-in, a new committee was created that was arguably more equitable in representation and provided for deliberations more in line with the values of mutual respect and reciprocity.[75]

The complexities Fung mentions echo the appeals for the institutionalization of requirements for deliberative reciprocity. Connecting deliberative democracy with consociational democracy is one possible method for institutionalizing deliberative reciprocity.[76] Studies of Macedonia's constitutional model and of the

Good Friday Agreement in Northern Ireland provide some support for this argument; however, both studies recognize that deliberative reciprocity is not a panacea—its institutionalization has drawbacks, such as adding a degree of elitism in the deliberative process and a more top-down approach to facilitating deliberations.[77] Such potential drawbacks notwithstanding, the institutionalization of deliberative reciprocity could assist in overcoming marginalization and exclusion by mandating the inclusion of marginalized voices and building tolerance for their expressions. The issues of reciprocity and cultural tolerance are inherently related to the issue of communication modes, which we discuss next.

Alternative Modes of Communication

Different modes of communication are relevant to understanding the deliberative experiences of diverse participants and to the effectiveness of various strategies used to alleviate inequalities and marginalization. (For a broader analysis of communication in deliberation, see Chapter 4.) Deciding on the acceptable forms of communication can be crucial in determining the final outcome of deliberations.[78] For Habermas, "authentic communication" is necessary in public discourses, and achieving "authentic communication" depends on satisfying a number of "validity claims," including "truth for statements or existential presuppositions, rightness for legitimately regulated actions and their normative context, and truthfulness or sincerity for the manifestation of subjective experiences."[79] Although critics argue that privileging rational-argumentation could be highly exclusionary to socially marginalized groups,[80] in arguing for validity claims, Habermas does not intend to exclude, but rather to provide conditions for substantive involvement in democratic deliberations.

To avoid internal exclusion problems, Young recommends supplementing rational argumentation with alternative modes of communication such as greeting, rhetoric, and narrative.[81] Greeting, or public acknowledgment, names the communicative political gestures through which those who have conflicts aim to solve problems by recognizing and including others in the discussion, and especially those with differing opinions, interests, or social locations. This mode of communication is essentially a form of culture recognition. The affirmative use of rhetoric is more strongly distinguished from the Habermasian notion of communicative action.[82] Rhetorical communication includes the use of emotional tone in discourse; figures of speech; nonverbal forms of communication such as visual media, signs, and demonstrations; and attention to the particular audience of one's communication.[83] Narrative and situated knowledge refers to the expression of personal experiences through storytelling or testimonies.

Few empirical studies have thoroughly examined which modes of communication are acceptable in specific policy contexts or how those modes influence the deliberative process and policy outcomes.[84] Ryfe, for example, recognizes that deliberations are inherently rooted in context and different kinds of contexts require different kinds of deliberations.[85] In his view, more rational deliberations about actions, plans, and policy proposals generally assume that participants share fundamental values. Alternative forms of communication are arguably more pertinent in situations when there are sharper divergences in values.[86] Ryfe's survey of sixteen deliberative organizations finds that sharing of personal experiences or stories is particularly common in deliberative forums that focus on building relationships rather than on achieving policy outcomes.[87] Furthermore, the use of rhetoric had an influence in "forcing the doors open," or increasing the diversity of views, in a Citizens' Jury process in England; however, rhetoric was not legitimately decisive in the decision-making process itself, which remained focused on reasoned debate.[88]

In short, allowing different forms of communication, in addition to more rational deliberations, addresses the issues of marginalization and exclusion by allowing, if not encouraging, diverse modes of expression, some of which may be "out of the mainstream" and challenging to the established conceptions of reasoned debate. Although additional communication modes can have negative effects and do not necessarily prevent marginalization, the inclusion of different forms of communication can also widen the discussion and challenge consensuses based on domination and exclusion.[89] As Walsh notes, the domination of already marginalized groups is not inevitable in deliberative democracy; listening and scrutiny can open up deliberations to excluded views.[90]

Consensus and Concurrent Decision Making

A common problem in participatory forms of democracy is the ability of majorities to marginalize or outvote the minorities, which can lead to "majority tyranny."[91] In response, theorists have argued for consensual decision making in the process of deliberative civic engagement.[92] Ideally, consensus building through the exchange of reasoned arguments is the most equitable method of developing mutual understandings. Consensus is perceived, in consensual models of deliberative democracy,[93] not as a mere agreement but rather as a further step wherein the support for a given outcome is made for the same reasons.[94] From this perspective, if all participants must mutually agree on a joint decision, then minorities can be better protected from majority tyranny.

Yet it remains questionable as to whether it is realistic to expect consensus building in a complex modern society with a plurality of differentiated voices. It is also unclear what effects the requirement of consensus building would have on inclusion in deliberative civic engagement events. A cluster of discursive theorists[95] has raised these questions in critiques of Habermas'[96] model of consensual deliberative democracy. For example, legal scholar Cass Sunstein observes a tendency toward group polarization within deliberative bodies, a type of a crowd mentality that could be detrimental to democracy.[97] A recent study of deliberative forums in Germany supports this observation, suggesting that polarization and lack of openness to changing one's opinions is more likely in more partisan deliberative forums.[98] Moreover, consensus building comes at the expense of diversity of views and places increased pressure on dissenters.[99] In fact, consensus is unattainable, unnecessary, and undesirable because negotiated agreements may be more feasible and attractive to participants even if they agree for different reasons.[100]

Some strategies have been suggested to avoid the problems related to both consensual decision making and majority tyranny. For example, Sunstein suggests concurrent deliberations, first among like-minded people, so-called enclave deliberations, followed by deliberations across cultural groups.[101] In such situations, group representation in deliberative bodies becomes important.[102] Young similarly acknowledges that differing and disagreeing people do not have to be discussing together all the time: "Sometimes it is better for relatively homogeneous groups to organize among themselves and deliberate about what they want, and then send representatives to more heterogeneous bodies."[103]

These theoretical arguments for concurrent deliberations are examined in a study of discursive councils in Miami-Dade County.[104] In this study, two levels of citizen deliberations are observed within the Community Relations Board, a citizen body within the county government. On one level, dialogue is facilitated by citizen volunteers within separate intracultural commissions, such as those for African Americans, Hispanics, Asian Americans, or women. These advisory commissions serve the purpose of identifying and expressing issues relevant to each cultural group. On the second level, the chairs of these commissions work on the broader Community Relations Board to deliberate about intercultural and other issues specific to the community at large. Both levels of discourse are embedded in the government structures and linked to the existing policy decision-making process, and both tended to be much more consensual than the less formal citizen forums that were facilitated in communities on particular issues.[105]

For Young, however, the trade-off of inclusion for efficiency or smooth rationality is undemocratic, and other more agonistic, nonrationalist theorists of discursive democracy agree.[106] For them, conflicts are inevitable in any open, pluralist democracy, and expressions and contestation of differences could lead to more informed perceptions, and eventually the reduction of agonistic tensions. These arguments are in line with Gutmann and Thompson's observation that in certain situations the value of deliberative civic engagement may be simply in initiating discussions and engaging the citizens in public discourses rather than in anticipating the development of agreements.[107]

The Limits and Prospects of Deliberative Civic Engagement in Divided Societies

Tolerance of cultural differences and willingness to include diverse voices in deliberative civic engagement processes is much easier when the divisions in cultural patterns are narrower and are not perceived as essential threats.[108] When cultural divergences touch on the "raw nerves" of the very fundamental subsistence of particular ways of living and established perceptions of cultural identity, the possibilities for reconciliation and deliberative engagement are diminished.[109]

The intractability, and often tragic consequences, of such deeply divisive ethnic, religious, and cultural conflicts are evident.[110] In the age of globalization, troublesome intercultural tensions are not restricted only to the world's familiar fault lines, like the Middle East, the Balkans, the Caucasus, sub-Saharan Africa, or the Indian subcontinent, but they are also emerging as significant issues in developed nations. For example, Switzerland is historically one of the most serene, multicultural consensual democracies, but it has recently experienced an explosion of intercultural tensions related to the growing Muslim population in the country. In particular, the desire of Muslim residents in Switzerland to build mosques with minarets was received with hostility by Switzerland's right wing, which initiated a referendum on the issue that banned building minarets and spurred violent riots.[111] If intercultural tensions are increasingly problematic even in one of the cradles of participatory democracy, what are the prospects for intercultural deliberations in more deeply divided societies?

The difficulties and limitations of multicultural discourses in deeply divided societies certainly should not be minimized; however, the increase in intercultural tensions may actually require more deliberative civic engagement rather than less, and may even necessitate the introduction of different forms of deliberation suitable to specific local contexts.[112] Indeed, empirical studies show that deliberative civic engagement is possible and can have beneficial effects in deeply divided societies, although difficulties remain. For example, the Good Friday Agreement in Northern Ireland provided for the establishment of a participatory Civic Forum, which serves as a vehicle for the deliberative engagement of citizens and as a consultative body of the government.[113] Research indicates that the Civic Forum has been relatively effective as a deliberative body.[114] In Macedonia, the so-called Ohrid Framework Agreement, which averted a violent conflict similar to those in the other former Yugoslav republics, also required strengthening the civil society, publicly recognizing cultural differences, and facilitating intercultural dialogue.[115] Some of the envisioned mechanisms for deliberative engagement in Macedonia include intercultural citizen commissions, citizen forums, and parliamentary bodies. The Framework Agreement and the efforts of Macedonian society toward intercultural dialogue were effective in sta-bilizing peace and improving the perceptions of inclusion among minority com-munities, even though divisions in the country still linger.[116]

Nevertheless, in both of these cases, the formal institutionalization of forums for intercultural deliberation was preceded by broader political agreements that ameliorated the intensity of intercultural conflicts. As such, these two cases dem-onstrate the important role of the political sphere and of government institu-tions in providing conditions for intercultural deliberative civic engagement in deeply divided societies.

So, we end the way we started, with lyrics from *Avenue Q*:

> If we could all just admit
> that we are racist a little bit,
> even though we all know that it's wrong,
> maybe it will help us get along . . .
> Everyone's little bit racist, it's true.
> But everyone is just about as racist as you!
>
> If we all could just admit
> that we are racist a little bit,
> and everyone stopped being so PC,
> maybe we could live in Harmony![117]

Though harmony may be too much to hope for, deliberations across cultural differences aspire to provide a model for mitigating intractable intercultural con-flicts. Deliberations across cultural differences have limitations, and in some cases may not be feasible, but other alternatives, such as open conflict or even warfare, may hold even less appeal. The suppression of latent tensions and the marginalization of cultural voices could have detrimental effects in the long term, such as explosion of violence.[118] Intercultural dialogue offers an opportu-nity to express individual differences without resorting to hostilities.[119]

We all have different cultural backgrounds, and—consciously or uncon-sciously, and to differing degrees—we perpetuate those reified stereotypes and biases that exist within our cultures. Representative deliberative bodies reflect social divisions, and given entrenched social inequalities, it is imperative that conveners of deliberative civic engagement processes devise and utilize strat-egies for overcoming exclusion and marginalization. The presence of impartial moderators to facilitate more equitable engagement in deliberations is perhaps the most vital.[120] Nonetheless, impartiality in intercultural deliberations is often not likely, and sometimes not desirable. Reciprocity and mutual respect for cul-tural differences offer more realistic criteria than impartiality for deliberative civic engagement across cultural differences.[121] Intercultural deliberations can increase familiarization with diverse views that might be less known outside specific cultural groups. Engaged deliberations may also expose unconscious biases, thus enabling intercultural learning. Having and sharing information is important for achieving these outcomes.[122] Likewise, using alternative modes of communication may further assist in the broader inclusion of marginalized voices, although it does not prevent internal exclusion.

Allowing for contestation of often partial cultural perspectives in intercultural deliberative settings provides an opportunity to potentially build a path to cultural tolerance. Building consensus and mutual agreements may not always be possible, and in some circumstances may even be disadvantageous.[123] It is perhaps sufficient to aspire for workable temporary agreements for action, while learning about and respecting each other's differences.[124]

In addition to the strategies elaborated in this chapter, future studies could also examine the role of government institutions in facilitating intercultural deliberations and investigate the strategies for impacting government decision making.[125] Furthermore, one of the key difficulties with institutionalizing deliberative civic engagement in deeply divided societies is that the divisions are often firmly rooted in history, past injustices, and stigmatizations.[126] Overcoming entrenched divisions may require not only inclusion and recognition but also a process of reconciliation that aims to build common understandings of past histories.[127] The Truth and Reconciliation Commission in South Africa is one notable example that points to the importance of connecting politics of reconciliation with theories of deliberative civic engagement.[128] Future studies could further examine the prospects of reconciliation approaches not only for addressing issues of marginalization and exclusion but also for other applications in the broader field of deliberative civic engagement.

Notes

1. Pincus-Roth (2006).
2. See Gutmann (1998).
3. On the cultural cognitive foundations of public opinion and the problems they present for governance, see Kahan (2007). In this chapter, we use the terms *dialogue* and *deliberation* interchangeably. For an elaboration of conceptual overlaps and distinctions between these two terms, see Levine, Fung, and Gastil (2005), Burkhalter, Gastil, and Kelshaw (2002), and the introductory chapter in this volume.
4. Gutmann and Thompson (1996).
5. Young (2000).
6. Gutmann and Thompson (1996); Fishkin (1991, 1995).
7. de Tocqueville ([1835/1840] 2000: 496–500); Pateman (1970).
8. Mill ([1862] 1962).
9. Mill ([1862] 1962: 79).

10. Mill ([1862] 1962: 79).
11. Fraser (1992, 2007).
12. Mill ([1862] 1962); de Tocqueville ([1835/1840] 2000); Young (1996).
13. de Tocqueville ([1835/1840] 2000); see also Mill ([1862] 1962).
14. Fraser (1992, 2007); Sanders (1997).
15. Young (2000).
16. Young (2000: 53–54).
17. Habermas ([1962] 1989: 27).
18. Fraser (1992, 1997, 2007).
19. Fraser (1992, 2007).
20 Mansbridge (2005).
21. Habermas ([1962] 1989: 176).
22. Young (2000: 55).
23. Young (2000: 22–23).
24. Young (2000); Fraser (1992, 2007); Sanders (1997); Mansbridge (1996, 2005).
25. Young (1996: 120).
26. Young (1996).
27. See Rai (2007).
28. Young (1996: 123); see also Gilligan (1982) and Tannen (1994).
29. Polletta (2006).
30. Strodtbeck and Mann (1956); Strodtbeck, James, and Hawkins (1957); James (1959); Hastie, Penrod, and Pennington (1983); Hans and Vidmar (1986); York and Cornwell (2006).
31. Hastie, Penrod, and Pennington (1983).
32. See, for example, Hans and Vidmar (1986).
33. Hastie, Penrod, and Pennington (1983).
34. Sanders (1997: 11).
35. See, for example, Strodtbeck, James, and Hawkins (1957).
36. Hastie, Penrod, and Pennington (1983); for a discussion of how these and other factors affect participation in deliberative civic engagement events, see Chapter 3.
37. Hastie, Penrod, and Pennington (1983); Hans and Vidmar (1986).
38. Strodtbeck, James, and Hawkins (1957).
39. Hickerson and Gastil (2008).
40. Siu (2009).
41. Nabatchi and Stanisevski (2008).
42. Participation had no effects on external efficacy, which concerns perceptions about the responsiveness of political officials and the political system.
43. Young (2004: 49).
44. Fishkin (1991, 1995); see also Fung (2003, 2006).
45. For a discussion, see Mansbridge (2005); see also Young (2000: 142).
46. Rai (2007).
47. Ackerman and Fishkin (2004); Fung (2003); Mansbridge (2004).
48. Fung, Lee, and Harbage (2008); Esterling, Fung, and Lee (2011); Leighninger (2006); Walsh (2007).
49. Leighninger (2006); Walsh (2007).
50. Fung and Lee (2008); Fung, Lee, and Harbage (2008); Esterling, Fung, and Lee (2011).
51. Nabatchi and Stanisevski (2008).
52. de Tocqueville ([1835/1840] 2000); Mill ([1862] 1962).
53. See Pateman (1970) and Barber (1984).
54. Gutmann and Thompson (1996).
55. On Citizens' Juries, see Crosby and Nethercut (2005). On Deliberative Polling, see Fishkin and Farrar (2005).
56. Fishkin (1995).

57. Fishkin, He, and Siu (2006); Luskin, Fishkin, and Jowell (2002).
58. Crosby and Nethercut (2005).
59. Jefferson Center (2002: 19).
60. Jefferson Center (2002: 19).
61. Fishkin (1995).
62. Mansbridge (2008).
63. Walsh (2007: 303).
64. Gutmann and Thompson (1996: 54–55); see also Gutmann and Thompson (2002).
65. Gutmann and Thompson (2002: 156).
66. Agné (2011).
67. Gutmann (1994); Habermas (1994); McBride (2005); Stanisevski (2008); Taylor (1994); Young (2000).
68. Galeotti (2002); Stanisevski (2010); Walzer (1997).
69. See McBride (2005).
70. For more, see Stanisevski (2008, 2010).
71. Stanisevski (2008); Stanisevski and Miller (2009).
72. Fung (2005); Stanisevski (2010).
73. Fung (2005).
74. Fung (2005: 409).
75. Fung (2005: 411).
76. O'Flynn (2010).
77. Stanisevski and Miller (2009); O'Leary (1999).
78. Young (1996).
79. Habermas (1984: 99).
80. Young (1996, 2000); Sanders (1997).
81. Young (2000).
82. Bohman (1988); Young (2000: 63).
83. Young (2000: 65).
84. See Fung (2003), Hendriks (2005a), and Ryfe (2002).
85. Ryfe (2002: 369).
86. Young (2000).
87. Ryfe (2002: 367); see also Levine, Fung, and Gastil (2005).
88. Parkinson (2003: 192).
89. Dryzek (2000); see also Young (2000, 2004: 49).
90. Walsh (2007).
91. de Tocqueville ([1835/1840] 2000); Mill ([1862] 1962).
92. See, for example, Habermas (1984, 1996a), Phillips (1995: 146), and Uhr (1998).
93. Habermas (1984, 1996a).
94. Dryzek (2000: 48).
95. Benhabib (1990); Dryzek (2000); Bohman (1995); Mansbridge (2004); Sunstein (2002); Young (2000, 2004).
96. Habermas (1984, 1996a). For responses to his critics, see Habermas (1979: 90; 1982: 257–258).
97. Sunstein (2002).
98. Hendriks, Dryzek, and Hunold (2007: 369–371).
99. Mansbridge (2004).
100. Dryzek (2000: 170).
101. Sunstein (2002).
102. Sunstein (2002: 192).
103. Young (2004: 50).
104. Stanisevski (2006).
105. Stanisevski (2006). The distinction between these two different forms of discursive arenas in Miami-Dade County—formal citizen boards and the less formal, ad hoc citizen

forums—is generally reflective of the differentiation between formal and informal, and micro and macro, discursive spheres discussed by Hendriks (2006).

106. Young (2004: 50); see also Connolly (1991); Dryzek (2000); Laclau and Mouffe (2001); Mouffe (2000, 2005).
107. Gutmann and Thompson (1996); see also Stanisevski (2010).
108. Benhabib (2002); Dryzek (2005); Stanisevski (2010).
109. Gilliatt (2002); Stanisevski (2010).
110. See, for example, Chua (2004); Glenny (2000); Kaplan (2005); Mamdani (2002).
111. Cumming-Bruce and Erlanger (2009); Husbands (2000); Traynor (2007).
112. Dryzek (2005); O'Flynn (2007); Young (2000).
113. See Dixon (1997, 2005); O'Leary (1999).
114. McCall and Williamson (2001).
115. Stanisevski and Miller (2009); for a discussion on culture recognition of Roma identities in Macedonia see Stanisevski (2008).
116. Stanisevski and Miller (2009).
117. Pincus-Roth (2006).
118. Stanisevski (2008, 2010).
119. Gutmann and Thompson (1996).
120. Mansbridge (2008).
121. Gutmann (1994); Gutmann and Thompson (1996); Habermas (1994); Young (2000).
122. Fishkin (1991); Fishkin, He, and Siu (2006); Luskin, Fishkin, and Jowell (2002).
123. Dryzek (2000); Mansbridge (1996); Sunstein (2002).
124. Gutmann and Thompson (1996); Dryzek (2000); Young (2000).
125. For examples, see Dryzek (2005); Gastil (2000); Hendriks (2005a); Levine, Fung, and Gastil (2005); Pierce, Neely, and Budziak (2008); Ryfe (2002); Stanisevski (2006).
126. Kymlicka and Bashir (2008); Stanisevski (2008).
127. Kymlicka and Bashir (2008); McCarthy (2002, 2004); Schaap (2004, 2005).
128. Kymlicka and Bashir (2008).

6

Online Deliberation Design

Choices, Criteria, and Evidence

TODD DAVIES AND REID CHANDLER

Creating democracy is . . . harder than rocket science.
—Ira Harkavy

As they evolve, information and communication technologies are providing numerous alternative ways for people to interact with each other and with information. In turn, this evolution is providing more choices for online deliberative civic engagement forums, sometimes called *deliberative e-democracy*. This chapter focuses on the questions, *How do we design deliberative e-democracy forums in the light of both available and prospective information/communication technologies? How does online deliberative civic engagement differ from face-to-face deliberative civic engagement in terms of both process and outcomes?* The space of design possibilities is vast, so we will touch on some of the more significant choices that must be made, as well as the current state of empirical research bearing on these choices.

We will take deliberation to denote "thoughtful, careful, or lengthy consideration" by individuals and "formal discussion and debate" in groups, without necessarily requiring a final decision or judgment.[1] We are therefore primarily interested in communication that is reasoned, purposeful, and interactive. (For a discussion about communication in deliberative civic engagement, see Chapter 4.) However, the power and predominance of other influences on political decisions and communication (e.g., mass media, appeals to emotion and authority, and snap judgments) are also relevant to deliberative e-democracy, both as contrasts to deliberative discourse and as potential influences on deliberation.

The term *online* as a modifier to "deliberation" could be read to indicate the mediation of deliberation among participants through one or more electronic communication technologies that augment our usual abilities to see or hear information separated from us in time or space. In addition to the Internet, this would include the telephone, "smart phones," teleconferencing systems, broadcasting (if used to facilitate communication between participants, e.g., "talking heads" debating over different satellite feeds), and even electronic tools, such as hand-held audience-response "clickers," through which participants interact in face-to-face meetings.

Design Choices

Once a decision is made to have online deliberation, the creators and conveners need to make several design choices. We discuss a set of broad design issues, grouped into categories. These have been selected for inclusion mainly because they have been the subjects of empirical research, although they represent a relatively small subset of all the potential choices a deliberation designer faces. Nevertheless, these issues do provide a way to organize the empirical literature relevant to deliberation design.[2]

The design choices are grouped under five categories representing the highest-level questions faced by the deliberation designer: (1) purpose (*Why* is the deliberation being designed—in other words, what objectives should the design reflect?); (2) population (*Who* will be involved?); (3) spatiotemporal distance (*Where* and *when* will participants be interacting with each other?); (4) communication medium (*How* will communication occur?); and (5) deliberative process (*What* will occur among the participants?). These categories, and all of the choice dimensions described within them (see Table 6.1 for a summary), could be applied both to off-line (i.e., face-to-face) and online deliberation. Our focus in what follows, however, will be on how the availability of communication technologies affects these choices. In the second section of the chapter, we discuss empirical findings related to each dimension. We conclude with a discussion of the main lessons that emerge from this empirical literature.[3]

Purpose

The purposive nature of deliberation is represented in our design space with two dimensions—the outcome of the deliberation and its collectivity.

Outcome. Does the deliberation aim to produce a decision, affect opinions or knowledge, or generate ideas? Whereas both decision making and brainstorming are legitimate goals for deliberation, it is generally easier to determine whether deliberation has reached its end state when one or more decisions are to be made. Deliberations undertaken to make decisions also tend to be different in character from those whose sole aim is idea generation, with the former being more oriented toward debating competing alternative solutions and the latter fostering sustained openness to different ideas and even an appreciation for their

Table 6.1 **Summary of Five Design Categories**

Category	Question	Design Dimensions
1. Purpose	*Why* is the deliberation being designed?	(a) Outcome (decisions-beliefs-ideas)
		(b) Collectivity (group-individual)
2. Population	*Who* will be involved?	(a) Recruitment (random-selected)
		(b) Audience (public-private)
3. Spatiotemporal Distance	*Where* and *when* will participants be interacting with each other?	(a) Colocation (face to face-telecommunication)
		(b) Cotemporality (synchronous-asynchronous)
4. Communication Medium	*How* will communication occur?	(a) Modality (speech-text-image-multimodal)
		(b) Emotivity (impeded-enabled)
		(c) Fidelity (transformed-unaltered)
5. Deliberative Process	*What* will occur between participants	(a) Facilitation (moderated-unmoderated)
		(b) Structure (rules-free form)
		(c) Identifiability (identifiable-anonymous)
		(d) Incentivization (reward-no reward)

variety. Decision making and belief formation are generally more demanding than brainstorming in an online environment because they are somewhat more likely to require access to tools (such as calculation aids) and information that participants may need to consult before reaching a decision.

Collectivity. Should deliberation's goal be an outcome for the whole group or just for the individuals within a deliberating group? Whether the outcome is a set of decisions, beliefs, or ideas is independent of whether those are associated with the group collectively or only with individual participants (or subgroups).

The collectivity dimension, like the outcome dimension, has deep implications for a deliberation's design. If the group must agree collectively on a set of decisions or ideas, more pressure to achieve mutual understanding is put on the process, and it will be harder to end the deliberation at an arbitrary point, such as when a time limit has been reached. Outcomes requiring collective agreement pose special challenges for an online environment because the tools required to reach consensus or to take a vote are more elaborate than a simple threaded conversation, which might be sufficient for idea generation.

Population

A consideration of the first question (the purpose of deliberation) entails some assumptions about whom the deliberation is for and who will participate (see Chapter 3). But the details are probably best considered only after the purpose of a deliberation has been determined. In our framework, population choices are represented by two dimensions—the recruitment of participants and the audience for the deliberative exercise.

Recruitment. Will participants represent a random sample, a self-selected group, or some other sampling criterion? The question of recruitment looms large for both off-line and online deliberations, especially when processes are meant to inform public policy. When information/communication technologies are involved, however, there are special considerations. Since not everyone has ready access to the Internet, for example, achieving a representative sample poses extra challenges for online deliberation. Still, participants in online public deliberations can be and have been given computers and Internet access in exchange for their participation, and other techniques such as adjusted sampling can be used to achieve representativeness when participant demographics are known.[4]

Audience. Will the deliberation process be visible to the public (either during or at some point after deliberation), or will it remain private to the deliberating group?[5] Even when the issue to be deliberated upon is a matter of public concern, the deliberation may be set up in a way that maintains confidentiality for the participants with respect to the larger public. A televised broadcast of a deliberation would not qualify under the definition of "online" given here unless the broadcast itself is integral to the deliberation (e.g., if viewers can be actively involved). But a broadcast deliberation can, in any case, greatly expand the audience for a deliberation, and communication technologies generally have the potential to make either passive or active participation much more widespread. The use of online tools has implications for the eventual audience, since online deliberation can generally be recorded, and it is difficult or impossible for participants to rely on assurances that their participation will not be shared with others when deliberation occurs online.

Spatiotemporal Distance

Information/communication technologies greatly expand the options for participants in a deliberation to be separated from each other in space and/or time. Our framework analyzes these possibilities in two choice dimensions—the colocation and the cotemporality of participants.

Colocation. Will the deliberation happen face-to-face (at the same time and place) or via some form of space- or time-shifted communication? "Location" here refers to a point or region in both space and time. If all participants are present in the same place at the same time, we will call this a face-to-face deliberation, even though the group might be sufficiently large so that not all participants can see each other. When some or all participants are spatially separated from each other, some form of telecommunication[6] technology is necessary. In either case, deliberation can happen "online." For example, in a face-to-face deliberation, a shared display can be used to record the proceedings for all to see, as it is happening. Participants can also interact with each other via devices that record survey responses displayed in real time, or via a chatroom that is accessed on individuals' laptops during a meeting. The use of these technologies in a face-to-face event might be somewhat distracting, but generally they do not remove the affordances of sharing space with other participants and can usefully augment face-to-face dialogue. In telecommunication deliberations, on the other hand, such as a teleconference, technology can be used that simulates face-to-face interaction to a greater or lesser extent. Colocation should probably therefore be viewed as a set of continua, depending on whether some, most, or all participants are colocated, and to what extent participants' behavior and subjective feeling during deliberation reflects colocation, regardless of whether they are physically co-present.[7]

Cotemporality. Will participation be synchronous or asynchronous? Once a decision has been made to use telecommunication, a forum designer must decide how much if any communication will be allowed to happen at some temporal distance, that is, asynchronously. Asynchrony allows participation to occur at different times for different people,—for example, with email or a message board. Synchronous or cotemporal participation implies that communication is received as soon as it is emitted. A face-to-face meeting is generally synchronous, but so is real-time text chat. Thus, cotemporality does not imply much about the medium or modality of communication. Asynchronous communication has traditionally been associated more with text than with speech, but technology has closed this gap. The advent of voice mail, for example, turned the telephone from a strictly synchronous medium into an asynchronous one as well. Some media afford both synchronous and asynchronous communication, depending on the participants. Text messaging, for example, can be considered a hybrid of the two, because a recipient of a text message can read and respond to it right away, or later. It might be termed "on demand" cotemporality. Thus, cotemporality, like colocation, should be seen as a continuum of possibilities.[8] Actual deliberations may also combine synchronous and asynchronous communication—for example, as when ideas from each table at an America*Speaks* event are submitted via laptops to "synthesizers" who combine and post ideas on a central display.[9]

Communication Medium

A deliberation designer also must make choices regarding the media through which deliberation will occur. Consistent with the rest of our framework, we consider just a few variables (dimensions) characterizing different media. This way of presenting the design space for communication media has been called "morphological analysis."[10] It is also in the tradition of "variable-based approaches" to the empirical study of communication technology.[11] We characterize communication media by their modalities, emotivity, and fidelity.

Modalities. Should communication occur through voice, text, images, or in a multimodal way? The modality of a communication is defined by the perceptual and cognitive faculties it engages, in contrast to the communication medium, which is the technology that delivers it. Here the range of design choices is truly vast. Participants can receive information through text (reading) and produce information through voice (speaking), or they can listen and write. They can be given a choice of several modalities, or be restricted to one. Prepared background information (e.g., materials provided prior to a deliberation) can be transmitted one way, while communication between participants can happen via a different modality. Information can be presented in multiple modalities (e.g., as audio and video) or as text with pictures. Again, technology keeps enhancing the possibilities. Speech recognition systems, for example, are beginning to offer the possibility of a textual transcript in real time as people speak.[12] Many technologies now make it increasingly possible to illustrate what someone is saying or writing pictorially or through video. Thus, the choice of modality is becoming truly independent of other choices, such as whether to colocate or synchronize a deliberation.

Emotivity. Will the medium encourage emotional involvement and/or expression, and if so, what kinds? In theory, deliberation connotes calm and relatively unemotional reasoning, but in practice, deliberation often engenders strong emotions (see Chapter 4). People's contributions or the results of deliberation may be enhanced if they find the experience fun, or at least pleasant. Or, they may learn more from encounters that are unsettling or even sad or angering.

That said, some researchers have argued that better decisions correspond to less emotional ones.[13]

The place of emotion is a question shared between online and off-line deliberation design, but online environments introduce their own issues related to emotion. Telecommunication can strip out emotionality, particularly if emotional cues (such as facial expressions and body language) are absent. On the other hand, the isolation of participants on the Internet, for example, might lead them to feel and/or express more emotion than they would face-to-face. Online forums sometimes provide features such as emoticons to enable emotional expression. Both off-line and online, then, whether and how much to encourage/enable emotional expression is an important design decision.

Fidelity. Will participants' communicative acts be transformed or left unaltered by the medium? This is a somewhat exotic dimension that seems likely to grow in importance in the future. "Transformed social interaction" (TSI) is communication in which some aspect of a communicator's message is systematically altered to change the experience of the recipient.[14] Examples of transformed communication include virtual reality systems, such as Second Life, in which avatars represent online participants. In such systems, it is possible for all participants to make (virtual) eye contact with each other at the same time.[15]

But transformation can and does occur without electronic technology. For example, when a newspaper editor alters the text of a submitted article or letter prior to publishing it, the result is transformed communication. Newspapers, then, can be a transformational medium. Technology has the potential to dramatically increase the scope and sophistication of transformed communication. For example, experiments are being conducted to simulate future artificial intelligence devices that correct one's grammar or word choices mid-communication.[16]

Deliberative Process

The final, and perhaps most important, design question concerns the deliberation process to follow during the interaction. Even if the designer has a process in mind, the participants themselves may choose one on their own, and they sometimes insist on doing so (as they may for some of the other design elements noted earlier). Planning for participants to design all or part of the deliberation process, however, remains a choice for the designer. Our framework includes four choice dimensions concerning the deliberative process: facilitation, structure, identifiability, and incentivization.

Facilitation. Will the deliberation be facilitated by a moderator, and if so how? Facilitation can occur in many different forms, or a designer may eschew facilitation altogether. If facilitators or moderators are present, they can take on many different combinations of roles. One researcher offers the following list of possibilities.

1. Greeter: making people feel welcome.
2. Conversation Stimulator: posing new questions and topics, playing devil's advocate in existing conversation.
3. Conflict Resolver: mediating conflicts toward collective agreements (or agreeing to disagree).
4. Summarizer of Debates.[17]
5. Problem Solver: directing questions to relevant people for response.
6. Supporter: bringing in external information to enrich debates and support arguments.
7. Welcomer: bringing in new participants, either citizens or politicians/civil servants.
8. 'Cybrarian': providing expert knowledge on particular topics.
9. Open Censor: deleting messages deemed inappropriate, normally against predefined rules and criteria. Feedback is given to explain why, and an opportunity to rewrite is provided.
10. Covert Censor: deleting messages deemed inappropriate, but without explaining why.
11. Cleaner: removing or closing dead threads, hiving off subdiscussions into separate threads.[18]

Since a facilitator can take on any subset of these roles, the possible combinations are quite numerous. In this chapter, we emphasize the online version of facilitation, but obviously many issues are shared with off-line deliberation. In face-to-face settings, facilitators may be able to interrupt or visually monitor and cue participants in a way that is not always possible online, depending on the medium and its affordances. Some online environments, however, afford the moderator a great deal of control not usually present in face-to-face deliberations, such as the power to censor comments before other participants are exposed to them. Additionally, advances in software make it possible to automate facilitation to a greater or lesser extent. Environments such as Slashdot.org contain built-in tools that aid people in classifying and giving provisional ratings to users' postings, which can both reflect and influence a user's reputation. Slashdot also recruits site members to assist in moderation, through simple feedback that is aggregated across users.

Structure. Will the deliberation be structured according to certain rules, follow an organized progression, or be left unstructured? Online environments, in some ways, make it easier to structure deliberation, as technology can be a

strong enforcer. In practice, however, imposing structure online can be more difficult than in a face-to-face meeting, especially if there is no moderator. We separate the issue of structure from facilitation, however, because structure can also
exist in software or in the minds of participants (e.g., as a social norm) without a
moderator being present.

Identifiability. Will participants be identifiable or anonymous? When each
act of communication can be tied to an individual, participation is identifiable.
Many forums, however, offer at least the option of contributing anonymously.
Anonymity can exist at different levels. For example, one's identity may be in-
visible to most or all participants, but visible to others, at least to those admin-
istering the forum. True anonymity is rare in an online space, due to the
traceability of Internet provider (IP) addresses and other mechanisms (login
requirements, HTTP cookies, browser fingerprinting, etc.) for identifying users
online. This may be one respect in which off-line deliberation, especially when
not done face-to-face, offers possibilities that are inherently difficult to achieve
if participants are online, since the world of bricks and mortar at least sometimes affords anonymous communication (e.g., anonymous postings on a wall
or graffiti).

Incentivizing. Will participants be rewarded/reinforced for contributing? This
has not often been an issue in face-to-face deliberations, but explicit reward or
points systems are commonplace online. Some systems award points toward
one's reputation and/or ability to contribute, and many make it possible to flag
one's messages positively or negatively.[19] Back-end computation makes the
necessary bookkeeping of such points and demerits much easier, and in principle, such techniques could be introduced into face-to-face deliberations, which
are increasingly augmented with electronic tools or decision aids.

Design Criteria

Of course, it is difficult to decide how to design a deliberation forum unless we
know how to assess its success. Here, we provide a brief discussion of some of
the criteria that have been applied in the past, especially by researchers evaluating different design choices. (For more on evaluation, see Chapter 10.) Which
criteria are used is, of course, another design choice to be considered.

Quantity

We can measure how much deliberation or participation is taking place in different ways—for example, by counting the total number of contributions, the
average number of comments per participant, the total and average lengths of
comments, and the number and proportion of participants who contribute.[20]

Quality

The quality of deliberative activity is more subjective than quantity, but it too can be measured in various ways. Metrics of quality include those that can be determined directly from the transcript(s) of a deliberation. One can count the average number of replies to each message, examine the distribution of contributions to a thread from participants with different viewpoints, or measure the length of replies by others to a message. Quality can also be assessed outside of the deliberation itself through methods such as asking participants to say or demonstrate how well they understood others, or to evaluate the quality of the deliberation.[21] In addition, one can use more qualitative or rhetorical methods of analysis to make more nuanced assessments of a given discussion's deliberative quality.

Regardless of one's method, a useful concept in assessing deliberative quality is *grounding*—the extent to which someone who says something knows that he or she has been understood correctly by those on the receiving end, and vice versa.[22] This differs from comprehension because, for example, a participant could be understood without knowing that he or she has been understood. Grounding is often assessed by inspecting a record of a dialogue (e.g., a transcript or video recording) and looking for markers of common understanding, such as mutual head nods, "yups" or "uh-huhs," and other linguistic acknowledgments. A few researchers have attempted to develop metrics for deliberativeness,[23] but as yet, no consensus measure or set of measures has emerged.

Inclusiveness

Measures of inclusiveness look at, for example, how closely the set of participants matches the demographics of a target population. This is referred to as "external inclusiveness."[24] Other measures are related to "internal inclusiveness," such as how often those who are in the minority, demographically or ideologically, contribute relative to other participants once they are part of a deliberation. (For more on diversity and inclusion in deliberative civic engagement, see Chapter 5.)

Preference

We can also ask whether participants or other stakeholders prefer a given type of deliberation over another, or prefer not deliberating at all. This can be measured prior to the deliberation itself, as a prospective choice, or during or after the experience, on a survey rating scale.

Efficiency

This criterion concerns the extent to which resources are optimally used. One measure is the speed with which deliberators can accomplish a task when time is allowed to vary. Other measures include cost and the number of people involved. The concept of "optimal" efficiency implies that this should be measured relative to the effective accomplishment of a goal, which can be harder to assess.

Efficacy

"Deliberative efficacy" refers to the consequences of the deliberation—whether and to what extent the deliberation accomplishes its purposes. If the purpose is to foster mutual understanding, then measures such as grounding and retention are good metrics for efficacy. Participants may understand each other but nevertheless fail to agree or come to a resolution on a decision or action. If this is the goal, efficacy must take into account whether the end result of the deliberation was consistent with that goal.

Empirical Findings from the Literature

Online deliberation is a relatively new field. Although the concept of public deliberation via electronic means was discussed as early as the 1970s,[25] and there was some early empirical study of deliberation online in the 1980s and 1990s,[26] investigations of structured or public online deliberation appear to have begun with work by Stephen Coleman and colleagues,[27] Lincoln Dahlberg,[28] and Vincent Price[29] around a decade ago. A review of empirical literature relevant to online deliberation therefore benefits from forays into adjacent fields, such as the study of online communities, social software, computer-supported cooperative work, human-computer interaction, psychology, education, information science, management science, political science, and media studies. What follows is a summary of some of the empirical work relevant to online deliberation, organized by the design choice dimensions defined in the previous section.

The focus in this chapter is on results that could not necessarily be known prior to empirical study. Much can be usefully said about the consequences of design choices that do not require such study. For example, online forums are easier and cheaper to set up for geographically dispersed participants, anonymity makes people less accountable for what they say, and Internet deliberation involves issues of accessibility and other digital divides. We have tried to limit ourselves to questions that require data analysis before we can answer them with confidence.

Purpose: Outcome and Collectivity

Whether a deliberation should be decision-, belief-, or idea-producing is partly determined by the context in which the need or desire for deliberation arises. However, there are some empirical results that bear on this question for deliberating groups. In comparisons of group versus individual brainstorming, the ideas generated have been found to be considerably less novel in group processes than when individuals are isolated,[30] because "deliberating groups discourage novelty."[31] Groups making decisions can similarly fail to reach good decisions when there is an initial bias among group members generally, or among its most influential members, away from the best outcome. In a typical study, business students were significantly more likely in groups than as individuals to invest more money in a failing project based on the "sunk cost fallacy."[32] The cognitive and motivational biases leading to "group polarization"—the tendency of groups to strengthen the average inclination of group members—can lead to *either* better or worse decisions after group discussion than in its absence.[33] When the right decision can be recognized easily by group members once it is identified (so-called "eureka problems"), group deliberation can outperform most if not all individuals within the group.[34] So these results, while they are not specific to the online case, suggest that deliberation has a better chance to improve decisions than to improve idea generation, but only if the decision is of the right type.

To the extent that deliberation is focused on participants' beliefs, we might ask whether it increases participants' knowledge (i.e., whether it creates more beliefs based on fact rather than on fiction or opinion). Common sense suggests that deliberation can sometimes have this effect, but it is not clear that group deliberation is better for this purpose than individual study in isolation. Experiments in public deliberation both online and off-line suggest that group deliberation does not improve knowledge acquisition over isolated study of briefing materials, and that attitude change may come primarily from the briefing materials and not from the influence of the group. Though as Peter Muhlberger points out, "deliberation may still be needed to motivate people to read the materials."[35]

The available literature on outcome quality focuses mostly on cases in which a social scientist can plausibly pass judgment on the quality of a group's decisions. But of course, often deliberation is needed most in cases where there is no objectively best decision or standard for what constitutes a good idea. In such cases, democratic deliberation may be needed for a decision to have perceived legitimacy.[36] Contemporary design teams utilize techniques to encourage novelty to improve group brainstorming (e.g., guidelines like "withhold judgment" and "encourage wacky ideas").[37] We are unaware of rigorous studies testing whether these techniques can overcome the social pressures that tend to discourage novel thinking in online brainstorming sessions, but there is some evidence that being able to see the contributions of others in an online setting improves brainstorming.[38]

As with the outcome dimension, whether a deliberation should result in a collective product is often dictated by context. To the extent that a deliberation designer has a choice, the available literature has shown more benefits to online deliberation for *individuals* who participate in online groups than it has for *group* online outcomes. In both online Deliberative Polls and scheduled political discussion online, individuals have been shown to have their attitudes affected by online discussion, and to evaluate the experience positively.[39] In contrast, research on online group decision making has yet to demonstrate consistent benefits. A meta-analysis published in 2002 concluded that the extant literature at that time generally showed worse objective and subjective outcomes for online versus face-to-face group decision making.[40] Since then, research comparing face-to-face and online decision making in groups supports a more nuanced view that places emphasis on the capacity of a medium to support the type of communication between group members necessary for them to make a decision or solve a problem, given the skills and attitudes of group members in relation to the medium.[41]

As noted earlier, the literature comparing group deliberation to statistical (nondeliberating) sets of individuals shows mixed results for decision making, primarily because groups can amplify biases. None of this amounts to a direct comparison of group versus individual outcomes as the goal of deliberation, but it does suggest, at least with the technology studied thus far, that online deliberation may have more benefits for individual learning and attitude change than for group-agreed outcomes, with the latter showing lesser or at best at par results in most online versus face-to-face studies. The latter results are limited by the quality of the technologies studied so far; however, they nevertheless provide evidence that group outcomes online show improvement as technology and the prevalence of skills to use it improve. It is also important to note that negative findings regarding group deliberation generally do not test deliberation structuring methods that have been developed to attenuate group biases.

Population: Recruitment and Audience

To our knowledge, no studies have systematically compared random versus nonrandom sampling for recruitment of participants in online deliberative forums. However, one of the arguments for random sampling is that if participants self-select, they will be less heterogeneous than the population as a whole (see Chapters 3 and 5). One study looked at registrants and participation in a national online dialogue organized by the US Environmental Protection Agency in 2000. Although participants were unrepresentative of the population as a whole in being heavy Internet users (and on related demographic measures), they were "representative of the broader public in the sense of bringing a diverse set of interest affiliations, attitudes about EPA, and geographical locations."[42]

A growing literature has looked at heterogeneity of self-selected groups in online forums. In Usenet groups, which tend to be focused on topics rather than defined by ideology, one study found that participants tend to be ideologically diverse and to reply more to opponents than to the like-minded.[43] On the Web, by contrast, there appear to be more pressures toward homophily (i.e., the tendency to connect with the like-minded), with some countervailing drivers of exposure to opposite viewpoints.[44] This may illustrate the sensitivity of Internet effects to specific technologies. Usenet forums historically have been organized by topic, bringing opposite sides together, while Web sites have loosely tended to reflect and serve particular points of view. In line with standard scientific practice, the designer of a deliberative forum should therefore be wary of selection biases in recruitment, and turn to random sampling or, less ideally, other techniques geared toward representative samples when inferences are to be drawn from the sample about a population, whether the deliberation is online or face-to-face.

The question of whether the audience for a public-interest deliberation exercise should be public or private has not, to our knowledge, been studied in an online context. But the results of Deliberative Polls that have been broadcast nationally in the United Kingdom and United States have shown large opinion change effects on participants similar to those found in polls that were not broadcast or recorded for public viewing.[45] This suggests that a public audience, at the least, does not inhibit participants from changing their views in a group deliberation exercise. Work on "accountability" by psychologists provides evidence that an audience whose overall viewpoint is unknown to those being watched can encourage people to consider countervailing arguments more seriously, justify their own views more thoroughly, and qualify their opinions.[46] Theoretical arguments have, however, questioned whether politicians are likely to be as forthcoming when they have expert knowledge the public lacks, if their deliberations are conducted in public.[47] Also, a passive audience is likely to follow and remember deliberation less well than active participants.[48]

Spatiotemporal Distance: Colocation and Cotemporality

A number of studies have specifically compared online with face-to-face deliberation. In this context, "online" usually means a form of deliberation that involves some sort of telecommunication, generally over the Internet. One such set of studies has looked at Deliberative Polling.[49] Deliberative Polls (DPs) have been conducted online using synchronous voice discussion combined with an interface that shows each talking participant on the "chat line." The results are reported to be "broadly similar" to those of face-to-face Deliberative Polls, although more modest in their effects. This last fact has been attributed to the reduced personal involvement of individuals as they participate. However, it has been speculated that a longer lasting online DP might well produce opinion shifts as large as those in face-to-face DPs.[50]

Another direct comparison of online versus face-to-face deliberation involved text-based instead of voice chat for the online condition. Online and face-to-face groups were randomly assigned, as was a control group. The deliberation was moderated and structured similarly in the two noncontrol conditions. This study found that both the online and face-to-face deliberations improved knowledge, efficacy, and political participation relative to the control group, and in about the same amounts. Opinion change did not show a similar pattern across the two groups, leading in opposite directions before and after, but the difference was not statistically significant.[51]

When combined, these studies suggest that online deliberation can produce outcomes that are similar to face-to-face deliberation, but that the level of involvement matters in the online case. Text-based chat may be less engaging than voice, and therefore less similar to face-to-face deliberation. Moreover, because the opinion shift in the face-to-face condition in the text-online study was not significant, the results indicate that at least in this exercise, online DPs are less effective than officially structured DPs. Before such broad-brush conclusions can be drawn, however, more research is needed.

One of the most systematic comparisons of online and face-to-face deliberation looked at the effects that face-to-face, synchronous online, and asynchronous online (over a twenty-four-hour period) deliberations, respectively, had on participants' deliberative behavior within each condition. The study found that online deliberators expressed a greater variety of viewpoints (less conformity to a group's most popular opinion) and showed more equality of participation than their face-to-face counterparts, but that face-to-face deliberation was of higher quality, more likely to refer to personal experiences, and more enjoyable for participants.[52] Other research has also found that computer-mediated communication (CMC) reduces individual conformity to the dominant opinion of a group, relative to face-to-face deliberation in deliberative judgment tasks.[53] But although online deliberation, particularly of the asynchronous variety (see later) tends to promote equal participation relative to face-to-face deliberation, it does not appear to reduce the aversion to conflict that characterizes people who do not like to deliberate.[54]

A large and growing literature compares face-to-face and computer-mediated communication more generally. Among the most interesting findings has been a study of group problem solving in the Lost at Sea task.[55] CMC participants were "significantly better judges of whether they made a successful decision and agree[d] on the success of their group's decision to a greater extent than [face-to-face] group members."[56] Recalling the lack of general support in the extant literature for superior decisions in CMC settings discussed earlier, this suggests nonetheless that the online context may attenuate the social biases and distractions that are more likely to be manifested in face-to-face settings and that can interfere with realistic judgments of group effectiveness.[57]

Another important issue for online communication is the extent to which users are satisfied with it relative to a face-to-face alternative. This is obviously quite dependent on the population of participants and the technology in question. CMC versus face-to-face studies of decision making and problem solving have generally found that CMC can be as satisfying as face-to-face communication for groups that are not anonymous and that have sufficient time to complete the task (which tends to take longer in CMC in these studies than face-to-face).[58] In a couple of studies from neighboring fields, students were reported to consider synchronous voice communication to be the next best thing after face-to-face communication.[59]

A useful framework for describing the results of online versus face-to-face studies of deliberation and decision making is the set of theories that have been referred to in the group processes literature as "media capacity theories." The shared features of these theories have been described as follows:

> CMC is a more restricted medium than FTF [face-to-face] communication; hence whether CMC groups are more effective than FTF groups depends a great deal on the complexity of their tasks. When the task is complex, FTF groups should perform much better than CMC groups because their members need rich media to engage in a great deal of coordination, persuasion, and expression of opinions in their group interactions. In contrast, when the task is simple, CMC should be a sufficient channel for groups to accomplish their tasks, and thus CMC groups will perform just as well as FTF groups.[60]

Two sets of findings support this pattern: (1) CMC groups can take four to ten times longer than face-to-face groups to finish assigned tasks due to the lack of nonverbal clues that aid understanding (grounding); and (2) CMC groups have often been found to have lower efficacy than face-to-face groups when performing tasks that require a lot of communication.[61]

Regarding cotemporality, a comparison of online discussion forums initiated by the city of Hoogeveen in the Netherlands in 2001–2002 provides some data on the synchronous versus asynchronous forum question.[62] On a number of measures, the asynchronous text forum showed similar patterns to two synchronous text forums (e.g., special treatment based on status occurred in both kinds of forums). However, the asynchronous forum generated much longer postings (179 words on average compared with 30 and 46 in the synchronous forums). Synchronous deliberation seemed to score modestly higher on grounding (i.e., "mutual understanding"). The asynchronous forum generated more deliberation (replies), but also more verbal attacks. Because these results are based on observations rather than a controlled experiment, however, it is possible that they can be accounted for by population differences (or selection bias) in the forums.

A more controlled comparison was recently done between synchronous and twenty-four-hour asynchronous deliberation forums about global warming and stem cell issues. While the asynchronous forum held over a twenty-four-hour period produced more equality of participation than the synchronous forum, this experiment's results were consistent with those of the Hoogeveen study in that discussion was less interactive in the asynchronous than in the synchronous online forum—with more repetitive postings and position statements than dialogue, indicating lower grounding, in the former.[63] It has also been noted that "synchronous deliberation gives facilitators control over who can speak and also permits them to monitor and guide the nature and flow of the deliberative conversations"[64] relative to asynchronous deliberation.

At least a few studies in related fields have looked at the effects of the cotemporality variable in general for computer-mediated communication, leading to pertinent findings. For example, asynchronous text usually generates the most significant information exchanges (barring, presumably, face-to-face communication),[65] and synchronous text communication tends to be selected more often than asynchronous text for "community-building" efforts, although it can exclude unskilled typists to some degree.[66]

Communication Medium: Modality, Emotivity, and Fidelity

Studies about the effects of different modalities that have focused specifically on online public deliberation have, to our knowledge, just looked at the relative effects of print versus online commenting on proposed regulations (e-rulemaking). None of the studies appear to have found large reliable differences in the quality or quantity of comments between these two media.[67] An interesting effect bearing on modality choice emerged from early structured deliberation experiments on political issues in the United States at the University of Pennsylvania. Text chat deliberators appeared more likely to show a pattern of more equal levels of contributions across participants, relative to face-to-face voice dialogue, and this modality appeared to draw out those with minority opinions more than in live spoken dialogue.[68] This result in a controlled setting differs from findings from organically occurring online forums in which women and African Americans were found to participate at disproportionately low levels.[69]

A large number of studies from computer-mediated communication and human-computer interaction bear on the choice of modality for a deliberative forum. The optimal modality for each communication situation is sensitive to many variables. Other things being equal, however, the available research supports the idea that people both prefer and are more productive when they are speaking rather than writing, probably because speech is less cognitively demanding than writing,[70] but that people who are high in literacy prefer and absorb more information per unit time when they are reading text rather than listening to speech.[71] This suggests a role for the developing technology of automatic speech recognition (ASR). If software can efficiently translate spoken words into text, then the users of an online system may be able to interact more optimally.

Much work in the study of computer-mediated communication has revolved around what we referred to earlier as "media capacity theories." *Media richness theory*, one well-known media capacity theory, has generated considerable research over the last three decades.[72] In this theory, a key variable predicting which modality a group will choose is *equivocality*, or the extent to which the correct solution to a group's task is ambiguous.[73] One formulation of media richness theory is the following:

> When equivocality is high, individuals are likely to have different interpretations of problems and may disagree as to what information is needed to shape a solution. These conditions require that individuals must first create a shared sense of the situation and then, through negotiation and feedback, formulate a common response. Daft and his colleagues argue that this requires a rich communication medium, one that, in our terminology, provides *interactivity* and *expressiveness*. A medium that provides interactivity permits communication partners to exchange information rapidly, adjusting their messages in response to signals of understanding or misunderstanding, questions, or interruptions [citation omitted]. A medium that permits expressiveness allows individuals to convey not only the content of their ideas but also intensity and subtleties of meaning through intonation, facial expression, or gestures. According to the contingency hypothesis, when task equivocality is high, media richness is essential to effective communication.[74]

Media richness theorists distinguish between "rich" and "lean" media, but this is usefully refined into the interactivity and expressiveness dimensions defined here. Modalities (text, speech, video, face-to-face) can be mapped onto expressiveness, and cotemporality can be mapped onto interactivity, thus defining a classification for two-way communication media under these two dimensions as shown in Table 6.2, with richness increasing as one moves from the upmost left toward the lowest right cell.

Both the interactivity/cotemporality and the expressiveness/modality dimensions correspond with trade-offs for the users of media. Higher expressiveness (video, and to a lesser extent speech) enables participants to communicate and understand subtleties of sentiment, but at the cost of greater parallel processing requirements for the recipient, and therefore, potential failure to communicate intended information because of distraction and information overload. Lower expressiveness (text, then speech) enables message senders to control more precisely the information that is communicated, but with potential loss of emotional nuance of which the sender may be more aware than the receiver. Lower expressiveness therefore places a higher demand on communicators to wisely choose and interpret words. Higher interactivity (synchronous, and to a lesser extent on demand) enables communicators to respond to each other more quickly, and therefore to avoid prolonged misunderstanding, but at the cost of greater cognitive demands on the sender, who must pay attention to the recipients' responses and reply to them under time pressure. Lower interactivity (asynchronous, and to a lesser extent on demand) gives both senders and receivers greater control over the pace at which they produce or understand a message, but with potential loss of communicative grounding. Additional important factors that may influence the choice of medium include whether communication is recorded and available for review later, and whether there is one, a few, or many recipients of a sender's message.

Media richness theory predicts that communicators will use rich media more when task equivocality (which may come from divergent preferences/emotions or from different beliefs/uncertainty) is high, and that they will use lean media

Table 6.2 **Two-Way Communication Media Representing Different Levels of Interactivity and Expressiveness**

		Expressiveness (modality)		
		Low (text)	*Moderate (speech)*	*High (video)*
Interactivity **(cotemporality)**	*Low* *(asynchronous)*	Email	Voice mail	Video mail
	Moderate (on *demand)*	Instant messaging (texting)	Instant voice messaging	Instant video messaging
	High *(synchronous)*	Synchronous text editing	Phone call (teleconferencing)	Video conferencing

more when task equivocality is low. Moreover, such theory suggests that measures such as quality, efficiency, efficacy, and satisfaction will improve for a communication if media richness and equivocality levels are well matched for a group's task. Many empirical studies have supported this theory at least to some extent, but the results overall have been mixed.[75] In a study of collaborative writing, for example, individuals who commented on a fictitious co-author's manuscript "preferred text only for commenting on problems of spelling and grammar and preferred voice for commenting on missing the main point of a passage, on project status, and on the success of the collaboration." The latter tasks were interpreted to be higher in equivocality.[76] The presence of variables other than task equivocality, however, can interact with media richness. An alternative vein of media capacity theory emphasizes the social influence of people's skills, habits, and attitudes within a group in helping to determine which medium will be most effective for a given task.[77]

In addition to modality, other important considerations include emotivity and fidelity. A number of studies of computer-mediated communication have looked at the use and effects of emoticons in text communication. Emoticons can be included within plain text without further facilitation by the interface, but an interface can make available more visible and detailed emoticons for use in a message board. One study found that participants in a computer-mediated decision-making session were more satisfied with their experience if emoticons were available to them.[78]

We have already touched on evidence, under Structure and Cotemporality, that free-flowing asynchronous text forums are associated with less civil behavior. This may therefore make participants less comfortable. A study by social psychologists showed that email users tend to misinterpret the tone of messages even though they think they are interpreting them correctly, and that this can result in flame wars.[79]

As was discussed under Modality, the choice of a medium that supports speech, as opposed to text-only media, tends to enhance the ability to communicate emotion accurately. Speech also appears more likely to prevent emotional blow-ups. In a study of collaborative writing using different modalities, those using speech were more likely to use mitigating phrases to smooth over interactions, whereas text users were more likely to use blunt or "almost hostile" phrases.[80]

Computer-mediated communication generally appears to be laden with emotion, with or without the use of emoticons. A review of the literature concluded that "there is no indication that CMC is a less emotional or less personally involving medium than F2F [face-to-face]. On the contrary, emotional communication online and off-line is surprisingly similar, and if differences are found they show more frequent and explicit emotion communication in CMC than in F2F."[81]

A growing body of research has looked at the effect of transformed social interaction (TSI) on users of virtual reality systems. As yet, it is unclear what effects this would have on online deliberation per se, but evidence is suggestive. A general finding, replicated in several studies with avatars, is that transformations of facial images designed to increase a feeling of connection between participants (e.g., blending the face one is looking at with one's own through computerized morphing, maintaining eye contact that cannot happen naturally) are not detected as transformations, do not disrupt communication, and can lead to more satisfying, persuasive experiences for participants.[82]

Deliberative Process: Facilitation, Structure, Identifiability, and Incentivization

We begin this section by considering the role of facilitation and structure. Studies of online public deliberation have shown that online discussions moderated by government officials resulted in more respectful behavior by participants than is found in spontaneous, unofficial online discussion.[83] In a study of online deliberation organized by the Hamburg city government, the researcher concluded that "the quality of debate was close to the rational-critical ideal of deliberative theory."[84] A few studies have looked systematically at the effect of moderators on online deliberative behavior. In an experimental study of Korean voters discussing an upcoming election, the presence of a moderator was found to significantly reduce the number of postings (pre-moderation), but improve deliberation quality and the likelihood that others' postings were read by a participant.[85] However, another study found that moderation involving censorship (i.e., the filtering of messages) can diminish trust in the forum.[86]

In a field experiment conducted in an online forum for discussing the future of New York's World Trade Center site, groups were given either "advanced" or "basic" facilitation, with the former involving professional facilitators who took a more active role in steering and summarizing discussions. Nonwhite (especially) and female residents were less likely to register for the discussions, but advanced facilitation appeared to boost participation for both groups relative to the basic condition, indicating that a more active approach might draw out underrepresented participants once they are part of the process.[87]

A growing volume of empirical study has focused on distributed moderation in systems such as Slashdot.org. Distributed moderation grew out of earlier work in "collaborative filtering"[88] that has found wide applications in electronic commerce, such as the Amazon.com system for suggesting items a user might like. Early analyses concluded that the Slashdot reputation and filtering system is relatively effective at identifying and directing users' attention to the highest value posts and comments, but with significant imperfections, such as biases created by earlier as opposed to later feedback.[89] More recent work has focused on making more efficient use of information in user behavior—for example, by letting all users benefit from the extra effort that some users exert in modifying filter settings.[90]

Few studies have systematically manipulated structure in online public deliberation, but a number of other studies of online forums provide insight into the structure question. For example, in the Hoogeveen, Netherlands, study, one of the two synchronous forums was much more restrictive in the postings it allowed.[91] This predictably led to fewer postings overall, and illustrates what may be a trade-off between structure and volume of participation. At the same time, more structure has been shown in several studies to lead to more deliberative behavior.[92] Many forum designs build in deliberative structure, but a common finding, at least anecdotally, is that these structures can be oppressive and prevent people from interacting in the ways that they want.[93] Nonetheless, there appears to be a growing consensus among deliberation advocates that the open Internet is not conducive to deliberation. This sentiment has even been expressed by German social theorist Jürgen Habermas:

> Use of the Internet has both broadened and fragmented the contexts of communication. This is why the Internet can have a subversive effect on intellectual life in authoritarian regimes. But at the same time, the less formal, horizontal cross-linking of communication channels weakens the achievements of traditional media. This focuses the attention of an anonymous and dispersed public on select topics and information, allowing citizens to concentrate on the same critically filtered issues and journalistic pieces at any given time. The price we pay for the growth in egalitarianism offered by the Internet is the decentralised access to unedited stories. In this medium, contributions by intellectuals lose their power to create a focus.[94]

Because "structure" is such a broad category of design possibilities, generic findings about structure are likely to be of less use to designers than are tests of particular techniques. Thus, this area is wide open for future research.

Another key feature of deliberation is identifiability. At least a few studies have looked specifically at the effect of forcing forum users to identify themselves. In a public deliberation context, Korean voters who were engaged in a controlled online discussion experiment about an upcoming election were found to be more engaged when allowed to post anonymously; however, identity cues were also found to improve externally rated discussion efficacy.[95] Consistent with these results, when a corporate online forum changed its policy so that employees could no longer post anonymously (measured by other participants' ability to see who they were), postings decreased significantly and became shorter, more narrowly focused, and less likely to generate a response.[96]

Early research on computer-mediated communication has generally found anonymity to boost CMC deliberation quality relative to face-to-face decision making and problem solving. As mentioned earlier, a majority of studies have found CMC groups to perform less well in making decisions than face-to-face groups, but this difference disappears when CMC groups are anonymous.[97] Somewhat paradoxically, however, anonymous groups under CMC show less satisfaction than do face-to-face groups in decision tasks.[98] Anonymity can also lead to more irresponsible behavior, such as showing up late for the deliberation or being a "troublemaker."[99] The effects of identifiability may also be culturally dependent. For example, anonymity or reduced identifiability has been posited to overcome "Confucian norms of social hierarchy and status" present in East Asian societies.[100]

Finally, we have found only one study that systematically manipulated the presence and absence of rewards in an online deliberation forum—the Korean voter experiment—which split participants randomly into conditions in which they received points that were "shown next to their login ID whenever they talked online." Points depended on their "frequency of postings, frequency of being read by someone else, and number of favorable replies." The points condition was found to produce more responses per message than the group without points. It also marginally improved a measure of "political discussion efficacy" that took account of "argument repertoire and other quality indices."[101]

A Note on Technology and Culture

The studies we have cited in this section, together with the design dimensions into which we have organized them, demonstrate that the main question facing designers of future online deliberations will increasingly be not *whether* but *how* to use online tools. Early research in this area tended to treat technology as "a dichotomous variable . . . either present or not."[102] But as technologies have evolved, the range of experiences they offer now span a broad spectrum from the simple and truncated text of a Twitter message to the high verisimilitude of the most advanced virtual reality environments, as well as augmented reality systems that attempt to give us the best face-to-face and online experiences simultaneously. Online deliberation and its public version—online deliberative civic engagement—are rich areas of study and design because of the huge space of possibilities within them.

At the same time, we should guard against techno-determinism, or the tendency to draw strict conclusions about the effects of technology, even when the technology being studied is narrowly circumscribed and the results are robust thus far. Cultural practices can change in response to technology and other factors, so that what holds today might cease to be the case in ten years, or in a culture not yet studied.

One researcher has characterized the pair of principles described above as "a culturalist perspective on technology," which "means that we take into account the complexity of the social practices of usage as well as its symbolic dimension. It also means that we have to be sensitive to the specific technology used in a given case, as the corresponding practices differ greatly."[103]

Conclusion

The literature relevant to the design of online deliberation processes is vast, and the empirical research discussed above is better seen as a sample than as a comprehensive guide to results across the several dimensions we have covered, which are themselves a small subset of the choices facing a designer. There is a large volume of literature that suggests some guidelines for online deliberation design, but relatively few of the questions have been adequately answered. Choices often involve trade-offs. Anonymity, for example, has been found to increase efficacy in decision making for online groups, but at the cost of a less satisfying experience for participants.[104]

Though the literature is complex, the general frameworks of media capacity theories and grounding provide a way to understand some of the findings we have discussed. In turn, these frameworks can assist online deliberation designers in making choices between different media or modalities. The environment for deliberation should be a good match for the needs and abilities of deliberators to resolve ambiguities and to achieve grounding, regardless of whether the task is to converge on a decision or just to hear each others' ideas. When a medium is insufficiently rich, or when participants are not able to use it effectively enough, it gets in the way of success and is likely to hurt the quality, efficiency, and efficacy of the deliberation, as well as subjective satisfaction with the process. This means, among other things, that the effectiveness of online deliberation can depend on the specifics of the online medium that go beyond the choice dimensions we have discussed here, such as details of interface design and the level of richness afforded to communication. As technology is continually advancing, it is therefore difficult to induce reliable principles about online versus off-line deliberation. Other sources of variation include differences across cultures[105] and time periods. Nevertheless, we believe that this literature has a few lessons to teach deliberative designers. A summary of four such lessons follows.

First, online forums can approach the impact of face-to-face deliberations if they are sufficiently engaging, if they are media-rich enough for the deliberative task, or if the standard for success is individual attitude change. So far, voice deliberation in real time seems to be more capable of achieving this than is asynchronous text deliberation.

Second, there appears to be a trade-off between media that give people more time (asynchronous, text) and those that stress more direct engagement (synchronous, voice). The former appear better for encouraging participation, including by those less represented in live discussions, and they lead to longer contributions. But, on average, they may be less effective at fostering mutual understanding or changing people's minds. Before substantive conclusions can be drawn, however, much more research is needed.

Third, unstructured dialogue on the Internet does not seem to foster deliberative behavior by the standards of deliberation advocates. Structure and human facilitation appear to be needed for high-quality deliberation in general and can produce it when serious purpose is evident, as in the case of government-organized and facilitated online forums. Structure, moderation, and facilitation can also be provided in distributed ways and can utilize software techniques that provide higher information value with less effort by users.

Fourth, allowing anonymous participation, even when users can be traced by administrators, appears to make people more willing to contribute to discussion, but it also lowers the sense of satisfaction participants feel, which is a common finding whenever a communication medium puts emotional distance between participants.

Theories such as media capacity, grounding, and the general findings of social and cognitive psychology suggest many questions and hypotheses that do not appear to have been well addressed in the literature we have seen. Examples of such questions include the following:

- What effects do different levels of media richness, or different modalities, have on deliberative outcomes? Do different media systematically produce different individual attitude changes or different group decisions?
- To what extent do characteristics of interfaces affect outcomes and the deliberative process? For example, does visually representing an individual participant make other participants more aware that the viewpoint of the focal participant is just one among many, and does this lead that viewpoint being discounted relative to an interface that decontextualizes the focal participant?
- If such effects are found, what normative implications does this have for deliberation design?

The field of online deliberation is young. We can look forward to learning much more as further studies are done, and as technology develops. For example, as speech recognition technology improves and becomes widely available, the advantages of online deliberation should increase, because users will be able to interact more flexibly and efficiently using both speech and text, switching between them as needed (e.g., speaking for production and reading for reception). At the same time, the necessary technology is not yet widely and easily available, and more research is needed to provide a compelling case that the classical goal of equivalent or better group decision making is reliably attainable through the use of an online system.

Meanwhile, there are other reasons that a deliberation designer might choose an online forum over, or in addition to, a face-to-face one. The most obvious reasons have to do with cost, personal convenience for participants, and the opportunity to involve more participants who cannot be present for face-to-face deliberative civic engagement. In contexts where face-to-face meetings create barriers for some users (due to shyness or other social dynamics, such as prejudice), structured online dialogue may provide a superior deliberative and democratic experience if the designer's modality choices match participants' skills and preferences.

Notes

1. "From Latin deliberare to consider well" (Hanks 1979). "Deliberation" can also refer to thinking processes within an individual mind. For this article, however, we focus on deliberation as a type of communication between people. Extensive definitions of deliberation have been proposed in the literature, e.g., Burkhalter, Gastil, and Kelshaw (2002), who focus on criteria for democratic deliberation in small face-to-face groups, as well as the literature on coding for deliberativeness or deliberative quality, in which measures could be said to constitute a definition of deliberation (see Graham and Witschge 2003; Stromer-Galley 2007; Trénel 2004).
2. For other dimensional analyses of communication forms in general, see Clark (1996) and Eckles, Ballagas, and Takayama (2009).
3. For some other typologies of issues in the design of online deliberation systems, see Rose and Sæbø (2010) and De Cindio and Peraboni (2010).
4. See, for example, Fishkin (2009b), Price (2009), and Cavalier (2009).
5. Eckles, Ballagas, and Takayama (2009: 14–21) distinguish the audience of a communication act from the "addressee," who may be an individual, a group, or a general audience. This is an example of further refinement that is possible in defining the design space for deliberation, but since the present volume is concerned with public deliberation, we felt it was outside the scope of this chapter to include cases where communication occurs between individuals privately. It should be noted, however, that a designer of a public deliberation system might want to allow for "backchannel" communication among individual participants. Thus, analyses like those of Eckles, Ballagas, and Takayama (2009) are relevant to the design of online deliberation systems at a more detailed level than we discuss here.

6. "Telecommunication" means communication "over a distance" (Hanks 1979). We include "temporal distance" in our use of this concept because the technologies that allow communication across time at the same location appear to be the same as those that allow it across space and time combined.

7. Clark and Brennan (1991) and Eckles, Ballagas, and Takayama (2009: 10) define a purely spatial dimension, which allows for the case of participants being in the same spatial location but separated in time. A stationary bulletin board or kiosk could facilitate deliberation in such a setting. We choose to treat this case together with space-shifted communication within our framework, but note that there is this further refinement that could be introduced if necessary.

8. Eckles, Ballagas, and Takayama (2009: 11) make a finer distinction here, between a "record" dimension (whether communication is ephemeral or available at an arbitrary time later) and a "synchronicity" dimension (whether a reply can be delayed or not).

9. See Lukensmeyer, Goldman, and Brigham (2005). Thanks to Peter Muhlberger for pointing out this possibility.

10. Zwicky (1967) and Card, Mackinlay, and Robertson (1991), both cited in Eckles, Barragas, and Takayama (2009: 4).

11. Nass and Mason (1990), cited in Eckles, Barragas, and Takayama (2009: 4).

12. See Anusuya and Katti (2009).

13. See Greene (2003).

14. Bailenson, Beall, Loomis, Blascovich, and Turk (2004).

15. Bailenson, Beall, Loomis, Blascovich, and Turk (2005: 511).

16. Yamada, Nakajima, Lee, Brave, Maldonado, Nass, and Morishima (2008).

17. For example, the "synthesizers" of discussions at town hall meetings. [This note is not in the original quotation.]

18. Wright (2009: 236).

19. See, for example, Slashdot.org.

20. See, for example, Kelly, Fisher, and Smith (2009).

21. See, for example, Stromer-Galley and Muhlberger (2009).

22. Clark and Brennan (1991).

23. See, for example, Jankowski and van Os (2004), Trénel (2004), Sack, Kelly, and Dale (2009), Steenbergen, Bächtiger, Spörndli, and Steiner (2003), and Stromer-Galley (2007). See Muhlberger and Stromer-Galley (2009) for an automated approach based on statistically examining concept-word linkages in text. Chapter 10 in this volume offers more detail on methods such as these.

24. Trénel (2009).

25. See, for example, Henderson (1970), Ohlin (1971), and Etzioni (1972, 1975).

26. See, for example, Asteroff (1982), Schneider (1997), and Wilhelm (1999).

27. See, for example, Blumler and Coleman (2001) and Coleman, Hall, and Howell (2002).

28. Dahlberg (2001).

29. Price and Capella (2002); Price, Goldthwaite, and Capella (2002).

30. Brown (2000: 176), cited in Sunstein (2006: 60).

31. Sunstein (2006: 60).

32. Whyte (1993), cited in Myers (2008: 278). For a case study of bias in real-world group decision making, see Whyte and Levi (1994).

33. Myers (2008: 278–284). For refinements and challenges to group polarization results in the context of deliberation online versus face-to-face, see Muhlberger (2003, 2005b).

34. For a discussion of the literature, see Sunstein (2006: 60–64).

35. Private communication; see also Muhlberger and Weber (2006).

36. See Tyler and Lind (2001) on "procedural justice."

37. Salustri (2005). An influential set of principles is the four rules for brainstorming proposed by Osborn (1957), cited in Sutton and Hargadon (1996: 685): "don't criticize, quantity is wanted, combine and improve suggested ideas, and say all ideas that come to mind, no matter how wild."

38. Michinov and Primois (2005).
39. See Fishkin (2009b) and Price (2009).
40. Baltes, Dickson, Sherman, Bauer, and LaGanke (2002).
41. Li (2007).
42. Beierle (2004: 159).
43. Kelly, Fisher, and Smith (2009).
44. Lev-On and Manin (2009).
45. See Fishkin (1996, 2006).
46. Lerner and Tetlock (1999: 256–257). Thanks to Peter Muhlberger for pointing us to this paper.
47. Stasavage (2004).
48. Schober and Clark (1989).
49. Luskin, Fishkin, and Iyengar (2006); Fishkin (2009b).
50. Fishkin (2009b: 31).
51. Min (2007).
52. Tucey (2010).
53. King, Hartzel, Schilhavy, Melone, and McGuire (2010).
54. Neblo, Esterling, Kennedy, Lazer, and Sokhey (2010: 574).
55. In this task, participants must collectively rank fifteen items in order of importance for survival from a yachting accident, and success is measured against a consensus of experts (Roch and Ayman 2005: 20).
56. Roch and Ayman (2005: 29).
57. Roch and Ayman (2005: 28).
58. See the literature reviewed in Li (2007: 598).
59. Brannon and Essex (2001); Lightner (2007).
60. Li (2007: 597).
61. Li (2007: 597–598).
62. Jankowski and van Os (2004).
63. Tucey (2010).
64. American Institutes for Research (2011: 131), citing Siu (2008).
65. Brannon and Essex (2001); Lightner (2007).
66. Brannon and Essex (2001).
67. Stanley, Weare, and Musso (2004); Schlosberg, Zavestoski, and Shulman (2009).
68. Price (2009).
69. Stromer-Galley and Wichowski (2010: 174).
70. Gould (1978) and Kroll (1978), cited in Kraut, Galegher, Fish, and Chalfonte (1992: 403).
71. Le Bigot, Rouet, and Jamet (2007).
72. For example, Daft and Lengel (1986).
73. Kraut, Galegher, Fish, and Chalfonte (1992: 378).
74. Kraut, Galegher, Fish, and Chalfonte (1992: 378).
75. See, for example, Dennis and Kinney (1998) and Kahai and Cooper (2003).
76. Kraut, Galegher, Fish, and Chalfonte (1992: 395).
77. See, for example, Fulk, Schmitz, and Steinfield (1990), cited in Li (2007: 597).
78. Rivera, Cooke, and Bauhs (1996).
79. Epley and Kruger (2005). For a more positive assessment of the ability of a text forum (Usenet) to foster community, see Baym (1998).
80. Kraut, Galegher, Fish, and Chalfonte (1992: 399).
81. Derks, Fischer, and Bos (2008: 766).
82. Bailenson, Beall, Loomis, Blascovich, and Turk (2005).
83. Coleman (2004), Jensen (2003), and Wright and Street (2007), all cited in Stromer-Galley and Wichowski (2010: 178).
84. Albrecht (2006: 75).
85. Rhee and Kim (2009).

86. Coleman, Hall, and Howell (2002); Wright (2009).
87. Trénel (2009).
88. Resnick, Iacovou, Suchak, Bergstrom, and Reidl (1994).
89. Lampe and Resnick (2004); Poor (2005).
90. Lampe, Johnston, and Resnick (2007).
91. Jankowski and van Os (2004).
92. See Janssen and Kies (2005) for an overview; see also Zhang (2005).
93. Schuler (2009).
94. Habermas (2006).
95. Rhee and Kim (2009).
96. Leshed (2009); cf. Lerner and Tetlock (1999).
97. Adams, Roch, and Ayman (2005), Baltes, Dickson, Sherman, Bauer, and LaGanke (2002), and Becker-Beck, Wintermantel, and Borg (2005), all cited in Li (2007).
98. Li (2007: 598).
99. Tucey (2010: 23–24).
100. Min (2009: 454).
101. Rhee and Kim (2009: 227, 230).
102. Albrecht (2006: 75).
103. Albrecht (2006: 75), who cites as an influence Suchman, Blomberg, Orr, and Trigg (1999).
104. Li (2007: 598).
105. See Fung (2002), Kulikova and Perlmutter (2007), and Robinson (2005), all cited in Stromer-Galley and Wichowski (2010: 180–181) and Min (2009).

PART THREE

OUTCOMES AND EVALUATION

7

Does Deliberation Make Better Citizens?

HEATHER PINCOCK

> Democracy of participation may have many beneficial consequences, but its main justifying function is and always has been, not the extent to which it protects or stabilizes a community, but the contribution it can make to the development of human powers of thought, feeling, and action.
>
> —Arnold Kauffman, *"Human Nature and Participatory Democracy"*

> Participating in democratic decisions makes many participants better citizens. I believe this claim because it fits my experience. But I cannot prove it. Neither, at this point, can anyone else.
>
> —Jane Mansbridge, *"On the Idea that Participation Makes Better Citizens"*

The summer of 2009 in the United States was dubbed by some "the summer of the town hall meeting," much to the horror of many advocates of deliberative civic engagement. After a failure to move forward on health care reform legislation, congressional representatives returned home to their districts for the summer recess in August to consult with constituents through a series of "town hall meetings."[1] But quite predictably, these public displays of shouting, insults, guns, fist fights, fear mongering, ideological extremism, and bald-faced irrationality were nothing like the ideal public fora democratic theorists envision. Some have warned that the meetings depicted on our television and computer screens *might* be a sensationalized rendering of what was really going on in many cities and towns across America, but "the summer of the town hall meeting" will not be remembered for inspiring confidence in the promise of deliberation in the United States. These spectacles are cast by democratic reformers as perfect foils or lessons in "what not to do" and serve as fodder for those eager to champion their own favorite procedural guidelines for making deliberative participation productive and worthwhile.[2]

They also serve to remind us, however, of a central truth about democracy, which has often been downplayed or sidelined by deliberative democrats: Democracy principally concerns the persistence and irrationality of human conflict. Conflict, especially when enacted in face-to-face discursive forms, is extremely difficult to manage with good results.[3] Though the scope of everyday citizen involvement in democratic procedures is a matter of continual debate, citizens surely require resources, capacities, skills, and dispositions that enable them to cope with conflict. How and where do they develop such capacities? Participatory and deliberative democrats have long claimed the developmental potential of participation, specifically deliberative civic engagement.

Despite having ancient origins and forming a recurring normative justification for participatory and deliberative processes, these developmental assumptions remain underscrutinized. If we take the role of conflict in democracy seriously, how do we expect citizens to manage it? What skills, dispositions, and relations should they have to best cope with its presence and effects? Furthermore, do their experiences in face-to-face deliberative civic engagement in conflictual settings improve their civic capacities to do so? In other words, does deliberation make better citizens? In this chapter, I address the normative and empirical aspects of the question, *What are the educative effects of deliberation on participants?* I review the current state of the field, highlight existing limitations, and suggest directions for future research.

First, I discuss the relationship between theories of participatory and deliberative democracy, arguing that educative assumptions are most compelling where these theories overlap. Second, I show how educative assumptions, that is, beliefs that deliberative participation will improve a citizen's civic capacities, are widely present in the canon of deliberative theory that has emerged in recent decades. Despite this, I argue that these "better citizen" claims have received relatively limited analytical attention from theorists. I argue that such attention is needed because "better citizen" claims form a recurring normative justification for why a practical deliberative turn[4] is needed in the design and implementation of democratic institutions.

Third, I turn to the existing empirical literature that has investigated these claims. I argue that although research has generated important insights about deliberation's effects on citizens, the literature is limited both by the way it conceptualizes educative effects and by the empirical contexts in which it tends to be situated. As a result, although we find some evidence to support "better citizen" claims, the research has neither adequately convinced the skeptics nor vindicated those who believe that deliberative civic engagement has educative potential.

Finally, I conclude with two suggestions for responding to these weaknesses and advancing our understanding of how deliberation does or does not make better citizens. First, future work on this question should begin with a clearer articulation of the kinds of changes that are expected and the mechanisms of the process theorized to produce them. Second, researchers should generate a map of the deliberative field that highlights the process design features considered most favorable to better citizen effects and identifies more and less appropriate empirical contexts to explore deliberation's educative potential. Following these steps will help to generate empirical insights about better citizen claims that are grounded in and can advance our assessments of the normative theories from which they originate.

Theorizing the Educative Benefits of Democratic Participation

There are long-standing claims about the educative effects of democratic participation, which are most clearly articulated in participatory theories of democracy. In contemporary democracies, citizens have few opportunities to exercise direct unfiltered self-government, that is, to have direct authority to make collective decisions about their shared problems. The realities of scale and complexity of governance preclude this as a general approach to democratic institutional design, and even make it challenging to incorporate in more partial or piecemeal ways.[5] This is to the dismay of those with participatory commitments who believe that political autonomy lies at the heart of democracy and should be prioritized in the design of democratic systems. Participatory democrats express their commitment to political autonomy as self-government in two key ways. First, they endorse the use, as much as possible, of collective decision-making processes that give citizens the opportunity to be directly involved in governing themselves by empowering them to make binding decisions about the shared problems they face. Second, they seek to establish collective decision-making processes that develop citizen capacities and competencies for self-governing, that is, to make these processes self-reinforcing through their educative effects.

This potential for citizens to learn through participation, such that participatory processes become self-reinforcing, is a core assumption for participatory democrats[6] who draw on claims put forward by ancient and modern political theorists (such as Aristotle, Rousseau, Mill).[7] Participatory democrats place considerable weight on deliberation as a method of citizen engagement. While some have associated "participatory democracy" with the political activism of direct action,[8] and partisan mobilization,[9] at its core participatory democracy requires direct citizen involvement, not simply as demonstrators in the streets or as guides or advisors to political officials, but as individuals directly empowered to make collective decisions regarding their shared concerns.[10] Although participatory democrats have sometimes called for reforms consistent with aggregative approaches to democracy such as referenda,[11] they more often focus on opportunities for relatively small groups to make collective decisions through face-to-face communication along the lines of the oft romanticized "town hall meeting."[12] In theory, it is in these discursive settings, where citizens are expected to explore their interests and engage in problem solving, that the educative goals of participation are best realized.

As a result, although the heyday of the participatory movements of the 1960s and 1970s has passed, the educative claims at the core of the theory have been kept salient by the so-called deliberative turn in democratic theory.[13] Like participatory democrats, deliberative democrats place significant weight on political autonomy and the transformative potential of democratic processes. Rather than focus on direct citizen self-government as an end in itself, however, they emphasize the need for reasoned decisions that can be accepted by all. They argue that under conditions of disagreement in a pluralist society, decisions are most legitimate when they are based on reasons that are developed and articulated through discursive processes and recognized by all who are affected.[14] Although some theories of deliberative democracy focus on elite and representative deliberation,[15] most theories (as well as much practice) require the involvement of lay citizens in decision-oriented deliberative processes.[16] Therefore, although often considered secondary to the goal of reasoned decision making, allusions to lasting individual effects are widely present in theories of deliberative democracy, thanks in great part to the legacy of participatory predecessors. Moreover, despite tensions and different foci between conceptions of participatory and deliberative democracy,[17] claims about the lasting educative potential of democratic participation are most compelling where these conceptions intersect—namely, in public decision-making processes that incorporate face-to-face deliberation among lay citizens.[18]

Despite being ubiquitous in the highly variegated literature on deliberative civic engagement, most claims about the educative effects of deliberation remain theoretically (and empirically) underscrutinized.[19] In particular, the shift of deliberative theory to acknowledge the persistence of conflict, jettison consensus as the aspirational ideal, and admit selfish and emotional expressions as permissible and valuable for the goals of political autonomy and equality has implications for the theoretical underpinning of educative claims that have not been fully articulated. In part as a result of these theoretical limitations, the growing empirical literature in deliberative democracy has not tended to focus on the concepts or contexts that are central to educative theories of deliberative participation. This absence of theoretical and empirical scrutiny must be addressed, not only to fill in gaps in our knowledge, but also because the normative justifications for participatory deliberative processes rest, in part, on these assumptions.

Key Assumptions of Deliberative Theory

The claims advanced by deliberative theorists can be divided into two general categories. First, and of critical importance for most theorists,[20] is the concern with producing better collective decisions. They claim deliberative decisions are "better" because they result from discursive processes of reason giving and mutual justification among all those subject to the decisions, and this renders them more legitimate.[21] These decision-oriented goals have been central to the work of deliberative practitioners and have been the focus of much empirical study of deliberation (see Chapters 9 and 10 for more discussion). Second, and the focus of this chapter, is the concern with producing better citizens. Here, "better" refers to a range of lasting changes that individuals experience as a result of their deliberative experience(s) that make them more capable citizens. This desire to make better citizens is widely shared by, and normatively significant for, deliberative theorists.

Although these theorists acknowledge their debt to republican theorists from Aristotle to Arendt who stress deliberative self-government as intrinsically valuable expressions of the "good life," much early theorizing about deliberative democracy concentrated on the foundations of its legitimacy claims.[22] Embedded in these arguments, however, are assumptions about how the deliberative process transforms individuals. For example, an early articulator of a deliberative conception of democratic legitimacy, Bernard Manin, stresses that political deliberations are "processes of education and training in themselves" and that the instrumental outcome is likely to follow in part because of the "educative effect of repeated deliberation."[23]

Most often stressed in such accounts is the expectation that through discursive interaction and as a result of reason giving, participants will come to conceptualize their preferences differently. Specifically, "the need to advance reasons that persuade others will help to shape the motivations that people bring to the deliberative procedure."[24] This expectation is based on the view that selfish arguments are illegitimate in a debate framed in terms of public good. Though this may begin as mere lip service to the common good, there is an assumption that over time, it becomes psychologically difficult to give public reasons without absorbing these other-regarding considerations.[25] Therefore, even the primary claim about how ideal deliberation leads to more legitimate decisions incorporates expectations about individual transformation that have implications beyond the particular decision at hand. This suggests that a public-spirited orientation may be a more general lasting effect of discursive preference formation under ideal deliberative procedures because these procedures are expected to "shape the identity and interests of citizens in ways that contribute to an attachment to the common good."[26]

Deliberative theorists also expect the opportunity to engage in discursive preference formation to contribute to the development of autonomy. According to Warren, autonomy refers to a "capacity of judgment" that enables the formation of preferences through examination and evaluation of "wants, needs, desires, values, roles, and commitments" instead of "manipulation, brainwashing, unthinking obedience, or reflexive acceptance of ascribed roles."[27] Similarly, in a summation of John Rawls, Joshua Cohen writes, "democratic politics should be ordered in ways that provide a basis for self-respect, that encourage the development of a sense of political competence, and that contribute to the formation of a sense of justice."[28] Rawls himself states that democratic politics ought to involve public deliberation oriented toward the public good because this "lays the foundations of civic friendship and [shapes] the ethos of political culture."[29] Therefore, in addition to its potential to make participants more public-spirited, deliberation is also suggested to have lasting effects on participants' autonomy and on the nature of their relations with other citizens.

These assumptions become more explicit in attempts to apply deliberative theories to real-world collective decision-making processes. Amy Gutmann and Dennis Thompson's classic contribution to deliberative theory acknowledges that deliberation will leave many moral disagreements unresolved; however, they maintain that the value of deliberation stems largely from its ability to "help citizens treat one another with mutual respect as they deal with the disagreements that invariably remain."[30] This mutual respect is sustained by the virtues of civic integrity and civic magnanimity.[31] Though they note that these civic virtues require explicit teaching in the schools,[32] Gutmann and Thompson also consider deliberation itself to be educative and stress the importance of deliberative decision making both inside and outside politics due to its educative function. They argue that citizens need to engage in deliberative decision making in the workplace and in their private lives to "cultivate the virtues of deliberation" and to "develop either the interest or the skill that would enable them to deliberate effectively in politics," because "the discussion that takes place in these settings not only is a rehearsal for political action, but also is itself a part of citizenship in deliberative democracy."[33]

Responding to Critics

Autonomy, a sense of political competence, attachment to the common good, the foundations of civic friendship, and mutual respect are all lofty educative claims embedded in these early articulations of deliberative theory. Such claims are no doubt part of the reason that deliberative theory has come under considerable attack from critics who find it naive, utopian, and even dangerous.[34] (For additional discussion about these critiques, see Chapter 11.) Some of these critics have narrowed in on deliberative theory's educative claims, including increased autonomy and an expanded sense of community, casting them as central normative justifications of the theory they are criticizing.[35] Several retrospective reviews have also noted how deliberative theory has shifted, adapted, and broadened to respond, at least in certain formulations, to these critiques[36] by (1) acknowledging a legitimate role for expressions of self-interest; (2) recognizing the value of a wide range of discursive forms including emotional appeals, storytelling, rhetoric, and narrative; and (3) clarifying the synergies between deliberative and nondeliberative decision procedures like voting, adjudicating, and bargaining.[37] Although this "coming of age" of deliberative theory[38] has not eclipsed the presence of educative claims, it has served to complicate the nature of these claims in some instances.

For example, in their corrective to the "classic ideal" of deliberation, which carves out a broad space for the legitimate expression of self-interest in deliberation, Jane Mansbridge and colleagues provide added theoretical complexity to the now familiar claim that participation in deliberation will change preferences for the better.[39] They make a distinction between opinion change and transformation with regard to interests, with the latter being the more significant, even if less likely, sort of individual change. While opinion change results from exposure to new information, discovery of logical mistakes in one's thinking, or adoption of a long-range view, "transformations in the direction of the common good" are produced by perspective taking, the development of new or strengthened understandings of justice, or strengthened ties to a newly formed or preexisting communal entity.[40] Deliberation is educative only when it produces these kinds of changes, and such outcomes are considered among "the most valuable features of deliberation" though they are expected to be much rarer than more straightforward changes in opinion.[41]

Emphasis on the normative importance of these deeper transformations has also been a feature of political philosopher Seyla Benhabib's recent work.[42] Benhabib develops the concept of "democratic iterations" to refer to "the complex processes of public argument, deliberation and exchange through which universal rights claims and principles are contested and contextualized, invoked and revoked, and posited and positioned throughout legal and political institutions, as well as in the associations of civil society."[43] Oriented toward debates about legal cosmopolitanism and transnational migration patterns, Benhabib aims to reconcile the tensions between universal human rights claims and the right to self-government of individual polities. Drawing on philosopher Jacque Derrida's concept of "iteration," she argues that the very meaning of rights claims is transformed through repetition and contestation in the public sphere.[44] In this view, deliberative processes not only offer a legitimate way to manage conflicts generated by competing rights claims, but in so doing they can also transform political identities and the quality and composition of the political community itself. In other words, when citizens learn through these iterations to be more inclusive and cosmopolitan, they are transformed into "better citizens."[45]

A second point of emphasis in more recent deliberative theory has stressed that in addition to generating attachment to shared understandings of the good, deliberation can be considered educative when it clarifies previously obscured conflicts and promotes further contestation. According to Mansbridge and her collaborators, the clarification of conflict becomes a normatively defensible outcome of deliberation once the legitimate place for a properly constrained self-interest is affirmed.[46] Ongoing contestation is also central to the transformative potential of democratic iterations as outlined by Benhabib.[47] This recent emphasis on conflict and contestation is motivated in part by a desire to address the criticisms of agonists who argue that deliberative theory fails to recognize the basic nature of politics as a contest between adversaries.[48]

In a similarly motivated response, political theorist John Dryzek recasts deliberative democracy in part as the engagement of discourses in a public sphere.[49] According to Dryzek, discourses underlie identities, but they are "amenable to reflection" and can change as a result of deliberative processes of persuasion.[50] Dryzek is skeptical about agonism's ability to convert enemies into adversaries and presents deliberation as a process of social learning that can better channel contestation and conflict in productive directions. The occurrence of this social learning therefore depends on continued engagement and contestation of discourses. The surfacing of conflict is considered educative when it prompts the reshaping of identities[51] and reconstructs relationships[52] in the direction of greater inclusion, or at least more "civilized engagement" (see Chapter 5 for additional discussion).[53]

As these examples illustrate, deliberative theorists continue to rely, in part, on educative assumptions to justify their theories even as they render those theories more complex. Overall, although "better citizen" outcomes are rarely, if ever, positioned as a primary purpose or goal in theories of deliberative democracy, they have nevertheless been invoked frequently from the outset and with increasing nuance to help make the normative case for deliberative democracy.

Empirical Evidence of Deliberation's Educative Effects

Not surprisingly, these claims have garnered attention in the burgeoning field of empirical research and captured the imagination of deliberative practitioners. As scholars have struggled to bridge the gap between the normative and empirical study of deliberation,[54] these claims have been given a place in the emergent research agenda. Some have insisted on the continued primacy of better collective decisions, stating that "learning about issues, gaining a sense of efficacy, or developing a better understanding of opposing views—should be regarded as instrumental to this aim,"[55] but most have posited better citizen claims as equally important avenues for empirical exploration. For example, one volume of empirical case studies notes the "schools of democracy" hypothesis as one of six questions about process and outcomes that shape the research agenda on deliberative civic engagement.[56] Likewise, in his edited volume advancing a research agenda for empirical scholars focusing on deliberative theory, political psychologist Shawn Rosenberg suggests that within the range of theoretical orientations to deliberative democracy, there is a consensus about its potential to contribute to

> (a) the making of more effective and just policy decisions, (b) the building of more united communities that embrace group and individual differences, (c) the facilitating of more equal, caring and cooperative social relations, and (d) the fostering of greater levels of cognitive and social development of individual citizens.[57]

The last three contributions are all forms of better citizen claims. In the same volume, Joshua Cohen, while reflecting on the empirical chapters, observes that while there is much attention on evaluating decision outcomes, there is little empirical study of the "intrinsic" virtues of deliberation including its capacity to generate mutual respect and a sense of community. He suggests that these claims account for the "intuitive attractions of deliberative democracy" and their purpose is to establish that "deliberative democracy is a compelling ideal," whereas other claims merely serve to "strengthen the case by showing the fit with justice and with effectiveness of policy."[58]

One survey of the social and political psychology research findings relevant to deliberative democracy outlines eight goals of deliberation that merit further study, six of which focus on presumed educative effects: increased engagement, tolerance, understanding of preferences, identification of common interests, empowerment, and social capital.[59] Even scholars who explicitly focus on the potential for citizen deliberation to influence policy decisions have noted its potential to empower citizens politically and psychologically.[60] In the practical field as well, deliberative practitioners adopt explicitly participatory orientations to their projects and articulate better decision and better citizen goals with co-equal weight. Take for example the mission statement of the Deliberative Democracy Consortium where both goals are advanced together:

> Central to our work is the conviction that the outcomes of deliberation result in qualitatively better, more lasting decisions on policy matters. Participation in such forums is central to democratic renewal. Essentially, our view is that democratic deliberation is a powerful, transformational experience for everyone involved—citizens and

leaders alike—which can result in attitudinal shifts toward the institutions and practice of democracy overall. . . . [The] Consortium has
embarked on an ambitious research agenda that will build knowledge
around the actual impact of deliberation upon civic attitudes and
behavior, and the sustainability of follow-on efforts. Our hypothesis in
this work is that, with expanded application, increased frequency and
greater visibility, deliberative democracy can invigorate and rekindle
the civic virtues of trust, participation and responsibility.[61]

As these statements imply, a growing body of empirical literature has emerged
and contributed much to our understanding about deliberation, including its
educative potential.[62] However, this literature continues to have blind spots concerning the way it specifies and operationalizes educative effects and the kinds of
deliberative venues where it looks for such effects. As a result, current research
does not yet fully respond to the calls for more fruitful collaboration between
the normative and empirical scholars of deliberation.

Research on Deliberation and Opinion Quality

Though recurrent in the literature, theorists rarely specify educative claims in ways
that lend themselves easily to empirical study. The claims reviewed above can be
divided into two broad categories: (1) those that relate to individual changes in
the attitudes and behaviors of participants,[63] and (2) those that relate to changes
in the social relations between citizens in a political community.[64] In trying to
operationalize these various claims, empirical scholars have largely focused on the
first set of categories relating to individual change. This is not surprising given that
many such scholars are working in the political behavior and public opinion field,
which has traditionally taken the individual as its unit of analysis. Aside from a
focus on the individual, however, these scholars have actually developed an "opinion track" in the deliberation research agenda that attends to related but different
concerns from those initially articulated by deliberative democrats.

Though deliberative theory is largely concerned with the problem of moral
disagreement[65] and the need to make legitimate collective decisions under
conditions of deep pluralism,[66] the opinion track has been more focused on
the symptoms of this problem. Noting low interest and participation in electoral politics on the part of the citizenry (and the American citizenry in particular), it begins from the problem presented by the "limitations of public
opinion as we find it in mass society,"[67] claiming that "the debate over the
process of opinion formation forms the foundation for discussions of deliberation."[68] This frame draws on several decades of public opinion research that
paints a picture of a rationally ignorant or uninformed public,[69] who express

meaningless doorstep opinions and nonattitudes,[70] or form their opinions through irrational and short-sighted processes[71] that are reinforced through homogenous networks[72] and highly susceptible to a constant onslaught of elite manipulation tactics.[73]

Concerned with these realities, the opinion track turns to deliberation as a way of generating meaningful public opinion that can serve as a reliable indicator to political representatives entrusted to carry out the public will. This emphasis on opinion formation situates the opinion track at a distance from the strand of deliberative theory focused on binding collective decisions and even further from the participatory strand of deliberative theory that seeks to empower citizens to make such binding decisions. This divergence has implications for better citizen claims. While not all empirical research has been conducted on the "opinion track," this perspective has greatly shaped the body of existing empirical research and resulted in notable blind spots with respect to the what and where of educative effects.

As a result of the opinion track's influence, much empirical study of deliberation is focused on opinion change and largely overlooks more foundational claims about the effect deliberation can have on a broader set of civic and political capacities. Instead, empirical scholars in this track are concerned with testing the effect of deliberation on opinion quality, or the extent to which opinions are more informed, consistent, and durable following deliberative experiences. They have found that citizens learn information as a result of deliberation,[74] including information that is adverse to their pre-deliberative opinions,[75] and that changes in their opinions are related to these information gains. Changes in voting intentions have also been shown to follow from information gains and policy opinion changes that occur during deliberation.[76]

Disagreements exist, however, about the specific mechanisms responsible for information gains and associated opinion changes. Robert Goodin and Simon Neimeyer find that these changes result from information sharing and individual internal "deliberation" rather than from the face-to-face discussions between participants in deliberative processes.[77] However, others have shown that, at least in some cases, the "on-site" portion of these deliberative experiences, rather than the briefing materials provided in advance, account for much of the learning and opinion change.[78] These and other findings support the self-reports of participants who themselves place the greatest emphasis on small group discussions; however, the findings do not hold for deliberation about high salience issues, where public discussion of the topic is relatively intense.[79] Evidence of deliberation's effects in low salience issue contexts and on individuals with weak opinion strength,[80] suggests, to the delight of opinion track scholars, that those most vulnerable to the doorstep opinion phenomenon[81] benefit the most from deliberation.

In addition to information gains, opinion track scholars have explored the quality of post-deliberative opinions by measuring their consistency and durability.[82] Consistency has been measured in numerous ways, including net opinion change, ideological consistency, social influence, and "single-peakedness" (the extent to which participants agree about the structure of preference ordering such that the probability of voting cycles is reduced and the meaning of majority rule is preserved). Net opinion change among group members in a particular direction, while controversial from a political standpoint, suggests that individual opinion changes are nonrandom. Aggregate changes are also encouraging for opinion track scholars concerned with capturing considered *public* opinion in ways that can inform political representatives. There is repeated evidence of net opinion change in some deliberative contexts,[83] suggesting that post-deliberative opinions are more consistent. Those examining consistency in ideological terms by looking at the match between issue opinions and broader ideological commitments, have found mixed results, raising doubts that deliberation increases opinion quality.[84] According to some, exposure to counterarguments does not yield more ideologically consistent results in the aggregate because those changing for the "right" reasons cancel out those changing for the "wrong" reasons.[85]

Other studies focus more specifically on "single-peakedness."[86] Like the link between information gains and opinion change, increased proximity to "single-peakedness" is most pronounced with low salience issues and among those who gain the most information.[87] Yet another approach has sought to uncover the mechanisms of social influence behind deliberative opinion change, finding some evidence that, in contexts of relatively high information and deliberative quality, such change is rooted in respect for one's interlocutor (as opinion track scholars have hoped) instead of in friendship, familiarity, personality, race, or gender (as critics have feared).[88]

Finally, increased opinion quality has been measured for its durability, or its ability to resist elite manipulation. For example, one study finds that cross-cutting, small-group discussions dampen the impacts of elite manipulation (measured through exposure to op-ed articles) on individual opinions.[89] Likewise, another study finds evidence to suggest that exposure to competing elite frames encourages deliberation, but that resulting opinions are ultimately shaped according to the strength and availability of those frames far more than their validity or relationship to evidence.[90]

Overall, this growing body of research has not managed to resolve questions about the effect of deliberation on opinion quality; instead, it has produced mixed results that suggest reasons for both skepticism and optimism. Although it appears clear that citizens can learn factual information in deliberative settings, and that changes in their opinions are related to this learning, opinion change may be primarily an internal process. While deliberation organizers and practitioners may be satisfied with these results, regardless of the phase of the process that produces them, such a finding would fundamentally challenge the heavy emphasis placed on discursive interaction by certain deliberative theorists.

To the extent that opinion change can be shown to be a relational process, there are mixed results concerning its likelihood to result from social pressure versus reason-giving. At best, aggregate opinion change may be a wash between these different processes. Indeed, a long-standing research agenda in social psychology on small group discussion casts doubt on the assumption that deliberation encourages citizens "to approach the discussion with a mind open to change" or that the observed changes actually result from "exchange of relevant and sound reasons" as opposed to "social pressures, unthinking commitments to social identities, or power."[91] This largely experimental research, along with some studies of real-world organizations and juries, suggests that observed opinion change most often results from social processes of conformity and domination.[92]

Some more recent deliberation research also finds that the greatest opinion changes result in groups where the balance shifts toward consensus (with two thirds or more in agreement),[93] suggesting a kind of bandwagon effect. Others find confirmation of group polarization resulting from unbalanced argument pools and social comparison effects.[94] Advocates of deliberation have argued that these findings are precisely why particular features of deliberative processes (such as balanced information, representative participation, and skilled moderation of discussions) are crucial for opinion quality to improve. According to their rubric, some of the "deliberations" being studied (particularly those set up solely for the purpose of research) do not qualify as deliberations at all. Indeed, if the research on opinion quality reveals anything, it is the importance of setting and context (for example, experimental versus real world, formal versus informal, Citizens' Jury versus Deliberative Poll) to the research findings.

These concerns point to the need to pay close attention to the structure and design of the different deliberative civic engagement processes to assess (1) how well they align with the regulative ideals articulated by normative scholars, and (2) what mechanisms of the process are theorized to produce particular outcomes. While some notable research has begun to attend to the "black box" of deliberation itself, yielding both optimistic[95] and pessimistic[96] appraisals of the quality of real-world deliberation, more work is needed to convincingly tie deliberative experiences to changes in opinion quality and to demonstrate that such changes approach the ideals of deliberative theory.

However, this sustained focus on opinion quality, though a major concern for opinion track scholars, is fairly peripheral to the core educative claims advanced by other deliberative theorists. To be sure, in some respects these studies of opinion change are related to the transformations that deliberative theory describes since they examine how individual preferences (most often in the form of policy opinions) change as a result of deliberation. Their focus, however, is on the relationship between factual information, opinions, and the "quality" of opinions in terms of their consistency and durability. This is not the sort of transformation with which deliberative scholars are primarily concerned because it does not analyze the content of these opinions in terms of their relationship to self-regarding or other-regarding interests.[97] These more ambitious transformations of the way citizens conceptualize their interests are at the core of "better citizen" claims advanced by deliberative democratic theory. Furthermore, studies of opinion quality do not examine changes in the attitudes or behaviors of participants that are associated with the capacities required for citizenship.

Research on Deliberation and Civic Capacities

Whereas studies of opinion quality have dominated the empirical literature, other researchers have attended to the attitudes and behaviors that are closer to the core educative claims of deliberative theory. A host of measures of "political capital" have been applied to capture deliberation's impacts on political attitudes.[98] These measures come from a long tradition of political behavior research that has most often conceptualized political attitudes as independent variables to explain political, and especially voting, behavior.[99] They include citizens' attitudes toward themselves and politics (internal political efficacy,[100] interest in politics, political attention, partisan and ideological strength) and toward government (external political efficacy, trust in government), as well as toward other citizens (empathy, political tolerance, social trust, sociotropism/ public-spiritedness). These attitudes are considered important because of their expected effect on political and civic participation, which is another measure of "better citizens" often introduced by empirical scholars. In some cases, researchers have combined many of these discrete measures into one index and found evidence of a causal relationship between participation in deliberation and increased political capital.[101] Others have disaggregated these attitudes and examined deliberation's effects on one or more of the factors separately.

Civic Attitudes toward Oneself, Politics, and Government

With respect to citizens' attitudes toward themselves and politics, there is evidence that deliberative participation increases political interest.[102] Studies also find statistically significant evidence to suggest that deliberation can strengthen the internal political efficacy of participants,[103] and of racial minorities in particular.[104] Others have presumed an effect on internal political efficacy based on observed changes in voting following jury deliberations.[105] Self-reports from other deliberative processes also provide anecdotal evidence of the effect of deliberative participation on internal political efficacy.[106] Several systematic assessments, however, have not found evidence of statistically significant positive relationships between deliberative participation and internal political efficacy.[107] In response to these negative findings and to social psychological theories of self-efficacy,[108] political theorist Michael Morrell developed a more situation-specific measure of efficacy that captures participants' assessments of their *deliberative competence*, and found evidence that face-to-face deliberative decision making can strengthen efficacy understood in this way.[109] Morrell's insight illustrates a limitation in the way educative effects have been conceptualized in much of the empirical literature on deliberation. Though his approach has promise, it is far more the norm to use standard measures developed in the political behavior literature to measure deliberation's educative effects. The few efforts to capture deliberation's discrete effect on attitudes toward government have followed in this vein, and demonstrated statistically significant effects on external political efficacy[110] and political trust[111] that hold up over time.

Attitudes toward Other Citizens

Assessments of deliberation's effects on participants' attitudes toward other citizens have been approached in several different ways,[112] but those focused on the way participants conceptualize their interests are most responsive to classic deliberative theory's claim that deliberation will generate public-spiritedness and attachment to the common good. General measures of what has been called "sociotropism"[113] (i.e., public-spiritedness) are operationalized with the question "when voting, people should always put the interests of the public as a whole before those of themselves and their family," and have been shown to increase as a result of deliberation.[114] But other efforts have focused instead on assessing the change in content of opinions for indications of greater public-spiritedness. Despite the evidence from experimental small group discussion research, which gives reasons to be skeptical that deliberation can "generate empathy and diminish narrow self interest,"[115] quasi-experimental research shows changes in the *content* of opinions that suggest the broadening of interests to encapsulate the fate of others.[116]

Empirical assessments about the content of opinions and one's understanding (or lack of understanding) of the interests that underlie those opinions are difficult. Scholars have generally not theorized about this in depth,[117] but Mansbridge has developed an analytically helpful way to empirically assess the content of interests.[118] In particular, her case study research reminds us that aside from a movement in the direction of common interests, there are several other ways deliberation might be expected to shift participants' understandings of their interests. While her fieldwork demonstrates that shifts toward common interests can occur with positive effect, it also reminds us that such shifts are not always normatively appealing, as classic deliberative theory implies. Mansbridge and her collaborators have shown that stronger attachment to self or sectional group interests can be a necessary and productive outcome of deliberation.[119]

Political and Civic Participation

Empirical research also conceptualizes better citizen claims by looking for evidence of changes in participants' political behavior, and specifically their political participation, as a result of deliberation. Some survey-based research on informal political talk indicates that exposure to different perspectives in informal discursive settings actually has a negative effect on rates of political participation.[120] Studies of this relationship in more organized deliberative settings have found the opposite. For example, researchers have found a direct causal relationship between jury duty and increased electoral participation.[121] Research on Deliberative Polls has found consistent evidence suggesting a modest relationship between deliberation and standard measures of political participation, including working on election campaigns, contacting government officials, donating to a political party, talking about politics, and voting.[122] A national US survey found a similar relationship between citizens who report participation within the last year in an organized face-to-face meeting to discuss a public issue and increased levels of electoral participation (voting and campaign work) and elite contacting (boycotting a product, signing a petition, contacting an official or a media outlet about a political issue).[123] That study also found a positive relationship between deliberation within the last year and forms of civic participation such as community service, community organizing, and problem solving.[124] These research designs control for selection effects through random sampling, control groups, and other statistical techniques designed to disentangle the reciprocal relationships between participation in deliberation and other forms of civic and political participation.[125] The different patterns of results between organized and informal forms of deliberation again suggest the need to attend carefully to the design and structure of the deliberative process under study, as well as the specific mechanisms theorized to produce particular impacts.

Limitations and Promise of Civic Capacities Research

Although the research on civic capacities and political capital conceptualizes "better citizen" claims more faithfully than opinion quality research, and provides some minimal support for the educative claims of deliberative theorists, it is also, in some ways, limited by blind spots in its categorization of these effects.

This is because existing research tends to overlook the more radical implications of the educative claims located at the intersection of participatory and deliberative theory. Deliberative theorists have suggested that participation in these experiences not only teaches people to be "better citizens," but also to be better in a *different* way, that is, to develop their deliberative and participatory capacities specifically, and aside from simply influencing their engagement with electoral politics.[126] This calls for a different way of conceptualizing the kinds of civic and political capacities that deliberation can generate. For example, in his comparative review of cross-national perspectives about the attitudes and behaviors that make a "good citizen," Jon Pammet includes the distinctly deliberative capacity to "try to understand the reasoning of people with other opinions" in his index.[127] But, as this review has shown, standard measures of political capital and behavior rarely capture these kinds of changes.

Attending to the most promising elements of existing research and noting those elements most conspicuously absent from it illuminates several avenues for the future study of deliberation's educative effects. For example, the notion of situation-specific efficacy holds promise and merits further development. Attention to public-spiritedness is directly linked to the transformative claims of deliberative theory, and in its more nuanced formulation, which gives a place to self-interest, it is ripe for further empirical exploration. Likewise, attention to civic participation and community service is a promising proxy for the more radical changes embedded in deliberative theory's educative claims, and though it has rarely been used, it may offer a way to capture "better citizen" effects at the behavioral level. Finally, despite the prominence of relational framing of "better citizen" claims by deliberative theorists, empirical research has focused almost exclusively on individual effects; this review has borne out that claim. Though a handful of studies have looked at the ability of deliberative processes to generate mutual understanding and acceptance of difference,[128] for the most part "better citizen" claims framed at the level of the social relations between citizens have remained the purview of theoretical speculation. This is another avenue in need of further empirical attention, and Chapter 8 in this volume, which uses the concept of community capacity building, offers one potentially promising approach to address these issues.

In sum, the existing literature presents decidedly mixed findings about the educative potential of deliberative civic engagement. The implications of this mixed record, however, are difficult to assess because so much of this research conceptualizes educative effects in ways that are heavily swayed by "opinion track" approaches to deliberation and leave aside the undertheorized and under-scrutinized claims at the core of deliberation's supposed educative potential. Thus far, I have treated as unproblematic the tendency of this literature to group a wide range of discursive processes under the heading of "deliberation" without

distinguishing between different structures and designs and their likely consequences. The conflicting empirical results, however, repeatedly illustrate the
need to make such differences explicit. Doing so will reveal that, in addition to
the limitations of the *what* of existing empirical research about deliberation's educative effects, there are significant problems introduced by the *where* of this
research as well.

Empirical Contexts and Venues

Observers have noted the growing presence of a "public deliberation movement"[129] in recent decades consisting of numerous organizations that routinely
design and implement deliberative venues throughout the United States and in a
number of other advanced democracies, as well as in developing nations (see
Chapter 2). These venues, in combination with long-standing participatory deliberative institutions like juries and the New England Town Meeting, as well as
those established more recently by governments and agencies experimenting
with avenues for broader citizen participation, provide a wide range of possibilities for the study of real-world organized deliberation among citizens.[130] Despite
the methodological challenges associated with this enterprise,[131] it is imperative
that the empirical study of deliberation attend to these real-world contexts, as they
are likely to be fruitful settings in which to assess the educative (and other) claims
of deliberative theory.[132] Although they all share basic features (everyday citizens
engaging in face-to-face discussions about matters of shared concern), they exist
for a number of different purposes and take many different forms, which no doubt
have serious implications for the outcomes they can be expected to produce.

Many surveys of empirical research have noted important differences among
the various ways that deliberation is conceptualized and the range of empirical
contexts where it is studied.[133] While some have addressed this variety by drawing
a hard line between what is and what is not appropriately considered democratic
deliberation,[134] others have attempted to make sense of this variety by mapping a
range of discursive forms in a wider deliberative system,[135] or by developing typologies to distinguish between various deliberative and/or participatory processes.[136] These efforts reveal that those venues receiving the greatest empirical
attention in the literature are not best suited to generate educative effects. On the
other hand, those venues that do present more appropriate settings to explore
educative claims typically have not been studied with these questions in mind.
Moreover, little effort has been given to categorizing these venues in ways that
help identify the mechanisms theorized to produce educative effects.

Most attempts to categorize deliberative civic engagement identify a number
of missions, goals, or purposes that are articulated by organizers and practitioners.[137] The focus is usually on the extent to which deliberative forums have

influence on public policy, and efforts to categorize them often turn heavily on this variable. According to this approach, the many deliberative forums that take place without any direct connections to the policy process are categorized as "educative forums." But a closer look reveals that "educative" is used here to refer primarily to information gains and opinion change instead of a wider set of democratic skills and dispositions.[138] Although some have included the cultivation of "civic habits" within their descriptions of these "educative forums," most researchers continue to conflate these categories with measures of opinion quality.[139] But presenting educative goals in this way—as the low end on a "policy impact" spectrum—is misleading. Not only does such a presentation incorrectly reduce or conflate educative effects with opinion quality but it also produces a typology of deliberative venues based on a variable of little consequence from the perspective of educative claims. This variable is especially problematic because many deliberative organizations have shifted over time to place increasing emphasis on their capacity to influence policy decisions in response to criticism that they are "just talk," making such categorizations open to contestation.[140] In short, sorting deliberative venues according to policy impact, as many typologies in the literature do, overlooks the most relevant criteria for educative claims.

A related but clearer variable from the perspective of educative claims is whether participants are asked to reach a collective decision.[141] The psychological conditions produced by collective decisions, particularly when they are binding on the group members in some meaningful way, are conducive to educative effects on deliberative skills and dispositions.[142] When the stakes are real for participants, and when they must reach a decision through discussion, they are more likely to engage in the process in a way that can foster deliberative skills.[143] Yet much of the empirical research is not focused on venues of deliberative decision making. In fact, much of the research cited so far is based on the study of deliberative venues that seek to explicitly eliminate the process of face-to-face collective decision making to keep measures of "considered public opinion" pure from the social pressures associated with face-to-face dynamics.[144] Although Fishkin has been the most explicit about this intention in his Deliberative Poll design,[145] many other deliberative forums are designed to conclude without a face-to-face collective decision being reached, instead relying on anonymous voting procedures. Forums organized by America*Speaks* (e.g., Americans Discuss Social Security), and those supported by the Kettering Foundation (e.g., National Issues Forum) or the Paul J. Aicher Foundation, formerly the Topsfield Foundation (e.g., Everyday Democracy), are all examples. Other deliberative civic engagement practices, such as the Citizen Juries process pioneered by Ned Crosby, do conclude with a face-to-face collective decision, but the outcomes have not tended to have meaningful consequences for the participants.[146] Despite the absence of this important condition, these venues are among the most frequently discussed in the empirical literature. These processes have important design variations in their own right, and the highly decentralized implementation structure in some cases is bound to produce even more diversity, yet they are alike in that they all lack a group decision that is binding in some meaningful way on the participants.

This may be for good reason. It is certainly not clear that a small group of citizens, no matter how representative they may be of the general population, and no matter how informed or considered their judgments become, should be legitimately authorized to make binding decisions on behalf of their fellow citizens.[147] Furthermore, there is good reason to be wary about the legitimacy of group decisions made in face-to-face settings even when the group members are only representing themselves. Jane Mansbridge most famously observed the tensions between unitary and adversary modes of democracy and the different purposes that face-to-face decision making can serve in these different contexts.[148] She stressed that, in contexts of conflict, face-to-face collective decision making can be a very risky business.

Consistent with the insights of her now classic study, political scientist Tali Mendelberg concludes her empirical literature review by stating:

> More than anything, the point to emerge from existing research is that the conditions of deliberation can matter a great deal to its success. . . . Other times, deliberation is likely to fail. This outcome is especially likely when strong social pressures or identities exist, conflict is deep, and the matter at hand centers on values rather than facts.[149]

But Mendelberg misses that these are the very conditions deliberative theory emerged to address (deep conflicts over values), and in so doing, filters out the conditions central to the participatory theories that generated educative claims in the first place. Focusing on deliberative processes that avoid the occasion for face-to-face collective decision making and are dedicated to different purposes, as much empirical research has done, means that when educative effects are studied, the findings are not well grounded in these original theories, and therefore, are not particularly illuminating tests of such theories.

The methodological challenges of capturing the subtle psychological processes associated with educative claims and isolating them to causal mechanisms connected with deliberative experiences[150] provide good reasons for looking in contexts where the conditions are theoretically most favorable to producing such changes. If such changes are not found in these contexts, where the conditions seem most favorable, then we must remain quite skeptical that they could occur anywhere. Alternately, if such changes are found in such contexts, these settings are best suited to teach us about the causal mechanisms that make them possible. Though some have argued that the "blunt instruments of social science" make it more fruitful to study this question in experimental settings,[151] I argue that the study of real-world contexts is needed, at the very least to complement experimental research, because of the difficulties of simulating collective decision-making experiences that have meaningful consequences for participants through experimental design.[152]

Fortunately, there are many deliberative venues where face-to-face collective decision making is central to the process design, and these have been the object of some empirical study. Some research focuses on well-established participatory deliberative institutions like juries[153] and the New England Town Hall Meeting.[154] A more recent body of research focuses on instances of "empowered participatory governance,"[155] such as participatory budgeting in Porto Alegre, Brazil,[156] and community policing in Chicago, Illinois, in the United States.[157] Citizens Assemblies in British Columbia and Ontario, Canada, which have been temporarily convened and given the power to determine referendum options concerning electoral reform, have also garnered significant attention.[158]

Research of these venues, however, has rarely focused systematically on the question of educative effects. Furthermore, little attention has been given to categorizing deliberative venues in ways that help identify the conditions expected to produce educative effects. Although face-to-face and binding collective decision making are important conditions, these indicators are too simplistic for effectively categorizing the wide range of processes found in current practice. With the exception of the efforts of Archon Fung,[159] I am aware of no attempts to develop typologies that are, at least in part, intended to clarify the educative potential of different deliberative venues.[160] Such an effort is necessary to advance our empirical understanding of this underscrutinized, but frequently touted, normative justification for deliberative civic engagement processes.

In sum, the mixed findings concerning deliberation's educative effects can be largely explained by the wide variety of contexts and venues being studied and compared. Real-world deliberative venues ought to take a central focus in the growing empirical research agenda. This is particularly important for the study of deliberation's educative effects because the conditions that are expected to generate high educative potential are not easy to simulate through experimental design. Real-world deliberative venues, however, exist in numerous forms, many of which are not ideal for the exploration of educative effects because they also lack real stakes for participants. Moreover, to the extent that the existing empirical literature focuses on real-world venues, it most often does so in contexts that are not best suited to generating educative effects. Given the methodological challenges of isolating deliberation's educative effects, which have been noted throughout this review and elsewhere,[161] future research should focus on contexts that are considered to have high educative potential. To do so requires a mapping of the deliberative field with close attention to the features of process design that are theoretically most conducive to generating these effects.[162]

Conclusion

For centuries, democratic theorists have claimed that participation is a developmental experience with the potential to cultivate desirable skills and dispositions among citizens. In the contemporary period, these "better citizen" claims have been most frequently advanced by advocates of participatory and deliberative democracy and have formed a reoccurring justification for why reform of existing democratic institutions ought to incorporate more deliberative participation from citizens.[163] Though the assumption of deliberation's educative potential is widely shared, it is theoretically and empirically underscrutinized. This is particularly problematic given the "heavy lifting," undercover as it may sometimes be, that such assumptions perform in the normative justifications offered for deliberation by theorists and practitioners.

Though a growing empirical literature aims to investigate deliberative theory, its attention to "better citizen" claims is hampered by several limitations. First, the conceptualization of educative effects has been heavily influenced by an opinion quality approach that fails to investigate the deeper set of transformative assumptions embedded in deliberative theory. Second, the enormous variety of deliberative venues and empirical contexts in which the question has been examined, without careful attention to variations in their process design and structure, make generalizations about deliberation's educative potential difficult. As a result, though evidence exists to support the contention that deliberation can improve opinion quality and strengthen civic capacities, these effects are not well connected to the normative theories from which better citizen claims originate. Therefore, skeptics remain unconvinced by better citizen claims and advocates have little ground upon which to account for where, when, why, and how such potential can be realized.

Researchers can begin to address these limitations in two ways. First, researchers must develop a set of analytical categories for describing and parsing the core educative claims made about participatory deliberative processes. These categories must be linked directly to the concerns of normative theorists who make better citizens claims.[164] Second, to locate the most appropriate real-world contexts for empirically testing such claims, researchers must develop a map of the deliberative field that pays attention to the differences among deliberative processes and the importance of those differences for educative claims.[165] Studies that follow these two steps will help bridge the normative-empirical divide that currently exists within the field of deliberative civic engagement research and transform optimistic assumptions into empirically grounded insights about the educative potential of deliberative civic engagement.

Notes

1. This is a misnomer for several reasons. Though it conjures images of the enigmatic New England town hall meeting (Mansbridge 1983; Bryan 2004), it was not intended, like those forums, to bring together the residents of a small town to deliberate and *decide* about matters of direct local concern. Instead, these were forums for voters to tell their elected representatives about their preferences and, perhaps more important, their fears about a matter of national policy. While the term is misleading in these ways, its use is likely a result of its ability to capture a popular conception of meaningful democratic participation, which has long been romanticized and idealized.
2. For examples, see Fishkin (2009a) and Susskind (2009).
3. See Warren (1996) for a theoretical elaboration of this described in terms of "social groundlessness of political space."
4. The term *deliberative turn* is used most often by political theorists to refer to the articulation of a theory of deliberative democracy that marked a challenge to and shift away from aggregative or minimalist conceptualizations of democracy (e.g., Dryzek 2000; Chambers 2003). There have also arguably been both practical and empirical deliberative turns, which have followed in part in response to these theoretical developments.
5. Mark Warren (2009) calls these piecemeal reforms "retrofitting" and notes that these initiatives themselves suffer from democratic deficits.
6. Hayden ([1962] 2005); Kaufman (1960, 1969); Pateman (1970).
7. For a review of the history of such claims, see Mansbridge (1999b).
8. Hayden ([1962] 2005).
9. Mutz (2006).
10. Kaufman (1960); Arnstein (1969).
11. Barber (1984: 281). By aggregative approaches to democracy, I refer to collective decision-making mechanisms that involve the collection and counting of individual fixed preferences (i.e., voting). Theories of deliberative democracy object to aggregative assumptions and emphasize that individual preferences are in fact constituted through deliberative processes.
12. Mansbridge (1983); Bryan (2004).
13. Chambers (2003); Dryzek (2000).
14. Habermas (1987, 1990); Cohen ([1989] 1997a, [1996] 1997b); Rawls (1993); Gutmann and Thompson (1996).
15. Bessette (1997); see also Steiner, Bächtiger, Spörndli, and Steenbergen (2004).
16. Gutmann and Thompson (1996); Fishkin (1995); Fung and Wright (2003).
17. Cohen and Fung (2004).
18. Fishkin (2009c: 78) agrees that "the educative function is most compelling for the face-to-face variants" of participatory democracy. See also Burkhalter, Gastil, and Kelhaw (2002).
19. For an exception, see Warren (1992).
20. Elster ([1986] 1997); Cohen ([1989] 1997a).
21. Such justifications for deliberative democracy are often called "epistemic." See Estlund (2008).
22. Cohen ([1989] 1997a, [1996] 1997b); Elster ([1986] 1997); Gutmann and Thompson (1996); Bohman (1998); Estlund (1997).
23. Manin, Stein, and Mansbridge (1987: 354, 363).
24. Cohen ([1989] 1997a: 76).
25. Elster ([1986] 1997:12).

26. Cohen ([1989] 1997a: 79); see also Gutmann and Thompson (2004: 11).
27. Warren (1992: 11–12); see also Warren (1996).
28. Cohen ([1989] 1997a: 69), citing Rawls (1971: 473–474).
29. Rawls (1971: 234).
30. Gutmann and Thompson (1996: 9).
31. Gutmann and Thompson (1996: 81–85).
32. Gutmann and Thompson (1996: 359).
33. Gutmann and Thompson (1996: 359).
34. Shapiro (1999); Przeworski (1998, 1999); Sunstein (2003); Knight and Johnson (1997); Sanders (1997); Fish (1999); Young (1999, 2001).
35. Sanders (1997).
36. Bohman (1998); Mansbridge, Bohman, Chambers, Estlund, Follesdal, Fung, Lafont, Manin, and Marti (2010); Bächtiger, Niemeyer, Neblo, Steenbergen, and Steiner (2010).
37. Dryzek (2000); Mansbridge (2003); Thompson (2008); Polletta (2008).
38. Bohman (1998).
39. Mansbridge, Bohman, Chambers, Estlund, Follesdal, Fung, Lafont, Manin, and Marti (2010).
40. Mansbridge, Bohman, Chambers, Estlund, Follesdal, Fung, Lafont, Manin, and Marti (2010: 78).
41. Mansbridge, Bohman, Chambers, Estlund, Follesdal, Fung, Lafont, Manin, and Marti (2010: 79). Much of the empirical work on deliberation's effects has emerged from the public opinion tradition and has therefore focused on testing more surface level opinion change instead of focusing on the transformative processes emphasized by normative theorists.
42. Benhabib (2004, 2006, 2007, 2008).
43. Benhabib (2004: 179).
44. For a compelling critique of Benhabib's reading of Derrida, see Thomassen (2010). Thomassen is skeptical of Benhabib's attempt to limit the effects of iterability. He argues instead that the positive potential of iterations can only be embraced in combination with their risks. See also Honig in Benhabib (2006).
45. According to Benhabib (2004: 57), this learning is mutual. Majorities learn to adjust their interpretation of universals to admit previously overlooked particulars, and minorities learn to adjust their particular claims in ways that attach to universals.
46. Mansbridge, Bohman, Chambers, Estlund, Follesdal, Fung, Lafont, Manin, and Marti (2010).
47. Benhabib (2004, 2006, 2007, 2008).
48. Mouffe (2000).
49. Dryzek (2000, 2005) uses the term *discursive democracy* to distinguish his theory from earlier articulations of deliberative democracy. According to this ideal, the public sphere can be more open to contestation because it is semi-detached from state institutions. In this way it can influence governmental actors without needing to succumb to the same decision-making pressures that apply to deliberation tied to sovereign authority.
50. Dryzek (2005: 225).
51. Dryzek (2005: 235).
52. Dryzek (2005: 225).
53. Dryzek (2005: 221). Note that while recent deliberative theorists assert the centrality and importance of contestation in an effort to address the agonist critique, they continue to see conflict as an outcome that serves the eventual realization of more inclusive identities. This is still in tension with agonism's conception of politics as always dependent on we/they distinctions. See Mouffe (2005: 24–25).
54. Thompson (2008); Mutz (2008); Rosenberg (2007a); Neblo (2005, 2007); Bächtiger, Niemeyer, Neblo, Steenbergen, and Steiner (2010); Neblo, Esterling, Kennedy, Lazer, and Sokhey (2010).

55. Thompson (2008: 502–503).
56. Fung and Wright (2003: 32). Despite this, however, the empirical case studies in their volume do not address educative questions.
57. Rosenberg (2007b: 14–15).
58. Cohen (2007: 229).
59. Mendelberg (2002: 153); the final two goals are improved political decision making and greater legitimacy for the constitutional order.
60. Goodin and Dryzek (2006).
61. http://www.deliberative-democracy.net/index.php?option=com_content&view=article&id=77&;Itemid=271, accessed January 21, 2010.
62. For a good overview of existing empirical research, see Abelson and Gauvin (2006).
63. Rosenberg (2007b); see part d of the list.
64. Rosenberg (2007b); see parts b and c of the list.
65. Gutmann and Thompson (1996).
66. Cohen ([1996] 1997b); Rosenberg (2007a).
67. Fishkin (2009c: 7).
68. Jacobs, Cook, and Delli Carpini (2009: 5).
69. Downs (1957); Delli Carpini and Keeter (1996).
70. Converse (1964); see also Bishop (2005).
71. Schumpeter (1942).
72. Mutz (2006).
73. Jacobs and Shapiro (2000).
74. Luskin, Fishkin, and Jowell (2002); Barabas (2004); Rose (2009).
75. Fishkin (2009c: 139); Hansen (2004: 135).
76. Luskin, Fishkin, Jowell, and Park (1999); Fishkin (2009c: 135–139).
77. Goodin and Neimeyer (2003).
78. Farrar, Fishkin, Green, List, Luskin, and Paluck (2010).
79. Fishkin (2009c: 120).
80. Barabas (2004).
81. Converse (1964).
82. Lindeman (2002).
83. Luskin, Fishkin, and Jowell (2002); Fishkin and Luskin (2005); Neblo (2010).
84. Sturgis, Roberts, and Allum (2005).
85. Jackman and Sniderman (2006). For an opposed perspective suggesting that opinion quality can be gauged by a *weakening* of the relationship between ideology and post-deliberative opinions, see Neblo (2010) and endnote 117 in this chapter.
86. Riker (1982).
87. Fishkin and Luskin (2005); List, Luskin, Fishkin, and McClean (2007).
88. Neblo (2010).
89. Druckman and Nelson (2003).
90. Chong and Druckman (2007: 652).
91. Mendelberg (2002: 181).
92. Sunstein (2003, 2009); Sanders (1997).
93. Barabas (2004).
94. Schkade, Sunstein, and Hastie (2006).
95. Siu (2009); see also Chapter 4 in this volume.
96. Rosenberg (2007b).
97. Mansbridge, Bohman, Chambers, Estlund, Follesdal, Fung, Lafont, Manin, and Marti (2010).
98. Jacobs, Cook, and Delli Carpini (2009). Though Jacobs and colleagues present the concept of "discursive capital" in their early chapters, they do not return to it in their empirical chapters. This is unfortunate because one key limitation of this literature is its failure to identify educative effects that are particular to *deliberative* participation. The concept of "discursive

capital" has promise to be just that kind of measure, but Jacobs and colleagues do not develop it further.

99. Campbell, Gurin, and Miller (1954); Campbell, Converse, and Miller (1960).

100. Internal political efficacy is a measure of citizens' beliefs about their own political competence, while external political efficacy is a measure of citizens' beliefs about government responsiveness to their participation. For discussion, see Balch (1974), Craig, Niemi, and Silver (1990), Niemi, Craig, and Mattei (1991), and Morrell (2003, 2005).

101. Jacobs, Cook, and Delli Carpini (2009: 101). Although this recent study represents a giant step forward for the systematic empirical study of deliberation, it illustrates several limitations of existing empirical research aiming to address the question of educative effects. First, the authors aggregate different categories of educative effects in ways that conceal the particular causal mechanisms associated with each. Second, they conceptualize and measure deliberation in an aggregated way. This overlooks important differences in the design features of these processes and their relevance to explaining educative effects.

102. Fishkin and Luskin (2002).

103. Fishkin (2009c: 141); Fishkin and Luskin (2002).

104. Nabatchi and Stanisevski (2008).

105. Gastil, Deess, Weiser, and Simmons (2010).

106. Gastil and Dillard (1999a); Doble, Higgins, Bagesse, and Fisher (1996); Smith (1999).

107. Gastil (2004); Morrell (2005); Nabatchi (2007, 2010b).

108. Bandura (1997).

109. Morrell (2005).

110. Nabatchi (2007, 2010b).

111. Fishkin and Luskin (2002).

112. Some have used measures of social trust and political tolerance, but do so in larger indices that conceal the direct effects on these attitudes specifically (e.g., Jacobs, Cook, and Delli Carpini 2009). Others have focused on political empathy, a capacity theorists argue is crucial to democratic practice (e.g., Morrell 2007, 2010). Some empirical research has suggested that empathy is a valuable deliberative capacity that should take the focus of democratic education (e.g., Mutz 2002a; Morrell 2010); however, some tests exploring deliberation's capacity to produce empathy have come up insignificant (e.g., Fishkin and Luskin 2002).

113. Kinder and Kiewet (1981).

114. Fishkin and Luskin (2002).

115. Mendelberg (2002: 181).

116. Fishkin (2009c: 142).

117. See Neblo (2010) for an exceptional effort in this regard. He argues that reduced influence of age, gender, race, political knowledge, negative affect/prejudice, and ideology on post-deliberative opinions demonstrate, in various ways, that deliberation has broadened participants' conceptions of their interests. While he finds moderate support for his hypotheses, his way of operationalizing the transformative claims of deliberative theorists is questionable. In particular, he makes the rather curious assumption that the reduced relevance of ideology on post-deliberative opinions is evidence of a frame shift from private to public interests.

118. Mansbridge (1983: 24–28).

119. Mansbridge (1983); Karpowitz and Mansbridge (2005b).

120. Mutz (2006).

121. Gastil, Deess, Weiser, and Simmons (2010).

122. Fishkin (2009c: 143).

123. Jacobs, Cook, and Delli Carpini (2009: 104–107).

124. Jacobs, Cook, and Delli Carpini (2009: 108–109).

125. For more discussion about who participates in deliberation and why, see Chapter 3 in this volume.

126. For empirical evidence regarding the important differences between traditional forms of political participation and deliberative forms of political participation, see recent work by Neblo, Esterling, Kennedy, Lazer, and Sokhey (2010).
127. Pammett (2009).
128. Walsh (2007).
129. Jacobs, Cook, and Delli Carpini (2009: 136); Gastil and Keith (2005). For a more critical perspective, see Lee (2008).
130. In this chapter, I do not include studies of informal talk (e.g., Mutz 2006; Jacobs, Cook, and Delli Carpini 2009; Walsh 2003) or elite deliberation (e.g., Steiner, Bächtiger, Spörndli, and Steenbergen 2004; Bessette 1997). I exclude cases of informal talk, disagreement concerning their inclusion in the study of deliberation notwithstanding (see Habermas [1962] 1989; Mansbridge 1999a; Thompson 2008; Mutz 2008), because such settings are not the most appropriate for exploring the specific claims about deliberation's educative effects. Given their ambitiousness, it is in contexts of more formalized deliberation, where structures are in place to support educative aims, that such claims can even begin to approach plausibility. I exclude cases of elite deliberation, because they shed little light on deliberation's educative effects for lay citizens.
131. Such challenges motivate some researchers to study deliberation in experimental settings. Some of this work is guilty of what Bächtiger and his colleagues call "concept stretching" (2010). For example, experiments where participants engage in no conversation at all (McCubbins and Rodriguez 2006), or "converse" only with a survey administrator (Jackman and Sniderman 2006) are misrepresented as tests of deliberation's impacts. Morrell (2005) and Neblo (2007) exemplify experimental designs that simulate "real-world" deliberation far more successfully, though they are still limited in their capacity to create "real stakes" for participants, a feature I argue is essential to deliberation's educative potential.
132. Levine, Fung, and Gastil (2005).
133. Bächtiger, Niemeyer, Neblo, Steenbergen, and Steiner (2010); Neblo (2007).
134. Cohen (2007); Thompson (2008).
135. Mansbridge (1999a); Hendriks (2006).
136. Fung (2006, 2007); Morrell (2005).
137. Fung (2007); Ryfe (2002); Button and Mattson (1999); Gastil (2000).
138. Fung (2007); Button and Mattson (1999).
139. Gastil (2000); Ryfe (2002).
140. Polletta (2008).
141. Morrell (2005).
142. Much argument has ensued over the definition of democratic deliberation and whether it requires an instance of collective decision making, can be merely "decision oriented," or can be any form of discussion about shared concerns. Chambers (2009) has made the important insight that although the presence of a binding decision is not a definitional constraint, it alters the psychological conditions of the deliberative experience and is therefore relevant to the outcomes that might be expected to follow.
143. Fung (2007: 169).
144. Fishkin (1995: 185; 2009c: 88, 133).
145. Fishkin (2009c: 25) refers to Deliberative Polling as a "quasi-experiment," which he argues gets at the best of both worlds by maximizing the capacity to control various conditions while also observing deliberation in the "real world." His aim, guided by the opinion track, is to design a counterfactual of what considered public opinion would look like in a way that can be generalized. As a result, the design is not well suited to the study of deliberation's educative effects because, oriented to different purposes, it lacks binding and face-to-face collective decision making.
146. Crosby and Nethercut (2005: 115).
147. Fung (2007: 165).
148. Mansbridge (1983).

149. Mendelberg (2002: 181).

150. Mansbridge (1999b).

151. Mansbridge (1999b: 291).

152. For an exceptional effort to overcome this limitation of experimental design while harnessing its benefits, see Morrell (2005).

153. Gastil (2008).

154. Mansbridge (1983); Bryan (2004).

155. Fung and Wright (2003).

156. Baiocchi (2001).

157. Fung (2004).

158. Warren and Pearse (2008); Rose (2009).

159. Fung (2007). For a discussion of the relationship between participatory design choices and the surfacing of public values in policy conflicts, see Nabatchi (2012b).

160. For another quite sophisticated effort to typologize public engagement mechanisms, see Rowe and Frewer (2005). They define effectiveness narrowly in terms of "information flow" and as a result, their typology sheds little direct light on the mechanisms most likely to produce educative effects that go beyond the exchange and processing of information.

161. Mansbridge (1999b).

162. For one such effort, see Fung (2007); see also endnote 164 for my own approach.

163. For an example, see Nabatchi 2010a.

164. In my own work, I argue that educative claims are best parsed into three categories: efficacy, interests, and relationships. I aim to show that claims about deliberation's potential to (1) strengthen citizens' subjective and objective sense of their deliberative competence (self-efficacy and skills), (2) help citizens develop enlightened preferences that incorporate their own interests and the interests of others (interest clarification), and (3) develop civic bonds between citizens (relationship building) encapsulate the range of "better citizen" claims advanced by participatory and deliberative theorists. I suggest that future research use these categories as a starting point for the empirical investigation of better citizen effects (see Pincock 2011).

165. Elsewhere I have presented three relevant dimensions upon which deliberative venues can be placed: (1) collective decision making, (2) issue scope, and (3) participative intensity. I argue that these dimensions highlight the conditions most suited to generating educative effects. Using these dimensions, I also identify empirical contexts ripe for study (see Pincock 2011).

8

Deliberation's Contribution to Community Capacity Building

BO KINNEY

> Like individuals, communities, too, have been transformed by deliberation. Citizens in communities that are accustomed to interactive public talk will not tolerate panel discussions and speeches. They insist instead on engaging one another. Indirectly, these citizens also are engaging in another, very innovative exercise. They are inventing a "civic super-highway," knitting together and linking all the civic organizations in their communities and providing a channel for information exchange and priority setting for common and cooperative work—what political economists call "social capital," and what the National Civic League calls "civic infrastructure."
>
> —David Mathews[1]

The claim that community is in decline raises few eyebrows. This argument was popularized by political scientist Robert Putnam, who cited decreasing political participation, civic engagement, organizational membership, and volunteerism as evidence of an overall decline in social capital—that is, "features of social organization such as networks, norms, and social trust that facilitate coordination and cooperation for mutual benefit."[2] The consequences of this decline are potentially dire, undermining democracy itself. As Christopher Lasch wrote, "Self-governing communities, not individuals, are the basic units of democratic society. . . . It is the decline of those communities, more than anything else, that calls the future of democracy into question."[3] Moreover, the modern democratic state has diluted participation to such an extent that citizens have become political consumers, rather than producers.[4] Compelling data and theory led the American Political Science Association's Standing Committee on Civic Education and Engagement to begin its 2005 report, *Democracy at Risk*, with the observation that "almost all agree that the fabric of our civic life has frayed significantly."[5]

Putnam's warning about the decline of social capital inspired a wave of research on the connection between community, public life, and economic vitality. One particularly ambitious study, the "Soul of the Community" research supported by the Knight Foundation and carried out by Gallup, claims to have found a statistically significant correlation between "community attachment" (defined as citizens' feelings toward the place where they live) and economic growth.[6] Numerous organizations and associations since have embraced this economic rationale for the importance of community, with the National League of Cities' *Governing Economies in the 21st Century* being but one example.[7]

The decline of community is of particular concern for practitioners of deliberative civic engagement for at least two reasons. First, healthy communities have a strong relationship with healthy democracies. This is perhaps best represented by John Dewey's belief that "democracy must begin at home, and its home is the neighborly community."[8] Second, deliberation is often invoked as a solution to the community crisis. For example, Kettering Foundation president David Mathews, in the quote that opens this chapter, credits deliberation with transforming communities and creating a "civic superhighway."[9] Likewise, King County, Washington, promotes its Countywide Community Forums as a "key to a sustainable community" that will build "social capital through both bonding and bridging dialogue and improving community mental health and happiness."[10]

In this chapter, I take a closer look at deliberation's relationship to community. Specifically, I address the question, *How does deliberative civic engagement contribute to community capacity building?*

To avoid the slipperiness of concepts like "community building" and "community capacity," I employ a framework developed in the field of social work that breaks the notion of community capacity into several more manageable (and observable) elements. Using this framework to understand community capacity and to examine deliberation results in two (perhaps unsurprising) findings: Deliberative civic engagement can build community capacity; however, there is a lack of systematic research on how this happens, and particularly on whether the effects are lasting. By describing some of the ways in which deliberative civic engagement can successfully build community capacity, I hope to refine our evaluation of deliberative practices so that we might better understand how to build sustainable deliberative communities.

A Framework for Community Capacity

To answer the question of whether deliberation can contribute to community capacity building, we first need to define and understand the concepts of community and community capacity building. Many definitions have been attempted, but I use as my starting point a framework outlined by a collaborative research team headed by Robert J. Chaskin, the deputy dean for Strategic Initiatives at the School of Social Service Administration at the University of Chicago.[11] This framework is helpful for several reasons: It is based on empirical evidence, attempts to synthesize existing research on community building, and breaks the concept of capacity building into discrete chunks that can be used to analyze community-building efforts. Additionally, it provides a foundation for a systematic understanding of the relationship of deliberative civic engagement to community capacity building.

The Community Capacity-Building Framework

The Community Capacity Building (CCB) framework uses a definition of community grounded both in common usage and in the community-building field: "A geographic area within which there is a set of shared interests or symbolic attributes."[12] Based on this definition, the CCB framework defines community capacity as

> the interaction of human capital, organizational resources, and social capital existing within a given community that can be leveraged to solve collective problems and improve or maintain the well-being of that community. It may operate through informal social processes and/or organized efforts by individuals, organizations, and social networks that exist among them and between them and the larger systems of which the community is a part.[13]

The framework identifies four component characteristics of community capacity, as well as four specific strategies for building community capacity. These are discussed in the following sections.

Characteristics of Community Capacity

The CCB framework identifies four key characteristics of community capacity: (1) a sense of community, (2) commitment to community among its members, (3) the ability to solve problems, and (4) access to resources (see Table 8.1).[14] Although these characteristics occur along a continuum and can exist in different degrees in different communities, "threshold levels of some are probably necessary if the community is to accomplish particular objectives."[15] For practitioners of deliberative democracy, breaking down the abstract concept of community capacity into more discrete components facilitates the evaluation

Table 8.1 **Characteristics of Community Capacity**

Characteristic	Definition
Sense of Community	The "degree of connectedness among members and a recognition of mutuality of circumstance."
Commitment	"The responsibility that particular individuals, groups, or organizations take for what happens in the community." This includes two aspects: (1) "that community members see themselves as stakeholders in the collective well-being of the neighborhood," and (2) "the willingness of these members to participate actively as stakeholders."
Ability to Solve Problems	The ability "to translate commitment into action."
Access to Resources	The "ability to make instrumental links with systems in the larger context (the city and region) and to access and leverage various types of resources located both inside and outside the neighborhood."

Source: Chaskin, Brown, Venkatesh, and Vidal (2001: 14–19).

of deliberative civic engagement initiatives in terms of community capacity building. Rather than asking simply, "Did this initiative build community capacity?" one can use the framework to ask more precise questions, such as, "Did this initiative strengthen participants' sense of community?" The second half of this chapter shows examples of how deliberation can build these elements of community capacity.

Strategies for Building Community Capacity

The CCB framework also identifies four specific strategies for building community capacity: (1) leadership development, (2) organizational development, (3) community organizing, and (4) organizational collaboration (see Table 8.2). While these strategies are not guaranteed to be successful, they "constitute the different ways in which communities can work intentionally to increase their ability to maintain and improve the well-being of their members, respond to changing circumstances, and achieve collective goals."[16] As with the

Table 8.2 **Strategies for Building Community Capacity**

Strategy	Definition
Leadership	The "skills, commitment, engagement, and effectiveness of individuals in the community-building process."
Organizational Development	The "creation of new organizations or the strengthening of existing ones so they can do their work better or take on new roles."
Community Organizing	"The associational aspects of community functioning and the mobilization of individual stakeholders for particular collective ends."
Organizational Collaboration	Building "the organizational infrastructure of communities through the development of relationships and collaborative partnerships on the organizational level."

Source: Chaskin, Brown, Venkatesh, and Vidal (2001: 25–26).

component characteristics of community capacity, the framework's identification of these specific strategies makes it easier to evaluate deliberative civic engagement initiatives in terms of their capacity-building potential and effectiveness.

The CCB framework is not beyond criticism. Despite the authors' claim that it is "comprehensive . . . dynamic and multidimensional,"[17] it is based primarily on qualitative interviews with practitioners and a small number of in-depth case studies, and it does not attempt to be representative of all possibilities.[18] It is, however, relatively consistent with other definitions of the term, and is useful for understanding, if not measuring or evaluating, the component parts of community capacity.[19] As a descriptive framework, it still does not address some critical issues: It does not speak to the transferability of community capacity from one issue to another,[20] the longevity of community capacity once a particular observed event is over,[21] and the appropriateness of community capacity building for the issue or problem at hand.[22] Tackling these problems is beyond the scope of this chapter, but deliberative practitioners interested in making use of community capacity-building techniques would do well to consider them. Despite this criticism, the CCB framework is quite useful as a starting point for evaluating the contribution of deliberative civic engagement to community capacity.

Assessing the Impact of Deliberative Civic Engagement on Community Capacity

Deliberative initiatives have rarely been systematically evaluated in terms of community capacity. (For more on evaluating deliberation, see Chapter 10.) Perhaps one reason for this is reluctance on the part of some deliberative organizers to participate in systematic evaluations, sometimes owing to a belief in the intrinsic benefits of deliberation regardless of instrumental outcomes. For example, when Paul Aicher, founder of the Topsfield Foundation, was asked in an interview how he measured deliberation's success, he replied, "I'm not quite comfortable with the premise of your question. You seem to be asking, 'Is it worth it?' Of course it is."[23] The true-believer attitude of many deliberative theorists has led some critics to comment that when negative effects of deliberation are discovered, they are often simply ignored.[24] (For more on critics' views of deliberation, see Chapter 11.)

Some deliberative practitioners are also skeptical of the validity of empirical research on processes as complex as deliberation.[25] The Jefferson Center, which promotes the Citizens' Jury deliberative process, notes on its Web site that whereas the Center's original mission focused on research, "the Center over the years did little research and concentrated mainly on developing the quality of the Citizens' Jury process and on getting it used in significant ways."[26] Likewise, a Topsfield Foundation report found that numerous community benefits resulted from the deliberative Study Circles they sponsored, but the direct connection between the events and community changes remained unclear and ungeneralizable.[27]

Even when practitioners see the value of systematic evaluation, they may view it as a luxury they cannot afford. Most projects are organized on a temporary, ad hoc basis, often under intense time pressures; the average budget of a deliberative initiative, according to a 2010 survey, is $6,000, and the median budget is zero.[28]

Finally, research on deliberative civic engagement and community capacity building, in particular, has been neglected because community capacity building is not always the primary goal of deliberation, but is viewed more commonly as a felicitous by-product.[29] When this is the case, systematic evaluation of community capacity building may not take place because it is not recognized as an important outcome until after the fact.

That said, there is a great deal of qualitative and anecdotal evidence to support the claim that deliberative civic engagement can contribute to community capacity building. Indeed, many of the reported outcomes of deliberation fit nicely into the CCB framework. Thus, I organize the following sections around the CCB framework's four characteristics of community capacity (sense of community,

commitment, ability to solve problems, and access to resources) and four strategies for building community capacity (leadership, organizational development,
community organizing, and organizational collaboration).

Sense of Community

Strengthening a sense of community among participants is a frequent goal of deliberative civic engagement. An implicit assumption by deliberative theorists is
that "people in conflict will set aside their adversarial, win-lose approach and
understand that their fate is linked with the fate of the other, that although their
social identities conflict they 'are tied to each other in a common recognition of
their interdependence.'"[30] Several reports of deliberative initiatives support this
assumption. For example, an evaluation of the National Issues Convention (the
first deliberative poll in the United States) found strong qualitative evidence that
strangers bonded and formed close ties.[31] Though these participants were from all
parts of the country, it seems reasonable that deliberative events could have similar effects on strangers within smaller communities. Likewise, a study of a group
of citizens who deliberated about community problems in Chattanooga, Tennes-
see, and devised and implemented solutions to the problems found that "deliberation both developed coherent collective interests and built strong bonds among
the citizens who pursued those interests together."[32] Similarly, a study about informal political talk found that such conversation strengthened both community
and social ties and reinforced group-based social boundaries.[33] Yet another study
of deliberative Study Circle programs found that participants reported forming
new, sometimes ongoing, relationships with other participants.[34]

Commitment

A second common goal of deliberative initiatives is to heighten participants'
feelings of commitment or responsibility toward their community. Public Agenda's case study about a tradition of deliberative civic engagement in Bridgeport,
Connecticut, reports that such participation can develop an "ethos of collective
responsibility" within a community, and that participants in deliberative processes increase their "willingness to take responsibility themselves."[35] One of the
ways in which these processes keep participants engaged is through their attention to concrete policy problems and changes.[36] For example, in a community-
initiated, deliberative strategic planning process for Bridgeport public schools,
eighty-four parents, community members, and educators crafted a mission
statement for the school system, developed core strategies, and wrote action
plans for each strategy; these activities positioned the community "as a partner
in education, rather than as a client or consumer."[37] The Bridgeport case does,
however, highlight the question of whether the effects of deliberation are limited

to a particular issue and time frame: A 2010 assessment of governance and collaboration in the city found little evidence to suggest heightened levels of commitment on issues other than education.[38]

The involvement of citizens in San Francisco's Long-Range Countywide Transportation Plan also appears to have helped develop a partnership between community members and policy makers, according to a Kettering Foundation study of deliberative exchanges between citizens and policy makers.[39] Citizens were invited to participate in a series of community workshops and meetings to identify important transit problems faced by residents of different San Francisco neighborhoods. While the workshops did not necessarily lead to successful implementation of solutions to the problems identified by participants, they may have increased a sense of community responsibility for solving problems. A Planning Department employee who helped coordinate the deliberations suggested that the success of the workshops "depended on how much of a true partnership the community group leaders wanted to forge."[40]

Participants in Study Circle programs report a number of examples of increased attachment to and investment in their communities. For example, researchers found that study circles contributed to increases in volunteering in Decatur, Georgia, and a successful school funding bond measure in Inglewood, California. Two participants in study circles ran for school board seats in North Little Rock, Arkansas, "after becoming more aware about what goes on in the schools and understanding the schools at a deeper level."[41]

Deliberation can also strengthen commitment to participate by helping to establish traditions of civic participation. At a conceptual level, deliberation is "self-reinforcing" for individuals and "participating in face-to-face public deliberation strengthens the cognitions, attitudes, and habits conducive to future deliberation."[42] Consequently, participants are led to see deliberation as typical and appropriate.[43] On a larger scale, deliberation can contribute to forming "collective habits."[44] For example, National Issues Forums have been found to stimulate the realization within a community that "it is possible to convene groups consisting of people who do not share the same views—and who come from very different circumstances—and create a civil atmosphere for talking about common concerns, even highly charged issues."[45] Similarly, the Gulf Coast Legislative Town Meetings "had such an impact on citizens (and, indirectly, legislators) that they have come to view it as a necessary part of the political process."[46]

A study of five American cities that had successfully maintained long-term commitments to participatory democracy found that

> through ongoing face-to-face collaboration [citizens] are unified as well as empowered. And the more accustomed they become to acting this way, the more impact they tend to have on the handling of civic affairs.

Public officials become accustomed to citizen involvement in public life, the result being that government becomes more responsive on an ongoing basis to community concerns. Power ends up being redistributed, and the more the effects of this are felt, the more motivation ordinary citizens have to believe in the responsiveness of government.[47]

In a widely cited Kennedy School of Government study, Elena Fagotto and Archon Fung observe that "embedded" deliberation—in which organizers attempt to instill deliberative practices into local organizations rather than holding isolated events—can lead to a greater degree of public action. However, they caution that "public deliberation rarely mobilized participants to *collective* action."[48] Rather, it tends to "facilitate action by enabling coordination, providing community input, involving decision-makers and exploiting synergies with other programs."[49] In their view, an investment of time and resources is required, in addition to the development of skills.

Numerous authors have suggested that deliberation can build commitment to participate by increasing the perceived legitimacy of policies (see Chapter 9). For example, several deliberative theorists suggest that

> faith in the democratic process will be enhanced as people who deliberate become empowered and feel that their government truly is "of the people" [and that] . . . [t]he legitimacy of the constitutional order will grow because people have a say in and an understanding of that order.[50]

In Fung's theoretical framework of varying modes of governance, there are two ways in which deliberative initiatives such as Deliberative Polls and Study Circles aim to bolster the legitimacy of public action: improving representativeness of participants and making discussions among participants more informed and reflective.[51] Empirical studies support these ideas. For example, one experimental study found that deliberation increased "perceptions of fairness" in decision making, as long as the deliberation took place before a decision was made.[52] However, another empirical study of individuals' preferences for political participation found that in most real-world situations, deliberation does not increase legitimacy, and if anything, it reduces people's satisfaction in the decision-making process.[53]

There is an important methodological point to be made here: Some studies of deliberation focus on informal political talk; some set up experimental deliberations solely for the purpose of research; and some examine actual deliberative initiatives taking place in communities. It is difficult to know how to weight the conclusions of these very different types of research. Furthermore, even when deliberation does increase the legitimacy or perceived legitimacy of decisions, it is unclear whether this leads directly to increased commitment of community members to participate. For example, one study of participatory budgeting in Brazil suggests that increases in participation take time to develop and tend to grow more quickly when the government commits significant support and resources.[54] And some researchers note that enhancing governmental legitimacy is a relative strength of deliberative civic engagement, whereas other approaches may effectively engage citizens without building this perception.[55]

Ability to Solve Problems

Some scholars suggest that deliberation should increase the ability of communities to solve problems. Ongoing participation in deliberative events leads citizens to "develop a more realistic understanding of the trade-offs involved in difficult public problems," which, in turn, "helps them learn to hold leaders accountable in realistic and effective ways."[56] Perhaps for these reasons, participants in the National Issues Convention and Deliberative Polls have reported an increased sense of "political efficacy."[57] (For more discussion on individual-level impacts resulting from deliberative civic engagement, see Chapter 7.) Similarly, Leighninger describes numerous deliberation initiatives enacted by governments, school systems, other organizations, and by citizens themselves that established knowledge, connections, and mutual accountability.[58]

These problem-solving efforts range from the simple to the complex. For example, the seven-state "Horizons" initiative launched by the Northwest Area Foundation to address rural poverty has produced community gardens, youth programs, new businesses, job training programs, food banks, cultural exchanges, farmers' markets, community centers, and community foundations.[59] In building participants' confidence in their abilities, deliberation can also lead to increased future participation, though once again, there has been scant research on these potential long-term impacts.[60]

Access to Resources

Perhaps the best example of deliberation contributing to increased resource access is participatory budgeting, a process by which citizens participate, through deliberation and negotiation, in the distribution of public resources.[61] The success of participatory budgeting depends on support from both the executive and legislative branches of government, as well as a strong civil society and financial resources to fund citizens' decisions.[62] Successful participatory budgeting makes the allocation of resources more just; that is, it increases access to resources for poorer communities.[63] In the dramatic case of Porto Alegre, Brazil, participatory budgeting resulted in increased access to running water, sewer coverage, public school enrollment, road maintenance, and housing assistance. Because of improved governmental transparency, participatory budgeting even increased citizens' willingness to pay taxes.[64] Similarly, Washington, DC's four large-scale Citizen Summits held from 1999 to 2005 allowed citizens to deliberate and provide input on the city's budgeting process, leading to budget allocations based on citizen priorities.[65] More recently, a participatory budgeting process in Chicago's 49th Ward has become a high-profile case.[66] The success of these initiatives appears to rely strongly on governmental support for the recommendations made by participants.

Deliberative civic engagement can also increase access to another important resource—information. For instance, the Study Circles program reports several examples of improved information available to community members as a result of such events in various cities, including: the creation of a report on racial disparities in Syracuse, New York; the initiation of televised school board meetings in North Little Rock, Arkansas; and the development of a public civic education class, as well as a printed guide to local government, in Decatur, Georgia.[67]

Deliberation also has the potential to increase ordinary citizens' access to community leaders. For example, due to continuing involvement of citizens in public decision making in Bridgeport, Connecticut, business and political leaders look at citizens differently, viewing them as necessary consultants and collaborators.[68] Similarly, participants in a Study Circles event in Fayetteville, North Carolina, report an improved relationship between neighborhoods and government.[69] In the case of Bridgeport, it seems that persistence, more than anything, has promoted this attitude among the city elite, whereas in Fayetteville, this relationship changed as the result of specific deliberative events.

Strategies for Building Community Capacity

The previous section showed that deliberative civic engagement has the potential to contribute to all four characteristics of community capacity outlined in the CCB framework. It can contribute to a sense of community by building bonds among participants and helping them to recognize commonalities. It can contribute to increased commitment to participate in the life of the community by strengthening collective responsibility for problem solving and community traditions of participation. Additionally, deliberative civic engagement can contribute to perceptions of government legitimacy, which may stimulate commitment to participate. It also can increase participants' ability to solve problems by helping them develop a realistic understanding of the problems and by building confidence in their problem-solving abilities. Finally, deliberative civic engagement can increase a community's access to resources by making distribution more just, by increasing information available to community members, and by making community leaders more accessible to ordinary citizens.

The next question is by what means could a deliberative civic reformer produce such effects. The CCB framework holds that an optimal strategy involves familiar elements, specifically leadership, organizational development, community organizing, and inter-organizational collaboration. In this section, I consider each of those factors in turn.

Leadership

Leadership development appears to be strongly related to both deliberation and community capacity.[70] Numerous case studies of deliberation events point out that training for citizen facilitators can build their individual leadership skills, which contributes to their participation in future events. For example, one convener of deliberations in Bridgeport, Connecticut, reported "we use the parents who have been trained to be our moderators and facilitators when we have other conferences, and their leadership skills have expanded dramatically."[71] The leadership training that occurs in deliberation can help embed deliberation within a community by creating deliberative "mavens," that is,

> people skilled and knowledgeable in the ways of deliberation who serve as an "information bank" and deliberative resource for the community. . . . They [begin] as importers of deliberation and [become], over time, a catalyst and resource for further deliberative practices across the community.[72]

Moreover, the design of deliberative processes greatly affects the influence that such processes have on leadership development, and deliberation is most likely to create mavens if it is user-friendly, adaptable, simple, and inexpensive.[73]

Participants in a two-day course for conveners, moderators, and recorders of National Issues Forums reported that since their involvement with the forums, they "were becoming more involved in community affairs" and "the concepts of public deliberation helped them in their leadership roles." The trainees identified four ways in which their involvement contributed to their leadership development: It improved their listening skills, increased their confidence in moderating deliberative forums on contentious issues, decreased their sensitivity during contentious discussions, and increased their open-mindedness.[74] In addition to its effects on facilitators, deliberation can also strengthen the leadership skills of participants. For example, participants involved in Study Circles on race and diversity report greater courage and confidence "to make changes they had long wished to make."[75]

Organizational Development

Deliberation can contribute both to the creation of new organizations and to the strengthening or changing of existing organizations. For example, participants in Chattanooga Venture "organized neighborhood associations, nurtured new nonprofit organizations, and spurred investment in the city" to combat the community problems they identified during deliberation.[76] The Study Circles Resource Center (now known as Everyday Democracy) reports examples of nine different ways in which study circle programs have contributed to organizational changes in communities. Specifically, organizations involved in study circles developed new purposes, found new allies, developed new ways of working, developed new capacity, hired new employees, identified new funding or resources, gained new credibility, developed new rules or procedures, and found new opportunities to teach other communities and groups.[77] Additionally, individual Study Circles participants report building new organizations or participating more in existing ones.[78]

Community Organizing

The relationship between deliberation and community organizing is complex. At first glance, the two techniques would seem to be in direct conflict: Most deliberative organizers focus their events on the discussion of issues and informed decision making rather than the advocacy for a particular position implied by community organizing. As public administration scholar Christopher Plein argues, a deliberative approach to public policy participation "borrows from the community organizing tradition" but is "*process* driven rather than issue or policy outcome oriented."[79] Communication scholar David Ryfe views this distinction between process and outcome as a "structural ambivalence within deliberative democracy about the relationship between talk and action," and notes that while deliberation is not always solely process (or talk) oriented, most initiatives, such as the National Issues Forums, "imagine that the ultimate impact of deliberation is on public opinion and not the policy-making process."[80]

Nevertheless, it is often difficult, in practice, to disentangle deliberation and community organizing. Some community organizers stress the deliberative nature of their work, and it also seems fair to say that community organizing has evolved and diversified into a wide range of activities.[81] For example, reform of the Chicago Police Department utilized community organizing techniques to involve citizens in a more deliberative approach to policing.[82] Likewise, the directors of Everyday Democracy argue that effective deliberation is not possible without community organizing to increase participation and generate successful action.[83] From a more theoretical perspective, advocates of Deliberation Day—a hypothetical national deliberation event—speculate that such an event would encourage community activists to get involved in local party matters, just as it would force national candidates to collaborate with local parties. For example, imagine "a host of community groups setting up tables at lunchtime, trying to gain the interest and support of deliberators for their activities. Casual connections made during the Day will deepen and grow in countless directions over extended periods."[84]

Organizational Collaboration

Community leaders in Bridgeport, Connecticut, note that collaboration among organizations increased as a result of deliberative civic engagement, "in large part because most now share the language of public engagement, and have the capacity to carry it out with some regularity."[85] Likewise, in an examination of the use of a Community Benefits Agreement model for land-use planning, in which community coalitions deliberate with private developers to make land-use decisions, deliberation led to "community empowerment" by bringing diverse community interests together as a coalition.[86] Moreover, a study of "community deliberation" initiatives reports that

> face-to-face meetings among neighbors and fellow citizens can build effective coalitions among active citizens and public and private organizations. In small but important ways, these groups can improve community life through coordinated voluntary activities, philanthropy, and policy initiatives.[87]

In sum, empirical research suggests that deliberative civic engagement can be an effective tool for building community capacity, and it bears a strong relationship with at least three of the four strategies outlined in the CCB framework. Specifically, it can build the leadership skills of facilitators and participants by developing their listening and discussion skills, open-mindedness, and confidence. It can contribute to organizational development by stimulating the creation of new organizations, as well as by strengthening or changing existing organizations. It also may contribute to community organizing when it focuses on action in addition to talk; however, deliberative theorists and practitioners disagree about the relationship between deliberation and community organizing. Finally, deliberative civic engagement can facilitate organizational collaboration by helping diverse organizations find common ground and creating coalitions.

Conclusion

Those who tout the power of deliberative civic engagement to build community capacity appear to have it right. By mapping the outcomes of deliberative initiatives in accordance with the CCB framework, it becomes clearer that deliberative practices can make contributions to each facet of community capacity and can support the strategies suggested for building such capacity.

That said, there is still a great deal of work to be done in understanding *how* deliberative civic engagement makes these contributions, and whether they are sustained beyond the scope and time frame of the original initiative. Though the deliberation literature benefits from a rich body of evidence about the effects that deliberation can have on communities, it suffers from a lack of research on what exactly makes those effects happen. The authors of the CCB framework note that all community-building initiatives face the challenges of "conditioning influences"—those factors that "facilitate or inhibit the development of community capacity and intentional efforts to build it."[88] These influences include characteristics such as safety, residential stability, and distribution of power and resources. Deliberative civic engagement may be helped or hindered by the existence of these (and other) influences in a community, which also may be beyond the power of conveners of deliberative initiatives to control. However, the design of deliberative practices, over which conveners do have control, also has a significant relationship with the outcomes of those practices.[89] (For a discussion of online design, with implications for face-to-face design, see Chapter 6.) In short, more research should be undertaken to better understand how deliberative civic engagement makes contributions to community capacity building.

Many case studies of deliberative events, including those cited in this chapter, highlight deliberation's contributions to the elements of community capacity building, but many others consciously ignore or simply overlook these effects. Additionally, some writers consider deliberation to be a part of, or synonymous with, community capacity or democracy in general,[90] which means the effects of deliberative activities are not always evaluated in terms of their contribution to communities—it is simply assumed that if deliberation took place, then the community is better off. It is beyond the scope of this chapter to analyze whether those studies that do not mention community capacity building contain systematic bias; instead, this chapter focuses on those cases where positive effects of deliberation were observed. However, deliberative civic engagement should not be assumed to produce community capacity by default; noneffects and negative effects of deliberation are certainly possible.[91]

Systematic testing of deliberation's contribution to community capacity building has not been conducted in proportion to the strength of claims made on deliberation's behalf. In the words of political scientist Tali Mendelberg, "Deliberation should not be attempted under all circumstances as a cost-free solution to costly problems, nor should it be rejected wholesale. Deliberation. . . . should be attempted only after careful analysis, design, and testing."[92] Likewise, while both theoretical and empirical research provide "a good deal of indirect support for the democratic potential of deliberation . . . this potential is highly context dependent and rife with opportunities for going awry."[93] The CCB framework used in this chapter provides a possible means for improving future study of deliberation's community effects.

Notes

1. Mathews (1994: 19).
2. Putnam (1995: 67).
3. Lasch (1995: 8).
4. Cortes (1996: 3).
5. Macedo (2005: 2).
6. www.soulofthecommunity.org.
7. National League of Cities (2008).
8. Dewey (1957: 213). The very term *healthy democracy* has been used frequently by Ned Crosby, who helped found Healthy Democracy Oregon, which created the Oregon Citizens' Initiative Review (www.healthydemocracyoregon.org).
9. Mathews (1994: 19).
10. http://www.countywidecommunityforums.org/ (accessed June 6, 2008).
11. Chaskin, Brown, Venkatesh, and Vidal (2001); see also Chaskin (2001). Throughout this chapter, I will refer to this as the "Community Capacity Building (CCB) framework."
12. Chaskin, Brown, Venkatesh, and Vidal (2001: 8).
13. Chaskin, Brown, Venkatesh, and Vidal (2001: 7).
14. Chaskin, Brown, Venkatesh, and Vidal (2001: 14).
15. Chaskin, Brown, Venkatesh, and Vidal (2001: 14).
16. Chaskin, Brown, Venkatesh, and Vidal (2001: 25).
17 Chaskin, Brown, Venkatesh, and Vidal (2001: 11).
18. Chaskin, Brown, Venkatesh, and Vidal (2001: 3–4).
19. Lempa, Goodman, Rice, and Becker (2008: 299–300). Two other frameworks for defining and understanding community capacity are Goodman, Speers, Mcleroy, Fawcett, Kegler, Parker, Smith, Sterling, and Wallerstein (1998), and Gibbon, Labonte, and Laverack (2002). In addition, Brinkerhoff and Crosby (2002: 77–78) list specific kinds of citizen capacities necessary for participation in policy making; Creasy, Gavelin, and Porter (2008) offer a framework for understanding and building "community cohesion;" and Stone (2001: 596) identifies components of "civic capacity."
20. Stone (2001: 597).
21. Stone (2001: 614).
22. See, for example, Brinkerhoff and Crosby (2002), Creasy, Gavelin, and Porter (2008: 7–8), and Fraser and Kick (2005). For a summary of some criticisms of community capacity building, see Saegert (2006: 275–278).
23. Flavin-McDonald and Barrett (1999: 34). The Topsfield Foundation (now known as the Paul J. Aicher Foundation) is the primary sponsor of Everyday Democracy, a deliberative democracy organization (see http://www.everyday-democracy.org).
24. Hibbing and Theiss-Morse (2002: 190–191).

25. See Crosby (2005) for a criticism of laboratory research on deliberation.
26. See http://www.jefferson-center.org (accessed September 19, 2008).
27. Roberts and Kay (2000: 219–252).
28. Lee and Polletta (2010).
29. See Gastil and Kelshaw (2000: 9–14).
30. Mendelberg (2002: 153–154).
31. Smith (1999: 52–53).
32. Gastil (2000: 119–121).
33. Walsh (2004).
34. Roberts and Kay (2000: 181–182).
35 Friedman, Kadlec, and Birnback (2007: 7).
36. Friedman, Kadlec, and Birnback (2007: 15).
37. Friedman, Kadlec, and Birnback (2007: 10).
38. Simmons and Mills (2010: 71–80).
39. Gastil and Kelshaw (2000: 9–14).
40. Gastil and Kelshaw (2000: 14).
41. Roberts and Kay (2000: 182–183).
42. Burkhalter, Gastil, and Kelshaw (2002: 413); cf. Pateman (1970).
43. Burkhalter, Gastil, and Kelshaw (2002: 414–415).
44. Melville, Willingham, and Dedrick (2005: 51).
45. Melville, Willingham, and Dedrick (2005: 51).
46. Gastil and Kelshaw (2000: 21).
47. Douglass (1994: 59)
48. Fagotto and Fung (2006: 26).
49. Fagotto and Fung (2006: 26).
50. Mendelberg (2002: 153).
51. Fung (2006: 70).
52. Sulkin and Simon (2001: 820).
53. Hibbing and Theiss-Morse (2002: 196–201).
54. Wampler (2007: 33–35).
55. Cooper, Bryer, and Meek (2006).
56. Friedman, Kadlec, and Birnback (2007: 7).
57. Fishkin and Luskin (1999); Luskin, Fishkin, Malhotra, and Siu (2007).
58. Leighninger (2006).
59. Morehouse (2009).
60. Burkhalter, Gastil, and Kelshaw (2002: 417–418).
61. Wampler (2007: 21).
62. Wampler (2007: 24).
63. Fung (2006: 71); Wampler (2007: 36). Gerlach-Kristen (2003) notes that Monetary Policy Committees make better decisions about setting interest rates if they deliberate beforehand, even without involving citizens.
64. Wagle and Shah (2003: 3); Fung (2006: 72).
65. America*Speaks* (2007).
66. Lerner and Altschuler (2011). As this book goes to press, participatory budgeting adapted from the Chicago model has spread to New York City. For updates on the spread of this process in North America, visit www.participatorybudgeting.org.
67. Roberts and Kay (2000: 192–193).
68. Friedman, Kadlec, and Birnback (2007: 7).
69. Roberts and Kay (2000: 190).
70. Other writers on community capacity have recognized the centrality of leadership; see, for example, Goodman, Speers, Mcleroy, Fawcett, Kegler, Parker, Smith, Sterling, and Waller-stein (1998: 260), Lempa, Goodman, Rice, and Becker (2008), and Gibbon, Labonte, and Laverack (2002: 487).
71. Friedman, Kadlec, and Birnback (2007: 7).

72. Friedman, Kadlec, and Birnback (2007: 14).
73. Friedman, Kadlec, and Birnback (2007: 15).
74. Daugherty and Williams (2007: 8).
75. Roberts and Kay (2000: 180–181).
76. Gastil (2000: 120).
77. Gastil (2000: 183–188).
78. Gastil (2000: 207–208).
79. Plein, Green, and Williams (1998: 515), emphasis in original.
80. Ryfe (2005: 61).
81. Leighninger (2010).
82. Fung (2001: 81–82).
83. McCoy and Scully (2002).
84. Ackerman and Fishkin (2002: 147).
85. Friedman, Kadlec, and Birnback (2007: 6).
86. Baxamusa (2008: 261).
87. Gastil (2000: 123).
88. Chaskin, Brown, Venkatesh, and Vidal (2001: 23).
89. Friedman, Kadlec, and Birnback (2007: 14–15); Kadlec and Friedman (2007); Roberts and Kay (2000: 219–252).
90. For example, Stone (2001: 611) equates "civic capacity" with "capacity for community-minded deliberation and action," and Dryzek (2007: 1) defines "democratization" as "the building of deliberative capacity in a political system."
91. Delli Carpini, Cook, and Jacobs (2004: 331); Creasy, Gavelin, and Porter (2008: 7–8).
92. Mendelberg (2002: 153–154).
93. Delli Carpini, Cook, and Jacobs (2004: 328).

9

Assessing the Policy Impacts of Deliberative Civic Engagement

Comparing Engagement in the Health Policy Processes of Brazil and Canada

GREGORY BARRETT, MIRIAM WYMAN, AND VERA SCHATTAN P. COELHO

> The strokes of the pen need deliberation as much as the sword needs swiftness.
>
> —Julia Ward Howe

Over the past three decades, societies in both "old" and "new" democracies have implemented many innovative deliberative civic engagement mechanisms.[1] Evaluations have shown that deliberation can reshape the attitudes and behaviors of participants (see Chapter 7), improve community capacity (see Chapter 8), reduce polarization on polemical issues,[2] and increase the political participation of traditionally marginalized groups (see Chapters 3 and 5).

The global promotion of deliberative civic engagement, however, has not been matched by sustained research demonstrating its tangible impact on policy. Consequently, disagreement persists over the conditions required to yield effective policy changes through deliberation. Factors such as the design of the deliberative mechanism, the level of public manager involvement, and the organizational features of civil society all come up as potential factors in whether deliberative civic engagement will produce policy change.[3]

This chapter enters this debate by addressing two questions, *What is the relationship between deliberation and the public policy process? And what is the impact of deliberative civic engagement on policy making?* Underlying these questions is a deeper, sometimes philosophical disagreement about whether citizen participation principally has intrinsic or instrumental value. Put another way, however, one might wonder whether governments (and citizens) can reap the instrumental value of deliberation without a prior commitment to securing its intrinsic value.[4] This question was recently articulated in a broad review of the literature on the relationship between public participation and policy:

> Democratic theory tells us that public participation is undertaken for different purposes and with different underlying goals. Tensions exist between views of participation as an essential element of successful democracy (and inherently desirable in its own right) and participation as a means of achieving something else, be it a specific decision outcome, a desire for more informed, accountable or legitimate decision making, or perhaps to share the blame for a difficult decision. Lying somewhere in between is the desire for public participation to contribute to a more educated and engaged citizenry.[5]

Again, much of the research on the quality of deliberation has been devoted to assessing the democratic performance of participatory mechanisms or their impacts on participants;[6] yet it should also be possible to assess impacts on policy and policy performance. Since most deliberations occur in a context in which an issue has policy implications, there is a great deal of variation in whether and how deliberative mechanisms are structured for or feed into the policy process. Such variation should provide fertile ground for comparative case study research and, eventually, more systematic large sample analyses. Measuring policy effects, however, has proven challenging, and few investigators have overcome the obstacles to tracking the impact of deliberative civic engagement on institutions and policy change.[7]

Rather than simply reviewing the limited research to date, this chapter addresses its central questions by presenting two in-depth cases of deliberative civic engagement. Both cases look at health policy processes, but each has distinctive features. Our Brazilian case examines local health councils that are part of an extensive national framework designed to promote accountability, priority setting, and local problem solving, whereas our Canadian case focuses on a national consultation concerning a policy response to an ethical problem. Examination of these cases sheds light on the kinds of policy proposals that are being generated by deliberative civic engagement and shows how they are (or are not) incorporated into public decision making.

Before delving into the details of these cases, however, we begin this chapter by discussing the presumed impacts of deliberation on policy processes and providing a conceptual overview of various features that influence the potential for policy impact. Next, we review the difficulties faced when assessing the impact of deliberation on policy and summarize some of the more recent literature that has addressed those challenges. Only then come the details from the Brazilian and Canadian case studies, followed by a conclusion examining the potential trade-offs between enlarging citizen input on policy issues and maintaining desirable standards of technical input and political representation.

From Deliberation to Policy Formulation?

Expected Impacts of Deliberation on Policy

The degree to which deliberative mechanisms link directly to policy makers/ policy making reflects, in part, whether the value of deliberation is conceived of as being intrinsic or instrumental. For some, the potential impact of deliberative civic engagement might be the gradual creation of a virtuous circle of citizen-state interaction.[8] In a sense, deliberative processes offer citizens a new feedback mechanism into the process of policy formulation.[9] Because deliberative civic engagement builds awareness and increases skills for citizenship, those new capacities, in turn, can be deployed in varied policy arenas. If public voice and participation increase across sectors, states respond by improving policy coherence and making public institutions more effective. As a result, social inclusion improves because a wider range of citizens have expressed (and, one hopes, examined) their concerns in a deliberative space. Throughout these iterative processes, democratic citizenship is strengthened.

For others, deliberative civic engagement is a mechanism available to governments for improving policy effectiveness. This perspective stresses participation as a means for governments to address citizens' concerns about democratic performance (via processes) and policy performance (via outputs). In this vein, deliberation gives governments a better understanding of people's evolving needs by responding to greater diversity in society and addressing inequalities in policy-making processes and public services. Governments can then leverage information, ideas, and resources held by citizens, civil society organizations, and the private sector as drivers for innovation to tackle complex policy challenges and improve the quality of public services. By galvanizing people to take action in policy areas where success requires changes in individuals' behavior, policy improves while costs drop. This reduces administrative burdens, compliance costs, and the risk of conflict or delays during policy implementation and service delivery.[10]

Regardless of whether deliberative civic engagement is used for its intrinsic or instrumental value—or some combination of the two—a lingering concern regarding its relationship to actual policy processes remains. To what degree are citizens' voices *actually* factored into final policy choices?

Features that Affect the Impact of Deliberation on Policy

We have identified at least three critical features of deliberative civic engagement as influencing policy impact: empowerment, embeddedness, and legitimacy. The relative strength of each within a deliberative process determines the quality of the process as well as the overall legitimacy of its outcome.

Empowerment. The degree to which deliberation is empowered to guide policy formulation has interested many researchers. Studies often conclude that citizen participants—though they may attribute certain individual and societal gains to deliberation—expect little in terms of policy impact.[11] This is often because deliberation is not always sequenced as an integral part of the policy process.

As communications scholar Martin Carcasson has noted,

> When the public is involved in institutional decision making, it is often too late in the process. The public is invited to respond to decisions that have already been made or perhaps to express their opinion right before the decision is made. At that point, the role of the public is reduced . . . to an extremely limited scope of potential action.[12]

Accordingly, the impacts of deliberative civic engagement will vary depending on where and when in the policy process it occurs and on the extent to which the stakeholders involved identify its aims within the policy-making process. To understand the degree to which a deliberative civic engagement is empowered, Carcasson developed a continuum of "authority and power" for participatory mechanisms. Moving from "least" to "most" authority, deliberation is a means of:

1. Deriving *personal benefits*, such as learning or fulfilling a sense of civic obligation;
2. Exerting *communicative influence* by aggregating public opinion on an issue;
3. Providing *advice and consultation* by feeding direct inputs into participatory fora;
4. Joining a *co-governing partnership* in which citizens join with officials to devise policy strategies for public action; and
5. Exercising *direct authority* over public decisions or resources.[13]

Although the cases in this chapter focus on intermediate processes in which citizens might hope to have influence on policy making, Table 9.1 illustrates several deliberative processes in which the impact is less ambiguous. These include the long-standing authority vested in citizens through the jury system to more recent innovations that give citizens the authority to direct local economic

Table 9.1 **Sample of Deliberative Civic Engagement Processes and Policy Impacts**

Deliberative Process	Initial Location	Inception	Number of Participants	Authority/ Influence	Legislative/Executive/ Judicial Check
Civil/ criminal jury[a]	London, England	1670	6–12 via random-selection (and usually voir dire)	Resolve matters of legal dispute	On specific points of law, judgments may be appealed to higher courts
Participatory Budgeting[b]	Porto Alegre, Brazil	1989	100s/1000s open, then elect delegates	Prioritize and allocate portion of city budget	Mayor may veto the budget
People's Campaign[c]	Kerala, India	1996	100s/1000s open, then elect delegates	Decide how to spend 1/3 of state planning budget	Legislative vote required to authorize spending
Deliberative Poll[d]	Wenling City, China	2005	235 via random-selection	Set priorities for economic development	Government action needed to implement priorities
Citizens' Assembly[e]	British Columbia, Canada	2003	160 via random-selection (+2 Aboriginal)	Send electoral reform referendum to electorate	Legislative vote required to trigger referendum
Citizens Initiative Review[f]	Oregon, USA	2010	24 via stratified random-selection	Present analyses/ recommendations through official Voters' Pamphlet	Secretary of State oversight (could be replaced by a board consisting of former panelists and state appointees)

[a] There is no definitive date for when the "modern civil jury" was established. The date given here is the year of "Bushel's Case," which established that juries could not be punished by the judge for rendering a "not guilty" verdict (Vidmar and Hans 2007: 27).

[b] Wampler (2009).

[c] Fischer (2006).

[d] Fishkin (2009c); Leib and He (2006).

[e] Warren and Pearse (2008).

[f] Gastil and Knobloch (2010).

Source: This table is adapted from John Gastil's October 2009 presentation, Giving power to public voice: A critical review of alternative means of infusing citizen deliberation with legal authority or influence, at Publics and Emerging Technologies: Cultures, Contexts, and Challenges, Banff, Canada.

development policy, among others. The point here is that deliberation can and does have clear and direct legal and policy consequences in these institutional settings, regardless of how likely those impacts might be in other cases.

Embeddedness. Another view suggests that deliberative civic engagement is a way for citizens to take "on an intermediary role in policy development, somewhere between utter ignorance and absolute control." This is likely to vary depending on the context.[14] Increasingly, we see that the degree of power and authority a deliberative mechanism has on the policy process is determined, in part, by the degree to which it is embedded in the community of practice.[15]

In some contexts, such as the participatory budgeting process in Porto Alegre, Brazil, citizen participation in policy making is part of a historically successful political platform, on which one of the country's main political parties has built much of its popular support. Therefore, the prerogative of public officials in a context where citizen participation in policy making has become much more embedded may be different from what it is in a context where such participation is a fresh innovation. Different contexts also have different starting points in terms of traditions of active citizenship, the strength of civil society, and the degree of "democratic space" in the public sphere, each of which helps embed citizen participation in the policy-making process.[16]

Legitimacy. Questions about the legitimacy of deliberative civic engagement are also important to consider. It is fine for citizens to monitor public service delivery or suggest actions for various social problems, but how much influence should these processes have over binding decisions concerning scarce resources? What weight should citizen advice have, for example, in defining who will receive antiviral medication for prevention in the event of an influenza pandemic? Legitimacy, it has been argued, can only be guaranteed if the public engagement process is "inclusive, voluntary, reasoned, and equal."[17] Thus, the outcomes of deliberative civic engagement may not be considered legitimate because the process did not adhere to these criteria.

In particular, the lack of inclusion is a persistent and abiding challenge to public involvement in deliberative processes (see Chapters 3 and 5). An inclusive process suggests a mix of participants from various backgrounds, ages, cultures, socioeconomic situations, education levels, and relevant geographic regions (e.g., rural versus urban areas). However, there is considerable debate as to what types of inclusion are ideal—or most needed—in deliberative civic engagement. Some authors highlight the need to actively promote the inclusion of groups traditionally marginalized from political processes—groups that may be poorly organized or not organized at all.[18] Other authors call for the use of random selection as a way of guaranteeing that the sociodemographic profile of the participants mirrors that of the population.[19] The expectation is that this approach avoids favoring those with more resources, as well as ensuring that debates are not monopolized by politicized collective actors with already strongly developed positions.

Each of these perspectives has a different understanding of what "a greater degree of inclusion" actually means. Those who argue for random selection suggest that the more the sociodemographic profile of the participants mirrors that of the population, the more inclusive the deliberative event will be. For those who argue for the need to include the marginalized, greater inclusion will finally take place when the neediest are "overrepresented." If deliberative civic engagement processes include certain design requirements, such as the adequate representation of civil society organizations (CSOs), the composition and number of CSOs participating might affect the degree of inclusiveness.

However, inclusion alone is not enough to guarantee legitimacy because it does not indicate the level of participation by those involved. In this context, level of participation refers to how the agenda is set and how the organization of the discussions and the practice of deliberation, bargaining, and confrontation happen in meetings. In essence, it considers the quality of the deliberative process and the extent to which citizens are able to understand the complexity of the issues and to enter deeply into discussion (see also Chapter 4).

Various authors who have analyzed deliberative civic engagement have observed that relationships between actors are marked by huge asymmetries, that government officials or public servants have excessive power, and that participatory forums are often "captured" or dominated by political interests or even by political parties.[20] This is all the more reason for working to include voices that go beyond "the usual suspects." Previous studies have suggested that deliberative civic engagement—if designed thoughtfully—can minimize some of these asymmetries and facilitate more inclusive deliberative processes.[21] In practice, however, most forms of engagement are still designed in ways that put more emphasis on technical and bureaucratic expertise than on the perspectives of the general public, thereby limiting the impact of the public's involvement in deliberative civic engagement.

Recent Evidence on the Impact of Deliberation on Policy Making

Against a backdrop of tightening fiscal constraints within many societies and demands for evidence-based policy making, it is important to include assessable outcomes for deliberative civic engagement. (For a discussion of evaluation, see Chapter 10.) If the potential impact of deliberative civic engagement on policy making is affected by how empowered, embedded, and legitimate it is, how can these qualities be assessed?

Most impact evaluations of deliberation have focused on the content and participants' experiences of the process rather than on the systematic tracking of their impact on policy outputs and outcomes. This is the result, in part, of the difficulty in demonstrating the causal links between participation and policy outcomes.

To begin, there is often ambiguity about what would constitute a substantial outcome. Deliberative mechanisms generate outcomes at many different levels, including individual, community, organizational, and policy levels. It is not always clear or feasible to track impacts on all of these levels, and focusing on one at the expense of the others might well miss significant and important outcomes. Impact then has to be considered in relation to initial goals. Public leaders and policy makers have diverse and sometimes poorly articulated goals for employing participatory mechanisms.[22] As a result, evaluators might not know what inputs or outcomes to track. Outcomes also are dependent, in part, on the goals—sometimes matched, sometimes not—of the various participants, including citizens, professional stakeholders, and public officials.[23] As a result, the legitimacy of the outcome might differ depending on whose goals were privileged in the deliberation.

The scope and level of analysis further complicates evaluation. Whereas inputs, processes, outputs, and outcomes from deliberations are all potentially important, piecemeal approaches to analyzing each of these poses difficulty in determining the relative importance to assign each.[24] Focusing on the first two tells us much more about an institution's democratic performance, while the latter two are more closely connected to policy performance.[25] Also, there are numerous questions regarding whether the focus should be on short-term, intermediate, or long-term results. Moreover, if the focus is on intermediate and/ or long-term results, the challenge of proving causal links due to the time lag and intervening events increases.[26]

Despite these challenges and the reality that evaluators are often precluded from assessing impacts thoroughly because of resource constraints, a number of recent studies have attempted to engage this issue using a variety of methodological approaches. Perhaps the most common approach to tracking the policy outcomes of deliberative exercises is case study analysis, such as the two presented later in this chapter. Case studies typically focus on a single deliberative civic engagement process or offer a comparison of two or more processes, and they rely on the analysis of varied sources of rich qualitative data (although there are some examples of mixed qualitative-quantitative approaches). The case study approach can make logical links between the internal features of a deliberative exercise and policy outputs, although these are often based on basic correlations and "most likely associations" rather than formal causal links.[27]

In a multiple-case study survey of nine successful community deliberations that led to "public action," the Keiki Caucus in the Hawaii (US) state legislature showed a particularly strong impact of deliberation on policy around public funding for children's welfare. While the results are impressive—the Caucus has been active for more than fifteen years "and most bills emerging from it are successful because of the reputation and legitimacy of the process"—the majority of nonlegislative participants came from professional civil society organizations rather than from the public at large. In the other more community-based cases, policy makers involved in deliberations tended to see the exercise as one of many influences on the eventual policy decision and only rarely admitted "that outcomes from deliberations played a dominant role in their decisions."[28] Nevertheless, many citizen participants throughout the case studies were positive about their engagement, and the deliberations were fairly well embedded in the official legislative process.

In another recent study of multiple cases of deliberation in two Dutch cities, citizens were very active in the participatory spaces and reported satisfaction with their engagement. At the same time, the researchers found that citizens saw their role primarily as information providers to government rather than as deliberators over policy outputs. In these cities, citizens contribute to decision making only occasionally, and usually only in cooperation with higher-level stakeholders, thereby leaving "vertical government decision making intact." The authors posit that this is the result of each deliberation being government-led, with a low level of empowerment from the perspective of citizen participants.[29]

There has also been an increase in the number of quantitative evaluations of participatory programs and their impact on various policy indicators. These evaluations can be particularly useful because they often draw from different data sources, such as administrative and public expenditure data. Many of these studies have focused specifically on the impact of participatory budgeting on policy by looking at changes in social spending and social welfare in communities using such mechanisms. In a desk review of work on participatory budgeting in Latin America, with a specific focus on Brazil, there are discernible effects on redistribution of public resources toward poor neighborhoods, based on the analysis of public expenditure flows.[30] There is also evidence that Brazilian municipalities that used participatory budgeting between 1996 and 2000 spent higher proportions of their budget on health care than municipalities that did not use participatory budgeting.[31] An international donor's evaluation of participatory budgeting in Porto Alegre also managed to trace a participatory impact on poverty reduction and improved access to water and sanitation.[32]

In addition to these quantitative studies, experimental approaches—such as the use of randomized controlled trials or "natural" policy experiments—have gained attention from governments and research funding agencies in recent years. These methods are considered particularly strong for assessing questions of impact because of their ability to isolate the impacts of an intervention using "treatment" and "control" groups—one group is exposed or "treated" with a policy intervention while another similar group is not. The differences in impact are then measured to understand the effects. For instance, an experimental study of the effects of community-based monitoring and deliberation in improving local health services in Uganda found positive effects on the groups that used deliberative mechanisms compared to those that did not. In fact, the impact on public service delivery was so pronounced that the "treatment" communities enjoyed statistically significant increases in infant weight and decreased child mortality, as well as higher utilization of local health services.[33]

Whereas the use of surveys and stakeholder interviews has tended to focus on the deliberative experiences of participants (both citizens and public officials), these studies sometimes include data on how and to what extent participants' perceived political efficacy changed as a result (see also Chapter 7). A survey of public administrators in US cities asked about the levels and types of citizen participation used in municipal policy and planning and the degree to which these were taken into account in decision making.[34] Though there appeared, in general, to be a wide range of participatory initiatives under way in many cities (ranging from "thin" forms of consultation to more robust forms of deliberative civic engagement), only one third of respondents agreed or strongly agreed that city management involved the public in identifying goals and objectives. A lack of interest in deliberation by public officials and the degree of political divisiveness over deliberation were two key challenges and impediments mentioned by respondents.

These various methodological approaches each have advantages and limitations, but it is apparent from scanning the literature that deliberative civic engagement can have an impact on policy processes. Nonetheless, the legitimacy of the outcomes is often unclear, even when deliberation is relatively empowered or embedded.

Health Policy in Brazil and Canada: Two Case Studies

In this section, we examine two large-scale deliberative civic engagement processes centered on health-policy issues. The first process engaged community health councils and focused on the core issues of accountability and priority-setting in the public health system in São Paulo, Brazil. The second process, undertaken by the Public Health Agency of Canada, engaged citizens and other stakeholders in developing a national pandemic influenza plan. For both cases, we briefly describe the deliberative civic engagement processes, the degree to which citizens were empowered, how their input was embedded in the policy process, and the policy proposals that were generated. We then assess the legitimacy of these processes and the resultant policy proposals by tracking how they were incorporated into the health policy decisions.

São Paolo, Brazil: Local Health Councils

Local Health Councils (LHCs) in Brazil are the result of civil society's historic struggle to achieve greater representation and accountability in the policy process. The democratic credentials of LHCs were earned through a process that began with re-democratization in the late 1970s as the community health movement began calling for "health for all." These calls continued through the 1980s and were eventually embedded in the 1988 Brazilian Constitution, which made public participation in health issues an official policy. LHCs became fully institutionalized components of the health policy-making process in the 2000s.

The mission of the LHCs is to bring together civil society organizations, service providers, and public officials in health co-governance. Specifically, they are designed to address the core issues of accountability, priority setting, and local problem solving on public health issues. LHCs are intra-municipal units that differ from the national, state, and municipal health councils in that they are consultative and have limited authority over the Health Secretariats' plans and accounts. The LHCs bring together thirty-two councillors, who are elected as LHC members and typically represent local associations or public institutions.

The case presented here is based on research conducted by the Centro Brasileiro de Análise e Planejamento (CIBRAP), which conducted a comparative study of six LHCs located in poor areas of São Paulo. Three of these areas— São Miguel, Cidade Tiradentes, and M'Boi Mirim—had strong histories of social mobilization over health demands, while the other three—Casa Verde, Vila Prudente/Sapopemba, and Parelheiros—had weaker histories of social mobilization.[35] The findings drew on a variety of qualitative methods that allowed for comparison of the six LHCs. First, the researchers analyzed eighty-three sets of LHC minutes, covering meetings from January 2006 to August 2007.[36] Second, they administered questionnaires to eighty-five participants—mostly service users (the majority of whom were representatives of local associations), councillors, and health managers.[37] Third, the researchers conducted participant observation of the six LHCs' meetings. Finally, secondary sources and historical documentation were reviewed to understand the history of social mobilization in each area.

Once the meeting minutes were analyzed, it became clear that the discussions that took place were not simply the presentation of health "shopping lists," characterized by citizens complaining and making demands. On the contrary, various types of issues were debated in the meetings, classified as (1) health issues, including discussions about health policies and programs; (2) problems with service delivery in the health sector; (3) participation issues, which focused on the procedures of the meetings and elections; and (4) other local problems with public health implications, including water supply, infrastructure, and security.

Regarding the discussions about "health issues," one of the key concerns voiced in the LHCs centered on outsourcing, strongly favored by the state and municipal governments of São Paulo during this period. Such outsourcing entailed the contracting of Organizações Sociais (OSs)—Health Organizations—to manage public hospitals and outpatient medical care units to provide rapid treatment of patients with problems of low and medium complexity. At the Municipal Health Conference held in December 2005, 700 health councillors from the LHCs rejected the use of these health organizations.[38] Criticisms focused on the grounds that the reliance on OSs signaled a process of privatization in health care services, which opponents claimed would exacerbate health inequities. In particular, all LHCs discussed the lack of representation in the new structures of outsourcing patient care.

Another topic discussed by the LHCs was the need to reduce patient absenteeism for specialist consultations, for which a range of solutions was suggested. Participants also organized a process of monitoring hospital construction and the availability of medicines in their submunicipalities. In some areas, the councillors were called to take part in the elaboration of the annual plan for health. In sum, the LHCs were involved in positioning, elaborating innovative proposals, and planning and monitoring health services.

To assess whether proposals made by the LHCs were incorporated into the policy process, the researchers assessed each LHC's connections to and interactions with other policy actors, including their engagement with the executive and legislative branches (at municipal, state, and national levels) and other participatory fora in the health sector, as well as their linkages to public and private community organizations. This established a basis for the level of embeddedness of each LHC in the broader policy context, and provided an opportunity to track different entry points for the take-up of the policy recommendations proposed by LHCs.

Overall, and as cited in the minutes, the inter-organizational linkages recorded across all LHCs is remarkable—these included health groups (971), state bodies (126), and participatory fora (36). Health councillors reported that nearly half of the associations they represent have interacted with branches of municipal executive and legislative authorities at least once during the last four years. In addition, thirty-seven politicians and 264 organizations were quoted in the interviews by councillors as persons or entities with which they interacted at least once in the last four years. Because of the clear linkages between each LHC and various policy spaces and institutions, one might expect that the debates held in the LHC would enter the policy process through the various councillors' networks, as well as have an impact on public health actions.

Interviews with public officials, however, presented a more mixed picture. In the localities where successful alliances were formed between the LHCs and Technical Supervision Units, the LHCs' proposals were brought more systematically into the policy decision-making process, which also contributed to increasing the amount of resources allocated for these areas. As an example, M'Boi Mirim—the only submunicipality where the LHCs supported the OSs— received twice the number of outpatient units managed by OSs than had been received, on average, by the other submunicipalities. Concerning the reduction of absenteeism, one out of four suggestions made by this LHC—to phone patients advising the date of the appointment—has been implemented. Their monitoring of the construction of the two municipal hospitals built during the period helped in speeding the process as, according to the managers of the Technical Supervision Units, the responsiveness of the Municipal Secretariat of Health grew once the claims were made or supported by civil society representatives.

Despite the small number of cases analyzed, the results suggest interesting relationships between LHCs, their level of mobilization, and distributive impacts. In the LHCs located in the submunicipalities with a stronger history of mobilization, researchers found greater socioeconomic inclusion, but less political and associative diversity. Also, the discussions in these LHCs were less deliberative, marked by more conflict and confrontation and greater resistance to changes in the procedures for participation. At the same time, better outcomes were presented in monitoring health care services and raising health expenditures. On the other hand, the LHCs located in areas with weaker histories of mobilization were more likely to forge agreements on changing procedures for participation, some of which could favor new and more deliberative dynamics. In particular, these LHCs were—and still are—concerned about the best procedures for selecting councillors and organizing meetings.[39] In sum, this case shows how the level of mobilization in communities using deliberative civic engagement affected the degree to which recommendations were incorporated into public policy and public action.

Canada: Consultations on Pandemic Influenza Planning

The Canadian case reflects a more specific event than the Brazilian case. Prompted by concerns expressed by the World Health Organization about a looming influenza pandemic—one potentially as devastating as the Spanish Flu pandemic of 1918–1919 which killed millions of people around the world, particularly children and young adults—Canada, like many other countries, undertook the development of a comprehensive pandemic influenza plan. From its inception, the Public Health Agency of Canada embraced a commitment to public involvement, with the then Secretary of State for Public Health clearly stating her desire to "embed public consultation into the DNA of the agency."

As part of the Canadian Pandemic Influenza Plan for the Health Sector, the Public Health Agency of Canada (PHAC) through its Pan-Canadian Health Network Council (PHNC) commissioned national public consultations to help inform its recommendations on the use of antiviral medication for prevention in the event of an influenza pandemic. Antiviral medication had not been used previously for preventive purposes; therefore, there was an insufficient scientific and technical basis for making decisions about its potential use in an influenza pandemic. The purpose of the consultation was to engage citizens in different parts of Canada in informed, constructive, and value-based dialogue on three key questions with which the network was struggling: Should governments provide publicly funded antivirals for prevention during an influenza pandemic? If yes, under what conditions? Specifically to whom should they be provided? While ordinary citizens might not have the scientific expertise to weigh various risk factors, it was understood that they can clearly express their preferences for the overarching values that should frame both the decision-making process and the decision itself. The information from these consultations was to be one of a number of streams of input into the ultimate decision.

Between December 2007 and March 2008, eleven full-day dialogues were conducted: seven with citizens, two with stakeholders,[40] and two with those in occupations that were considered prime recipients for antivirals. An extensive evaluation process was planned from the outset, grounded in an evaluation framework that tied areas of inquiry to clearly defined objectives for each aspect of the consultations and defined the kinds of information needed, as well as appropriate tools for identifying them. Individual sessions were evaluated by participants who also provided an overall evaluation following both the consultations and the public release of the consultation report. A post-process evaluation was undertaken with the planning team to identify key findings, lessons learned, and implications for the topic of the consultations, as well as for future citizen engagement efforts in public health. The deliberative civic engagement process was also intended to encourage a "culture of reflection" in an organization committed to public involvement. As in the São Paulo study, researchers also examined the impact of the consultations on PHAC's decision related to the use of antivirals in a pandemic, how this input was weighted against other inputs, and the factors contributing to good dialogue and deliberation.

To discern whether citizen and stakeholder advice influenced the policy process, researchers did several things. In the sessions, participants were asked how seriously they expected their advice to be taken and the extent to which they would trust the ultimate recommendations, knowing how much advice was being sought. Researchers followed the work of the planning team as communications were developed about the consultations for decision makers. Researchers also interviewed policy makers to identify how and when the proposals entered the decision-making process and how well citizen and stakeholder input was considered alongside legal, ethical, scientific, and financial streams of evidence, and input from international organizations and agencies.

Using all available input, a national policy recommendation was developed, which has since become part of Canada's pandemic planning strategy. All relevant information about the consultations, as well as the recommendation and ensuing decision, are public and were communicated directly to all participants in the engagement process.[41]

Impact Factors: Achieving Legitimacy through Inclusion and Deliberation Dynamics

The preceding sections described the deliberative features of the cases, degrees of empowerment and embeddedness in the policy-making process, and some outcomes. In both cases, deliberative civic engagement led to policy recommendations that were brought into, and had some impact on, the policy process. At the same time, there was varied success in translating public voices into final policies, and accounting for this difficulty requires looking more closely at the cases' success at achieving legitimacy, inclusion, and high-quality deliberation.

What remains debatable, however, is the degree to which policy recommendations were translated into final policies, as well as the overall legitimacy of each process. In Brazil, for example, policy recommendations are certainly a central element of the LHCs, but the degree to which they are incorporated into policy is more difficult to assess. In contrast, the PHAC used all available input, including citizen recommendations, to form a national policy for Canada's pandemic planning strategy. In part, we believe the resultant legitimacy issues are a function of inclusion and the dynamics of deliberation in the processes. Each of these elements is discussed below.

Inclusion. In the Brazilian study, inclusion was measured using indicators that reflected a profile of each LHC—its levels of associational and political plurality, its demographic profile and whether it represented the local population, and a socioeducational profile—to assess the presence of the poor and less educated. The socioeducational and demographic indicators point to some interesting findings about inclusion. First, there is a notable participation of nonwhite individuals in the

LHCs, particularly in Cidade Tiradentes, where 70 percent of the councillors were identified as "black" or "brown." Second, 23 percent of the LHC councillors had not completed primary education. Third, there was a good gender balance in the LHCs.

These observations suggest that the LHCs studied were successful in reflecting the sociodemographic profile of the local population. The findings also challenge the more established view of participation, namely, that people who participate in political activities, including deliberative civic engagement, tend to be advantaged members of society in terms of socioeconomic, educational, and racial characteristics (see Chapter 3). While it may be the case that many deliberative civic engagement events often lack participants from traditionally underrepresented groups, it is also likely that this differs depending on the context and design of the deliberation.[42] Thus, it appears that in the case of LHCs, the design was successful in bringing ordinary citizens on board.

With respect to the political profile of the LHCs, the data suggest a predominance of councillors affiliated with or sympathetic to the PT (the more leftist Workers' Party) in five of the six LHCs. The presence, albeit less intense, of other parties was reported in two of the *sub-prefeituras*. Concerning the types of association included in the LHCs, researchers found important differences across the sample—half included a high plurality of association types while the other half did not.

In Canada, even when there are guidelines or recommendations for participation, there are rarely legal requirements for ensuring inclusion. In most cases, where organizations or institutions want to go beyond stakeholders or "the usual suspects," the aim is to recruit a group that reflects the overall population of Canada, and decisions are made in each case about how best to achieve this. In the PHAC case, the intent was to foster a values-based dialogue among randomly selected citizens (the "unorganized" public) to develop and prioritize potential decision options on the use of antivirals for prevention of influenza. Citizens' input, along with information about the scientific, ethical, and legal aspects of the issue, as well as input from international agencies, was then to be used to develop a national policy recommendation.

Participants in the citizen sessions were recruited by telephone and asked a series of questions including a few demographic items and a handful of knowledge and attitudinal measures to ensure that their "top of mind" views on key issues were largely the same as those of the population from which they were drawn. They were invited to provide input as "ordinary citizens" on the kinds of value-based considerations governments should keep in mind as they make decisions about this challenging issue.

The recruitment of stakeholders and target groups was undertaken in a rather different manner. PHAC had in place lists of stakeholder groups to whom invitations were sent. Target groups, or those potentially eligible to receive antivirals, were identified through the development of a selection matrix intended to solicit the participation of a wide cross-section of the target populations. These participants were specifically asked to participate as individuals rather than as advocates for their company, organization, or association. For the First Nations session, recruitment took place through organizations and established contacts in First Nations communities, both urban and rural, within commuting distance of the host city.

There were many challenges in the recruitment process, primarily with respect to random selection, where enormous resources of time and energy were expended to recruit the required number of participants. It was also recognized in the post-process discussions that random recruitment is increasingly difficult to achieve in an era where so many people have unlisted phone numbers or use cell phones rather than landlines.

Despite these efforts, and regardless of the recruitment approach, a number of inherent biases are encountered in searching for participants for public processes. For example, in Canada, participants must be fluent in English or French, unless specific arrangements are made to accommodate other languages (this does tend to be "routine" in large diverse urban centers such as Toronto where materials are routinely prepared in at least five languages); they must be comfortable speaking with strangers, often in an unfamiliar setting; they must be willing to essentially donate their time (in the PHAC case, small honoraria were provided to non-stakeholders along with accommodation and travel costs if needed); and they must be able to take the required time away from their daily responsibilities. In the PHAC situation, each session was a full day; for many participants who had to travel, this essentially involved at least two full days of their time.

One of the questions participants were asked as part of their evaluation was the extent to which they felt their group was a reasonable reflection of the community in which they lived. Despite the challenges identified, most felt that this was the case. However, as practitioner/researchers, we are increasingly sensitive to the need for a number of approaches to engaging participants. As with many dimensions of planning and implementing participatory processes, we know that there is no "cookie cutter" approach—each situation has its particular characteristics and needs and these must be thought through carefully in advance, ideally with a subset of those to be involved.

In sum, the inclusion practices in both cases have implications for the legitimacy of the processes. In the Brazilian case, given the relatively simple and inexpensive way that LHCs recruit councillors, researchers expected to find a participant profile strongly biased by councillors. In fact, the results suggest a more mixed profile, in which the councils reflected the sociodemographic characteristics of the population, but were more biased in terms of political and associational characteristics. In Canada, the recruitment process was more sophisticated and expensive, and researchers expected a more inclusive profile of participants. However, the experience suggested that even under these conditions it was difficult to build a fairly inclusive group. Together, the distinctive recruitment approaches of the two cases show how difficult it is to translate inclusionary goals into practical procedures. Building on these findings, we suggest that an approach emphasizing more inclusive recruitment procedures can lead to greater legitimacy.

Deliberation Dynamics. Moving from inclusion to deliberation, in the Brazilian case, the deliberative dynamics were assessed using four indicators: the design features of how meetings are facilitated and how a meeting's agenda and themes are coordinated; discursive practices, or how participants speak and deliberate in the LHC; the accountability of the councillors to their constituencies; and the councillors' satisfaction with the LHC process.

The results suggested that all of the LHCs suffered with respect to at least some of these variables. For example, in regard to discursive dynamics, the number of contributions councillors made to LHC meetings suggested that deliberation is limited, with only a few councillors raising issues. Moreover, in 60 percent of these cases, councillors spoke only once, suggesting that they are not participating in sustained discussions. With respect to accountability and satisfaction, councillors use a great variety of media to keep their constituencies informed, and approximately half of them are satisfied with the performance of their LHCs.

In the Canadian case, the situation was quite different. Recruitment posed some challenges, though overall there was a good representation of the population in each community. Because this was a cross-country consultation, it was important to have a systematic, consistent, and replicable process. An information presentation was developed for use in each session, complemented by a presentation of activities specific to each region. The sessions themselves adhered to the same agenda and were carefully designed and pilot tested. A deliberative dialogue methodology was used, with each session facilitated by a team of skilled professionals to enable full and equal participation. In addition, participants were informed that their input would be considered along with other sources of input (previously identified), and integrated into the ultimate decision about the use of antivirals for prevention in the event of an influenza pandemic.

With respect to the dynamics of who spoke and how they did so, participants were prepared for the dialogue sessions with a set of ground rules for dialogue and information about the differences between dialogue and debate. They were also encouraged to draw on their own experience of successful and less successful conversations to help understand how they would be engaging with one another.

Common information was prepared and delivered in presentations and in printed material to ensure that all participants had the information and support they needed to participate effectively. The day included presentations (with time for questions and answers and ongoing access to experts and other resource people), along with a mix of small group and whole group discussion. Participants were involved in helping to synthesize their discussions and in articulating what they held in common as well as key areas of difference. Overall, participants felt that they had a fair opportunity to share their ideas, thoughts, and concerns. By and large, they felt that their input would be taken seriously by decision makers, and they were very willing to participate in a similar venture in the future.

Likewise, the Canadian process was different from the LHCs in Brazil in terms of accountability. Participants were involved as individuals and did not have to account to a formal constituency. Not surprisingly, there was a range of views with respect to how seriously decision makers would consider their input. Overall, however, participants did feel positive about this, largely because they perceived the process to be fair, and felt that facilitators and note-takers were doing a good job of capturing and recording their deliberations. They also felt that they would trust the ultimate decision; they were glad to know that citizens' values were being considered along with other streams of input, and that, together, these would provide a sound basis for decision making. And, given that at least one decision maker attended each session, they acknowledged the commitment of decision makers to the national consultation process.

Decision makers themselves described how much they learned from helping to plan the consultation process and from observing sessions. In the Canadian PHAC case, key scientific and communications experts were involved throughout the process. Not only did they help to frame the issue, develop background materials, and fine-tune agendas and presentations, but they also worked inside the agency with relevant committees, as well as across the country with their counterparts in the provinces and territories. As noted, experts and decision makers attended each session. A number commented that a direct result of their involvement was to consider all other streams of input through a "citizens' lens," and that the values articulated in this process would definitely be useful in other health policy arenas. They also felt that their experience with this process— along with the subsequent assessment and reporting—added considerably to the agency's capacity to design and implement future participatory processes. Finally, they noted that their informal communication networks across jurisdictions were greatly improved over the course of the process, an impact that has been ongoing. In short, from the standpoint of accountability, PHAC was able to demonstrate to politicians and citizens that they had consulted broadly and that their decisions about how best to use antivirals for prevention were well founded in the best information available, as well as in societal values.

In terms of legitimacy, the degree of methodological sophistication present in the Canadian case, including the use of facilitators, helped to ensure the contributions of participants and their satisfaction with the process. In contrast, trained facilitators were not used in Brazil; thus, participants were not stimulated to position themselves and share their views in LHCs, and the dialogue was constrained to only the more active and politicized councillors. These findings highlight the importance of facilitation in encouraging active participation, reducing asymmetries, and ensuring the legitimacy of the process.

Implications

Both cases expose a crucial aspect of deliberative civic engagement in policy making. Each process was concerned—directly or indirectly—with the negotiation and definition of patterns for the distribution of public goods, which adds complexity to concerns about legitimacy and reinforces the question, legitimacy for whom?

In Brazil, the LHCs acted, at times, as "good" members of a deliberative body—for example, by engaging in deliberation about how the public good should be defined. At other times, however, they violated the theoretical norms of deliberation by pressing and arguing quite directly—and probably legitimately—for narrow self-interests to draw increased health resources to their areas. Relative to municipal, state, and national health councils, LHCs are not particularly directly connected to the policy-making process, as these councils are not expected to make binding decisions over public health accounts and plans.

In Canada, despite the evidence that the PHAC worked to provide a sense of societal values, concerns, and questions on the issue under consideration, there is limited evidence about how citizens' recommendations were balanced with the more technical ones during the decision-making process. Nevertheless, it is very clear—based both on the ultimate decision and on information from decision makers—that citizens' advice and recommendations influenced the decision about antivirals, as well as communication strategies related to pandemic influenza.

Together, these cases suggest that even with efforts to make deliberative civic engagement processes transparent and inclusive, there are questions concerning their real impact on policy. In particular, the cases reveal the importance of design, not only in terms of how deliberative civic engagement process are linked or connected to the policy process and decision making, but also in terms of inclusion (i.e., *who* participates) and deliberative dynamics (i.e., *how* people participate). Given the complexity of the policy process and the variation among deliberative processes, more research is needed not only to determine which deliberative design factors are best for influencing policy but also to determine when and for whom legitimacy is attained with such influence. Inclusion and the dynamics of deliberation are likely to be only two of several variables that affect the ability of deliberative civic engagement processes to impact policy making.

Conclusion

The Brazilian LHC and the Canadian PHAC cases, along with the other examples and reviews provided in this chapter, offer evidence that citizens are participating directly in the process of health policy decision making. In both countries, this has been a welcome innovation compared to the more usual technocratic ways of discussing (and making) health policy. Despite these important and relatively novel examples, the cases also demonstrated that the connection between deliberative civic engagement and the policy-making process remains, to date, quite informal and dependent on the disposition of public officials and politicians to hear (and act upon) the recommendations that emerge in such forums.[43]

If deliberative citizen engagement is legitimate when the process is inclusive, voluntary, reasoned, and equal, one must ask where the policy process begins and ends. Where ultimately does citizen engagement fit into the spectrum of the policy process? A number of authors and stakeholders suggest that once deliberative civic engagement is in place, it will become a major driver in decision making; however, this is not what our cases suggest. To the contrary, the Brazilian and Canadian cases suggest that the input from deliberative civic engagement is rarely the principal factor in policy decision making. Accordingly, these cases reinforce our call for more elaboration about how citizen input can be effectively balanced alongside other decision-making considerations. In this sense, the challenge is to find a fair method of weighing the different contributions made in these settings and, at the same time, demonstrating that citizens' input is genuinely taken into account.

The cases also suggest that becoming an effective part of the policy process depends not only on the empowerment, embeddedness, and legitimacy of deliberative civic engagement but also on how the outcomes of these processes are synthesized, made accessible, and fed into policy making. In the Brazilian case, for instance, LHCs produce a myriad of recommendations on health services, but there is too little evidence of how these are digested and made comprehensible in a policy-relevant manner. More investment is this area would go some distance in helping to preserve the richness of involving citizens, managers, researchers, service providers, and others in policy debates, as well as in preparing the materials resulting from deliberative civic engagement to be used more effectively throughout other stages of the policy-making process.

Notes

1. See Habermas (1984); Fung and Wright (2003); Dryzek (2000); Gaventa (2006). The Brazilian case presents results of the project "Participation and Health Policy" coordinated by Vera Schattan P. Coelho and developed at CEM/CEBRAP and the CDRC/IDS with support from CEPID-Fapesp, INCT-CNPq and DFID. The chapter also presents results from the project "Defining Indicators for Evaluation of Participatory Experiences," coordinated by Miriam Wyman and Vera S. P. Coelho with support from DDC/Hewlett Foundation. Note that the views expressed herein are those of the authors and do not necessarily reflect the views of the United Nations.
2. Abelson and Gauvin (2006).
3. Abers (2001); Wampler and Avritzer (2004); Coelho and Nobre (2004).
4. OECD (2009).
5. Abelson and Gauvin (2006).
6. See Gastil (2000); Delli Carpini, Cook, and Jacobs (2004); Beierle and Cayford (2002).
7. Rocha Menocal and Sharma (2008).
8. Gaventa and Barrett (2010).
9. Boulding and Wampler (2010).
10. OECD (2009).
11. Fung (2006).
12. Carcasson (2009).
13. Carcasson (2009). For a similar continuum, see the International Association for Public Participation (IAP2) Spectrum of Public Participation (2007).
14. Leighninger (2006: 117).
15. Fagotto and Fung (2009).
16. Gaventa and McGee (2010); Gaventa and Barrett (2010); Roberts (2004).
17. Button and Ryfe (2005: 27).
18. Gaventa (2006); Cornwall (2007).
19. Fishkin and Luskin (1999).
20. See Coelho and Nobre (2004).
21. Coelho (2011); Ansell and Gash (2008).
22. See Nabatchi and Farrar (2011) for a discussion of policy makers' perceptions of participation and deliberation.
23. Cunningham and Leighninger (2011).
24. Abelson and Gauvin (2006).
25. OECD (2009).
26. Chess (2000).
27. McGee and Gaventa (2010).
28. Fagotto and Fung (2009: 36).
29. Michels and de Graaf (2010: 488).
30. Marquetti (2002); Serageldin, Driscoll, Meléndez San Miguel, Valenzuela, Bravo, Solloso, Solá-Morales, and Watkin (2003), as cited in Goldfrank (2006).
31. Boulding and Wampler (2010).
32. World Bank (2008).
33. Björkman and Svensson (2007).
34. Wang (2001).
35. This classification, based on secondary research, was checked in interviews with Carlos Neder, ex-councillor, state deputy, and a specialist on social health movements in the city of São Paulo, as well as Nabil Bonduki, an ex-municipal councillor and a research specialist on social movements in São Paulo.
36. A standard form was created to guide the analysis and the collection of data from these minutes. To see the distribution of the minutes in the subdistricts, as well as the data

gathered and used in this research, see http://www.centrodametropole.org.br/v1/dados/saude/Anexos_Artigo_Saude_CDRCCEM.pdf.

37. According to the Municipal Law 13,716 from 2002, regulated by the Municipal Decree 44,658 from 2004, CLSs should have twenty-four effective and twenty-four substitute councillors, half of whom represent civil society, with the other half split between government and service providers, and health workers.

38. Teixeira, Kayano, and Tatagiba (2007).

39. Coelho, Ferraz, Fanti, and Ribeiro (2010).

40. A distinction was made between ordinary (unorganized) citizens and stakeholders (organized citizens) who typically have well-established ways of making their concerns known to decision makers.

41. Materials related to the PHAC consultation process can be found at http://www.phac-aspc.gc.ca/influenza/antiviralprev-eng.php.

42. Davies, Blackstock, and Rauschmayer (2005).

43. There is some evidence that this is beginning to change in Canada. By way of example, the Government of Ontario legislated the creation of a Citizens' Council for the Ministry of Health and Long Term Care specifically to allow citizens to provide input on key issues related to drug policy. Information about the Ontario Citizens' Council can be found at http://www.health.gov.on.ca/en/public/programs/drugs/councils/citizens_council.aspx.

10

Evaluating Deliberative Public Events and Projects

JOHN GASTIL, KATIE KNOBLOCH, AND MEGHAN KELLY

> It is difficult to make the people participate in the government; but it is
> still more difficult to supply them with experience, and to inspire them
> with the feelings which they need in order to govern well.
> —Alexis de Tocqueville, *Democracy in America*[1]

Turning the clock back just twenty years, one would have difficulty finding a person in public office, academia, or civil society talking about the virtues of "citizen deliberation." At that time, there were a few innovative public deliberation programs, such as the Citizen Juries in the United States and Planning Cells in Germany, but these efforts were isolated and often overlooked, even by those who would develop other deliberative programs in later years.[2]

The present landscape could not be more different. A proliferation of deliberative practices has coincided with a growing interest in citizen engagement. Some of the most widely recognized contemporary approaches include the Deliberative Poll,[3] the Citizens' Assembly,[4] Participatory Budgeting,[5] 21st Century Town Meetings,[6] and many others. These deliberative projects draw on different understandings of deliberation and how it should be practiced (see Chapter 2), yet they have begun to coalesce into something like a civic-intellectual movement. Networks of deliberative practitioners and scholars connected through organizations such as the Deliberative Democracy Consortium all aim toward creating more widespread "discursive participation."[7]

Along with this move toward more widespread deliberation, however, comes the question, *What research designs and evaluation methods are used to assess the processes and outcomes of deliberative projects and programs?* With a wide diversity of agencies and organizations deploying different approaches to deliberative civic engagement, it has become more important than ever to take seriously the *evaluation* of these deliberative processes. At present, no systematic comparisons of alternative deliberative methods exist, though many civic reformers, researchers, and agency officials have ideas about when to use one process over another.[8] Aside from those produced by the sponsors themselves, there are very few detailed and complete evaluations of individual deliberative projects. The main exceptions include interesting but incommensurate collections of analyses, such as those on the 1996 National Issues Convention in Austin, Texas (USA)[9] and the 2004 Citizens' Assembly on Electoral Reform in British Columbia (Canada).[10] Although several deliberative scholars have relied on more comprehensive case studies to analyze deliberative forums,[11] their varying methodology has not provided a clear picture of the best way to perform an evaluation.

More often than not, the research on deliberative projects has severe limitations, at least when judged as comprehensive evaluations. Typical studies and reports, including some by the first author of this chapter, include one or more of the following features: a narrow focus on a particular aspect of the event, such as its deliberative quality; the exclusion of attention to important elements of deliberation, such as participant selection and speaking opportunities; an overreliance on first-person interviews and self-report data; selective vignettes that usually showcase specific participants' positive experiences; particularly compelling moments in an uneven process; the favorable summary judgments of officials or witnesses with no training in ethnography or evaluation; and the optimistic and unsubstantiated attributions of policy or cultural impacts, as proclaimed by public agency staff, columnists, or event organizers. Such reports lack credibility and comparability across projects, so they do little more than continue to highlight the best-case potential of such processes to favorably impress participants, organizers, and officials. These reports tell only a fraction of the entire story, and event organizers do not reap the benefits of constructive criticism. When the stakes are high, as when Healthy Democracy Oregon convinced the Oregon state legislature in 2009 to enact the Citizens' Initiative Review, only a rigorous and thorough review will help organizers see and address the flaws in their design and convince policy makers of the quality and impact of a process.[12]

For a time, these limited evaluations may have served a useful function by sweeping away undue skepticism about the value of citizen deliberation. To improve our understanding of the strengths, weaknesses, and varied impacts of deliberative projects, however, we must begin to evaluate more systematically the design, processes, and outcomes of such activities. This chapter aims to facilitate such comparisons through three main sections. We begin by reviewing briefly the purposes and pitfalls of evaluation to clarify why and how it should be done. We then propose a set of three general evaluation criteria based on past theory, research, and practice. Finally, we suggest measurement approaches for each criterion that can be combined to produce robust evaluations with either small or large research budgets.

Brief Reflections on Evaluation

At the outset, we recognize that deliberation practitioners and researchers some-times have conflicting goals in evaluation. Before discussing evaluative criteria and methods of measuring these, we wish to make a brief argument for how evaluation can simultaneously meet the needs of both parties.

Process and Outcome Orientations to Evaluation

Those who design and implement a deliberative project typically have a very limited budget, almost all of which goes into building and promoting a process (e.g., advertising and recruitment, rental of the meeting space, preparing mate-rials, and providing lodging, expenses, and sometimes compensation for partic-ipants). This often leaves only a pittance for research and evaluation. Moreover, practitioners logically reserve that small portion of funds remaining for targeted evaluations to gather only those kinds of evidence most relevant to prospective funders (or in pursuit of renewal from a current funder). These interest-driven reviews typically focus on whether a project achieves the specific and often narrow goals of the organizer and/or funder.[13] By contrast, researchers often concern themselves with drawing out causes and effects, which makes them par-ticularly interested in measuring inputs and process elements—the indepen-dent and mediating variables that ultimately help to explain variations in project outcomes.[14]

More generally, this reflects a basic distinction between process- and out-come-oriented evaluations. Process evaluations examine the implementation and unfolding character of a project, looking at how the structure of the event and the way that discussion takes place affect its deliberative quality. Also known as "formative" evaluations, the process assessment asks critical ques-tions such as, What aspects of the process were not as strong as hoped? Which planned-for aspects did not actually happen? Prospectively, they also address how to make improvements for the next implementation.[15] By contrast, out-come evaluations focus on the end results and long-term consequences, partic-ularly as they relate to the project's original intended effects.[16] Sometimes called "summative" assessments, these evaluations ask, Did the event 'work'? Did it achieve its goals (e.g., policy impact, increased community support, more enlightened citizens)?[17] Thus, a summative evaluation defines "success" and determines whether the outcomes met that threshold.

When these two forms of evaluation are coupled together, they can try to link process faults to any failures in achieving desired outcomes. In other words, there can be a convergence of interest in making a more thorough evaluation—one that measures the practitioner's key outcome variables and the researcher's process variables. In a sense, the ongoing study of the 2009 Australian Citizens' Parliament illustrates this partnership, with the new Democracy Foundation (the nongovernmental sponsor of the event) having ensured adequate outcome measures, and grants from the Australian Research Council and National Science Foundation (USA) providing the funds for detailed measures of the process itself.

Pragmatic Theoretical Foundations

An evaluation including both process and outcome elements may still be somewhat arbitrary or at least ad hoc if it is not grounded in a foundational theoretical framework, and the continued disconnect between normative and empirical studies of deliberation[18] make determining a standard of deliberation particularly difficult. If practitioners hope to learn from a growing body of evaluations, they will need a framework that allows assessments to be commensurate across a range of different issues, contexts, and deliberative methods. Researchers, meanwhile, already have the burden of tying their particular hypotheses to larger theoretical frameworks, such that we might even develop a stable and conceptually rich deliberative democratic theory "research program."[19]

Some of the earliest efforts to build normative and empirical theories of deliberation began with grand theoretical foundations on the wide-reaching works of Jürgen Habermas and John Rawls.[20] Some early studies of deliberation tried to derive evaluative principles and methods directly from early philosophical work, such as the twin principles of "fairness" and "competence" identified by Thomas Webler and Ortwin Renn.[21] More recently, Habermas' writings provided the inspiration for the first systematic coding scheme for deliberative talk—the Discourse Quality Index (DQI).[22] In both cases, however, we believe the abstractness and foci of the original theories limit the comprehensiveness of these approaches for evaluating deliberation. In particular, they represent a theoretical basis for looking at information, reasoned argument, and procedural safeguards in a deliberative process, but they downplay other design and structural features and treat outcomes as exogenous to evaluation. These efforts seek to evaluate outcomes via the quality or justness of the process, as when Jacob Cohen argues that "outcomes are democratically legitimate if and only if they could be the object of a free and reasoned agreement among equals."[23]

Some practitioners resist evaluative approaches that focus on narrow process elements linked to philosophical theory; however, the result of untethering assessments from theories is that evaluation drifts across a sea of disparate process and outcome indicators. Replacing theoretical abstractions with purpose-driven criteria, such as "success" and "effectiveness," quickly reveals the difficulty of reconciling conflicting values and priorities among practitioners and key stakeholders.[24] A review of thirty evaluation studies of participation highlighted this difficulty, as shown by the considerable range of terminology used to capture process or outcome effectiveness.[25] Incommensurate studies used more than twenty different indicators of process (e.g., inclusivity, comfort, participation rate, structured decision making) and just as many outcome measures (e.g., cost-effectiveness, perceptions of consultation by public officials, time to develop regulations, staff awareness, public trust). Several of the criteria used in deliberation research (e.g., fairness, social impact) remain too broad to allow consistent interpretation, and the inconsistent methods in how evaluators operationalize those criteria make it impossible to draw reliable comparisons or generalizations.[26]

Thus, in the following section, we aim to introduce a set of criteria that both have academic moorings in the larger theories of deliberative democracy *and* have direct significance for practitioners. Moreover, we introduce criteria broad enough to be measurable in a wide range of different deliberative contexts, and we recognize that the purposes of different deliberative designs will make one or another criterion more relevant in an overall assessment of both process and outcomes.

Four Evaluative Criteria

The following criteria should prove useful for evaluating a wide range of projects designed to promote deliberative civic engagement. In designing these criteria, we have drawn on research concerning the wider range of public engagement, participation, and consultation methods, but we intend our criteria to apply specifically to *official or quasi-official processes whereby lay citizens play a central role, often in concert with policy makers and/or stakeholders, in devising solutions to a public problem through a democratic and deliberative process.*[27] (For more discussion about what constitutes deliberative civic engagement, see Chapter 1.) If a deliberative engagement program, project, or event aspires to this general purpose and design, then the following evaluative criteria are appropriate for assessing its overall quality.[28]

At the outset, we wish to stress that *any* deliberative civic engagement process should, at least to some, be evaluated on its own terms. To call themselves deliberative civic engagement projects, however, such efforts either do, or should, share concern with four basic procedural principles: (1) maintaining design integrity, and (2) producing sound deliberation and judgments. In addition, projects can be assessed in terms of the outcomes they engender. Here, more variation occurs between different program objectives, but nearly all projects seek to generate (3) influential conclusions and/or actions. For some processes, it will be enough for deliberation to yield recommendations that carry influence,[29] whereas other programs will emphasize taking direct action, whereby citizens not only talk but *work* together to exert their influence.[30] Finally, the greatest variation in purposes comes from the wide range of (4) long-term effects on public life that deliberative engagement processes hope to realize. Herein, we will consider methods for evaluating a range of these, from beneficial effects on individual citizen participants to broader impacts on the community or even the larger political culture. Chapters 7 and 8 of this volume provide more detailed descriptions of benefits to the individual and community, respectively, but these benefits are also often the concern of evaluators. We label these as long-term effects because they reach beyond the immediate purpose and impact of citizen deliberation, but nearly every deliberative enterprise carries ambitions that extend outward in this way.[31] Deliberative theory and research often concern themselves with such distal impacts.[32]

Criterion 1: Design Integrity

A high-quality deliberative engagement process gains its power partly from the integrity of its development, design, and implementation. This subsumes a number of criteria in the theoretical literature, including procedural "fairness"[33] and "acceptance,"[34] the latter referring to whether the public will perceive a process as fair (and thereby "accept" it as legitimate). We further break down this criterion of design integrity into three more specific subcriteria.

Unbiased framing. The process by which issues are framed for deliberation should be transparent, that is, subject to open criticism by all interested parties. The resulting issue frame should be a fair representation of conflicting views and arguments. Even when the organizers imagine that they have an undefined, "open" issue frame (e.g., "political reform," without specifying any options), it is still the case that they selected that issue and generated language to describe it.

Procedural design involvement. The deliberative procedures themselves should be developed in consultation with (or at least subjected to comment from) interested parties, particularly those with different points of view on the issue at hand, and the resulting process should be consistent with the best practices for deliberation (e.g., rigorous analytic process for studying the problem and generating and evaluating solutions, along with respectful and egalitarian relations among participants). For recurring forums, project designers and evaluators may consider working collaboratively through developmental evaluation, which allows evaluators to continually provide feedback on process design, utilizing the insights gained through evaluation to improve the process.[35] Ideally, this would also include consultation with deliberative participants, whose understanding of deliberation may be more in line with the normative goals of deliberation than that of the organizers.[36]

Representativeness. The selection of citizen participants should give broad opportunity to all potentially interested parties (excluding only those with public offices or unusually high personal/financial stakes in an issue). The resulting body of citizen participants (hereafter called simply a "citizen panel") should prove representative of the general population and, in particular, include representatives from any permanent minorities (i.e., groups for whom public policy consistently goes against their interests) and even smaller-numbered culturally relevant identity groups (i.e., subpublics or communities that seek visible representation in any public deliberative body). (For further discussions of representation and inclusion in deliberative events, see Chapters 3 and 5.)

The integrity of the design constitutes the most fundamental criterion for assessment because it determines whether a process meets the professional standards of deliberative civic engagement practitioners and the philosophical aspirations of deliberation advocates. Moreover, if a process does not manifestly adhere to a sound procedure, policy makers and citizens alike will question its legitimacy and give less credence to any recommendations that may be developed.[37]

Criterion 2: Democratic Deliberation and Judgment

If one can generally assess design integrity prior to the beginning of a deliberative civic engagement event, this second criterion of democratic deliberation and judgment stands out as the *process criterion* in our scheme. We break it into two subparts, first requiring the evaluation of the talk that takes place, then seeking to assess the quality of the judgments that result.

Deliberative analytic process. To count as an instance of "democratic deliberation," a project must meet a high standard for the quality of the talk in which its citizen participants and other actors engage. We use a definition of deliberative public meetings adapted from the one Gastil offered in *Political Communication and Deliberation.*[38] As shown in Table 10.1, a deliberative meeting involves a rigorous analytic process, with a solid information base, explicit prioritization of key values, an identification of alternative solutions (sometimes preconfigured beforehand, but often still subject to amendment), and careful weighing of the pros and cons. Research on group decision making has found that of these analytic elements, careful consideration of *cons* is often the key to a high-quality process, and the emphasis on "hard choices" and "trade-offs" in many deliberation processes reflects this.[39]

Democratic social process. Exclusive focus on problem-solution analysis, per se, would make our conception of deliberation overly rationalistic and ignore the social aspect of deliberation. One might say that the social component of deliberation is what makes it *democratic* deliberation. Requirements of equal opportunity, mutual comprehension and consideration, and respect attempt to mitigate the marginalizing effects of traditional power inequalities and make clear the implicit emphasis on inclusion and diversity in deliberation (see also Chapter 5).[40]

Table 10.1 **Key Features of Democratic Deliberation and Judgment in Public Meetings**

Analytic Process	
Create a solid information base	Combine expertise and professional research with personal experiences to better understand the problem's nature and its impact on people's lives.
Prioritize the key values at stake	Integrate the public's articulation of its core values with technical and legal expressions and social, economic, and environmental costs and benefits.
Identify a broad range of solutions	Identify both conventional and innovative solutions, including governmental and nongovernmental means of addressing the problem.
Weigh the pros, cons, and trade-offs among solutions	Systematically apply the public's priorities to the alternative solutions, emphasizing the most significant trade-offs among alternatives.
Social Process	
Adequately distribute speaking opportunities	Mix unstructured, informal discussion in smaller groups with more structured discussion in larger groups. Create special opportunities for the reticent.
Ensure mutual comprehension	Ensure that public participants can articulate general technical points and ensure that experts and officials are hearing the public's voice.
Consider other ideas and experiences	Listen with equal care to both officials and the general public. Encourage the public to speak in their authentic, unfiltered voice.
Respect other participants	Presume that the general public is qualified to be present, by virtue of their citizenship. Presume officials will act in the public's best interest.
Final Decision-Making Process	
	The decision should be the solution that best addresses the problem, often incorporating complementary approaches when they are mutually reinforcing.
	Final decision-making stages should remain noncoercive and use one of any possible democratic voting systems and decision rules (consensus, majority rule, proportional outcomes, etc.).

Sound judgment. We single out one final element of the deliberative civic engagement process: the quality of the final decision or judgment reached. The concern here is with "competence"—how well the citizen participants are able to reach a sound decision based on the information available to them[41]—as well as equality in decision making. In a sense, this is the logical output of deliberative analysis: Participants weigh a mix of high-quality data, meaningful personal experiences, and diverse perspectives in the course of establishing priorities, forming well-reasoned judgments, and participating in a fair process of decision making. Independent of assessing deliberation, however, deliberative civic engagement programs should show signs of high-quality judgment reached under egalitarian methods.

In moving toward sound judgment, deliberation sustains a healthy tension between clash and consensus. On the one hand, public deliberation should include periods of manifest disagreement among the citizens (or "panelists") on both questions of fact and more fundamental moral issues. During deliberation, disagreements will arise, and panelists must be willing to dispute each other's claims and offer competing moral and values arguments. The absence of such a clash would suggest excessive consensus-seeking among citizens who surely have genuine differences in experiences and values. On the other hand, deliberative groups should be able to work through their differences in a process of learning from and understanding the perspective of other panelists, allowing them to shift their opinions and often reach broad agreement when assessing initiatives. Narrow majority views should sometimes grow into large majorities, and minority viewpoints should sometimes grow into successful majorities (see Chapter 5).

In sum, citizens' judgments should become more "enlightened" because of the information presented, the views put forward, and the careful, honest discussions among participants.[42] After deliberating, participants should demonstrate more informed and coherent views on initiative-related issues after participating in panel discussions. Partipants should be able to give reasons for their views, and they should be able to explain the arguments underlying alternative points of view.

Criterion 3: Influential Conclusions/Actions

Once implemented, a successful deliberative civic engagement process should show clear evidence of impact. Depending on the particular design and mission, for example, a process might directly establish policy, shape the policy-making process, or influence the actions of the wider public, among other possible goals. We again identify two subparts to this criterion: influential recommendations and effective action.

Influential recommendations. A handful of citizen deliberative processes, such as the jury system in the United States, already have a direct means of impact—rendering verdicts in a particular case. Likewise, participatory budgeting has a direct means of exercising citizen authority.[43] In most other cases, however, deliberative projects simply aim to advise or offer policy proposals, similar to the role of the forums designed to advise health policy makers discussed in Chapter 9. Influence in these cases amounts to affecting the odds that a policy proposal will succeed or fail in light of citizen recommendations. Specifically, when a clear majority of panelists favors a particular policy initiative, its chances of prevailing should increase, and the reverse should be true when citizens oppose a policy. Thus, when the 2002 "Listening to the City" town meeting rejected plans for developing the World Trade Center site, it had the effect of scuttling designs that might well have gone forward otherwise.[44] More affirmatively, Deliberative Polls held in Texas led that state's public utilities to follow citizen recommendations to increase their emphasis on renewable resources.[45]

Effective, coordinated action. Deliberative bodies that attempt to generate change through direct action should be able to coordinate their post-deliberative efforts to thereby change the relevant voluntary actions taken by the larger public, which may indirectly spark policy changes (depending on whether the citizens' action plan involves public policy change). Such projects are the focus of organizations like Everyday Democracy, which aims to empower communities not only to advocate policy changes but also to transform their civic culture and mobilize the public to take direct action to address local problems.[46]

Criterion 4: Long-Term Effects

If deliberative processes are implemented and the evidence shows that citizens are reaching sound and influential judgments and/or transforming public action, that would be enough to warrant their widespread adoption. Nonetheless, it is important to examine other potential outcomes because many deliberative civic engagement programs stress the impact they have on the participants themselves, the wider public, or macro-level political processes. To give a sense of the range of these secondary, long-term effects in relation to governance, we describe and suggest evaluation approaches for three such benefits: transforming public attitudes and habits, changing public officials, and altering strategic political choices.

Transforming public attitudes and habits. In the long term, deliberative civic engagement efforts could transform not only their participants but also the larger public.[47] Those participating in, engaged with, or captivated by such efforts should report stable (or rising) levels of public trust and signs of reduced civic neglect. Voter turnout in elections might increase, and citizens should develop political beliefs (e.g., a sense of political self-confidence or efficacy) conducive to varied forms of public participation (e.g., attending public meetings, using public affairs media). Chapter 7 provides a more detailed description of potential cognitive and behavioral benefits of deliberation, as well as measures for gauging change.

Changing public officials' attitudes/behavior. Citizen deliberation could also change how public officials think and behave in relation to the larger public. Government officials could develop more favorable views of the judgments that citizens make during deliberative events. Officials should also demonstrate an awareness of the importance of citizen deliberation and come to respect judgments made through such efforts. As a sign of improved leadership, elected representatives (and agency officials) could also begin to step away from conventional public opinion on initiatives in anticipation of deliberatively produced judgments to the contrary. Effective deliberation can even change officials' attitudes toward the prospects of deliberation itself, as happened in Oregon, where some legislators opted to support renewal of the Citizens' Initiative Review in 2011 after seeing the success of its first round of deliberations.[48]

Altering strategic political choices. In addition, public deliberation could change the strategic choices made by political campaign professionals during elections. For instance, deliberative processes will have transformed the electoral environment if initiative and policy campaigns begin to focus more of their energy on addressing the issues raised by deliberative panels (e.g., holding debates focused on panel issues) and incorporating deliberative panel results into campaign advertising. A more far-reaching effect could be the emergence of routine pilot-testing of potential initiatives with low-cost varieties of "deliberative polling" or citizen review panels in an effort to understand how the public will view a prospective initiative after deliberating.[49]

Sequential Elements of a Multimethod Evaluation

At this point, we have introduced the four evaluative criteria but only in conceptual terms. In the remainder of this chapter, we offer ways to *measure* each of these criteria. Sensitive to the constraints most deliberative events face, we also suggest low-budget, minimally satisfactory evaluative approaches for each criterion. Table 10.2 summarizes our measurement recommendations, matching the criteria for deliberation with each (approximately) sequential element of a deliberative civic engagement process—from project set-up to long-term effects. Before detailing measurement methods, we first describe these sequential elements of public deliberation in more detail, as well as the appropriate means for collecting data during each stage of evaluation.

Cultural/Political Contextual Analysis

Though we do not choose to include it in Table 10.2, we begin by noting that a thorough evaluation begins with an appreciation for the context in which a deliberative civic engagement event takes place. If one indulges the postmodern impulse to think of a deliberative event as a "text," it should be clear that the social context in which the text is embedded shapes the meaning of the event itself and the discussions that take place.[50] The context influences how deliberative events come into being, their structure, and their process and outcomes.[51] Taking context into account simply makes the other data found in the course of an evaluation more meaningful and interpretable.

Project Setup

The remaining forms of data follow the course of a deliberative civic engagement project from its inception to its aftermath, beginning with its initial design and implementation. Project setup involves the selection of materials and participants, as well as the selection and framing of topics. The study of the project requires scrutinizing everything from archival materials to census data for the target population for the event. Usually done post hoc, this can involve third-party interviews with organizers and interested parties; at other times, direct observation of the project setup will be possible, such as when the organizers themselves are conducting a self-assessment.

Structural Features

Studying the structure of the deliberation means looking at the framework within which the public conducts its discussions. This includes: attention to the presentation of information, values, and solutions; instructions and logistical designs for using information and interacting with other participants; and the formal role of facilitators (if present). Researchers must consider how organizers deploy background materials or witnesses in the event, as well as how they allocate time for specific tasks such as values clarification and the weighing of trade-offs. A final consideration is the physical setting used for deliberation, such as the official markers of authority (quality of furniture, seating arrangements of citizens and officials) that may serve as indicators of preferred values or ways of interacting. Assessing these structural features requires looking not only at the official agenda but also at some record of the proceedings, whether first-hand observation by the evaluator or another basic record of the setting and sequence of events.

Table 10.2 **Methods for Evaluating Each of the Criteria and Subcriteria (Low-Cost, Minimal Measures in Bold) for a Deliberative Civic Engagement Project**

	Project Setup	Structural Features of Agenda	Discussion Process	Subjective Experience	Final Output	Policy Impact	Long-Term Effects
Sequential Elements of the Deliberative Process and Outcomes							
	Archival documents and interviews	Official agenda and record of proceedings	Video, transcript, and/or direct observation	Participant surveys and interviews	Final participant recommendations, judgments, or public statement	Policy analysis, elite interviews, and media accounts	Surveys and interviews with participants, public, and/or officials
1. Design Integrity							
1a. Unbiased Framing	**Review planning documents and** interview planners and interested parties						
1b. Procedural Design Involvement							
1c. Representativeness	**Compare participant demographics with census data and** compare participant attitudes with population survey data						

(continued)

Table 10.2 (continued)

		Sequential Elements of the Deliberative Process and Outcomes					
	Project Setup	Structural Features of Agenda	Discussion Process	Subjective Experience	Final Output	Policy Impact	Long-Term Effects
2a. Democratic Deliberation and Judgment: Analytic Process							
2a.1. Information	**Adequate of search and selection of informative materials and witnesses**	**Adequate time for testimony and cross-examination**	Scrutinizing information (and adding personal experience when appropriate)	Surveys assessing increased knowledge			
2a.2. Values Evaluations		**Adequate time for considering deeper values**	Explicit discussion of values	Surveys assessing values-basis of choices	Presence of clear values in statement (if appropriate)		
2a.3. Range of Alternatives	**Sufficiently broad range of approaches included in materials and embodied in witnesses**	Diversity of views presented by witnesses; time reserved for identifying new solutions (if appropriate)	Exploration of full spectrum of alternatives available				
2a.4. Weighing Pros and Cons		Structuring time for weighing the pros and cons and the cross-examination of witnesses	**Explicit discussion of trade-offs;** connection of values and information to choices				

Sequential Elements of the Deliberative Process and Outcomes

	Project Setup	Structural Features of Agenda	Discussion Process	Subjective Experience	Final Output	Policy Impact	Long-Term Effects
2b. Democratic Deliberation and Judgment: Social Process							
2b.1 Equality of Opportunity to Speak		Procedural safeguards meant to ensure equality (e.g., round-robins)	Assess frequency of talk by individuals and by viewpoints; note interruption patterns and facilitator behavior	**Assessment of whether one had an adequate chance to express views, particularly dissenting ones**			
2b.2 Comprehension	Clarity of briefing materials	Witness contextualization of information	Noting when people ask for clarifications	Understanding of issue complexities			
2b.3 Consideration		Time to reflect; Not in debate format too long	Presence of questions, feedback, reflective talk	Consideration of other views			
2b.4 Respect		Dis/respectful behavior modeled by witnesses and staff; rules for talk	Dis/respect shown directly in talk	Sense of feeling respected by other participants			

(*continued*)

Table 10.2 (*continued*)

	Sequential Elements of the Deliberative Process and Outcomes						
Criterion/Data	Project Setup	Structural Features of Agenda	Discussion Process	Subjective Experience	Final Output	Policy Impact	Long-Term Effects
2c. Democratic Deliberation and Judgment: Final Decision	Clear articulation of the charge/question put to the citizen deliberators	**Adequate time allotted for making final decisions**	Substantive discussion of clear points of disagreement	Recognition of trade-offs and downsides of preferred choice; satisfaction with and commitment to decision	**Check for supermajority; third-party assessment of decision in light of available information**		
3. Influential Conclusions/Actions							
3a. Influential Recommendations						**Third-party assessment of policy impact**	
3b. Effective, Coordinated Action							Large-scale, longitudinal population surveys and case study analysis

220

Sequential Elements of the Deliberative Process and Outcomes

Criterion/Data	Project Setup	Structural Features of Agenda	Discussion Process	Subjective Experience	Final Output	Policy Impact	Long-Term Effects
4. Secondary Benefits							
4a. Transforming Public Attitudes and Habits							**Post-deliberation participant survey;** Longitudinal survey (and analysis of voting records) for both deliberation participants and wider public
4b. Changing Public Officials' Attitudes/ Behavior							**Interviews with public officials;** Legislative and institutional policy analysis
4c. Altering Strategic Political Choices							Intensive interviews and strategic document analysis within policy-relevant interest groups

Discussion Process

The evaluation of deliberation requires examining directly its content and social dynamics. Questions, claims, narratives, and reflective talk that include explicit discussions of information, values, and trade-offs can unveil the analytic processes. Similarly, the presence of turn taking, interruptions, and references to others and their ideas can indicate levels of equality, comprehension, consideration, and respect. The form of decision making, whether through majoritarian voting, consensus, or some other means, may also indicate the quality of deliberation, particularly if minorities are silenced in the process. Two approaches to examining the discourse of deliberation are generally undertaken: content analysis[52] and discourse/narrative analysis.[53] Although a comprehensive method for coding the content of deliberation has not yet been developed, the adaptation of a coding scheme such as the DQI[54] to include alternative ways of speaking and a means for measuring the democratic quality of the discourse may allow for uniform comparisons of deliberative talk across contexts. One can further distinguish between micro-analytic approaches that closely examine the transcripts through content or discourse analysis and macro-analytic approaches that use coders to measure the degree of deliberation in the process as a whole.[55] These methods reveal how deliberation operates and how individuals interact when engaged in deliberation.

Because the meaning of texts can be revealed only by attention to the particular context in which it is embedded, qualitative discourse analysis is the most thorough means of examining deliberation, but it is also the most intensive and interpretive methodology, requiring considerable skill and time. Similar drawbacks accompany attempts to analyze transcripts through content analysis, and these are coupled with the difficulty of creating a replicable coding scheme that adequately captures the multiple requirements of deliberative discussion. Thus, although a low-budget evaluation may maintain its quality through the inclusion of the other evaluative criteria discussed in this chapter, it might unfortunately (but often necessarily) include little systematic analysis of the deliberation itself.

Subjective Experience

A thorough evaluation of deliberation must differentiate between the manifest features of talk and the subjective experiences of deliberators themselves. The satisfaction rating popular among deliberation practitioners represents a minimal form of this assessment method.[56] Revealing participants' perceptions and recollections of trade-offs, values, and disagreements can add value, but self-report data have particular salience when trying to assess the distribution of speaking opportunities, the depth of comprehension and consideration, and measures of whether participants felt treated with respect.

Final Output

The product of the deliberation, whether a written statement, verbal decision, press release, or other form of discourse, merits analysis in its own right. Researchers evaluating output may again turn to either discourse analysis or content analysis. The output of deliberation indicates the quality of the decision and may include markers of information, values, and trade-offs considered in the deliberation. Whether the output mentions or provides space for opposing views or minority opinions may also testify to the level of equality in the deliberation and reveal the presence (or lack) of mutual comprehension, consideration, and respect.

Policy Impact

It is often difficult to establish baseline probabilities for policy outcomes, and this complicates the assessment of policy impact.[57] The most effective approach is probably to employ a third-party evaluator who combines all relevant documentation with interviews, preferably both before and well after a deliberative event (Chapter 9 provides examples of such assessment). Long-term assessment, in particular, could determine whether the influence of the deliberative engagement builds (or erodes) over time, for both participants and conveners. The same basic methods apply when attempting to trace collective action back to a deliberative project, with the emphasis shifting from policy analysis to sociological investigation. The latter might entail large-scale longitudinal surveys to assess public behavior because it becomes more critical that the investigator look beyond the choices made by key strategic actors.

Long-Term Effects

Well after a deliberative event has concluded, an evaluation can continue if organizers wish to assess the impact that a project had over a longer time frame. Longitudinal studies of the participants can show how deliberation reshapes attitudes and behaviors, such as research showing how criminal jury deliberation produces changes in jurors' voting frequency years after having completed their service at the courthouse.[58] Similarly, Gastil has conducted a study of how participants in the Australian Citizens' Parliament had changed a full year after completing their deliberations,[59] and Nabatchi has examined the longer-term impacts of deliberation on participants' perceptions of political efficacy.[60] Tracing effects beyond the event participants themselves requires the addition of population surveys, interviews with key public actors or officials, and other intensive follow-up analyses—rarely done by researchers seeking closure on case studies and practitioners who have moved onto the next project even before the first one ended.

Measurement Methods for Evaluation

Table 10.2 provides measurement notes broken down by each of the four evaluation criteria and subcriteria, but here we add more detail about design integrity, the deliberative process, the soundness of citizens' judgments, and long-term impacts.

Measuring Design Integrity

In general, one can assess these design features through direct inspection of relevant project records, along with interviews of organizers and interested third parties. Each of the three elements of design integrity, however, requires different forms of data.

Whenever possible, the fairness of the "issue frame" should be evaluated before the deliberative body convenes and reaches its conclusion. (A "frame" is the way in which a problem is described and potential solutions are arrayed.) This way, evaluations of the frame will not constitute post hoc reactions to the outcomes. A neutral third party (e.g., unaffiliated university researcher or program evaluation specialist) can do such evaluation independently, through inspection of project documents and procedures, to judge whether the framing process was neutral and transparent. Ideally, however, this process is evaluated by interested parties from all relevant perspectives. The latter approach offers a more varied perspective on the procedure's fairness to the particular concerns of different interest/advocacy groups.

Assessing procedural design involvement follows the same basic protocol as issue frame evaluation, with two exceptions. First, it is useful to get preliminary process assessments before deliberation begins, but whenever possible, it is helpful to complement these with assessments during and after deliberation. The actual implementation of the deliberative procedures may shape the final evaluations thereof. Second, to ensure commensurate evaluations, it is also important to discuss with each evaluator—including interested parties—the conception of deliberation underlying the process design.

With regard to representativeness, the final body of citizens who attend the event (versus those who register or pledge to attend) should be surveyed to determine their relevant demographic and ideographic (attitudinal) characteristics. These characteristics can then be compared against relevant census and survey data for the targeted geographic/political region. This can be more expensive when the target area does not have a readily available census or survey profile, as in the case of a watershed, transit-area, "biozone," or other nonstandard region.

Measuring Democratic Deliberation

Because of the complexity of democratic deliberation, it is exceedingly difficult to reduce evaluations of the different processes into one aggregate score.[61] Further muddying the evaluative process, the quality of deliberation does not solely depend on the communication that takes place. The context and structure of the discussion, as well as the decision reached and the participants' experiences, affect the completeness of a deliberative act. Operationalizing deliberation necessitates attention to these and other elements. Recognizing this, scholars have broken deliberation into three dimensions: input, process, and outcome.[62] Along similar lines, Table 10.2 suggests that measures of deliberation can include many elements—from a project's setup to its final output—with the greatest emphasis on the content of the deliberation itself and participants' subjective experiences thereof.

Measuring Soundness of Judgments

We place special emphasis on the final element of deliberation—the final statement, recommendation, or judgments reached in the course of a deliberative project. Here, we suggest more details on how to make this difficult evaluation. First, systematic coding of an audio (or preferably video, for ease of transcription) record of the deliberation can establish whether disagreement took place. This can be complemented with interviews of participants to determine whether they subjectively experienced such disagreements and whether there were any *potential* disagreements that they chose not to bring forward (i.e., internally censored).

Second, the presence of supermajority support for a recommendation is assessed directly from the event records when formal votes are taken by the citizen deliberators. In all cases, it helps to survey the participants afterward, to learn the degree to which they (privately) supported any final recommendations. More indirect survey items can measure the extent to which participants recognize the trade-offs they faced, the downsides of the choice they made, and the best arguments for each alternative.[63] Other indirect measures of judgment quality include assessing participants' political reflections and decision knowledge, which should have developed as a result of their having participated in a deliberative process with others.[64]

Third, participants' final judgment can be evaluated by a neutral third party, as well as interested parties, to obtain their varied assessments of its soundness. In these cases (and those where no final judgment is reached), it is also helpful to combine an analysis of the deliberation with a survey of participants, so that one can assess the degree to which the information and perspectives provided in the event shaped citizens' individual views on the issue. In particular, post-deliberation citizens should be more knowledgeable, have better correspondence between their views and relevant facts, and understand the *cons* of whatever recommendation they ultimately made.

Evaluating Long-Term Effects

The methods of evaluation used to assess these secondary outcomes can be as varied as the potential impacts themselves. One can assess impacts on participants and the larger public through survey research and the inspection of election records (in those countries where voting is not mandatory). Examples abound for what to include in such surveys and how to assess it, but the best examples include longitudinal assessment (to establish change over time), comparison groups (to differentiate deliberation's impact from those effects of other social/political forces), and a wide variety of measures (e.g., breaking down efficacy into multiple subcomponents, such as self-efficacy versus collective efficacy or the sense of effectiveness when acting in a group).[65] Again, Chapter 7 provides a more thorough discussion of potential individual level changes and the some options for measurement.

To assess changes in public officials, survey methods likely will fail, owing to poor response rates conventionally obtained among elites. Instead, one should assess these outcomes through interviews with public officials and in-depth, longitudinal legislative and policy analyses that compare processes before and after the deliberative civic engagement, in light of other changes in the political/legislative environment.

Finally, one can assess these outcomes through interviews with public officials, lobbyists, campaign officials, and political activists. This can prove especially challenging, as it requires accessing internal strategic decisions (or documentation thereof) within organizations whose interests may not be well served by such investigation. If one can obtain such data, however, it is possible to detect signs of the deliberative process exerting its influence. For instance, policy initiatives that fail to pass muster in trial runs (i.e., in the mock deliberative polls described earlier) are subsequently withdrawn. This can indicate that anticipation of the eventual deliberative civic engagement process is causing more careful vetting of the proposals such a group might put before policy makers and the general public.

Conclusion: Integrating Evaluative Methods into Overall Assessments

Once again, Table 10.2 summarizes the preceding discussion to show how the different elements of evaluation correspond to the four criteria. The most low-budget evaluation should still contain the elements of Table 10.2 that are highlighted in bold type. Those pieces are important and inexpensive in terms of both cost and time. The rest of the table augments these basic methods with additional assessment tools, which may require more labor, money, and time. Whether one's evaluation requires more than a basic method depends on one's resources and goals, but it is important to recognize the limitations of the basic evaluation approaches in terms of their reliability and validity.

In addition, it is important to consider how one *integrates* these various evaluation metrics. That is, how does one move from separate assessments of each criterion (or subcomponent) to an evaluation of the deliberative civic engagement project as a whole? This depends, again, on one's conception of the project, but the approach outlined in this chapter and summarized later will apply to many such programs.

Each of the three elements of the Design Integrity criterion count as pass-fail elements, and a subpar evaluation on any one of these yields a negative summary evaluation of the entire process. That is, if any aspect of the design failed to meet basic standards for integrity, the other outcomes of the process are all suspect.

The three elements of the Sound Deliberation and Judgment criterion are parts of a coherent whole, such that one arrives at a single assessment of Deliberation/Judgment in light of each element. The third of these might be most important (i.e., the coherence and soundness of the group's judgments), but this should be weighed by how rich the disagreement was and how effectively the group could move toward a supermajority. Outstanding performance on two of these criteria might obviate poor performance on another, but outright failure on either the first (disagreement) or third (quality of judgment) should yield an overall assessment of program failure.

The Influential Conclusions/Actions criteria are different, in that some programs will emphasize only one—or even *neither*—of these criteria. All deliberative civic engagement programs, however, should orient toward one or the other to at least a degree, lest deliberation become seen as "merely" discussion, disconnected from action. Even then, however, poor performance on a program's relevant influence criterion does not impugn the entire exercise; rather, it suggests the need for improving the component of the program that leverages influence.

Finally, the Long-Term Effects criterion stands apart from all these other criteria, in that program success may not require evidence of these impacts. If a program is well designed, deliberative, and influential, these become "bonus" effects, not strictly necessary for justifying the citizen engagement program, per se. In the long run, however, these secondary benefits could be of tremendous value for the public and its political culture. A more engaged public, legitimate institutions, and responsible, deliberative politics could dramatically increase the capacity for shared governance and public action and, ultimately, yield much better public policy. Such potential impacts should be assessed, because evidence of these changes could increase the estimated value of deliberative civic engagement, thereby warranting the time and resource expenses it requires.

As the number and type of deliberative civic engagement forums proliferates, understanding what works best requires a standardized means for evaluating deliberation. In this chapter, we have tried to provide a framework for future researchers and practitioners and hope that by applying this evaluative scheme to a number of different cases, we can begin to more systematically assess best practices and better understand both the processes and outcomes of deliberative events.

Notes

1. Portions of this essay are adapted from Gastil (2009a).
2. For the history of a variety of deliberative public engagement practices, see Gastil and Levine (2005).
3. Fishkin (2009c).
4. See Warren and Pearse (2008).
5. Baiocchi (2001, 2003).
6. Lukensmeyer, Goldman, and Brigham (2005).
7. The term comes from Jacobs, Cook, and Delli Carpini (2009), as discussed in Chapter 3 of this volume.
8. Examples of such process-choice charts include those produced by McMaster University (http://www.vcn.bc.ca/citizens-handbook/compareparticipation.pdf), the National Coalition for Dialogue and Deliberation (http://www.thataway.org/?page_id=1487), and the International Association for Public Participation (http://www.iap2.org/associations/4748/files/spectrum.pdf and http://www.iap2.org/associations/4748/files/toolbox.pdf).
9. McCombs and Reynolds (1999).
10. Warren and Pearse (2008). An edited volume on the 2009 Australian Citizens' Parliament being led by Australian deliberation scholar Lyn Carson is also in production. See Dryzek (2009) and Hartz-Karp and Carson (2009).
11. Button and Mattson (1999); Edwards, Hindmarsh, Mercer, Bond, and Rowland (2008); Hartz-Karp (2005); Mendelberg and Oleske (2000).
12. Gastil and Knobloch (2010).
13. Beierle and Konisky (2000: 589); see also Chess (2000: 775).
14. For example, Farrar, Fishkin, Green, List, Luskin, and Paluck (2010).
15. Rossi, Lipsey, and Freeman (2004: 34).
16. Weiss (1998: 334–335).
17. Rossi, Lipsey, and Freeman (2004: 36).

18. Thompson (2008). For examples of process and impact evaluation frameworks for citizen participation, see Nabatchi 2012a.
19. We use the term in the general sense meant by Lakatos (1978: 83–104). For an example of this concept's application to a social scientific theory, see Gastil (1994).
20. See Habermas (1979, 1984, 1987) and Rawls (1971, 1993). For their use and critique, see Benhabib (1996), Joshua Cohen ([1989] 1997a), and Pellizzoni (2001).
21. Webler and Renn (1995).
22. Steenbergen, Bächtiger, Spörndli, and Steiner (2003).
23. Cohen ([1989] 1997a: 21).
24. Abelson and Gauvin (2006: 7).
25. Rowe and Frewer (2004); see also Rowe and Frewer (2000).
26. Rowe and Frewer (2004); see also Abelson and Gauvin (2006).
27. This definition is adapted from Gastil (2008).
28. After all, nothing is learned when one's research simply establishes that a program intended simply to "inform" the public does not engage citizens in a meaningful dialogue. Similarly, little is gained when a program with no clear values or intentions—but clearly no deliberative element in its design—turns out, on closer inspection, to *indeed* lack deliberative features.
29. For instance, Citizen Juries have traditionally played this advisory role (Crosby and Nethercut 2005). Fishkin (2009c) emphasizes this consultative role for Deliberative Polls.
30. To get a sense for more action-oriented engagement, see examples in Leighninger (2006).
31. Leighninger (2006) stresses such impacts. For a readable account of the wider aims of deliberative democracy, see Gutmann and Thompson (2004).
32. See Burkhalter, Gastil, and Kelshaw (2002), Delli Carpini, Cook, and Jacobs (2004), Gastil (2008), Mendelberg (2002), and Ryfe (2005).
33. Webler and Tuler (2000: 568) define fairness as "the opportunity for all interested or affected parties to assume any legitimate role in the decision-making process."
34. Rowe and Frewer's (2000: 12–15) acceptance criteria include representativeness, independence, early involvement, influence, and transparency.
35. Patton (1994).
36. Polletta (2008).
37. Rowe and Frewer (2004). A concern about design integrity is part of what motivated practitioners to service mark Citizens' Jury and Deliberative Poll, lest those terms be used too loosely to describe low-quality processes.
38. Gastil (2008).
39. Orlitzky and Hirokawa (2001).The National Issues Forums is one such process that stresses trade-offs (http://www.nifi.org).
40. Dahlberg (2005).
41. Webler and Tuler (2000: 571) say that a competent process should provide "access to information and its interpretations" while employing "the best available procedures for knowledge selection."
42. In the sense of Dahl's (1989) "enlightened understanding."
43. Baiocchi (2001, 2003).
44. Lukensmeyer, Goldman, and Brigham (2005).
45. Fishkin (2009c).
46. Numerous cases are available at everydaydemocracy.org; see also Scully and McCoy (2005).
47. This is sometimes called "community impact," which includes a variety of indicators, including higher voter turnout, increased cooperation between sectors (public, private, non-profit) and greater community capacity (Friedman, Kadlec, and Birnback 2007: 7–8).
48. When the first two authors of this chapter presented our evaluation of the Oregon Citizens' Initiative Review (CIR), we witnessed first-hand the changing attitudes of some skeptical legislators, who were impressed both by the output of the CIR citizen panels and by the impact the process had on public opinion, which we were able to demonstrate (see Gastil and Knobloch 2010). For a discussion about what legislators want and need to know about public deliberation, see Nabatchi and Farrar (2011).

49. This would be lower-grade equivalents of the polls described by Fishkin and Farrar (2005) or the Citizens' Initiative Review implemented in Oregon.
50. Halliday (1978); Foucault (1980).
51. Mendelberg and Oleske (2000); Muhlberger (2005a).
52. Steiner, Bächtiger, Spörndli, and Steenbergen (2004).
53. See Black (2008); Ryfe (2006).
54. Steenbergen, Bächtiger, Spörndli, and Steiner (2003); see also Steiner (2012).
55. Black, Burkhalter, Gastil, and Stromer-Galley (2010).
56. For instance, the Crosby and Nethercut (2005) report found consistently high satisfaction ratings with Citizen Juries. Process/decision satisfaction was also a primary measure in Gastil, Burkhalter, and Black's (2007) evaluation of jury deliberation.
57. For a good example of an attempt to assess a range of policy-relevant impacts, see Guston (1999).
58. Gastil, Deess, Weiser, and Simmons (2010).
59. This research is in progress. For more information, contact the first author at jwg22@psu.edu.
60. Nabatchi (2007, 2010).
61. Burkhalter, Gastil, and Kelshaw (2002: 418) recommend studying deliberation as a "multi-dimensional concept, rather than simply seeking an aggregate 'deliberation score.'"
62. Black, Burkhalter, Gastil, and Stromer-Galley (2010); Edwards, Hindmarsh, Mercer, Bond, and Rowland (2008).
63. On the development of argument repertoires, see Cappella, Price, and Nir (2002).
64. Muhlberger and Weber (2006:11, 18).
65. On varied measures of attitudinal impact in longitudinal data, see Gastil, Black, Deess, and Leighter (2008). On assessing change in voting behavior resulting from deliberation, see Gastil, Deess, Weiser, and Simmons (2010). On different approaches to measuring efficacy, see Gastil (2004).

PART FOUR

CONCLUSION

11

Listening and Responding to Criticisms of Deliberative Civic Engagement

LOREN COLLINGWOOD AND JUSTIN REEDY

> Public deliberation falls short of meeting the lofty hopes of democratic theorists who imagined it would . . . resurrect the citizen-ruler of ancient Athens.
> —Lawrence R. Jacobs, Fay Lomax Cook, and Michael X. Delli Carpini, in *Talking Together: Public Deliberation and Political Participation in America.*

Picture a national deliberative forum that has been scheduled to discuss issues of the day, such as national security or health care, with the ultimate goal of providing sound policy recommendations to legislators. The event's organizers work studiously to set up a very good convention, but they must still clear numerous obstacles to succeed. What if the citizens who show up to the forum do not constitute a representative sample of the population, resulting in some voices being under- or overrepresented? What if small discussion groups in the forum fall into rancorous discord rather than reasoned debate, or simply fail to reach a meaningful consensus? What if participants' policy recommendations fall flat with legislators, who question the viability of the citizens' proposals? Such hazards worry even the most experienced deliberative practitioner.

As the previous chapters have helped illustrate, deliberative civic engagement can have advantages over some other systems of governance, such as the traditional representative republican government found in many democracies. Chief among these are the tenets on which deliberative civic engagement rests—deeper citizen involvement, thoughtful dialogue, respect for diverse viewpoints, and smarter policy decisions that garner democratic legitimacy.

Whereas previous chapters in this compendium have touched on challenges facing deliberative civic engagement, this chapter focuses entirely on the criticisms leveled against such processes. Specifically, this chapter addresses the

Table 11.1 **Summary of the Major Criticisms of Deliberative Civic Engagement and Responses**

Theoretical Criticisms	*Evaluation and Response*
Citizens are disengaged from politics and are not motivated to participate in deliberative civic engagement processes.	Participants in deliberative civic engagement processes value the experience precisely because it engenders the sense of efficacy they do not feel in conventional politics. Moreover, some deliberative processes require intensive engagement only from a smaller segment of society willing to participate.
Deliberative civic engagement is too idealistic in its goals of intense, equitable, dispassionate participation by the citizenry.	Deliberation has shown itself to be a practical, achievable public practice. While the ideal descriptions advanced by theorists may not be compelling to average citizens, their frustrations with conventional politics and their appreciation for deliberation have made it possible to recruit and retain large, diverse numbers of participants.
The approach of reasoned, fact-based argumentation in deliberative civic engagement favors some groups in society over others.	Deliberative practitioners have worked earnestly to accommodate alternative styles of communication, argumentation, and evidence, trying to ensure that groups are not systematically disadvantaged by the format of deliberation. Critiques of power imbalances caused by deliberation have little empirical support, and evidence suggests deliberation can be effective in addressing these imbalances. Enclave deliberation among societal groups can help these groups see some benefits of deliberation before entering into discussions in the wider public sphere.
People are too prone to preconceptions and prejudices that keep them from having an open mind, and group discussion leads to disagreement and a deepening of existing divisions.	Because deliberative forums are designed to encourage deeper analysis and open-mindedness, they seem to be more effective than conventional political processes at dealing with prejudices and implicit attitudes. In practice, deliberation tends to produce common ground, shared goals, and consideration of many views and alternative options.

Practical Criticisms	Evaluation and Response
No single model of deliberation is most effective.	A patchwork of deliberative reforms may be more appropriate than focusing on a single cure-all approach.
The structure of particular deliberative events can introduce bias, for example, through the selection of topics or participants.	Deliberative scholars should be wary of allowing any event to claim the mantle of deliberation without ensuring that it is fair and unbiased. Organizers should ensure they allow for the representation of a wide range of views.
Deliberation is disconnected from public policy formation.	Policy-related deliberative forums have been successful, and practitioners are working to tie deliberation more strongly to policy making and direct democracy.
Deliberation many have negative individual-level effects, and deliberative forums are too costly for regular use.	Evidence shows that deliberative civic engagement can benefit participants. The costs of such processes vary considerably. Given the benefits, and the potential to reduce costs in the longer term, upfront costs may be worthwhile.
Deliberation detracts from efforts to address more fundamental conflicts among political groups and views.	Deliberative scholars and practitioners should work to ensure representation of diverse viewpoints. Deliberative civic engagement can help mobilize minorities, thereby giving more attention to their concerns.

questions, *What are the critics' views on deliberative civic engagement, and given what we know, what, if any, are the most persuasive counterarguments?* To this end, we focus first on theoretical concerns, including citizen motivation and aptitude, idealism, deliberation as reason-based argumentation, and cognition and open-mindedness. We then turn to practical concerns, including models of deliberation, the ability to represent diverse viewpoints, public policy outcomes, and individual benefits from deliberation. Finally, we take on a political concern, namely, that policy deliberation draws attention away from more fundamental issues of inequality and social justice. These criticisms and rebuttals are summarized in Table 11.1. In examining the views of critics, this chapter provides a wider perspective on the potential pitfalls of deliberative civic engagement, as well as its prospective advantages in producing effective, legitimate policy, and in helping citizens become better connected to governance.

Theoretical Criticisms

There are four broad theoretical arguments against deliberative civic engagement. First, some scholars wonder whether citizens are motivated sufficiently to participate in civic engagement processes. Second, some argue that the goals of deliberative engagement are too idealistic. Third, some believe that the nature of deliberation, with its rational, reason-based argumentation, privileges some members of society over others, and consequently suggest that reasoned argument may not be the best approach for discussing public issues. Finally, some question whether people come to a group discussion and remain open-minded, and whether group decision making helps people decide on contentious issues or merely deepens existing divisions.

Citizens' Motivation and Aptitude

The first criticism, that voters are not willing or motivated enough to meet the participatory requirements of deliberative civic engagement, has been put forth by several scholars. One notable example is a critique that received mention in Chapters 1, 3, and 8. In *Stealth Democracy: Americans' Beliefs about How Government Should Work*, political scientists John R. Hibbing and Elizabeth Theiss-Morse argue that voters simply do not want to participate at the levels that direct democracy enthusiasts appear to encourage. They claim that most voters would prefer to participate less in the political process. People lead busy lives and overall do not have the time or energy to devote to a participatory lifestyle. Moreover, voters are self-conscious not only about their own ability to participate effectively, but also about the ability of the American public writ large. That is,

Hibbing and Theiss-Morse claim that voters' interest in more participation is "tempered by worries over their own ability and the ability of the American people to understand the issues involved." The disengagement of the public from political matters lends credence to these claims. Hibbing and Theiss-Morse thus argue, "real-life deliberation can fan emotions unproductively, can exacerbate rather than diminish power differentials among those deliberating, can make people feel frustrated with the system that made them deliberate, is ill-suited to many issues, and can lead to worse decisions than would have occurred if no deliberation had taken place."[1]

According to this argument, most citizens find political disagreements unnecessary. They do not follow politics too closely, so when drawn into a discussion involving contrary viewpoints, they become frustrated with the details and tune out of the conversation. In other words, people would rather continue to believe that others maintain a similar worldview than be faced with the reality that others' worldviews are significantly different from their own. These critics point to research showing that more deliberation does *not* lead to greater satisfaction with the democratic process. If anything, weaker democratic practices produce higher levels of collective decision-making acceptance and perceived process legitimacy than do stronger democratic procedures.[2]

But Hibbing and Theiss-Morse's claims have been challenged, and considerable evidence stacks up against them. A wide body of research, ranging from general public surveys to analyses of National Issues Forums to studies of jury service, shows that deliberation can encourage greater support for participation in public life and politics.[3] Indeed, one key argument against deliberative procedures advanced by Hibbing and Theiss-Morse—that deliberation leads to greater frustration—is contested by political scientist Donald Searing and his colleagues, who found that "encounters with citizens expressing multiple viewpoints in public discussions, and the challenge of defending one's own views, can set participants on edge and thereby stimulate learning."[4]

The critiques would be stronger if these scholars could find substantial public opposition to participating in *deliberative* civic engagement; rather, it seems that many citizens enjoy taking part in deliberative processes because the engagement enhances their sense of political self-confidence.[5] Indeed, recent survey evidence suggests that the people most unlikely to participate under status quo conditions are those who are interested in participating in deliberative forums.[6] It is somewhat unsurprising that citizens find politicians and representative systems to be unsatisfactory and that they respond by wanting to tune out of politics. To be sure, that is exactly what deliberation scholars hope to remedy.

In addition, even if most citizens do not want to participate more deeply in government, many deliberative procedures—such as randomly selecting voters to participate in focus groups resulting in policy proposals—do not require all voters to participate more. Statistical advancements like random sampling allow practitioners to glean the insights of the entire public even if the wider public would decline a mass invitation to deliberate.

Is Deliberative Civic Engagement Too Idealistic?

The foregoing critique suggests that there may be a mismatch between deliberative democrats' participatory expectations and reality. Political philosopher John Mueller, in the wonderfully titled essay, "Capitalism and Ralph's Pretty Good Grocery Store," makes precisely this point. He argues that "the fault in the mismatch between democracy's image and its reality lies more with the ideals than with the facts." Deliberative activists are unrealistic in their assessments, not so much of the people's ability but rather of institutional possibilities. Institutional constraints provide serious barriers to massive participation; thus, theorists, practitioners, and the public should be more or less content with the political and economic systems we have. "Putting it more gently," Mueller writes, "since human beings are a flawed bunch, an institution will be more successful if it can work with human imperfections rather than requiring first that the race be reformed into impossible perfection."[7] Deliberative theorists, on the other hand, aim and hope for humans to reach what may be just unnatural to them—more active involvement in the public sphere.

In his final analysis, Mueller claims that democracy works despite vast under-participation. Over the past 200 years, democracy—in all its messiness—still exists despite the fact that truly significant participation has not been achieved in many countries. Because democracy endures despite its imperfections, it is simply not true that wider participation is a requirement. Rather, it is simply a philosopher's ideal: "One would think that it would be obvious by now that democracy works despite the fact that it often fails to inspire or require very much in the way of responsibility and knowledge from its citizenry. . . . Democracy does not require that people generally be well informed, responsible, or actively attentive."[8]

Judge Richard Posner agrees with Mueller. In his book, *Law, Pragmatism, and Democracy*, Posner argues that deliberative theorists set the bar too high in their expectations that people want to participate broadly. Instead, critics and commentators should view democracy realistically. Pragmatism, Posner argues, is at "its core . . . merely a disposition to base action on facts and consequences rather than on conceptualisms, generalities, pieties, and slogans. Among the pieties rejected is the idea of human perfectibility; the pragmatist's conception of human nature is unillusioned."[9] Thus, when pragmatists look at American democracy and historic levels of public participation, they see a system that has functioned effectively for centuries with no particular need for dramatic reform.

Posner also attacks one of deliberation's key tenets—that open-minded people can come together to arrive at policy solutions. This argument is often leveled against the deliberative process, and Posner makes the point by way of a hypothetical: "Suppose a person from a culture where suicide is considered immoral confronts one who considers it moral . . . both agree on relevant facts, to what can they appeal to resolve their dispute . . . disagreement will be incapable of resolution by rational methods." Thus arises the need for government, and specifically representative democracy. Its job is "to manage conflict among persons who, often arguing from incompatible premises, cannot overcome their differences by discussion." In Posner's view, representative democracy solves this problem, whereas deliberative civic engagement, with its town hall meetings, demands a much more substantial investment of time by private citizens who would rather, for the most part, tune out of politics. Similar to Madison's argument in the *Federalist Papers*, Posner claims that demographic and socioeconomic heterogeneity will produce political factions with varying interests. Under these conditions, many issues can only be solved by majority vote. The theoretical foundations of deliberative civic engagement are simply utopian ideals, unworkable in modern conditions.[10]

The idea that deliberative theory does not take into account the complexities of modern society is also expounded upon by political theorist Emily Hauptmann.[11] Her critique focuses more on participatory theory—the idea that voters should participate more. She suggests that deliberative civic engagement does not take sufficient account of the complexity of modern society and is, therefore, an unrealistic prospect for modern governance. Similarly, political scientist Mark Warren, in one of his less optimistic turns, writes that "the transformative ideals of radical democracy often seem beset by a fuzzy utopianism that fails to confront limitations of complexity, size, and scale of advanced industrial societies."[12] It seems, then, that these authors are advancing the notion that citizens do not have the *time* to participate more in public affairs, and hence deliberation is too idealistic. In fact, as Warren argues, the burden of constant decision making may even make citizens *less* inclined to participate in the political process.

Along similar lines, political communication scholar Diana Mutz asks, in her book *Hearing the Other Side*, whether ideal deliberative discussion is even possible in the "real" world. She also questions whether results from a deliberative event can generalize to the wider public. "For most of us," she writes, "the ideal deliberative encounter is almost otherworldly, bearing little resemblance of the conversations about politics that occur over the water cooler, at the neighborhood bar, or even in our civic groups. The consequences of an ideal deliberative encounter will make little difference if there are few, if any, such exchanges."[13] This criticism, aimed primarily at "representative sample" forms of deliberation, suggests that even if such deliberative processes do work, the overall ends and societal benefits may be minimal if the results cannot be extrapolated to the public.

Although the work of these critics unmistakably addresses some of the theoretical challenges facing deliberative civic engagement, deliberation in the field has shown itself to be a feasible, achievable public practice. As described in earlier chapters in this volume, a variety of local leaders and practitioners have been able to attract large, diverse numbers of citizens to deliberative events to considerable effect. The critics are right that many citizens have an indifference toward politics that may make it difficult to achieve strong participation in deliberative systems; however, some evidence suggests that citizens' lack of interest stems mainly from problems associated with traditional representative government.

Thus, political philosopher Robert Talisse argues that the public sphere is rife with signs of *citizen interest* in the ideals of deliberation, and rejection of other systems of governance. Television news shows, Web sites, and other outlets take great steps to position themselves as independent, balanced, and free of political spin, and citizens often turn to these outlets for information presented as the unvarnished truth and free of political "bull." Talisse points out that in the United States the "various media outlets promote a unified view of what proper democratic politics should be. Specifically, it should be a fair and balanced ongoing critical exchange of reasons and arguments among epistemically honest and earnest political inquirers."[14] Rather than turning away from politics entirely, the electorate is eager for facts and reasoned arguments, and the media are marketing themselves as providing just that. Thus, the rhetoric of deliberation is taking hold in society.

Others, such as public policy scholar Robert Durant, point out the severe shortcomings of the media, the public, and the government in actually engaging in deliberative practices in some instances—for example, with environmental regulation and enforcement.[15] However, Talisse's point remains valid: The public cannot be faulted for being disgusted with a political system that is often nondeliberative and out of touch with citizen concerns. Thus, despite the "democratic deficit" in the United States, Durant asserts that citizens show signs of interest in deliberation, as the lay public is trying to get involved in decision making about environmental regulation and wants to provide an alternative view in a debate dominated by bureaucrats, scientists, and corporate interests. Likewise, surveys have found widespread participation in various forms of public talk in the United States, which also suggests a great deal of public interest in deliberative forms of politics.[16]

The concerns raised by Posner about the ability of deliberative discussions to reach the ideals described by theorists also seem misplaced. His hypothetical scenario about the morality of suicide does not seem to trouble deliberative practitioners; there is strong evidence to show that deliberation can change people's attitudes.[17] It is also true that many issues are less divisive, such as underage drinking, and agreement or compromise can likely be achieved.[18] For instance, suppose a group of people get together to debate the allocation of educational resources. One part of the group may want money for a playground and another may want greater resources allocated to teacher salaries. It seems plausible that this group of people could arrive at some sort of agreement through both reasoned discussion and simple compromise. Indeed, many issues seem to follow this model.[19]

Only the critique raised by Mutz poses into a major challenge to deliberative democracy in practice. As she suggests, deliberations are starkly different from typical conversations, and their conclusions cannot be taken as representative of the broader public. Practitioners are struggling to bridge this gap between the relatively ideal setting of a deliberative discussion and the distinctly imperfect world of conventional politics. For some practitioners, this is part of the rationale for "critical mass" approaches rather than representative-sample models (see Chapters 2 and 3), and there is some evidence that, at least at the local level, deliberative processes can reach enough people to change the political equation and achieve various policy outcomes (see Chapter 9). Many advocates of representative-sample models of deliberation have concluded that these projects require substantial efforts to communicate the conclusions reached by participants to the public at large. Some studies have shown that when citizens learn that a randomly selected set of their peers has taken part in an intensive, nonpartisan deliberation, they value—and can be persuaded by—the recommendations made by the participants in those processes.[20]

Deliberation, Reasoned Argument, and Privilege

The third broad theoretical critique addresses whether deliberation's focus on reasoned argument is the most appropriate method of civic engagement. Do certain forms of deliberative engagement privilege some groups and put others at a disadvantage? Is such talk the best method to encourage citizen participation? Chapters 4 and 5 address this controversy in depth, but we revisit it here to offer our own thoughts on these questions.

The deliberative process is generally presumed to be a "rational" one, in which competing arguments are analyzed, weighed against one another, and debated with the goal of achieving the best public policy for the common good. If certain groups of people are disproportionately better at this approach, however, one could argue that those groups will have an unfair advantage in obtaining their desired results, which would contradict the egalitarian goals of deliberation. Advantaged groups can define what knowledge is, how to attain it, and the parameters within which reason is defined.

In this view, deliberation simply becomes another tool of social control.[21] Moreover, some cultures and segments of society tend to favor argumentative or conversational approaches that differ from the reasoned, cool-headed analysis that tends to be preferred in deliberative environments. Ultimately, participants from such subgroups may struggle to achieve their aims in a deliberative forum or may have their views discounted or delegitimized.

Political theorist Lynn Sanders offers this critique in suggesting that rational argumentation may not be the most appropriate type of discussion for collective decision making. The highly structured style of deliberation may be advantageous to some groups and disadvantageous to others:

> The [deliberative communication] model . . . does not take sufficient account of the ways that status and hierarchy shape patterns of talking and listening to ensure that all perspectives are considered, that participation in a public discussion instills a sense of autonomy, and that the pursuit of a common interest does not coincide with the promotion of the views of the dominant.[22]

Sanders concludes that many citizen engagement processes may work to silence particular subgroups—namely women, minorities, and the poor—who tend to utilize emotional appeals, narrative storytelling, personal testimony, and other forms of argument that can be discounted or delegitimized in deliberative civic engagement processes.

In addition to this silencing problem, Sanders also notes that some people are better arguers and articulators than others, and that those people are more likely to hold sway and power in a deliberative setting. If, for instance, one member of a deliberative group appears as an expert in the collective mind of the other group members (while lacking actual expertise), this one person may then hold disproportionate sway. This may happen even if the group does not share that person's views, or if her or his policy suggestions are not the most appropriate course of action. If this is indeed the case, the group's decision may not be a result of deliberative, egalitarian processes but rather a result of an individual's undue influence. In short, the premise of Sanders' argument is that inequality and difference exist not only in society but also in a deliberative setting. This lack of equality may result in asymmetrical deliberative outputs that benefit those who are stronger at reasoned argumentation. Thus, Sanders concludes that reason-based deliberation may not be the most appropriate path to collective decision making.

Other scholars make similar arguments about structural inequalities and different communication styles. For example, education scholar Anne Newman critiques the use of deliberation in government meetings to make policy on public education. She suggests that these public forums are not necessarily the best way to address education, which is itself full of inequalities, because the people who could benefit the most from changes to education are less able to effect change through deliberative civic engagement.[23] Likewise, political philosopher Iris Marion Young argues that "structural inequalities operate effectively to block the political influence of some while magnifying that of others, even when formal guarantees of political equality hold."[24] Although Young is not opposed to deliberative practices, per se, she argues that theory and practice should not be confused, that "we should resist the temptation to consider that ideals of deliberative democracy are put into practice when public officials or foundations construct procedures influenced by these ideas."[25]

Although there are strong arguments about deliberation and its focus on reasoned debate, these critiques have lost some power in recent years. Practitioners are increasingly using alternative forms of discourse in deliberative forums, such as personal narrative or testimony, and scholars have grown more accepting of these varying kinds of communication (see Chapters 4 and 5).[26] For example, a study citing the Indigenous Issues Forums in South Dakota described that deliberative process as using a circle technique wherein "participants are encouraged to listen with respect and empathy to all individuals and to suspend assumptions in order to be open to what others have to say." The Forums "also involve the elderly to share their stories and use visual arts, movies, games, and music to stimulate discussion."[27]

Similarly, models developed by the National Issues Forums (NIF) include an "integrative model" of deliberation.[28] This model is less idealistic than the rational model and allows for multiple, heterogeneous views. Participants do not speak according to deliberative ideals but rather obtain information about various policy choices and their consequences and trade-offs, and then discuss that information using multiple forms of communication. So it appears that practitioners, scholars, and activists are responding to these critiques by suggesting and designing new ways for citizens to communicate during deliberation.

The claims that some groups are disadvantaged in deliberative events would also benefit from more empirical evidence, as well as confirmation that the context under study is truly deliberative. For example, although Newman provides some evidence for her claims, her research examines governmental meetings, which may not meet the criteria of a true deliberative civic engagement event. In contrast, Sanders provides at least indirect empirical evidence; however, she softens her critique by arguing that if the structure of group deliberations can be altered, then democratic discussion may be improved and thus become more equitable. Here, Sanders turns to the research on jury studies to show that some forms of group deliberation elicit more egalitarian interactions than others:

When jury deliberations are focused more on eliciting a range of views instead of on the common problem of arriving at a verdict, they appear likely to provoke both a more considerate discussion and one that leaves jurors more satisfied with their participation: Jurors on evidence-driven juries report thinking they have done a good job more frequently than do jurors on verdict-driven juries.[29]

Other studies support this claim. For example, research about gender and ethnic differences among jury members found that, by and large, people in disadvantaged groups do not report discrimination in their experiences with jury deliberation.[30] In short, the research on jury deliberation suggests that status inequalities can be minimized or overcome entirely if the deliberative *process* is robust and if conditions are favorable to creating an egalitarian discussion.

Concerns about equality in deliberation are also found in international, non-Western contexts. Scholars have raised concerns about potential biases in discussion processes, and warned against seeing any event that strives for the ideals of deliberation as a truly deliberative forum.[31] For example, after conducting dozens of interviews with Philippine activists, Peter Levine and Rose Marie Nierras find worries about bias entering into the deliberative process. As one respondent said, "The problem is that deliberation privileges reasonableness. And that's why I have asked, 'does deliberation exclude struggle? . . . If I ask a hungry person who's been put in jail to be reasonable, he'll give me the finger." Other Philippine activists worried that some deliberation participants could not express themselves effectively in a group situation: "The discourse of peasants is often not explicit—often hard to understand."[32] Furthermore, structural inequalities often go unnoticed because they are ingrained at a somewhat unconscious level for conveners and participants. Thus, the discussion arrangement is often predicated on these rather insidious and ostensibly innocuous inequalities, which may contain "falsifications, biases, misunderstandings, and even contradictions" that too often go unnoticed because they represent the existing status quo.[33]

At the heart of many of these international critiques is the suggestion that because democracy is a product of Western history and institutional development, deliberation is either irrelevant or less useful for non-Western polities. This argument implies that democracy may not work for all countries or regions of the world; accordingly, invoking deliberation may reek of paternalism. However, economist Amartya Sen suggests that this argument tends to conceptualize democracy as strictly voting and the ballot box.[34] Pointing to India as the best example of successful democracy in a non-Western country, Sen argues that when we envision democracy more broadly to include political discussions, the citizenry—regardless of Western affiliation—can advance their interests and obtain political power and influence. In *Collective Decision Making around the*

World, several examiners find that deliberative practices operate effectively in various parts of the world, including Cameroon, Colombia, Albania, and Russia.[35] Deliberation may have historically been widespread; thus, at least some evidence suggests that deliberative engagement may not be strictly a Western practice and idea after all.

Nevertheless, we must take seriously these concerns about deliberation, reasoned argument, and privilege. In addition to using various forms of discourse, scholars and practitioners have suggested other potential solutions to this problem. For example, Young argues for more transparent deliberation procedures that acknowledge the potential for subconscious inequalities with the goal of improving the process.[36] Others, including Young and Sanders, suggest using "enclave deliberation" wherein members of a societal subgroup deliberate alone rather than—or prior to—participating in a forum involving a wide range of people. Allowing people to deliberate in these enclaves may help societal subgroups gain some benefits of deliberative processes before entering into discussions in the wider public sphere.[37]

Open-Mindedness and Group Polarization

The final theoretical concern spans two related questions: Can people truly come to a deliberative forum and be open-minded about new opinions and ideas? If so, does group discussion tend to lead to agreement and common ground, or does it tend to sow discord among discussants?

Malcolm Gladwell's book *Blink* popularized the large body of psychological research suggesting that under certain circumstances, human brains seem incapable of the type of open-mindedness required by deliberative civic engagement.[38] For example, Gladwell discusses a card game experiment conducted by University of Iowa researchers. Essentially, the experiment demonstrates that people subconsciously figure out rules to games faster than they do consciously. Thus, Gladwell concludes that people instinctively and subconsciously know what is going on before they can reason and act on it. In other words, our brains reach conclusions without immediately telling us at the conscious level. If this is the case, then people may actually come into deliberative settings with conclusions about other group participants already formed, or they may form such opinions in the preliminary stages of a deliberative process. This subconscious attitude formation may make it difficult for some participants to be open to contrary opinions.

Further, the idea that participants can lay stereotypes and preconceptions aside and engage in open, honest dialogue has come under scrutiny based on recent work in social psychology. The Implicit Attitudes Test (IAT) developed by psychologist Tony Greenwald and his colleagues reveals that most members of a population hold hidden prejudices against lower-status racial groups and have preferences for higher-status racial groups.[39] The IAT uses unconscious associations between objects to measure speed time of pairings—the faster participants make a connection between two paired objects, the more tightly those objects go together in that participant's mind, and vice versa.

The most famous IAT is the race test, whereby positive or negative words are paired with two categories—usually white or black. The test reveals that many participants have an implicit bias in favor of white people. For example, participants more quickly pair 'hurt' or 'bad' with African Americans than they pair 'hurt' or 'bad' with European Americans. Even though most subjects do not consciously admit they prefer one race to another, the IAT suggests that people have a latent preference for whites.

This may affect deliberative processes because although people may think they are coming to a deliberative forum with an open mind, they may, in fact, be arriving with latent biases or opposition toward particular social groups. In short, people could come to a deliberative forum, and subconsciously make snap judgments about the topic under discussion, the other participants in the group, or other factors.

On the surface, snap judgments and implicit attitudes may be worrisome; however, they may not have a strong effect on deliberations. Research shows that people can and do change their implicit attitudes over time. As Gladwell himself concludes, "Our first impressions are generated by our experiences and our environment, which means that we can change our first impressions by changing the experiences that comprise those impressions."[40] Deliberative forums provide for different experiences. They are designed to provide equal standing and foster positive interactions with people from widely varying ethnic or social backgrounds, and give people a great deal of time to share experiences, analyze information, consider other points of view, and discuss potential solutions. In short, deliberative civic engagement aims to get people to think more deeply about an issue than they did before.

But even if deliberation makes participants more open-minded, that does not mean the experience will necessarily result in consensus or common ground. It may be more likely that groups will struggle to reach a decision, and split into opposing camps. Some research maintains that group and dyadic discussion can more often lead to dissensus and polarization rather than consensus or compromise.[41] The term *group polarization* can have two distinct meanings. The more colloquial understanding is that the group splits along fault lines, with each camp taking up positions at opposing poles and refusing to budge. The other definition, which is more common in small group research, applies when a group of like-minded people discuss a decision and the moderate group members shift toward the most extreme members, making the overall group decision more extreme than the initial average position—that is, the group has polarized to an extreme choice. Either case could be a problem for deliberative civic engagement, since the goal is to reach legitimate agreed-upon solutions that are thought out and promote the common good.

Regardless of its specific definition, polarization suggests that exposure to oppositional viewpoints may stimulate hardened disagreement as opposed to mutual understanding and agreement.[42] Political theorist Ian Shapiro argues along these lines when he states, "Once honest exchange gets under way, they might unearth new irreconcilable differences, with the effect that the relationship worsens and perhaps even falls apart in acrimony."[43] Oppositional polarization occurs, in part, because most people do not want to expose themselves to others who disagree with them. People tend to self-select—when they engage in political conversations it is most likely to be with a friend or family member, and in the context of agreement. Similarly, some research has shown that greater heterogeneity in political discussion tends to drive down the participation rate of voters, because exposure to opposing viewpoints makes people more frustrated with politics.

Legal scholar Cass Sunstein argues that group political discussion can result in the other type of polarization, where a group shifts to an extreme. According to Sunstein, when group members are exposed to new information, they may collectively move to more extreme positions relative to their pre-deliberation tendencies."[44] In Sunstein's view, polarization occurs primarily for two reasons. First, people want to maintain their reputations and self-conception and thus are more likely to acquiesce to the dominant view; and second, each group has only a limited pool of arguments, thereby cutting down on the number of new ideas exposed to the group as a whole. This results in a polarizing shift in which intra-group opinion variance and individual differences decrease, and the group converges on a more extreme position.[45]

Concerns about polarization potentially create real problems for deliberative civic engagement in practice. They also point to a paradox—there is a normative desire to increase and improve dialogue among people who disagree, but people who disagree are less likely to talk with one another. However, several responses to these critiques lessen their impacts. First, some critics actually discuss the benefits of exploring heterogeneous views. For example, Mutz argues that such exposure can increase the strength and legitimacy of certain arguments, which can in turn reduce animosity and produce a more civil political culture. She finds that "the capacity to see that there is more than one side to an issue, that a political conflict is, in fact, a legitimate controversy with rationales on both sides, translates to greater willingness to extend civil liberties to even those groups whose political views one dislikes a great deal."[46]

Second, most of these critiques are focused on general political discussion, as opposed to discussion in deliberative events. Moreover, research focused on

deliberative civic engagement has generally not supported concerns about polarization. For example, in a study of National Issues Forums, McAfee finds that
"even in the face of trenchant disagreement, participants would focus on coming
up with a direction that would accommodate the plural concerns in the room."[47]
Thus, although opinion polarization may occur, because deliberative forums
tend to remind participants that others' views are legitimate, the negative effects
of polarization can conceivably be contained and contravened.

Likewise, the composition of the deliberating group may determine the
extent of polarization. If conveners can recruit a suitably diverse group, then deliberation should be less polarizing. For example, some studies show that groups
that include women behave quite differently from groups that exclude women.
Groups with women have a stronger orientation toward consensus, equality, and
intimacy, whereas all-male groups are less conflict avoidant.[48]

Even Sunstein acknowledges that deliberation can work in large-scale heterogeneous settings so long as like-minded people are not walled off from alternative
points of view.[49] In fact, an important part of deliberation is the careful analysis of
multiple arguments or options, and consideration of other groups' concerns—
both of which would be invaluable in preventing the form of group polarization
in which members shift toward an extreme opinion. Posner, in his critique of
deliberation, latches onto Sunstein's concerns about group polarization and
applies them to nearly *any* group discussion, including political deliberation—
ignoring the fact that Sunstein raised his concerns about polarization to point out
the importance of divergent views and dissent being raised in discussion.[50]

In sum, although we should be concerned about group polarization in political
discussion—whether in the form of opposing camps refusing to meet in the
middle, or a group of like-minded people shifting to an extreme—deliberation is
well-equipped to face these troubles through its structures of careful consideration, weighing of opposing arguments, and many other forms of analysis that may
not arise in everyday group discussion. Rather than asking simply whether group
discussion can sow conflict and disagreement, or engender compromise and mutual consideration, a more appropriate question is whether *deliberation* tends
toward one of those outcomes—and evidence abounds in this volume and many
other sources that it can help people find common ground on contentious issues.[51]

Practical Criticisms

Beyond these theoretical concerns, deliberation faces many practical questions. First, are some forms of deliberative civic engagement better than others,
and how can the structure and process of a deliberative forum affect citizens'
experiences and final outcomes? Second, how can practitioners represent a
wide range of viewpoints in a deliberative forum, and how can deliberation

deal with the issue of inequality in terms of who shows up, who participates, and who runs an event? Third, can deliberation affect public policy and lead to better, more legitimate policy outcomes? Fourth, what kinds of practical benefits can citizens receive from deliberation, and what other practical disadvantages are there to deliberative civic engagement? Finally, does deliberative civic engagement distract citizens from addressing more fundamental conflicts about power and politics?

Effects of Different Models of Deliberation

Different forms of deliberation may provide various benefits, such as increases in political knowledge, civic skills and dispositions, or group camaraderie (see Chapter 7). But it bears asking whether some methods of deliberative civic engagement are more effective than others. If no one model of deliberative civic engagement has been shown most effective, perhaps this undermines the credibility of all methods. After all, should not one or another practitioner be able to demonstrate that a particular model of deliberation tends to produce better outcomes?

One response might be that different models have distinct advantages and achieve qualitatively different goals. For instance, Citizen Juries bring together a randomly selected group of participants to analyze a public policy question, with the hope of producing broad agreement within the group and influencing public opinion and/or policy makers.[52] In contrast, Conversation Cafés are open processes that bring together a nonrepresentative sample of people to discuss issues of concern. They are not designed to influence public policy but rather to facilitate dialogue among ordinary people and help them to (perhaps) find common ground.[53] Similarly, Jane Mansbridge points out that although Deliberative Polling may be the "gold standard" for representative-sample deliberation, it does not help mobilize the wider citizenry to participate. Thus, although it is one of the most researched models of deliberation, it is not sufficient for changing the nature of governance as desired by deliberation's advocates.[54]

Following the argument that different processes are better suited to achieving different goals, it is important to examine the various structures and features of particular deliberative models. Such examinations are arguably most important when deliberative processes are aimed at affecting policy outcomes. Some have raised concerns about how the choice of topic and organization of discussion may subtly introduce bias into the process. For example, America*Speaks* drew criticism for its 21st Century Town Meeting on the United States budget deficit, called "Our Budget, Our Economy." Some scholars argued that the focus of this event on "cutting the deficit" cued budget-conscious ideals for participants and shifted their attention away from costly government programs they may actually support. Others charged that the written background materials and selection of "expert witnesses"—typically expected to be balanced and neutral—subtly promoted a point of view favored by the organizers.[55] Other features of deliberative processes should also be given attention. For example, some scholars have urged that we closely analyze the position of the deliberation moderator, who faces the difficult task of remaining neutral while keeping the discussion on track and preventing any outspoken members from shutting down discussion. If moderators are not careful, or not earnestly concerned with remaining neutral, they can introduce bias into the process.[56]

The point here is that one size does not fit all: Given the multiple goals for deliberative civic engagement (see Chapters 1 and 2), deliberative processes need to come in multiple forms. This multimethod approach is popular with many deliberation practitioners, who create their own processes or sequences of processes to take advantage of the strengths of different approaches to deliberation.[57]

Representing Diverse Viewpoints in Deliberative Forums

Another area of practical concern is the representation of a diverse range of viewpoints in the deliberative forum. Two potential benefits of deliberative civic engagement are that it can represent the will of the people and incorporate the voices of a diverse body of citizens. Because of this, the recruitment of participants is a serious concern, lest participants be as demographically skewed as is commonly the case for other forms of civic engagement (see Chapter 3). If insufficient attention and resources are devoted to outreach, deliberative events are likely to underrepresent the exact groups of people who have traditionally been underrepresented in society (e.g., in the United States, this means Native Americans, African Americans, Latinos, and other ethnic minorities).[58]

Fortunately, there are some strategies that can contravene this participation paradox (see Chapters 3 and 5). One commonly used approach is to map community networks, form relationships with network leaders, decide which elements of the population seem least likely to participate, and spend greater time and energy recruiting through the networks favored by those populations. Deliberative projects using this strategy typically produce a far more diverse turnout of participants than take part in conventional political activities like public hearings. Random selection is another strategy used to recruit a diverse body of participants. In this strategy, each citizen has an equal chance of selection, which is equivalent to an equal probability sample in random sampling methodology. If there are still representation issues under this design, then targeted sampling can be employed. Here, citizens that fit certain characteristics (demographic, ideological, or otherwise) can be targeted with extra phone calls, mailings, and greater incentives to increase the likelihood that they participate in the forum.

Beyond the concerns about inclusivity and recruitment are concerns related to the diversity of views necessary for vibrant deliberation. One criticism of deliberative events is that their neutral or nonpartisan stance is actually closely related to the views of mainstream political elites—that the "neutral" stance is actually just a moderate consensus of political leaders, neatly balanced with partisans on both the right and left.[59] This could exclude some important viewpoints that are not politically centrist, or represented by mainstream partisans, thus artificially limiting the range of views that participants discuss and consider.[60]

For instance, consider a hypothetical debate about the United States taking military action against a foreign nation. A deliberative forum may provide background materials and advocates from a hawkish pro-war camp as well as from a more doveish camp that calls for economic sanctions instead of war. Though the forum is seemingly balanced between pro- and antiwar groups, it could omit the views of antiwar groups that are pushing for nonintervention, or those calling for diplomatic solutions without sanctions. Consequently, participants may not consider those views at all. An argument in a similar vein is that organizers may co-opt the framing of the issue, forcing participants to deliberate about something with which they may have initially disagreed. For example, organizers may charge the participants with devising a fair way to charge patients co-payments for government-provided health care, even though some participants may have advocated other ways to raise money and financially stabilize the health system.[61]

The forgoing discussion leads to the critique that deliberative civic engagement may, at times, struggle with issues of legitimacy. Mark Button and David Ryfe contend that deliberative processes are legitimate when "fair procedures of public reasoning are, in principle, open to everyone." This should, in turn, lead to the outcome of the event as legitimate because the process was "inclusive, voluntary, reasoned, and equal."[62] Moreover, deliberative processes should leave open the possibility for alternative framings of issues. Efforts to make deliberative processes transparent in these and other ways may increase the likelihood that legislators and policy makers respond to and implement participants' recommendations.

Deliberation and Public Policy Outcomes

In many cases, deliberative civic engagement is ultimately meant to influence public policy in some way, so an important question is whether such systems help produce "better" policy solutions and outcomes that are seen as being democratically legitimate (see Chapter 9). Two issues are important in addressing this concern.

First, democratic legitimacy arises, in part, when policy solutions are formulated through an inclusive process and when they are based on common ground and shared conceptions of the public good. Nevertheless, some groups may be underrepresented or less effective in deliberative venues. As a consequence, their views may not be well reflected in the proposed solution or final policy outcome. To mitigate this possibility, practitioners can take steps to ensure the inclusion of a wide range of groups and viewpoints in the deliberative process and a wide range of interests in the policy options.

For example, organizers may start by building a deliberative body from a random sample of the general population and add other representatives from segments of society or ethnic minority groups to ensure broad representation. This strategy was employed in the 2009 Australian Citizens' Parliament to guarantee representation of the nation's Aboriginal population.[63] Organizers can also encourage a deliberative forum to consider many views by doing research *before* the event to identify numerous options to present to participants for analysis and discussion.[64]

A second criticism leveled against the aim of developing or influencing public policy through deliberation is that citizens may settle on solutions that are politically untenable, difficult to enact, or simply unfeasible.[65] As a result, legislators and decision makers may ignore citizen recommendations. Several responses to this critique are worth noting. First, while ordinary people may not have scientific or technical expertise, they are able to clearly express their preferences for the values that should frame and guide even the most complex of policy issues.[66] Such input can help elected representatives and administrative officials better understand the public's interests and priorities and provide a guiding framework for decision and policy making.

In addition, research shows that citizens can make reasonably good decisions based on limited information, and that the quality of those decisions can be improved when more and better information is available.[67] Thus, to help overcome some of the limitations of citizen knowledge, organizers of deliberative events can provide informational materials that are consistent with the issue at hand and the work that participants have been asked to do. Such materials should be of high quality and provide "sufficient context and history on the issues, be neutral and fair to all perspectives, leave room for citizens to create new options, and have credibility with all audiences."[68]

Finally, there is evidence that deliberative forums have produced solid public policy recommendations and have successfully influenced policy decisions on a variety of matters at all levels of government (see Chapter 9). For example, in New Haven, Connecticut—a racially diverse community— policy makers, citizen activists, and community leaders used public deliberation to address issues concerning inadequate schools and racial inequality. Lawmakers paid attention, as evidenced by their use of deliberation to overcome legislative logjams.[69] In Canada, the British Columbia Citizens Assembly successfully investigated and made recommendations about changing the province's electoral system.[70] In the United States, the Oregon Citizens' Initiative Review, a statewide, government-sponsored reform process, was recently launched. In this process, a randomly selected panel of citizens deliberates about a ballot measure and issues a "Citizens' Statement" with its findings. The 2010 pilot project was lauded as a huge success and as a fair way to improve the state's initiative process, and in 2011, the state decided to make the process a permanent fixture of its government.[71] Finally, consider the cases discussed in Chapter 9 of this volume, where citizens deliberated about and influenced health policy making in Brazil and Canada.

The Effects and Costs of Deliberation

Another set of practical criticisms concerns the effects and costs of deliberative civic engagement. Many critics point to the possibility of negative effects, particularly for individuals. For example, some critics argue that deliberation can injure citizens by causing them to feel frustrated, inefficacious, and powerless.[72] In turn, others suggest that this will discourage further political participation. However, evidence presented in Chapter 7 shows that deliberation has several educative effects for participants. Other research suggests that deliberative civic engagement may be especially meaningful to historically underprivileged segments of society. For example, research shows that the aforementioned Indigenous Issues Forums helped indigenous groups come together and discuss important issues, resulting in "a process of individual transformation that may well be a precondition to increased civic engagement."[73]

Moreover, evidence in Chapter 8 suggests that deliberation can help develop leadership skills and encourage community organizing to address other political issues. Research supports these assertions. For example, after a National Issues Forum in West Virginia, one study found that college students mobilized "to work on issues that emerged from deliberations, conduct[ed] additional forums, and even frame[d] new issues."[74] As a result, deliberation became embedded in parts of the political process in West Virginia, which resulted in both policy and personal effects. As Fagotto and Fung note, "The forums on domestic violence contributed to raising awareness on the issue (domestic violence), and provided the convening organization with important information on the public understanding of the phenomenon."[75]

It is important to note that despite these findings, deliberative civic engagement does not generally address the problem of declining rates of participation in other political arenas. Nevertheless, some deliberative processes, coupled with other democratic reforms, could be employed to help encourage wider participation.[76] One option to foster mass deliberation is to use a smaller, randomly

selected deliberative forum or panel that shares its findings and recommendations with the general public through the Web, or a government-provided voter
guide—as was done with the British Columbia Citizens' Assembly or the
Oregon Citizens' Initiative Review.[77]

A related criticism suggests that deliberative civic engagement is too costly to
put into practice.[78] In terms of money, Gastil reports that high-quality Citizens'
Juries can cost $50,000 to $150,000 for the five-day intensive event.[79] Bigger deliberative reforms, such as a nationwide "Deliberation Day" in which citizens are
paid to participate in small, local discussions on national issues, would prove to
be even more expensive.[80] However, a recent study of a variety of deliberative
forums found that many organizers had little to no financial support for the
events—the average budget for a deliberative project was $6,000, and the me-
dian cost was zero.[81] This suggests that cost need not be as big a barrier to deliberative reforms as critics say.

Critics also claim that deliberation has too many transaction costs for both
citizens and government officials. The participation level required of citizens in
deliberative civic engagement is higher than in other kinds of governance, and
many citizens might prefer not to be involved because of time, costs (e.g., lost
wages or child care or transportation expenses), or forgone opportunities.[82]
Likewise, government officials must spend time and money to develop and/or
use deliberative processes, which may adversely affect their ability to broker
policy compromises and satisfy citizen demands.[83]

Though these arguments certainly have merit, research shows that when they
take deliberative civic engagement seriously, both citizens and governments can
benefit in many ways. Over time, deliberative efforts may reduce policy conflicts,
increase the perceived legitimacy of policies, ease implementation difficulties,
and improve the effectiveness of public action. More research is needed to prove
the frequency of these benefits, but if such outcomes do regularly result from
deliberative civic engagement, then the upfront costs and investments would be
a small price to pay for better, more thoughtful governance.

Distraction from Fundamental Conflicts and Community Politics

A final criticism can be summarized as the conviction that focus on "talk"
across lines of political difference can dilute or distract from real conflicts
about power in society. This set of concerns takes a variety of forms. One
variant is the complaint that when civic deliberation directly involves government, citizens' views always end up "in the hallway" rather than in the main
room where the real discussion takes place.[84] More strident critics have
argued that the structural inequalities in a community or the wider society

persist—and perhaps even get enhanced—in deliberation because deliberation replaces voting equality and the raw political power of social movements with unequal expression and influence among socially advantaged and disadvantaged groups. In other words, deliberation hides social inequalities while operating through them.[85]

These concerns will have to be addressed by the track record of deliberative civic engagement as it builds over time. Meanwhile, however, systematically improving the *practice* of deliberation will be critical to shaping its outcomes and effects. To take a long-standing example of institutionalized citizen deliberation, the jury system has at times reinforced biases and inequalities, but it has also advanced minority rights, civil rights, and the interests of those who would have suffered gravely had their fate not been in the hands of sympathetic peers.[86] Key reforms to improving the jury as a check on state power have been ensuring that the jury pool includes a broad cross-section of the public and avoiding racial bias during jury selection.[87] These and other efforts have helped improve the deliberative potential of juries and increased the odds that jury members will stand up for the rights of those who had previously been excluded from the jury room— left "in the hallway" as it were.

One deliberative practice with potential to address concerns about social conflicts and power inequalities is the aforementioned "enclave deliberation." This practice can be particularly fruitful within subpublics (as opposed to the "mass public"), as group members select and deliberate about an issue and their collective interests before discussing it with, or taking action in, the larger public. For those who doubt the efficacy of full-scale deliberation, such enclave deliberation may be an acceptable alternative, as it can sharpen the arguments and strengthen the position of a minority group in advance of (or in the course of) a political conflict.[88]

To shift deliberation entirely into enclaves, however, would miss the potential for fusing radical and deliberative politics—something that political theorists Joshua Cohen and Archon Fung have attempted.[89] In their view, a two-track process can harness both the mobilizing power of mass politics and the critical insight of reasoned discussion. First, mass-scale deliberation can occur through the same institutions and processes as social movements. This would include enclave deliberation but also involve clashes between competing arguments and narratives. Second, citizens would be given powerful roles and a direct voice in the executive, legislative, and judicial branches through processes such as participatory budgeting, citizen assemblies, and juries. Such an approach would bring to the table a range of concerns, including those steeped in social movements and informal sectors, and subject government decisions to direct public scrutiny, making the exercise of power more—not less—visible.

Conclusion

This chapter has outlined a series of criticisms often leveled against deliberative civic engagement. It also evaluated those criticisms in light of deliberative theory and research, and explored counterarguments to some critiques. The general goal of this approach was to help practitioners and theorists better implement and analyze deliberative procedures.

Overall, the criticisms fall into two broad categories—theoretical and practical concerns. Regarding the theoretical criticisms, scholars have argued that citizens are too politically disengaged and too ignorant of public policy to participate effectively in deliberation. However, these claims ignore the growing public interest in deliberative civic engagement and the success of deliberative systems in encouraging citizens to take an active role in governance. Some scholars have argued that deliberation focuses too much on reasoned argument and cool-headed analysis, leading to discrimination against some societal groups. These claims are troubling, but deliberation practice and theory has shifted to include alternative ways of speaking and reasoning, ensuring the inclusion of individuals from many walks of life. Finally, other scholars have suggested that people may be unable to enter group discussions with an open mind, or that group discussion itself is predisposed to create conflict and discord. These concerns are valid, but deliberation takes places in an egalitarian discussion environment that exposes people to a wide range of views, which seems ideally suited to helping people overcome implicit biases and preconceived notions. In addition, research that suggests group discussion encourages the polarization of members into opposing camps, or the shift of like-minded groups to an extreme, are more applicable in *nondeliberative* groups—the safeguards of deliberative discussion are intended to counteract just such phenomena. Future research may undertake more longitudinal designs to see how members of opposing camps may change opinions or become less extreme over time as a result of engaging in deliberative programs.

There are also practical concerns about deliberation. First, some believe that certain forms of deliberative civic engagement are more effective than others and may consequently have different effects on citizens' experiences and final outcomes. Moving forward, researchers should examine the effects of different deliberative design choices, the appropriate applications for different deliberative models, and the ways that different models can be used together to produce a stronger democracy. In addition, research should examine issues of bias vis-à-vis various factors of structure and process (e.g., topic selection, background materials, and moderators) to ensure that public forums claiming the mantle of deliberation are, in fact, strongly deliberative.

Second, there are practical concerns about issues of recruitment and representation. Tailoring deliberative discussion so that it is compelling to a broad range of people is essential. Future research can employ quantitative methods to measure the variation in deliberative group participation as a function of different recruitment approaches and discussion formats.

Third, critics question whether deliberation influences and increases the democratic legitimacy of policy making. Numerous success stories involving deliberative policy solutions and recommendations tell of influencing government leaders. Future research should examine what policy areas are most susceptible to the influence of deliberative civic engagement and how stronger connections to the policy process can be made.

Fourth, critics question the effects of deliberation on individuals and worry about its costs. However, numerous studies show that deliberative civic engagement can increase participants' civic skills and dispositions, as well as their interest and activity in politics and governance. Longitudinal research should be done to examine how different types of forums create and sustain long-term civic capacity in different groups and in different parts of the world. Moreover, most deliberative processes can be (and are being) done with very little money, but even the most expensive deliberative processes may be worthwhile in light of their potential benefits, as well as the long-term costs of not resolving political and policy conflicts.

Finally, skeptics worry that deliberative civic engagement will obscure more serious conflicts and exacerbate inequalities in social power. This concern requires both vigilance and an ecumenical mind-set among deliberation practitioners. Deliberative processes must be designed carefully with existing power relations in mind, including the tendency of public officials to avoid bringing to the fore the most controversial issues that affect disadvantaged social groups. An ecumenical disposition will also safeguard against building deliberative structures in isolation from—or even in opposition to—preexisting community traditions and social/political movements, processes that may not privilege deliberation but do draw in the concerns and voices of marginalized and disadvantaged groups.

All in all, the theory and practice of deliberative civic engagement have adapted over time to address many concerns raised by critics. Though some obstacles have proven formidable, practitioners of deliberation have been fairly successful in making deliberative ideals a reality for many citizens. Nonetheless, much work remains in answering these and other critiques and implementing deliberative civic engagement in a wider variety of forms and settings. Citizens have become very pessimistic about government and politics in the modern age, but if deliberation scholars and practitioners can meet these challenges, they could help deliver the promise of deliberative civic engagement to more people and more levels of government in countries across the globe.

Notes

1. Hibbing and Theiss-Morse (2002: 91, 191).
2. Morrell (1999); Hibbing and Theiss-Morse (2002).
3. Gastil (2008); Gastil, Deess, Weiser, and Simmons (2010); Neblo (2010); Neblo, Esterling, Kennedy, Lazer, and Sokhey (2010).
4. Searing, Solt, Conover, and Crewe (2007: 602).
5. Gastil (2008); Gastil, Deess, Weiser, and Simmons (2010); Nabatchi (2007, 2010b); Nabatchi and Stanisevski (2008); Searing, Solt, Conover, and Crewe (2007).
6. Neblo, Esterling, Kennedy, Lazer, and Sokhey (2010).
7. Mueller (1999: 9, 12).
8. Mueller (1999: 183–184).
9. Posner (2003: 3)
10. Posner (2003: 8, 112, 113, 138).
11. Hauptmann (2001).
12. Warren (1996: 242).
13. Mutz (2006: 8).
14. Talisse (2005: 192).
15. Durant (1995).
16. Jacobs, Cook, and Delli Carpini. (2009).
17. Abelson, Eyles, McLeod, Collins, McMullan, and Forest (2003); see also Gastil (2009b) and Fishkin (2010).
18. Fagotto and Fung (2006).
19. Think of the US Congress and all the ostensibly contentious issues on which it deliberates. While Congress, as of this writing, is not viewed in a positive light, its members decide outcomes of issues and the government still works.
20. Gastil and Knobloch (2011); Warren and Pearse (2008).
21. Levine and Nierras (2007: 8).
22. Sanders (1997: 370).
23. Newman (2009); see also Mendelberg and Oleske (2000).
24. Young (2001: 117).
25. Levine and Nierras (2007: 118).
26. Burkhalter, Gastil, and Kelshaw (2002: 402); Polletta and Lee (2006).
27. Fagotto and Fung (2006: 13).
28. McAfee (2004).
29. Sanders (1997: 366–367).
30. Hickerson and Gastil (2008).
31. Page and Jacobs (2010); Baker (2010).
32. Levine and Nierras (2007: 7–8).
33. Young (2001: 686).
34. Sen (1999).
35. Martin (2006).
36. Young (2001).
37. Karpowitz (2009).
38. Gladwell (2005).
39. Greenwald, Nosek, and Banaji (2003). One can take an IAT test online at https://implicit.harvard.edu/implicit/.
40. Gladwell (2005: 97).
41. Mutz (2006).
42. Mutz (2006).
43. Shapiro (2002: 199).
44. Sunstein (2002: 178).

45. Karpowitz and Mendelberg (2007: 175).
46. Mutz (2006: 85).
47. McAfee (2004: 54).
48. Karpowitz and Mendelberg (2007: 647).
49. Sunstein (2002).
50. Talisse (2005: 194).
51. Gastil (2008); Fishkin (2009a).
52. Gastil (2008: 204).
53. See www.conversationcafe.org.
54. Mansbridge (2010).
55. Baker (2010); Page and Jacobs (2010).
56. Guttman (2007: 421).
57. Carson and Hartz-Karp (2005).
58. Davies, Blackstock, and Rauschmayer (2005).
59. Page and Jacobs (2010).
60. Guttman (2007).
61. Guttman (2007).
62. Button and Ryfe (2005: 27).
63. Dryzek (2009).
64. Mansbridge (2010: 56); see also Fishkin (2009a).
65. Irvin and Stansbury (2004); see also Nabatchi and Farrar (2011) for a discussion of this concern from the perspective of legislators.
66. For a discussion, see Nabatchi (2011, 2012b).
67. See, for example, Delli Carpini (2000), Riggle, Ottati, Wyer, Kuklinski, and Schwarz (1992), and Sniderman, Brody, and Tetlock (1991).
68. Lukensmeyer and Brigham (2002: 355).
69. Fagotto and Fung (2009).
70. Ratner (2005).
71. For details, see www.healthydemocracyoregon.org.
72. See, for example, Hibbing and Theiss-Morse (2002).
73. Fagotto and Fung (2006: 12–13).
74. Fagotto and Fung (2006: 11).
75. Fagotto and Fung (2006: 12).
76. Mansbridge (2010).
77. Gastil and Knobloch (2011); Warren and Pearse (2008).
78. Irvin and Stansbury (2004).
79. Gastil (2010, personal correspondence).
80. Ackerman and Fishkin (2004).
81. Lee and Polletta (2009).
82. Posner (2003).
83. Irvin and Stansbury (2004).
84. Levine (2006: 2); see also Levine and Nierras (2007).
85. Kadlec and Friedman (2007).
86. Dwyer (2002).
87. For an overview, see Vidmar and Hans (2007).
88. Karpowitz, Raphael, and Hammond (2009).
89. Cohen and Fung (2004). Boyte (2011) emphasizes the first of the two tracks Cohen and Fung identify by stressing the need for meaningful community-level engagement in the tradition of local movement politics, albeit tempered by a more reflective, deliberative impulse.

12

Advancing the Theory and Practice of Deliberative Civic Engagement

A Secular Hymnal

G. MICHAEL WEIKSNER, JOHN GASTIL, TINA NABATCHI,

AND MATT LEIGHNINGER

> Deliberation and debate is the way you stir the soul of our democracy.
> —Jesse Jackson, *American civil rights leader*

We come to the end of this book having covered vast ground with the aid of dozens of authors, critics, and reviewers who made possible the insights of the preceding chapters. We now seek to answer one final set of questions, *How should the findings in the previous chapters influence the practice and study of deliberative civic engagement? And what should be the agenda for the future?* As we draw together key findings and nagging uncertainties from those chapters, we have come to view these as the elements of a secular songbook, a hymnal of sorts for deliberative democrats. Instead of lyrics and notes, this hymnal offers themes and refrains, useful research findings and observations addressing the "big questions" of deliberative civic engagement.

To stretch the metaphor mercilessly, we realize that you may be reading this chapter either before or after making your way through each section of the hymnal. Whether you have arrived at this page as a patient, linear reader or as an anxious parishioner peeking ahead, you may wonder whether you are a "member of the congregation" for which we prepared this songbook. Rest assured, *Democracy in Motion* speaks for an inclusive community, welcoming into its fold any and all. There is much to be learned here if you are a government official considering using deliberative civic engagement to fulfill public participation obligations and responsibilities or to help avoid backlash on a tough political decision. There is much to learn if you are leader in a nongovernmental organization (NGO), hoping to tap deliberative civic engagement to address an important community issue. And there is certainly much to learn if you are a student or researcher who wants to come up to speed quickly on the large and dispersed literature on deliberative civic engagement.

In this concluding chapter, we offer two final contributions—a review of key findings and questions from the preceding chapters, and a look forward to unresolved questions and directions for future study. In a sense, we hope to guide you back through the greatest hits in this humble hymnal and to make notes of our own about which songs are yet unsung and where, it seems, a few of the songbook's pages have gone missing.

Main Findings

The first job of *Democracy in Motion* has been to integrate the literature from the dozen or more academic fields that have embarked on the study of deliberative civic engagement.[1] Looking across the previous chapters, the following conclusions stand out:

- Deliberative civic engagement is rapidly proliferating and evolving in response to the changing expectations and capacities of ordinary people and to the new political, social, and economic conditions facing leaders and managers in many different types of organizations around the world (see Chapter 2).
- Like virtually all forms of political participation, people of higher socioeconomic status get overrepresented in deliberative civic engagement; however, practitioners have shown that they can increase the representativeness of deliberative civic engagement significantly by using random sampling (at a cost) or targeted, network-based recruitment (to a point) (see Chapter 3).
- Well-structured deliberative events generally produce high-quality discussion, even among diverse participants. Such events distinguish themselves from more commonplace public meetings by their emphasis on deliberative communication norms, trained facilitators, and a degree of concern about facing trade-offs and finding common ground (see Chapter 4).
- Deliberative civic engagement can help alleviate social problems of exclusion, marginalization, and inequality, particularly when proactive design strategies are employed, such as the use of impartial moderators, the facilitation of reciprocity and mutual respect, having and sharing balanced information, and using alternative modes of communication (see Chapter 5).

- Early research suggests that online deliberation is already an effective complement to face-to-face deliberation because it is more convenient and effective for certain tasks, such as brainstorming. As a replacement for face-to-face deliberation, online deliberation can be effective for group decision making when it allows participants to hear and see each other synchronously (in real time). There are, however, trade-offs: Text-based, asynchronous deliberation may be less effective for fostering mutual understanding or changes in opinion, but it seems to compel broader participation and a greater variety of viewpoints (see Chapter 6).
- Deliberative civic engagement can have educative effects for individual participants, particularly in terms of opinion quality and civic capacities (see Chapter 7).
- Deliberation provides a powerful tool for increasing community capacity. As our sense of community declines, deliberative civic engagement can revive a sense of shared mission and lead people to expect themselves and their leaders to work together to solve common problems (see Chapter 8).
- Deliberative civic engagement can have short, medium, and long-term policy impacts, although more research is needed to empirically demonstrate these outcomes (see Chapter 9).

Among the many useful insights *Democracy in Motion* provides, two chapters pull together suggestions and findings from each section of the book. Chapter 10 synthesizes the research from the preceding chapters into a comprehensive evaluation tool that we hope future practitioners and researchers will seriously consider using in their projects. The chapter recommends readily available methods for evaluation that can be used for projects with very small budgets that must focus on only one or two evaluation criteria, as well as for projects with larger budgets that are seeking deeper and more innovative evaluations. The chapter does not offer novel instruments and metrics but instead provides a common language that could be used to frame and then integrate studies across a wide range of deliberative civic engagement efforts.

If these evaluation suggestions are adopted, *Democracy in Motion* will go a long way toward resolving several problems for both researchers and practitioners. For researchers, the practices and outcomes of deliberations seem so varied that describing a consistent "deliberation effect" proves difficult. Establishing a set of shared evaluation tools will help researchers determine what works, when, and why. For practitioners, these tools will clarify the goals of deliberation and provide rigorous feedback about whether goals were achieved.

Chapter 11 also provides a unique synthesis of the findings in *Democracy in Motion* by directly tackling some of the strongest criticisms of deliberative civic engagement. That chapter catalogs a litany of concerns, ranging from apprehension about the motivation and capacity of citizens to deliberate, to anxieties about the feasibility and cost of creating deliberative forums. The well-informed responses to these criticisms vary depending on their nature. The concerns about how citizens experience deliberation, for instance, get evaluated by empirical data: By and large, it turns out that citizens are eager to participate in deliberative events, capable of doing so, and routinely benefit from them.

Critics' concerns about process are less easily evaluated. Some of the criticisms already have inspired improvement in how deliberative events are organized. For example, organizers have enhanced their capacity to assemble a diverse and demographically representative body of participants, either through random sampling methods or a focus on community mapping that helps organizers better recognize underrepresented constituencies for targeted recruitment. Many deliberation formats now include storytelling and welcome other modes of expression beyond formal argument to lessen inequalities across social groups with different speaking traditions.

Some important criticisms, however, remain unanswered, and we will review some of those—and suggest some of our own—in the following sections. The more important lesson may be to forgo the temptation to divide into critics and advocates. The findings thus far suggest that the practice of deliberative civic engagement benefits tremendously from both external and internal criticism. In the end, it pays to bring the outsiders in (as project consultants) and for the insiders to step outside their own projects. The authors of Chapters 10 and 11 (along with their outside reviewers) have done so effectively, as they have both sought out criticism and helped engineer deliberative projects that profit from such critique. This should also spur more critically informed evaluations of deliberative events, as is proposed in Chapter 10, which, in turn, will help us weigh the merits of criticisms expressed in Chapter 11, as well as the issues discussed next.

Unresolved Questions

Democracy in Motion also hopes to set an agenda for studying the most important questions that remain unanswered. Three central questions about the outcomes and impacts of deliberation remain unresolved. First, Chapter 7 shows that it is unclear precisely when and how deliberation transforms participants into better citizens. Though some persuasive evidence has accumulated to show that deliberation renders more reflective, informed, and coherent judgments, most aspects of "better citizenship" remain insufficiently tested. Even those who advocate the intrinsic merits of deliberation often have an implicit assumption that it necessarily comes with straightforward benefits to participants. That assumption remains one worthy of continued testing across different deliberative designs, different subgroups of the public, and the full range of civic attitudes and habits that deliberation might transform.

Second, Chapter 8 shows that deliberative civic engagement has the potential, to which it often rises, to build community capacity. Nevertheless, important questions remain about *how* deliberative civic engagement makes these community capacity contributions, and whether such contributions are sustained beyond the scope and time frame of the initiative. Future research will benefit from systematically adopting and applying the Community Capacity Building Framework,[2] as well as examining other community characteristics, to investigations of the effects of deliberative civic engagement on community capacity.

Finally, Chapter 9 leaves us wondering how often and under what circumstances public deliberation influences public policy. This chapter contributes to improving how we think about policy impacts, particularly in terms of the timing of deliberative events in the policy making cycle and the different roles that citizens can play in different institutional designs. Moreover, the chapter offers strong evidence that deliberation *can* have considerable impact, from the direct and obvious impacts of empowered citizen deliberation (for example, in criminal/civil juries and participatory budgeting) to the ongoing impact of other embedded deliberative processes. When one creates a deliberative innovation, however, such as a one-time event or a more elaborate round of deliberation, it may or may not yield policy results depending on its inclusivity, legitimacy, deliberativeness, and other as-yet-unclear factors.

The other chapters in this volume also raise unresolved issues. How representative must a deliberation be—and how closely must the participants match the demographic characteristics of the larger population—to be considered legitimate, and to produce policy impacts? Can we rely on equitable deliberations, in which a wide range of people participate and have an equal opportunity to be heard, to produce equitable outcomes? How does participation in deliberation vary across countries (e.g., those with more or less communitarian traditions) and institutional contexts (e.g., those with weaker or stronger representative institutions)? Can we institutionalize deliberative civic engagement in deeply divided societies? How do the dynamics of deliberation differ between online and face-to-face formats, and how can we achieve the significant promise of online deliberative civic engagement? These are just a few of the ample theoretical and empirical questions to keep research in the field growing and providing meaningful insights for years to come.

Going Farther and Going Further

Yet we can and should go farther and further than we have in this volume. In defining our target audience for the book, we have risked singing with the choir in the interest of creating a common songbook. After all, this book project was born at a meeting of researchers and practitioners interested in deliberation and public life. And given how such works circulate, most readers already have a good idea about deliberative civic engagement and why it is important. After all, even the harshest critics of deliberation already care enough about democracy and public participation to take the deliberative approach seriously. Most readers take for granted that democracy faces fresh challenges and new opportunities and that deliberation factors into conversations about both. Next, we identify but a few areas where we could extend our study of deliberation.

The Rhetorical Problem of Deliberative Advocacy

If we step outside the deliberative cathedral and seek to sing with ever wider circles of concerned citizens, civic reformers, and public-minded scholars, we will need to address other issues that this volume set aside. Who has the problem that deliberative civic engagement solves? Is it government officials or leaders of NGOs? Is it average citizens? Is it researchers? All of the above? If we presume that is officials and NGO leaders, how many of these leaders are aware that they have a "deliberation gap?" How would they think about the problem—as a way to get reelected, to control or improve public participation, or something else? Those who already see deliberation as a solution may not know whom to persuade and whether there is a persuasive argument to present. As an irreverent investor might say, "Your solution is not my problem!"

To the extent that the research compiled in this volume has shown many of deliberation's strengths and benefits, the present challenge constitutes a *rhetorical* problem—specifically that of knowing one's audience, establishing one's ethos, and determining what constitutes a convincing appeal. From a scholar's perspective, such problems call for more focused research on how potential stakeholders in deliberative civic engagement frame their problems. It may turn out that citizens view their problems and needs differently from government officials, and both of these groups view the problem differently from leaders of NGOs.[3] For example, the methods of evaluation presented in Chapter 10 may mesh more with how elites view deliberation than how citizens do. Citizens would likely favor engagement that allows a greater role to set agendas and to frame issues, and they would view the quality of discussions based on how naturally they flow and the degree to which they are engaging.

Research on this might start with interviews and surveys. Chapter 2 took a move in that direction by providing descriptive information about who is organizing deliberative events and their motivations for doing so. It may well prove true, as that chapter suggests, that the primary driver for local leaders to adopt deliberative civic engagement is to avoid political backlash on tough decisions and to avoid painful experiences with town hall meetings and other ad hoc forms of engagement. By contrast, nonprofit leaders may be turning to deliberation with a thinly veiled agenda—to advance a specific cause or conclusion that they intend the process to validate.

Since sponsors of events view deliberation primarily as a means not an end, the interests of sponsors and the ideals of deliberation may clash. Even if sponsors abide by the internal tenets of deliberation—such as unbiased facilitation and discussion materials—they may still seek to manipulate the process from the outside by managing how it is presented through the media, or by failing to include a wide range of organizations and people in the recruitment process.

Similarly, we should be concerned about why advocates of deliberation, particularly at the state/provincial and federal/national levels, commonly favor left-leaning causes. Some of the most important deliberative innovations, such as the British Columbia Citizens' Assembly, came from the imaginations of right-of-center public officials, and direct evidence on deliberation's aggregate impact on opinion does *not* suggest a clear left-leaning bias.[4] As Chapter 2 argues, it is also true that many local deliberative projects have been initiated by moderate or even conservative leaders. Nonetheless, there exists the stereotype of deliberation as a liberal project.

Consider the recent case of the Oregon Citizens' Initiative Review. This process was established with strong bipartisan support in 2009, and the evidence of its impact on the 2010 election showed that it turned voters against one conservative initiative (instituting mandatory minimum sentencing) and against one liberal measure (to expand medical marijuana access). When the process was made permanent in 2011, it passed with bi-partisan support in an evenly divided legislature, but its only opposition votes came from a large bloc of conservative Republicans. Though none spoke out against the measure, its support was not universal.[5]

One explanation might be the implicit cultural language commonly used to advance deliberation.[6] The deliberative cause is often framed as one of equality (of voice and opportunity), concern for the disenfranchised, and appeals to consensus and community. These cultural themes make sense, but one can also make appeals for deliberation that respect NGO action, local control, and the power of citizens to control public spending.

More broadly, one can appeal to the values of hierarchy and individualism—the twin values that complement equality and community. Sensible appeals to more hierarchical values include the special recognition deliberation affords professional expertise, from the policy elites who answer questions during Deliberative Polls, to the witnesses in Citizen Juries, to the behind-the-scenes advocates and experts who help write briefing materials at virtually every well-structured deliberative event. More fundamentally, deliberation asks for the creation of *informed* public voices, a clear admission that one can distinguish the shout of the mob from the "mild voice of reason."[7]

As for celebrating the individual, deliberation's advocates could make clearer that seeking a "reasoned consensus" does not mean permitting a premature consensus. For instance, even when the criminal jury system requires unanimity for a verdict, judges accept hung juries in roughly 10 percent of cases. When deliberating juries reach an impasse, it is common for a judge to both encourage further deliberation but also to admonish jurors not to yield for the sake of agreement.[8] In this sense, the appeal to reasoned argument grounds itself in a radical individualism, one that asks each person to yield only to the force of the better argument, rejecting the impulse to conform or the urge to belong.

With greater understanding of the interests and cultural language of prospective sponsors, we can tune deliberative civic engagement processes to their frequency. With greater understanding of these interests, we can figure out how best to reach them and use their own words in our messages. In any case, understanding these kinds of motivations will reveal missed opportunities for deliberation, but it will also illuminate (and hopefully help to forestall) potential abuses of deliberative processes.

Understanding the Deliberative Moment

A less obvious consequence of "preaching to the choir" is that this book has only partially answered the question, *Why now?* It is true, as stated in Chapter 1, that there is a growing movement for deliberative civic engagement among researchers and practitioners from "America to Zimbabwe." It is also true (as stated in Chapter 2) that in the past few decades, surveys show growing support for policies that seek to increase civic engagement. Yet the idea of deliberative civic engagement dates back at least to ancient Athens, after which its appeal has ebbed and flowed. A deliberative moment came and went early in the twentieth century, only to return in the late 1980s.[9]

In part, technological changes in communication media have driven the current renewal. The Internet, and social media in particular, have accelerated the growth of citizen capacities, connectedness, and attitudinal change. As discussed in Chapter 6, new technologies also present new opportunities to deal with the challenges of scale and cost.[10] As deliberation becomes cheaper and better, it is an increasingly viable alternative for public participation.

But only a small subset of deliberation research projects focus on technological innovations, and the general practice of deliberation reflects the low priority typically placed on innovation and technology. Returning to the example of the Oregon Citizens' Initiative Review, this week-long analysis of complex ballot measures used hand-held "clickers" for tabulating votes, but it principally relied on oversized Post-its and easels to exhibit participants' comments on the walls. Such experiences raise important questions. How do we better utilize mobile computing to improve deliberation, particularly with participants and audiences of widely varying comfort with new technologies? To reach beyond the smaller set of deliberators at any given event, how do we leverage online social networking to reach and engage wider audiences? Answering questions like these should be at the core of the field and require the insights of everyone from new-technology pioneers to classical political philosophers.

Understanding Designs and Outcomes in Context

As is evident from the many chapters in this book, advocates of public deliberation—scholars, practitioners, and civic leaders alike—have suggested that deliberative engagement can lead to numerous benefits for individual citizens, public officials, communities, policy, and governance. And while the preceding chapters often point to empirical evidence of such benefits, they also report mixed results. These mixed results, along with critics' concerns (see Chapter 11), suggest at least one sure conclusion: Not all deliberative processes are created equal in terms of their ability to generate specific outcomes.

This conclusion should not be surprising. John Dewey recognized long ago that the challenge of public participation lies in "the improvement of the methods and conditions of debate, discussion, and persuasion."[11] While much progress has been made since Dewey's time, there is still tremendous multiplicity in the design and goals of deliberative processes due to the wealth of tools, techniques, and procedures available. Moreover, there is almost exponential variety in such efforts because of the possible contexts and policy areas where deliberation can be used. This raises the issue of how to design deliberative civic engagement processes to maximize the likelihood of achieving desired goals and other positive outcomes. Or, posed as research questions: What deliberative design choices are best for attaining specific goals? And what design choices are most likely to lead to what outcomes? The logic behind these questions is simple: It is likely that the outcomes of deliberative civic engagement (good, bad, or inconclusive) are, in part, a function of design.

Some theoretical work about the connection between participatory design and outcomes has been done. For example, using the term *minipublics* to describe the convening of citizens in self-consciously organized public deliberations, public policy scholar Archon Fung has identified eight important institutional design choices (vision and type of minipublic, how participants are recruited and selected, the subject and scope of deliberation, deliberative mode, frequency of recurrence and iteration, the stakes, degree of participant empowerment, and extent of monitoring) and has hypothesized how these design choices affect the quality of democratic governance in terms of ten functional outcomes (civic engagement as quantity of participation, participation bias, quality of deliberation, informing officials, informing citizens, democratic skills and socialization, official accountability, justice of policy, effectiveness of public action, and popular mobilization).[12] Similarly, chapter co-author Tina Nabatchi has generated a theoretically based list of propositions about how some of these and other participatory design choices are likely to affect the ability of public administrators to identify and understand the public values in play for a given controversial policy issue.[13] Other design choices are also likely to matter—for example, the instruments and materials given to participants, the role of facilitators and moderators, and implementation issues such as logistics, venues, timing, and reporting.

Such theoretical work provides numerous areas ripe for future research about the effects of design choices on outcomes, but we think three areas are particularly exciting. First, we must recognize that design choices are not made in a linear fashion. Instead, they are interrelated, made through an iterative and integrative process, and completed under consideration of numerous other factors, such as: the goals for deliberative engagement (i.e., why deliberation is wanted or needed and the hopes about what it will accomplish); the stakes for participants (i.e., why participants want to deliberate and their perceptions about the importance of the issue); timing (i.e., how quickly a decision needs to be made or an outcome reached); mandates, laws, rules, and/or regulations; and organizational context and conditions (e.g., budget, human and other resources, available technologies, and logistical constraints). Understanding these contextual factors and their impacts on both design opportunities and outcomes will be an important area of research.

Second, research connecting design and outcomes should not simply focus on issues of *process design* (i.e., choices about specific elements within an individual participatory event) but also must look at issues of *systems design* (i.e., choices made about the overall structure of participatory endeavors).[14] Issues of systems design will be particularly important when deliberative civic engagement is used in a governmental arena (e.g., by legislative or administrative bodies) as opposed to a civil society arena (e.g., by an NGO or community, nonprofit, or academic organization).

Finally, it is important to recognize that context matters. Though deliberation has value in a wide range of settings, we believe the governmental context is particularly important to examine, as this is where we are likely to see deliberation used to make real changes to policies that have broad impacts on citizens. Specifically, we believe that scholars and practitioners need to give critical and sustained attention to the role of public administration and administrative agencies in deliberative civic engagement. Such attention is vital given the rapidly changing political, social, economic, and environmental landscape of this new governance era.[15] Several research agendas for deliberation in public administration have been offered elsewhere, so only a few points are covered here.[16]

First, and perhaps most important, we cannot neglect what may be the ultimate systems and process design choice in public administration—the connection to the policy process. Specifically, we need to understand the point(s) in the policy cycle at which deliberative processes are most effective. Are certain processes more effective at certain points? Does the policy issue and context within which deliberation occurs affect the outcomes? Some scholars have provided theoretical work that may be useful for answering these and related questions. For example, some scholars have distinguished between deliberative processes that are quasi-legislative (i.e., deliberations that occur "upstream" in the policy-making process as prospective activities that help set standards, guidelines, expectations, or rules and regulations for behavior) versus quasi-judicial (i.e., deliberations that occur "downstream" in the policy-making process as retrospective, fact-based, and/or that determine the rights or obligations of selected citizens or stakeholders).[17] Fung provides a different way of thinking about the connection between deliberation and the policy process: His "democracy cube" maps the institutional possibilities for engaging citizens in democratic governance in different areas of public sector decision making.[18] Such frameworks may be helpful in examining the connection of deliberative civic engagement to the stages in and domains of the policy process.

Second, we "need comparative research to determine whether modern deliberative processes are more effective, less effective, or even different from other modern non-deliberative citizen participation processes, as well as older processes such as community boards, advisory commissions, and even the notion of representative bureaucracy (i.e., Jacksonian participation)."[19]

Third, we need to focus on different levels of analysis—from the *micro level* (e.g., at the level of the individual citizen, do these processes affect the public's understanding of its roles in government and governance? Do they change individual perceptions of government and governance?), to the *group level* (e.g., how do deliberative groups function and to what end?), to the *organizational level* (e.g., how does deliberative engagement foster or hinder institutional capacities for collaboration, conflict resolution, decision making, and effective public action?), and to the *macro level* (e.g., what are the impacts of larger political, technological, economic, historic, and other social forces on deliberative civic engagement?).

Fourth, we need research useful to public leaders and managers. For example, "What are the obstacles to greater use of deliberative processes? How should managers decide on what processes to use when? How do (or might) deliberative processes affect the discretion, power, and control of administrators and other public decision makers? How and how effectively are decisions from these processes implemented and monitored over time?"[20] How might legal frameworks for deliberative engagement be bolstered to improve the authority of agencies and administrators to engage in such work?[21]

Finally, we need research that explores deliberative civic engagement vis-à-vis public affairs education. Specifically, what are the skills, abilities, and areas of knowledge required of public managers who utilize deliberative civic engagement, and how do we train the next generation of public leaders and managers to do such work?

In sum, we in the field of deliberative civic engagement need to make progress on issues of design, outcomes, and context. Specifically, we need to know what deliberative design choices are best for attaining specific goals, and what design choices are most likely to lead to what outcomes. Such research will be particularly important within the domain of public administration. There is a need to move toward consilience in the accumulation and integration of theory and empirical evidence, particularly concerning the connection between design and outcomes, but also in other areas of deliberative civic engagement.

Conclusion

Trying to capture all of the insights and questions emerging from the development of deliberative civic engagement is an ambitious project. There will always be a tension—one hopes it will be a creative and dynamic one—between research and practice and among academic fields. But we should recognize that the limitations of this book are actually an opportunity.

Whether we are researchers, practitioners, public officials, or advocates, we should first develop a better understanding of why deliberative work matters, why it is proliferating, and why it makes political sense for the people who initiate, support, or take part in these projects. Next, we should confront the reasons that—despite the proliferation of these efforts—most people are still unaware of deliberative civic engagement, its tenets, and its basic strategies. We need to push farther and further on the research questions, especially the critical ones about whether deliberation creates better citizens and better policy. We should use the new evaluation tool proposed in Chapter 10 to accelerate learning. We should do our best to guide and ground future innovations, especially those that attempt to harness the potential of new interactive and social technologies.

Though the leaps forward in technology and citizen capacity make predictions and prescriptions difficult, we can at least help innovators avoid the most obvious mistakes, and lay out the lessons from practice and scholarship that can drive future experimentation. Finally, we should more closely consider and examine issues of design, outcomes, and context.

Most of the people drawn to deliberative civic engagement possess some combination of critical, clear-eyed scholarship and fervent, open-eyed advocacy. This makes sense, because the changes in citizen expectations and the questioning of traditional forms of expertise are among the primary pressures now reshaping democracy. Deliberative civic engagement is happening because it responds to practical problems and resonates with the desires of citizens. It is a cause that is compelling to both the heart and the mind. It seems important that we carry on in this spirit, retaining a combination of criticism and passion, and communicate it more effectively to others. Let us sing the hymns of deliberative civic engagement, write new songs, and teach them to others. After all, it's likely the best way to keep democracy in motion.

Notes

1. Carcasson (2008).
2. Chaskin, Brown, Venkatesh, and Vidal (2001).
3. For a discussion of what types of information would be convincing to elected officials, see Nabatchi and Farrar (2011).
4. Gastil, Bacci, and Dollinger (2010); Gastil and Dillard (1999b).
5. See Gastil and Knobloch (2010) and the news archive at the Healthy Democracy Oregon Web site.
6. Gastil, Reedy, Braman, and Kahan (2008); see also Kahan (2007).
7. Bessette (1997).
8. Gastil, Deess, Weiser, and Simmons (2010).
9. Gastil and Keith (2005); Keith (2007).
10. *The Guardian* provides a glimpse of one such process in Iceland at http://www.guardian.co.uk/world/2011/jun/09/iceland-crowdsourcing-constitution-facebook.
11. John Dewey (1927 [1988]: 365).
12. Fung (2003).
13. Nabatchi (2012b).
14. Nabatchi (2011).
15. Bingham, Nabatchi, O'Leary (2005); Bingham, O'Leary, and Nabatchi (2005); (Nabatchi 2010a).
16. See, for example, Bingham, Nabatchi, and O'Leary (2005); Bingham and O'Leary (2006); CDN (2006); Roberts (2008). The list of research questions below is adapted from Nabatchi (2010a).
17. Bingham, Nabatchi, and O'Leary (2005); Bingham, O'Leary, and Nabatchi (2005).
18. Fung (2006).
19. Nabatchi (2010a: 390).
20. Nabatchi (2010a: 392).
21. For discussions, see Bingham (2008, 2010) and Bingham, Nabatchi, and O'Leary (2005).

REFERENCES

Abelson, Julia, John Eyles, Christopher B. McLeod, Patricia Collins, Colin McMullan, and Pierre-Gerlier Forest. 2003. Does deliberation make a difference? Results from a citizens panel study of health goals priority setting. *Health Policy* 66(1): 95–106.

Abelson, Julia, and Francois-Pierre Gauvin. 2006. *Assessing the impacts of public participation: Concepts, evidence, and policy implications.* Ottawa: Canadian Policy Research Networks.

Abers, Rebecca. 2001. *Inventing local democracy: Grassroots politics in Brazil.* Boulder: Westview Press.

Ackerman, Bruce, and James S. Fishkin. 2002. Deliberation day. *Journal of Political Philosophy* 10(2): 129–152.

Ackerman, Bruce, and James S. Fishkin. 2004. *Deliberation day.* New Haven: Yale University Press.

Adams, Susan J., Sylvia G. Roch, and Roya Ayman. 2005. Communication medium and member familiarity: The effects of decision time, accuracy, and satisfaction. *Small Group Research* 36: 321–353.

Agné, Hans. 2011. Answering questions in parliament during budget debates: Deliberative reciprocity and globalisation in Western Europe. *Parliamentary Affairs* 64(1): 153–174.

Albrecht, Steffen. 2006. Whose voice is heard in online deliberation? A study of participation and representation in political debates on the internet. *Information, Communication, & Society* 9(1): 62–82.

Alesina, Alberto, and Eliana La Ferrara. 2000. Participation in heterogeneous communities. *Quarterly Journal of Economics* 115(3): 847–904.

American Institutes for Research. 2011. Community forum deliberative methods literature review. Working draft February 7.

America*Speaks.* 2007. *DC Citizen Summit—Neighborhood Action Initiative.* Washington, DC: America*Speaks.* http://www.americaspeaks.org/index.cfm?fuseaction=Page.viewPage&pageId=638&grandparentID=473&parentID=499. September 19, 2008.

Ansell, Chris, and Alison Gash, 2008. Collaborative governance in theory and practice. *Journal of Public Administration, Research and Theory* 18(4): 543–571.

Anusuya, M. A., and Shriniwas K. Katti. 2009. Speech recognition by machine: A review. *International Journal of Computer Science and Information Security* 6(3): 181–205.

Arnstein, Sherry R. 1969. A ladder of citizen participation. *American Institute of Planners Journal* 35(4): 216–224.

Asteroff, Janet F. 1982. Electronic bulletin boards, a case study. *Columbia University Center for Computing Activities.* Spring 1982. http://www.columbia.edu/acis/history/bboard.html.

Bächtiger, André, Simon J. Niemeyer, Michael Neblo, Marco R. Steenbergen, and Jürg Steiner. 2010. Disentangling diversity in deliberative democracy: Competing theories, their blind spots and complementarities. *Journal of Political Philosophy* 18(1): 32–63.

Bailenson, Jeremy N., Andrew C. Beall, Jack Loomis, Jim Blascovich, and Matthew Turk. 2004. Transformed social interaction: Decoupling representation from behavior and form in collaborative virtual environments. *Presence: Teleoperators and Virtual Environments* 13: 428–441.

Bailenson, Jeremy N., Andrew C. Beall, Jack Loomis, Jim Blascovich, and Matthew Turk. 2005. Transformed social interaction, augmented gaze, and social influence in immersive virtual environments. *Human Communication Research* 31(October): 511–537.

Baiocchi, Gianpaolo. 2001. Participation, activism, and politics: The Porto Alegre experiment and deliberative democratic theory. *Politics and Society* 29: 43–72.

Baiocchi, Gianpaolo. 2003. Emergent public spheres: Talking politics in participatory governance. *American Sociological Review* 68(1): 52–74.

Baker, Dean. 2010. America speaks back: Derailing the drive to cut social security and Medicare. *Huffington Post*, June 21. http://www.huffingtonpost.com/dean-baker/america-speaks-back-derai_b_619465.html. August 20, 2010.

Balch, George I. 1974. Multiple indicators in survey research: The concept of "sense of political efficacy." *Political Methodology* 1: 1–43.

Baltes, Boris B., Marcus W. Dickson, Michael P. Sherman, Cara C. Bauer, and Jacqueline S. LaGanke. 2002. Computer-mediated communication and group decision making: A meta-analysis. *Organizational Behavior and Human Decision Processes* 87(January): 156–179.

Bandura, Albert. 1997. *Self-efficacy: The exercise of control.* New York: W. H. Freeman.

Barabas, Jason. 2004. How deliberation affects policy opinions. *American Political Science Review* 98(4): 687–701.

Barber, Benjamin. 1984. *Strong democracy: Participatory politics for a new age.* Berkeley: University of California Press.

Bartels, Larry. 2008. *Unequal democracy: The political economy of the new gilded age.* Princeton: Princeton University Press.

Baxamusa, Murtaza H. 2008. Empowering communities through deliberation: The model of community benefits agreements. *Journal of Planning Education and Research* 27: 261–276.

Baym, Nancy. 1998. The emergence of community in computer-mediated communication. In *Cybersociety 2.0: Revisiting computer-mediated communication and community,* ed. Steven G. Jones, 35–68. Thousand Oaks, CA: Sage.

Becker-Beck, Ulrike, Margret Wintermantel, and Anna Borg. 2005. Principles of regulating interaction in teams practicing face-to-face communication versus teams practicing computer-mediated communication. *Small Group Research* 36: 499–536.

Beierle, Thomas C. 2004. Digital deliberation: Engaging the public through online policy dialogues. In *Democracy online: The prospects for political renewal through the internet,* ed. Peter M. Shane, 155–166. New York: Routledge.

Beierle, Thomas C., and Jerry Cayford. 2002. *Democracy in practice: Public participation in environmental decisions.* Washington, DC: Resources for the Future Press.

Beierle, Thomas C., and David M. Konisky. 2000. Values, conflict, and trust in participatory environmental planning. *Journal of Policy Analysis and Management* 19(4): 587–602.

Bellah, Robert N., Richard Madsen, William M. Sullivan, and Ann Swidler. 1984. *Habits of the heart: Individualism and commitment in American life.* Berkeley: University of California Press.

Bellah, Robert N., Richard Madsen, Steven M. Tipton, William M. Sullivan, and Ann Swidler. 1989. *The good society.* New York: Knopf.

Benhabib, Seyla. 1990. Communicative ethics and contemporary controversies in practical philosophy. In *The communicative ethics controversy,* ed. Seyla Benhabib and Fred Dallmayr, 330–371. Cambridge: MA: MIT Press.

Benhabib, Seyla, ed. 1996. *Democracy and difference: Contesting the boundaries of the political.* Princeton: Princeton University Press.

Benhabib, Seyla. 2002. *The claims of culture: Equality and diversity in the global era.* Princeton, NJ: Princeton University Press.

Benhabib, Seyla. 2004. *The rights of others: Aliens, residents, and citizens.* Cambridge, UK: Cambridge University Press.

Benhabib, Seyla. 2006. *Another cosmopolitanism.* New York: Oxford University Press.

Benhabib, Seyla. 2007. Democratic exclusions and democratic iterations. *European Journal of Political Theory* 6(4): 445–462.

Benhabib, Seyla. 2008. The legitimacy of human rights. *Daedalus* 137(3): 94–104.

Berry, Jeffrey M., Kent E. Portney, and Ken Thomson. 1993. *The rebirth of urban democracy.* Washington, DC: Brookings Institution.

Bessette, Joseph M. 1997. *The mild voice of reason: Deliberative democracy and American national government.* Chicago: University of Chicago Press.

Beierle, Thomas C., and Jerry Cayford. 2002. *Democracy in practice: Public participation in environmental decisions.* Washington, DC: Resources for the Future Press.

Bingham, Lisa Blomgren. 2008. Legal frameworks for collaboration in governance and public management. In *Big ideas in collaborative public management,* ed. Lisa Blomgren Bingham and Rosemary O'Leary, 247–269. Armonk, NY: M. E. Sharpe.

Bingham, Lisa Blomgren. 2010. The next generation of administrative law: Building the legal infrastructure for collaborative governance. *Wisconsin Law Review* 2010(2): 297–356.

Bingham, Lisa Blomgren, Tina Nabatchi, and Rosemary O'Leary. 2005. The new governance: Practices and processes for stakeholder and citizen participation in the work of government. *Public Administration Review* 65: 528–539.

Bingham, Lisa Blomgren, Rosemary O'Leary, and Tina Nabatchi. 2005. New governance processes for stakeholder and citizen participation in the work of government. *National Civic Review* 94(1): 54–61.

Bingham, Lisa Blomgren, and Rosemary O'Leary. 2006. Parallel play, not collaboration: Missing questions, missing connections. *Public Administration Review* 66 (Suppl. 1): 161–167.

Bishop, George. 2005. *The illusion of public opinion: Fact and artifact in American public opinion.* Lanham, MD: Rowman and Littlefield.

Björkman, Martina, and Jakob Svensson. 2007. Power to the people: Evidence from a randomized field experience of a community-based monitoring project in Uganda. Policy Research Working Paper Series No. 4268, World Bank, Washington, DC.

Black, Laura W. 2008. Deliberation, storytelling, and dialogic moments. *Communication Theory* 18: 93–116.

Black, Laura W. 2009. Listening to the city: Difference, identity, and storytelling in online deliberative groups. *Journal of Public Deliberation* 5(1): Article 4.

Black, Laura W., Stephanie Burkhalter, John Gastil, and Jennifer Stromer-Galley. 2010. Methods for analyzing and measuring group deliberation. In *The sourcebook for political communication research: Methods, measures, and analytic techniques,* ed. Eric P. Bucy and R. Lance Holbert, 323–345. New York: Routledge.

Black, Laura W., Howard T. Welser, Jocelyn DeGroot, and Daniel Cosley. 2008. "Wikipedia is not a democracy": Deliberation and policy making in an online community. Paper presented in the Political Communication division of the International Communication Association annual convention, Montreal.

Blumler, Jay G., and Stephen Coleman. 2001. Realising democracy online: A civic commons in cyberspace. IPPR/Citizens Online Research Publication No. 2, March. http://www.citizensonline.org.uk/site/media/documents/925_Realising%20Democracy%20Online.pdf.

Bobbio, Norberto. 1987. *The future of democracy: A defense of the rules of the game.* Trans. Roger Griffin. Cambridge: Polity.

Bohman, James. 1988. Emancipation and rhetoric: The perlocutions and illocutions of the social critic. *Philosophy and Rhetoric* 21(3): 185–203.

Bohman, James. 1995. Public reason and cultural pluralism: Political liberalism and the problem of moral conflict. *Political Theory* 23: 253–279.

Bohman, James. 1998. Survey article: The coming of age of deliberative democracy. *Journal of Political Philosophy* 6(4): 400–425.

Bohman, James. 2007. Political communication and the epistemic value of diversity: Deliberation and legitimation in media societies. *Communication Theory* 17: 340–347.

Bojer, Marianne Mille, Heiko Roehl, Marianne Knuth, and Colleen Magner. 2008. *Mapping dialogue: Essential tools for social change.* Chagrin Falls, OH: Taos Institute Publications.

Bottger, Preston C. 1984. Expertise and air time as bases of actual and perceived influence in problem-solving groups. *Journal of Applied of Psychology* 69: 214–221.

Boulding, Carew, and Brian Wampler. 2010. Voice, votes and resources: Evaluating the effect of participatory democracy on well-being. *World Development* 38(1): 125–135.

Boyte, Harry. 2011. *We the people politics: The populist promise of deliberative public work.* Dayton, OH: Kettering Foundation. http://www.kettering.org/media_room/publications/We-the-People-Politics.

Brannon, Rovy F., and Christopher Essex. 2001. Synchronous and asynchronous communication tools in distance education: A survey of instructors. *TechTrends* 45(1): 36–42.

Briggs, Xavier de Souza. 2008. *Democracy as problem solving: Civic capacity in communities across the globe.* Cambridge, MA: MIT Press.

Brinkerhoff, Derick W., and Benjamin Crosby. 2002. Citizen participation in the policy process. In *Managing policy reform: Concepts and tools for decision-makers in developing and transitioning countries.* Bloomfield, CT: Kumarian Press.

Brown, Rupert. 2000. *Group processes.* 2nd ed. Oxford: Blackwell.

Bryan, Frank M. 2004. *Real democracy: The New England town meeting and how it works.* Chicago: University of Chicago Press.

Burkhalter, Stephanie, John Gastil, and Todd Kelshaw. 2002. A conceptual definition and theoretical model of public deliberation in small face-to-face groups. *Communication Theory* 12: 398–422.

Burnheim, John. 1985. *Is democracy possible? The alternative to electoral politics.* Berkeley: University of California Press.

Burns, Nancy, Kay L. Schlozman, and Sidney Verba. 2001. *The private roots of public action: Gender, equality, and political participation.* Cambridge: Harvard University Press.

Button, Mark, and Kevin Mattson. 1999. Deliberative democracy in practice: Challenges and prospects for civic deliberation. *Polity* 31: 609–637.

Button, Mark, and David M. Ryfe. 2005. What can we learn from deliberative democracy? In *The deliberative democracy handbook: Strategies for effective civic engagement in the 21st century,* ed. John Gastil and Peter Levine, 20–33. San Francisco: Jossey-Bass.

Cacioppo, John T., and Richard E. Petty. 1982. The need for cognition. *Journal of Personality and Social Psychology* 42: 116–131.

Cacioppo, John T., Richard E. Petty, Jeffrey A. Feinstein, and W. Blair G. Jarvis. 1996. Dispositional differences in cognitive motivation: The life and times of individuals varying in need for cognition. *Psychological Bulletin* 119: 197–253.

Callenbach, Ernest, Michael Phillips, and Keith Sutherland. 2008. *A citizen legislature/A people's parliament.* Charlottesville, VA: Exeter.

Campbell, Andrea Louise. 2003. *How policies make citizens: Senior political activism and the American welfare state.* Princeton: Princeton University Press.

Campbell, Angus, Philip E. Converse, and Warren E. Miller. 1960. *The American voter.* New York: Wiley.

Campbell, Angus, Gerald Gurin, and Warren E. Miller. 1954. *The voter decides.* Evanston, IL: Row, Peterson.

Cappella, Joseph N., Vincent Price, and Lilach Nir. 2002. Argument repertoire as a reliable and valid measure of opinion quality: Electronic dialogue during campaign 2000. *Political Communication* 19: 73–93.

Carcasson, Martin. 2008. *Democracy's hubs: College and university centers as platforms for deliberative practice.* Dayton, OH: Kettering Foundation.

Carcasson, Martin. 2009. Beginning with the end in mind: A call for goal-driven deliberative practice. *Public Agenda.* Online. www.publicagenda.org/cape.

Card, Stuart K., Jock D. Mackinlay, and George G. Robertson. 1991. A morphological analysis of the design space of input devices. *ACM Transactions on Information Systems* 9(2): 99–122.

Carr, Deborah S., and Kathleen Halvorsen. 2001. An evaluation of three democratic, community-based approaches to citizen participation: Surveys, conversations with community groups, and community dinners. *Society and Natural Resources* 14: 107–126.

Carson, Lyn, and Janette Hartz-Karp. 2005. Adapting and combining deliberative designs: Juries, polls, and forums. In *The deliberative democracy handbook: Strategies for effective civic engagement in the 21st century*, ed. John Gastil and Peter Levine, 120–138. San Francisco: Jossey-Bass.

Carson, Lyn, and Brian Martin. 1999. *Random selection in politics.* Westport: Praeger.

Cavalier, Robert, with Miso Kim and Zachary Sam Zaiss. 2009. Deliberative democracy, online discussion, and project PICOLA (Public Informed Citizen Online Assembly). In *Online deliberation: Design, research, and practice*, ed. Todd Davies and Seeta Peña Gangadharan, 71–79. Stanford, CA: CSLI Publications.

Chambers, Simone. 2003. Deliberative democratic theory. *Annual Review of Political Science* 6: 307–326.

Chambers, Simone. 2009. Deliberation and mass democracy: Counting voices and making voices count. Paper presented at the American Political Science Association Annual Meeting, Toronto, ON.

Chaskin, Robert J. 2001. Building community capacity: A definitional framework and case studies from a comprehensive community initiative. *Urban Affairs Review* 36: 291–323.

Chaskin, Robert J., Prudence Brown, Sudhir Venkatesh, and Avis Vidal. 2001. *Building community capacity.* New York: A. de Gruyter.

Chess, Caron. 2000. Evaluating environmental public participation: Methodological questions. *Journal of Environmental Planning and Management* 43(6): 769–784.

Chong, Dennis, and James N. Druckman. 2007. Framing public opinion in competitive democracies. *American Political Science Review* 101(4): 637–655.

Chua, Amy. 2004. *World on fire: How exporting free market democracy breeds ethnic hatred and global instability.* New York: Anchor.

Clark, Herbert H. 1996. *Using language.* Cambridge, UK: Cambridge University Press.

Clark, Herbert H., and Susan Brennan. 1991. Grounding in communication. In *Perspectives on socially shared cognition*, ed. Lauren B. Resnick, John M. Levine, and Stephanie D. Teasley, 127–149. Washington, DC: American Psychological Association.

Clary, E. Gil, Mark Snyder, and Arthur A. Stukas. 1996. Volunteers' motivations: Findings from a national survey. *Nonprofit and Voluntary Sector Quarterly* 25: 485–505.

Coelho, Vera. 2011. Is social participation democratizing politics? In *Accountability through public opinion: From inertia to public action*, ed. Sina Odugbemi and Taeku Lee, 333–347. Washington, DC: World Bank.

Coelho, Vera S., Alexandre Ferraz, Fabiola Fanti, and Meire Ribeiro. 2010. Mobilization and participation: A win-win game? In *Mobilizing for democracy: Citizen action and the politics of public participation*, ed. Vera S. Coelho and Bettina von Lieres. London: Zed Books.

Coelho, Vera S., and Marcos Nobre, eds. 2004. *Participação e deliberação: teoria democrática e experiências institucionais no Brasil contemporâneo.* São Paulo: 34 Letras.

Coelho, Vera S., Barbara Pozzoni, and Mariana Cifuentes Montoya. 2005. Participation and public policies in Brazil. In *The deliberative democracy handbook: Strategies for effective civic engagement in the 21st century*, ed. John Gastil and Peter Levine, 174–184. San Francisco: Jossey-Bass.

Cohen, Arthur R. 1957. Need for cognition and order of communication as determinants of opinion change. In *The order of presentation in persuasion*, ed. Carl Iver Hovland, 79–97. New Haven, CT: Yale University Press.

Cohen, Arthur R., Ezra Stotland, and Donald M. Wolfe. 1955. An experimental investigation of need for cognition. *Journal of Abnormal and Social Psychology* 51: 291–294.

Cohen, Joshua. [1989] 1997a. Deliberation and democratic legitimacy. In *Deliberative democracy: Essays on reason and politics*, ed. James Bohman and William Rehg, 67–92. Cambridge, MA: MIT Press.

Cohen, Joshua. [1996] 1997b. Procedure and substance in deliberative democracy. In *Delibera-tive democracy: Essays on reason and politics*, ed. James Bohman and William Rehg, 407–438. Cambridge: MIT Press.

Cohen, Joshua. 2007. Deliberative democracy. In *Democracy, deliberation, and participation: Can the people govern?* ed. Shawn W. Rosenberg, 219–236. London: Palgrave Macmillan.

Cohen, Joshua, and Archon Fung. 2004. Radical democracy. *Swiss Journal of Political Science* 10(4): 23–34.

Coleman, Stephen. 2004. Connecting parliament to the public via the internet: Two case studies of online consultations. *Information, Communication, and Society* 7: 1–22.

Coleman, Stephen, Nicola Hall, and Milica Howell. 2002. *Hearing voices: The experience of online public consultations and discussions in UK governance*. London: Hansard Society.

Collaborative Democracy Network (CDN). 2006. A call to scholars and teachers of public admin-istration, public policy, planning, political science, and related fields. *Public Administration Review* 66 (Suppl. 1): 168–170.

Connolly, William. 1991. *Identity/difference*. Ithaca, NY: Cornell University Press.

Cornwall, Andrea. 2007. Negotiating participation in a Brazilian municipal health council. In *Spaces for change: The politics of participation in new democratic arenas*, ed. Andrea Cornwall and Vera S. Coelho, 155–179. London: Zed Books.

Converse, Philip E. 1964. The nature of belief systems in mass publics. In *Ideology and discontent*, ed. David E. Apter, 206–261. New York: Free Press.

Converse, Phillip E. 1972. Change in the American electorate. In *The human meaning of social change*, ed. Angus Campbell and Phillip E. Converse, 263–338. New York: Russell Sage Foundation.

Conway, M. Margaret. 2000. *Political participation in the United States*. 3rd ed. Washington, DC: CQ Press.

Cooper, Terry L., Thomas A. Bryer, and Jack W. Meek. 2006. Citizen-centered collaborative pub-lic management. *Public Administration Review* 66(s1): 76–88.

Cooper, Terry L., and Pradeep Chandra Kathi. 2005. Neighborhood councils and city agencies: A model of collaborative coproduction. *National Civic Review* 94(1): 43–53.

Cooper, Terry L., Juliet A. Musso, and Alicia Kitsuse. 2002. Faith organizations and neighborhood councils in Los Angeles. *Public Administration and Development* 22: 83–94.

Cortes, Ernesto J. 1996. Community organization and social capital. *National Civic Review* 85(3): 49–53.

Costa, Dora L., and Matthew E. Kahn. 2003. Understanding the American decline in social capi-tal, 1952–1998. *Kyklos* 56: 17–46.

Craig, Stephen C., Richard G. Niemi, and Glenn E. Silver. 1990. Political efficacy and trust: A report on the NES pilot study items. *Political Behavior* 12: 289–314.

Creasy, Stella, Karin Gavelin, and Dominic Porter. 2008. *Everybody needs good neighbors? A study of the link between public participation and community cohesion*. London: Involve.

Creighton, James L. 2005. *The public participation handbook: Making better decisions through citizen involvement*. San Francisco: Jossey-Bass.

Crosby, Ned. 1995. Citizen juries: One solution for difficult environmental questions. In *Fairness and competence in citizen participation: Evaluating models for environmental discourse*, ed. Or-twinn Renn, Thomas Webler, and Peter Wiedemann, 157–174. Boston: Kluwer Academic.

Crosby, Ned. 2005. *Research relevant to sound deliberative practice*. Minneapolis, MN: Jefferson Center. http://www.jefferson-center.org/vertical/Sites/%7BC73573A1-16DF-4030-99A5-8FCCA2F0BFED%7D/uploads/%7BA546CA10-77D4-4075-BEB6-1B9251985E62%7D. PDF. September 19, 2008.

Crosby, Ned, and Doug Nethercutt. 2005. Citizen juries: Creating a trustworthy voice of the peo-ple. In *The deliberative democracy handbook: Strategies for effective civic engagement in the 21st century*, ed. John Gastil and Peter Levine, 111–119. San Francisco: Jossey-Bass.

Cumming-Bruce, Nick, and Steven Erlanger. 2009. Swiss ban building of minarets on mosques. *New York Times*, November 30.

Cunningham, Kiran, and Matt Leighninger. 2011. Research for democracy, and democracy for research. In *Educating for deliberative democracy*, ed. Nancy Thomas, 59–66. San Francisco: Jossey-Bass.

Cutler, Stephen J., and Nicholas L. Danigelis. 1986. Age-differences in voluntary association memberships: Recent trends. *Gerontologist* 26: A213–A213.

Daft, Richard L., and Robert H. Lengel. 1986. Organizational information requirements, media richness and structural design. *Management Science* 32: 554–571.

Dahl, Robert A. 1989. *Democracy and its critics*. New Haven, CT: Yale University Press.

Dahlberg, Lincoln. 2001. The internet and democratic discourse: Exploring the prospects of online deliberative forums extending the public sphere. *Information, Communication, & Society* 4: 615–633.

Dahlberg, Lincoln. 2005. The Habermasian public sphere: Taking difference seriously. *Theory and Society* 34: 111–136.

Daugherty, Renée A., and Sue E. Williams. 2007. Applications of public deliberation: Themes emerging from twelve personal experiences emanating from National Issues Forums training. *Journal of Public Deliberation* 3(1): Article 10.

Davies, Ben B., Kirsty Blackstock, and Felix Rauschmayer. 2005. "Recruitment," "composition," and "mandate" issues in deliberative processes: Should we focus on arguments rather than individuals? *Environment and Planning C: Government and Policy* 23: 599–615.

Davies, Todd, and Seeta Peña Gangadharan, eds. 2009. *Online deliberation: Design, research, and practice*. Stanford, CA: CSLI Publications. http://odbook.stanford.edu.

De Cindio, Fiorella, and Cristian Peraboni. 2010. Design issues for building deliberative design habitats. In *Proceedings of the Fourth International Conference on Online Deliberation (OD2010)*, ed. Fiorella De Cindio, Ann Machintosh, and Cristian Peraboni, 41–52. Leeds, UK: University of Leeds and Università Degli Studi Di Milano.

Delli Carpini, Michael X. 2000. In Search of the informed citizen: What Americans know about politics and why it matters. *Communication Review* 4(1): 129–164.

Delli Carpini, Michael X., Fay L. Cook, and Lawrence R. Jacobs. 2004. Public deliberation, discursive participation, and citizen engagement: A review of the empirical literature. *Annual Review of Political Science* 7: 315–344.

Delli Carpini, Michael X., and Scott Keeter. 1996. *What Americans know about politics and why it matters*. New Haven: Yale University Press.

Dennis, Alan R., and Susan T. Kinney. 1998. Testing media richness theory in the new media: The effects of cues, feedback, and task equivocality. *Information Systems Research* 9: 256–274.

Derks, Daantje, Agneta H. Fischer, and Arjan E.R. Bos. 2008. The role of emotion in computer-mediated communication: A review. *Computers in Human Behavior* 24: 766–785.

Dewey, John. 1910. *How we think*. New York: D. C. Heath.

Dewey, John. [1927] 1988. The public and its problems. In *The later works of John Dewey, 1925–1952*, Vol. 2, ed. Jo Ann Boydston, 238–372. Carbondale: Southern Illinois University Press.

Dewey, John. 1957. *The public and its problems*. Denver: A. Swallow.

Dixon, Paul. 1997. Paths to peace in Northern Ireland (I): Civil society and consociational approaches. *Democratization* 4: 1–27.

Dixon, Paul. 2005. Why the Good Friday agreement in Northern Ireland is not consociational. *Political Quarterly* 76: 357–367.

Doble, John, Damon Higgins, Jennifer Begasse, and Celeste Fisher. 1996. *The public's capacity for deliberation: What can we learn from NIF?* Englewood Cliffs, NJ: John Doble Research Associates.

Douglass, R. Bruce. 1994. The renewal of democracy and the communitarian prospect. *Responsive Community* 4(3): 55–62.

Downs, Anthony. 1957. *An economic theory of democracy*. New York: Harper.

Druckman, James N., and Kjersten R. Nelson. 2003. Framing and deliberation: How citizens' conversations limit elite influence. *American Journal of Political Science* 47(4): 729–745.

Dryzek, John S. 1990. *Discursive democracy: Politics, policy, and political science*. Cambridge: Cambridge University Press.

Dryzek, John S. 2000. *Deliberative democracy and beyond: Liberals, critics, contestations.* Oxford: Oxford University Press.

Dryzek, John S. 2005. Deliberative democracy in divided societies. *Political Theory* 33: 218–242.

Dryzek, John S. 2007. Democratization as deliberative capacity building. Conference paper presented to Political Science Seminar, Research School of Social Sciences, Australian National University, Canberra, Australia. http://deliberativedemocracy.anu.edu.au/documents/Dryzek2007_000.pdf.

Dryzek, John. 2009. The Australian Citizens' Parliament: A world first. *Journal of Public Deliberation* 5(1): Article 9.

Dudley, Larkin S., Ricardo S. Morse, and James P. Armstrong. 2008. Comparing content of two NIF forum formats: Face-to-face group versus online. *International Journal of Public Participation* 2: 84–86.

Durant, Robert F. 1995. The democracy deficit in America. *Political Science Quarterly* 110: 25–47.

Dwyer, William L. 2002. *In the hands of the people.* New York: St. Martin's.

Eckles, Dean, Rafael Ballagas, and Leila Takayama. 2009. The design space of computer-mediated communication: Dimensional analysis and actively mediated communication. Paper presented at the Social Mediating Technologies Workshop, CHI 2009, Boston, April. http://personalpages.manchester.ac.uk/staff/vmgonz/documents/smt/31Eckles,%20Ballagas,%20Takayama%20-%20Design%20Space%20of%20CMC.pdf.

Edwards, Peter B., Richard Hindmarsh, Holly Mercer, Meghan Bond, and Angela Rowland. 2008. A three-stage evaluation of a deliberative event on climate change and transforming energy. *Journal of Public Deliberation* 4(1): Article 6.

Ehrlich, Thomas, ed. 2000. *Civic responsibility and higher education.* Westport, CT: Oryx Press.

Eliasoph, Nina. 1998. *Avoiding politics: How Americans produce apathy in everyday life.* Cambridge: Cambridge University Press.

Elster, Jon. [1986] 1997. The market and the forum: Three varieties of political theory. In *Deliberative democracy: Essays on reason and politics,* ed. James Bohman and William Rehg, 3–34. Cambridge, MA: MIT Press.

Elster, Jon, ed. 1998. *Deliberative democracy.* Cambridge: Cambridge University Press.

Epley, Nicholas, and Justin Kruger. 2005. When what you type isn't what they read: The perseverance of stereotypes and expectancies over e-mail. *Journal of Experimental Social Psychology* 41(July): 414–422.

Esterling, Kevin, Archon Fung, and Taeku Lee. 2011. *How much disagreement is good for democratic deliberation? The CaliforniaSpeaks health care reform experiment.* http://archonfung.net/docs/share/EfungLee_disagreement_2011.pdf.

Estlund, David. 1997. Beyond fairness in deliberation: The epistemic dimension of democratic authority. In *Deliberative democracy: Essays on reason in politics,* ed. James. Bohman and William Rehg, 173–204. Cambridge, MA: MIT Press.

Estlund, David. 2008. *Democratic authority.* Princeton: Princeton University Press.

Etzioni, Amitai. 1972. MINERVA: An electronic town hall. *Policy Sciences* 3: 457–474.

Etzioni, Amitai. 1975. Participatory technology. *Journal of Communications* 25(2): 64–74.

Fagotto, Elena, and Archon Fung. 2006. *Embedded deliberation: Entrepreneurs, organizations, and public action.* Boston: Taubman Center for State and Local Government.

Fagotto, Elena, and Archon Fung. 2009. Sustaining public engagement: Embedded deliberation in local communities. Everyday Democracy and the Kettering Foundation Occasional Paper, October. http://www.everyday-democracy.org/en/Resource.136.aspx.

Farrar, Cynthia, James S. Fishkin, Donald P. Green, Christian List, Robert C. Luskin, and Elizabeth Levy Paluck. 2010. Disaggregating deliberation's effects: An experiment within a deliberative poll. *British Journal of Political Science* 40: 333–347.

Finkel, Steven E. 1985. Reciprocal effects of participation and political efficacy: A panel analysis. *American Journal of Political Science* 29(4): 891–913.

Fiorina, Morris. 2003. Parties, participation, and representation in America: Old theories face new realities. In *Political science: The state of the discipline,* ed. Ira Katznelson and Helen V. Milner, 511–541. New York: W.W. Norton.

Fischer, Frank. 2006. Participatory governance as deliberative empowerment: The cultural politics of discursive space. *American Review of Public Administration* 36: 19–40.

Fish, Stanley. 1999. Mutual respect as a device of exclusion. In *Deliberative politics*, ed. Stephen Macedo, 88–102. New York: Oxford University Press.

Fishkin, James S. 1991. *Democracy and deliberation: New directions for democratic reform.* New Haven: Yale University Press.

Fishkin, James S. 1995. *The voice of the people: Public opinion and democracy.* New Haven: Yale University Press.

Fishkin, James S. 1996. The televised deliberative poll: An experiment in democracy. *Annals of the American Academy of Political and Social Science* 546(July): 132–140.

Fishkin, James S. 2006. The nation in a room: Turning public opinion into policy. *Boston Review* (March/April). http://bostonreview.net/BR31.2/fishkin.php.

Fishkin, James S. 2009a. Town halls by invitation. *New York Times*, August 15. http://www.nytimes.com/2009/08/16/opinion/16fishkin.html?scp=1&sq=fishkin,%20james&st=cse.

Fishkin, James S. 2009b. Virtual public consultation: Prospects for internet deliberative democracy. In *Online deliberation: Design, research, and practice*, ed. Todd Davies and Seeta Peña Gangadharan, 23–35. Stanford, CA: CSLI Publications.

Fishkin, James S. 2009c. *When the people speak: Deliberative democracy and public consultation.* Oxford: Oxford University Press.

Fishkin, James S., and Cynthia Farrar. 2005. Deliberative polling: From experiment to community resource. In *The deliberative democracy handbook: Strategies for effective civic engagement in the 21st century*, ed. John Gastil and Peter Levine, 68–79. San Francisco: Jossey-Bass.

Fishkin, James S., Baogang He, and Alice Siu. 2006. Public consultation through deliberation in China: The first Chinese deliberative poll. In *The search for deliberative democracy in China*, ed. Ethan J. Leib and Baogang He, 229–245. New York: Palgrave Macmillan.

Fishkin, James S., and Robert C. Luskin. 1999. Bringing deliberation to the democratic dialogue. In *The poll with a human face: The National Issues Convention experiment in political communication*, ed. Maxwell McCombs and Amy Reynolds, 3–38. Mahwah, NJ: Lawrence Erlbaum.

Fishkin, James S., and Robert C. Luskin. 2002. *Deliberation and "better citizens."* Stanford, CA: Center for Deliberative Democracy, Stanford University. http://cdd.stanford.edu/research/papers/2002/bettercitizens.pdf.

Fishkin, James S., and Robert C. Luskin. 2005. Experimenting with a democratic ideal: Deliberative polling and public opinion. *Acta Politica* 40: 284–298.

Flavin-McDonald, Catherine, and Molly Holme Barrett. 1999. The Topsfield Foundation: Fostering democratic community building through face-to-face dialogue. *New Directions for Adult and Continuing Education* 81: 25–36.

Foucault, Michel. 1980. *The history of sexuality.* Vol. 1, *An introduction.* New York: Vintage.

Frank, Thomas. 2004. *What's the matter with Kansas?* New York: Metropolitan Books.

Fraser, Jim, and Edward Kick. 2005. Understanding community building in urban America. *Journal of Poverty* 9(1): 23–43.

Fraser, Nancy. 1992. Rethinking the public sphere: A contribution to the critique of actually existing democracy. In *Habermas and the public sphere*, ed. Craig Calhoun, 109–142. Cambridge, MA: MIT Press.

Fraser, Nancy. 1997. *Justice interruptus: Critical reflections on the "postsocialist" condition.* New York: Routledge.

Fraser, Nancy. 2007. Transnationalizing the public sphere: On the legitimacy and efficacy of public opinion in a postwestphalian world. In *Identities, affiliations, and allegiances*, ed. Seyla Benhabib, Ian Shapiro, and Danilo Petranovic, 45–66. Cambridge: Cambridge University Press.

Freeman, Samuel. 2000. Deliberative democracy: A sympathetic comment. *Philosophy and Public Affairs* 29: 371–419.

Friedman, Will. 2006. Deliberative democracy and the problem of scope. *Journal of Public Deliberation* 2(1): Article 1.

Friedman, Will, Alison Kadlec, and Lara Birnback. 2007. Transforming public life: A decade of citizenship engagement in Bridgeport, CT. Case Studies in Public Engagement No. 1, Center for Advances in Public Engagement, Public Agenda.

Fulk, Janet, Joseph Schmitz, and Charles W. Steinfield. 1990. A social influence model of technology use. In *Organizations and communication technology*, ed. Janet Fulk and Charles W. Steinfield, 117–140. Newbury Park, CA: Sage.

Fung, Archon. 2001. Accountable autonomy: Toward empowered deliberation in Chicago schools and policing. *Politics and Society* 29(1): 73–103.

Fung, Archon. 2002. One city, two systems: Democracy in an electronic chat room in Hong Kong. *Javnost/The Public* 9: 77–94.

Fung, Archon. 2003. Survey article: Recipes for public spheres: Eight institutional design choices and their consequences. *Journal of Political Philosophy* 11: 338–367.

Fung, Archon. 2004. *Empowered participation: Reinventing urban democracy*. Princeton, NJ: Princeton University Press.

Fung, Archon. 2005. Deliberation before the revolution: Toward an ethics of deliberation in an unjust world. *Political Theory* 33(2): 397–419.

Fung, Archon. 2006. Varieties of participation in complex governance. *Public Administration Review*, 66: 66–75.

Fung, Archon. 2007. Minipublics: Deliberative designs and their consequences. In *Democracy, deliberation and participation: Can the people govern?* ed. Shawn W. Rosenberg, 159–183. Oxford: Palgrave Macmillan.

Fung, Archon, and Elena Fagotto. 2009. Sustaining public engagement: Embedded deliberation in local communities. Everyday democracy and Kettering Foundation.

Fung, Archon, and Taeku Lee. 2008. *The difference deliberation makes: A report on CaliforniaSpeaks statewide conversation on health care reform*. Washington, DC: AmericaSpeaks. http://archonfung.net/docs/reports/CASpeaksReportFinalv3.pdf.

Fung, Archon, Taeku Lee, and Peter Harbage. 2008. *Public impacts: Evaluating the outcomes of the CaliforniaSpeaks statewide conversation on health care reform*. http://californiaspeaks.org/wp-content/_data/n_0002/resources/live/CaSpks%20Evaluation%20Report.pdf.

Fung, Archon, and Erik Olin Wright, eds. 2003. *Deepening democracy: Institutional innovations in empowered participatory governance*. The Real Utopias Project, Vol. 4, ed. Erik Olin Wright. London: Verso.

Galeotti, Anna E. 2002. *Toleration as recognition*. Cambridge: Cambridge University Press.

Gastil, John. 1994. An appraisal and revision of the constructivist research program. In *Communication Yearbook 18*, ed. Brant R. Burleson, 83–104. Newbury Park, CA: Sage.

Gastil, John. 2000. *By popular demand: Revitalizing representative democracy through deliberative elections*. Berkeley: University of California Press.

Gastil, John. 2004. Adult civic education through the national issues forums: Developing democratic habits and dispositions through public deliberation. *Adult Education Quarterly* 54: 308–328.

Gastil, John. 2005. Deliberation. In *Communication as . . .: Perspectives on theory*, ed. Gregory J. Shepherd, John St. John, and Ted Striphas, 164–173. Thousand Oaks, CA: Sage.

Gastil, John. 2008. *Political communication and deliberation*. Thousand Oaks, CA: Sage.

Gastil, John. 2009a. A comprehensive approach to evaluating deliberative public engagement. In *Engaging with impact: Targets and indicators for successful community engagement by Ontario's Local Health Integration Networks*, ed. MASS LBP, 15–27. Toronto, Ontario.

Gastil, John. 2009b. Giving power to public voice: A critical review of alternative means of infusing citizen deliberation with legal authority or influence. Presentation given at Publics and Emerging Technologies: Cultures, Contexts, and Challenges, October, Banff, Canada.

Gastil, John. 2010. *The group in society*. Thousand Oaks, CA: Sage.

Gastil, John, Chiara Bacci, and Michael Dollinger. 2010. Is deliberation neutral? Exploring patterns of attitude change during "The Deliberative Polls™." *Journal of Public Deliberation* 6(2): Article 3.

Gastil, John, and Laura W. Black. 2008. Public deliberation as an organizing principle for political communication research. *Journal of Public Deliberation* 4(1): Article 3.

Gastil, John, Laura W. Black, E. Pierre Deess, and James Leighter. 2008. From group member to democratic citizen: How deliberating with fellow jurors reshapes civic attitudes. *Human Communication Research* 35: 137–169.

Gastil, John, Stephanie Burkhalter, and Laura W. Black. 2007. Do juries deliberate? A study of deliberation, individual difference, and group member satisfaction at a municipal courthouse. *Small Group Research* 38: 337–359.

Gastil, John, Eugene P. Deess, Phil Weiser, and Cindy Simmons. 2010. *The jury and democracy: How jury deliberation promotes civic engagement and political participation.* New York: Oxford University Press.

Gastil, John, and James P. Dillard. 1999a. The aims, methods, and effects of deliberative civic education through the National Issues Forums. *Communication Education* 48: 1–14.

Gastil, John, and James P. Dillard. 1999b. Increasing political sophistication through public deliberation. *Political Communication* 16: 3–23.

Gastil, John, and William M. Keith. 2005. A nation that (sometimes) likes to talk: A brief history of public deliberation in the United States. In *The deliberative democracy handbook: Strategies for effective civic engagement in the 21st century*, ed. John Gastil and Peter Levine, 1–19. San Francisco: Jossey Bass.

Gastil, John, and Todd Kelshaw. 2000. *Public meetings: A sampler of deliberative forums that bring officeholders and citizens together.* Dayton, OH: Kettering Foundation.

Gastil, John, and Katie Knobloch. 2010. *Evaluation report to the Oregon State Legislature on the 2010 Oregon Citizens' Initiative Review.* Unpublished manuscript, Department of Communication, University of Washington.

Gastil, John, and Peter Levine, eds. 2005. *The deliberative democracy handbook: Strategies for effective civic engagement in the 21st century.* San Francisco: Jossey-Bass.

Gastil, John, Justin Reedy, Donald Braman, and Dan Kahan. 2008. Deliberation across the cultural divide: Assessing the potential for reconciling conflicting cultural orientations to reproductive technology. *George Washington Law Review* 76: 1772–1797.

Gaventa, John. 2006. Finding the spaces for change. IDS Bulletin 37(6): 23–33.

Gaventa, John, and Gregory Barrett. 2010. So what difference does it make? Mapping the outcomes of citizen engagement. IDS Working Paper Vol. 2010 No. 347, Development Research Centre on Citizenship, Participation and Accountability. http://www.ids.ac.uk/files/dmfile/Wp347.pdf.

Gaventa, John, and Nicholas Benequista. 2009. Reversing the flow. *Alliance Magazine*, June 1.

Gaventa, John, and Rosemary McGee, eds. 2010. *Citizen action and national policy reform: Making change happen.* London: Zed Books.

Gerlach-Kristen, Petra. 2003. Monetary Policy Committees and the benefits of deliberation. Working paper, University of Basel. http://wwz.unibas.ch/fileadmin/wwz/redaktion/makro/Papers/pgk2003a.pdf.

Gibbon, Marion, Ronald Labonte, and Glenn Laverack. 2002. Evaluating community capacity. *Health and Social Care in the Community* 10(6): 485–491.

Gilliatt, Stephen. 2002. No surrender? The attachment to identity and contemporary political thought. *Contemporary Politics* 8: 23–35.

Gilligan, Carol. 1982. *In a different voice.* Cambridge: Harvard University Press.

Gladwell, Malcolm. 2005. *Blink: The power of thinking without thinking.* New York: Little, Brown.

Glenny, Misha. 2000. *The Balkans: Nationalism, war, and the great powers: 1804–1999.* New York: Viking.

Goldfrank, Benjamin. 2006. Lessons from Latin American experience in participatory budgeting. Presentation at the Latin American Studies Association Meeting, San Juan, Puerto Rico, March.

Goodin, Robert E. 2003. *Reflective democracy.* Oxford: Oxford University Press.

Goodin, Robert E., and John S. Dryzek. 2006. Deliberative impacts: The macro-political uptake of mini-publics. *Politics and Society* 34(2): 219–244.

Goodin, Robert E., and Simon J. Niemeyer. 2003. When does deliberation begin? Internal reflection versus public discussion in deliberative democracy. *Political Studies* 51: 627–649.

Goodman, Robert M., Marjorie A. Speers, Kenneth Mcleroy, Stephen Fawcett, Michelle Kegler, Edith Parker, Steven Rathgeb Smith, Terrie D. Sterling, and Nina Wallerstein. 1998. Identifying and defining the dimensions of community capacity to provide a basis for measurement. *Health Education and Behavior* 25: 258–278.

Gould, John D. 1978. An experimental study of writing, dictating, and speaking. In *Attention and performance VII*, ed. Jean Requin, 299–319. Hillsdale, NJ: Lawrence Erlbaum.

Graham, Todd, and Tamara Witschge. 2003. In search of online deliberation: Towards a new method for examining the quality of online discussions. *Communications* 28: 173–204.

Greene, Joshua D. 2003. From neural "is" to moral "ought": What are the moral implications of neuroscientific moral psychology? *Nature Reviews Neuroscience* 4: 847–850.

Greene, Robert. 2004. Not in my neighborhood council: What can save L.A.'s broken neighborhood councils? *LA Weekly*, August 26.

Greenwald, Anthony G., Brian A. Nosek, and Mahzarin R. Banaji. 2003. Understanding and using the Implicit Attitudes Test: I. An improved scoring algorithm. *Journal of Personality and Social Psychology* 85(2): 197–216.

Guston, David H. 1999. Evaluating the first U.S. consensus conference: The impact of the citizens' panel on telecommunications and the future of democracy. *Science, Technology, and Human Values* 24: 451–482.

Gutmann, Amy. 1994. Introduction. In *Multiculturalism: Examining the politics of recognition*, ed. Amy Gutmann, 3–25. Princeton: Princeton University Press.

Gutmann, Amy, ed. 1998. *Freedom of association*. Princeton: Princeton University Press.

Gutmann, Amy, and Dennis F. Thompson. 1996. *Democracy and disagreement*. Cambridge, MA: Harvard University Press.

Gutmann, Amy, and Dennis F. Thompson. 2002. Deliberative democracy beyond process. *Journal of Political Philosophy* 10(2): 153–174.

Gutmann, Amy, and Dennis Thompson. 2004. *Why deliberative democracy?* Princeton: Princeton University Press.

Guttman, Nurit. 2007. Bringing the mountain to the public: Dilemmas and contradictions in the procedures of public deliberation initiatives that aim to get "ordinary citizens" to deliberate policy issues. *Communication Theory* 17: 411–438.

Habermas, Jürgen. [1962] 1989. *The structural transformation of the public sphere: An inquiry into a category of Bourgeois society*. Trans. Thomas Burger. Cambridge, MA: MIT Press.

Habermas, Jürgen. 1975. *Legitimation Crisis*. Cambridge, MA: Beacon.

Habermas, Jürgen. 1979. *Communication and the evolution of society*. Boston: Beacon Press.

Habermas, Jürgen. 1982. Reply to my critics. In *Habermas: Critical debates*, ed. John B. Thompson and David Held, 219–283. Cambridge, MA: MIT Press.

Habermas, Jürgen. 1984. *The theory of communicative action*. Vol. 1. Trans. Thomas McCarthy. Boston: Beacon Press.

Habermas, Jürgen. 1987. *The theory of communicative action*. Vol. 2. Trans. Thomas McCarthy. Boston: Beacon Press.

Habermas, Jürgen. 1990. *Moral consciousness and communicative action*. Trans. Christian Lenhardt and Shierry Weber Nicholson. Cambridge, MA: MIT Press.

Habermas, Jürgen. 1994. Struggles for recognition in the democratic constitutional state. In *Multiculturalism: Examining the politics of recognition*, ed. Amy Gutmann, 107–149. Princeton: Princeton University Press.

Habermas, Jürgen. 1996a. *Between facts and norms: Contributions to a discourse theory of law and democracy*. Trans. William Rehg. Cambridge, MA: MIT Press.

Habermas, Jürgen. 1996b. Three normative models of democracy. In *Democracy and difference: Contesting the boundaries of the political*, ed. Seyla Benhabib, 21–30. Princeton: Princeton University Press.

Habermas, Jürgen. 2006. Towards a United States of Europe. Bruno Kreisky Prize Lecture, March 9. Trans. http://www.signandsight.com/features/676.html.

Halliday, Michael A. K. 1978. *Language as social semiotic: The social interpretation of language and meaning.* Baltimore: University Park Press.

Han, Hahrie. 2009. *Moved to action: Motivation, participation and inequality in American politics.* Stanford: Stanford University Press.

Hanks, Patrick, ed. 1979. *Collins dictionary of the English language.* Glasgow: William Collins Sons.

Hans, Valerie P., and Neil Vidmar. 1986. *Judging the jury.* New York: Plenum Publishing.

Hansen, Kasper M. 2004. *Deliberative democracy and opinion formation.* Odense: University Press of Southern Denmark.

Hart, Roderick, and Sharon Jarvis. 1999. We the people: The contours of lay political discourse. In *The poll with a human face: The National Issues Convention experiment in political communication,* ed. Maxwell McCombs and Amy Reynolds, 59–84. Mahwah, NJ: Lawrence Erlbaum.

Hartz-Karp, Janette. 2005. A case study in deliberative democracy: Dialogue with the city. *Journal of Public Deliberation* 1(1): Article 6.

Hartz-Karp, Janette, Patrick Anderson, John Gastil, and Andrea Felicetti. 2010. The Australian Citizens' Parliament: Forging shared identity through public deliberation. *Journal of Public Affairs* 10: 353–371.

Hartz-Karp, Janette, and Lynn Carson. 2009. Putting the people into politics: The Australian Citizens' Parliament. *International Journal of Public Participation* 3(1): 9–31.

Hastie, Reid, Steven Penrod, and Nancy Pennington. 1983. *Inside the jury.* Cambridge: Harvard University Press.

Hauptmann, Emily. 2001. Can less be more? Leftist deliberative democrats' critique of participatory democracy. *Polity* 33(3): 397–421.

Hayden, Tom. [1962] 2005. *The Port Huron statement.* New York: Thunder's Mouth Press.

Hayes, Andrew F., Dietram A. Scheufele, and Michael E. Huge. 2006. Nonparticipation as self-censorship: Publicly observable political activity in a polarized opinion climate. *Political Behavior* 28: 259–283.

Henderson, Hazel. 1970. Computers: Hardware of democracy. *Forum* 70(2): 22–24, 46–51.

Hendriks, Carolyn M. 2005a. Participatory storylines and their influence on deliberative forums. *Policy Sciences* 38: 1–20.

Hendriks, Carolyn M. 2005b. Consensus conferences and planning cells: Lay citizen deliberations. In *The deliberative democracy handbook: Strategies for effective civic engagement in the 21st century,* ed. John Gastil and Peter Levine, 80–110. San Francisco: Jossey-Bass.

Hendriks, Carolyn M. 2006. Integrated deliberation: Reconciling civil society's dual role in deliberative democracy. *Political Studies* 54: 486–508.

Hendriks, Carolyn M., John S. Dryzek, and Christian Hunold. 2007. Turning up the heat: Partisanship in deliberative innovation. *Political Studies* 55: 362–383.

Hibbing, John R., and Elizabeth Theiss-Morse. 1995. *Congress as public enemy. Public attitudes toward American political institutions.* Cambridge: Cambridge University Press.

Hibbing, John R., and Elizabeth Theiss-Morse. 2002. *Stealth democracy: Americans' beliefs about how government should work.* Cambridge: Cambridge University Press.

Hickerson, Andrea, and John Gastil. 2008. Assessing the difference critique of deliberation: Gender, emotion, and the jury experience. *Communication Theory* 18: 281–303.

Hill, Kim Q., and Jan E. Leighley. 1999. Racial diversity, voter turnout, and mobilizing institutions in the United States. *American Politics Quarterly* 27: 275–295.

Huckfeldt, R. Robert, and John Sprague. 1995. *Citizens, politics, and social communication: Information and influence in an election campaign.* New York: Cambridge University Press.

Husbands, Christopher. 2000. Switzerland: Right-wing and xenophobic parties, from margin to mainstream? *Parliamentary Affairs* 53: 501–516.

International Association of Public Participation (IAP2). 2007. IAP2 Spectrum of Participation. http://www.iap2.org/associations/4748/files/spectrum.pdf.

Involve. 2008. *Deliberative public engagement: Nine principles.* London, UK: National Consumer Council. http://www.involve.org.uk/wp-content/uploads/2011/03/Deliberative-public-engagement-nine-principles1.pdf. March 30, 2011.

Irvin, Renee A., and John Stansbury. 2004. Citizen participation in decision making: Is it worth the effort? *Public Administration Review* 64: 55–65.

Jackman, Simon, and Paul M. Sniderman. 2006. The limits of deliberative discussion: A model of everyday political arguments. *Journal of Politics* 68(2): 272–183.

Jacobs, Lawrence R., Fay Lomax Cook, and Michael X. Delli Carpini. 2009. *Talking together: Public deliberation and political participation in America.* Chicago: University of Chicago Press.

Jacobs, Lawrence R., and Robert Y. Shapiro. 2000. *Politicians don't pander: Political manipulation and the loss of democracy responsiveness.* Chicago: University of Chicago Press.

Jacobs, Lawrence R., and Theda Skocpol, eds. 2005. *Inequality in American democracy: What we know and what we need to learn.* New York: Russell Sage Foundation.

James, Rita. M. 1959. Status and competence of jurors. *American Journal of Sociology* 64(6): 563–570.

Jankowski, Nicholas W., and Renee van Os. 2004. Internet-based political discourse: A case study in online civic engagement. In *Democracy online: The prospects for political renewal through the internet,* ed. Peter M. Shane, 181–193. New York: Routledge.

Janssen, Davy, and Raphaël Kies. 2005. Online forums and deliberative democracy. *Acta Politica* 40: 317–335.

Jefferson Center. 2002. *Citizen Jury: Global climate change.* Minneapolis/St. Paul, MN: Jefferson Center. http://www.jefferson-center.org/vertical/Sites/%7BC73573A1-16DF-4030-99A5-8FCCA2F0BFED%7D/uploads/%7BF29315AB-1654-4CBB-B29B-C8A9FEFC2C15%7D. PDF. August 5, 2011.

Jensen, Jakob L. 2003. Public spheres on the internet: Anarchic or government-sponsored—a comparison. *Scandinavian Political Studies* 26: 349–374.

Kadlec, Alison, and Will Friedman. 2007. Deliberative democracy and the problem of power. *Journal of Public Deliberation* 3(1): Article 8.

Kahai, Surinder Singh, and Randolph B. Cooper. 2003. Exploring the core concepts of media richness theory: The impact of cue multiplicity and feedback immediacy on decision quality. *Journal of Management Information Systems* 20: 263–299.

Kahan, Dan. 2007. The cognitively illiberal state. *Stanford Law Review* 60: 115–154.

Kaplan, Robert D. 2005. *Balkan ghosts: A journey through history.* New York: Picador.

Karpowitz, Christopher F., and Jane Mansbridge. 2005a. Disagreement and consensus: The importance of dynamic updating in public deliberation. In *The deliberative democracy handbook: Strategies for effective civic engagement in the 21st century,* ed. John Gastil and Peter Levine, 237–253. San Francisco: Jossey-Bass.

Karpowitz, Christopher F., and Jane Mansbridge. 2005b. The importance of dynamic updating in public deliberation. In *The deliberative democracy handbook: Strategies for effective civic engagement in the 21st century,* ed. John Gastil and Peter Levine, 120–138. San Francisco: Jossey Bass.

Karpowitz, Christopher F., and Tali Mendelberg. 2007. Groups and deliberation. *Swiss Political Science Review* 13(4): 645–662.

Karpowitz, Christopher F., Chad Raphael, and Allen S. Hammond IV. 2009. Deliberative democracy and inequality: Two cheers for enclave deliberation among the disempowered. *Politics & Society* 37: 576–615.

Kathi, Pradeep Chandra, and Terry L. Cooper. 2008. Connecting neighborhood councils and city agencies: Trust building through the Learning and Design Forum process. *Journal of Public Affairs Education* 13 (3/4): 617–630

Katz, Elihu. 1994. Introduction: The state of the art. In *Public opinion and the communication of consent,* ed. Theodore L. Glasser and Charles T. Salmon, xxi–xxxiv. New York: Guilford.

Kaufman, Arnold S. 1960. Human nature and participatory democracy. In *Responsibility, NOMOS III,* ed. Carl J. Friedrich, 266–289. New York: Liberal Arts Press.

Kaufman, Arnold S. 1969. Participatory democracy: Ten years later. In *The bias of pluralism,* ed. William E. Connolly, 201–212. New York: Atherton Pres.

Keith, William. 2007. *Democracy as discussion: The American forum movement and civic education.* Lanham, MD: Lexington Books.

Kellstedt, Paul M., Sammy Zahran, and Arnold Vedlitz. 2008. Personal efficacy, the information environment, and attitudes toward global warming and climate change in the United States. *Risk Analysis* 28: 113–126.

Kelly, John, Danyel Fisher, and Marc Smith. 2009. Friends, foes, and fringe: Norms and structure in political discussion networks. In *Online Deliberation: Design, Research, and Practice*, ed. Todd Davies and Seeta Peña Gangadharan, 83–93. Stanford, CA: CSLI Publications.

Kelshaw, Todd. 2007. Understanding "abnormal" public discourses: Some overlapping and distinguishing features of dialogue and deliberation. *International Journal of Public Participation* 1. http://www.iap2.org/displaycommon.cfm?an=1&subarticlenbr=252.

Kinder, Donald R., and D. Roderick Kiewiet. 1981. Sociotropic politics: The American case. *British Journal of Political Science* 11(2): 129–161.

King, Ruth C., Kathleen S. Hartzel, Richard A.M. Schilhavy, Nancy P. Melone, and Timothy W. McGuire. 2010. Social responsibility and stakeholder influence: Does technology matter during stakeholder deliberation with high impact decisions? *Decision Support Systems* 48: 536–547.

Kirchler, Erich, and James H. Davis. 1986. The influence of member status differences and task type on group consensus and member position change. *Journal of Personality and Social Psychology* 51: 83–91.

Klein, Joe. 2010. How can a democracy solve tough problems? *Time Magazine*, September 6.

Knight, Jack, and James Johnson. 1997. What sort of equality does deliberative democracy require? In *Deliberative democracy: Essays on reason and politics*, ed. J. Bohman and W. Rehg, 279–320. Cambridge, MA: MIT Press.

Knoke, David. 1986. Associations and interest groups. *Annual Review of Sociology* 12: 1–21.

Knoke, David. 1990. *Political networks: A structural perspective*. New York: Cambridge University Press.

Knoke, David, and Randall Thomson. 1977. Voluntary association membership trends and the family life cycle. *Social Forces* 56: 48–65.

Krassa, Michael A. 1990. Political information, social environment, and deviants. *Political Behavior* 12: 315–30.

Kraut, Robert, Jolene Galegher, Robert Fish, and Barbara Chalfonte. 1992. Task requirements and media choice in collaborative writing. *Human-Computer Interaction* 7: 375–407.

Kroll, Barry M. 1978. Cognitive egocentrism and the problem of audience awareness in written discourse. *Research in the Teaching of English* 12: 269–281.

Kulikova, Svetlana V., and David D. Perlmutter. 2007. Blogging down the dictator? The Kyrgyz Revolution and Samizdat websites. *International Communication Gazette* 69: 29–50.

Kumlin, S. 2002. The personal and the political: How personal welfare state experiences affect political trust and ideology. PhD diss., Götteberg University.

Kymlicka, Will, and Bashir Bashir. 2008. *The politics of reconciliation in multicultural societies*. Oxford: Oxford University Press.

Laclau, Ernesto, and Chantal Mouffe. 2001. *Hegemony and socialist strategy: Towards a radical democratic politics*. 2nd ed. London: Verso.

Lakatos, Imre. 1978. *The methodology of scientific research programmes*. Cambridge: Cambridge University Press.

Lampe, Cliff, Erik Johnston, and Paul Resnick. 2007. Follow the reader: Filtering comments on slashdot. In *Proceedings of the ACM Conference on Human Factors in Computing*. San Jose, CA: CHI 2007.

Lampe, Cliff, and Paul Resnick. 2004. Slash(dot) and burn: Distributed moderation in a large online conversation space. In *Proceedings of the ACM Conference on Human Factors in Computing*. Vienna, Austria: CHI 2004.

Lasch, Christopher. 1995. *The revolt of the elites and the betrayal of democracy*. New York: W.W. Norton.

Lawless, Jennifer L., and Richard L. Fox. 2001. Political participation of the urban poor. *Social Problems* 48: 362–385.

Lazer, David, Michael E. Neblo, Kevin M. Esterling, and K. Goldschmidt. 2009. *Online townhall meetings: Exploring democracy in the 21st century*. Washington, DC: Congressional Management Foundation.

Le Bigot, Ludovic, Jean-François Rouet, and Eric Jamet. 2007. Effects of speech- and text-based interaction modes in natural language human-computer dialogue. *Human Factors* 49 (December): 1045–1053.

Lee, Caroline. 2007. Is there a place for private conversation in public dialogue? Comparing stakeholder assessments of informal communication in collaborative regional planning. *American Journal of Sociology* 113(1): 41–96.

Lee, Caroline W. 2008. Disciplining democracy: Market logics in the public deliberation industry. Paper presented at the Northeast Law and Society Association Meeting, Amherst, MA, October.

Lee, Caroline W. 2011. Five assumptions academics make about public deliberation, and why they deserve rethinking. *Journal of Public Deliberation* 7(1): Article 7.

Lee, Caroline, and Francesca Polletta. 2009. The 2009 dialogue and deliberation practitioners survey: What is the state of the field? Easton, PA: Lafayette College. http://sites.lafayette.edu/ddps/.

Leib, Ethan J. 2004. *Deliberative democracy in America: A proposal for a popular branch of government*. University Park: University of Pennsylvania Press.

Leib, Ethan J., and Baogang He, eds. 2006. *The search for deliberative democracy in China*. New York: Palgrave Macmillan.

Leighley, Jan E. 1990. Social interaction and contextual influences on political participation. *American Political Quarterly* 18: 459–75.

Leighley, Jan E. 2001. *Strength in numbers? The political mobilization of racial and ethnic minorities*. Princeton: Princeton University Press.

Leighninger, Matt. 2006. *The next form of democracy: How expert rule is giving way to shared governance—and why politics will never be the same*. Nashville, TN: Vanderbilt University Press.

Leighninger, Matt. 2009a. Democracy, growing up: The shifts that reshaped local politics and foreshadowed the 2008 presidential election. Occasional Paper No. 5, Center for Advances in Public Engagement, Public Agenda.

Leighninger, Matt. 2009b. *The promise and challenge of neighborhood democracy: Lessons from the intersection of government and community*. Austin, TX: Grassroots Grantmakers.

Leighninger, Matt. 2010a. *Creating spaces for change: Working toward a "story of now" in civic engagement*. Battle Creek, MI: Kellogg Foundation.

Leighninger, Matt. 2010b. *Recentering democracy around citizens*. Report presented at the Deliberative Democracy Consortium, Cantigny Conference Center, February 17.

Leighninger, Matt. 2010c. Teaching democracy in public administration. In *The future of public administration around the world: The Minnowbrook perspective*, ed. Rosemary O'Leary, David Van Slyke, and Soonhee Kim, 233–244. Washington, DC: Georgetown University Press.

Leighter, James L. 2007. Codes of commonality and cooperation: Notions of citizen personae and citizen speech codes in American public meetings. PhD diss., University of Washington.

Leighter, James L., and Laura W. Black. 2010. "I'm just raising the question": Terms for talk and practical metadiscursive argument in public meetings. *Western Journal of Communication* 74: 547–568.

Leistner, Paul, and Amalia Alarcon de Morris. 2009. From neighborhood association system to participatory democracy: Broadening and deepening public involvement in Portland, Oregon. *National Civic Review* 98(2): 47–55.

Lempa, Michele, Robert M. Goodman, Janet Rice, and Adam B. Becker. 2008. Development of scales measuring the capacity of community-based initiatives. *Health Education and Behavior* 35: 298–315.

Lerner, Jennifer S., and Philip E. Tetlock. 1999. Accounting for the effects of accountability. *Psychological Bulletin* 125(2): 255–275.

Lerner, Josh, and Daniel Altschuler. 2011. Government can't solve budget battles? Let citizens do it. *Christian Science Monitor* April 5.

Leshed, Gilly. 2009. Silencing the clatter: Removing anonymity from a corporate online community. In *Online deliberation: Design, research, and practice,* ed. Todd Davies and Seeta Peña Gangadharan, 243–251. Stanford, CA: CSLI Publications.

Levine, Peter. 2010. The path not taken (so far): Civic engagement for reform. *Huffington Post,* January 26.

Levine, Peter, Archon Fung, and John Gastil. 2005. Future directions for public deliberation. In *The deliberative democracy handbook: Strategies for effective civic engagement in the 21st century,* ed. John Gastil and Peter Levine, 271–288. San Francisco: Jossey-Bass.

Levine, Peter, and Rose Marie Nierras. 2007. Activists' views of deliberation. *Journal of Public Deliberation* 3(1): Article 4.

Levine, Peter, and Lars Hasselblad Torres. 2008. Where is democracy headed? Research and practice on public deliberation. Deliberative Democracy Consortium. http://www.deliberative-democracy.net/index.php?option=com_docman&Itemid=93.

Lev-On, Azi, and Bernard Manin. 2009. Happy accidents: Deliberation and online exposure to opposing views. In *Online deliberation: Design, research, and practice,* ed. Todd Davies and Seeta Peña Gangadharan, 105–122. Stanford, CA: CSLI Publications.

Li, Shu-Chu Sarinna. 2007. Computer-mediated communication and group decision making: A functional perspective. *Small Group Research* 38: 593–614.

Lichterman, Paul. 2005. *Elusive togetherness: Church groups trying to bridge America's divisions.* Princeton: Princeton University Press.

Lightner, Carol J. 2007. Student perceptions of voice and their experiences in an asynchronous/synchronous voice/text environment: A descriptive study. PhD diss., Capella University.

Lindeman, Mark. 2002. Opinion quality and policy preferences in deliberative research. In *Political decision-making, deliberation, and participation,* ed. Michael X. Delli Carpini, Leonie Huddy, and Robert Y. Shapiro, 195–221. Oxford: Elsevier Science.

Lippmann, W. 1955. *Essays in the public philosophy.* New York: Little, Brown.

List, Christian, Robert C. Luskin, James S. Fishkin, and Iain McClean. 2007. Deliberation, single-peakedness, and the possibility of meaningful democracy: Evidence from deliberative polls. PSPE Working Paper No. 1, Center for Deliberative Democracy, Stanford University.

Lukensmeyer, Carolyn J., and Steve Brigham. 2002. Taking democracy to scale: Creating a town hall meeting for the twenty-first century. *National Civic Review* 91(4): 351–366.

Lukensmeyer, Carolyn J., Joe Goldman, and Steven Brigham. 2005. A town meeting for the twenty-first century. In *The deliberative democracy handbook: Strategies for effective civic engagement in the 21st century,* ed. John Gastil and Peter Levine, 154–163. San Francisco: Jossey-Bass.

Luskin, Robert C., and James S. Fishkin. 2003. Deliberation and "better citizens." Unpublished manuscript, Center for Deliberative Democracy, Stanford University. http://cdd.stanford.edu/research/papers/2002/bettercitizens.pdf.

Luskin, Robert C., James S. Fishkin, and Shanto Iyengar. 2006. *Considered opinions on U.S. foreign policy: Face-to-face versus online deliberative polling.* Center for Deliberative Democracy, Stanford University. http://cdd.stanford.edu/research/papers/2006/foreign-policy.pdf.

Luskin, Robert C., James S. Fishkin, and Roger Jowell. 2002. Considered opinions: Deliberative polling in Britain. *British Journal of Political Science* 32: 455–487.

Luskin, Robert C., James S. Fishkin, Roger Jowell, and Alison Park. 1999. Learning and voting in Britain: Insights from the deliberative poll. Center for Deliberative Democracy, Stanford University. http://cdd.stanford.edu/research/papers/2000/general_election_paper.pdf.

Luskin, Robert C., James S. Fishkin, Neil Malhotra, and Alice Siu. 2007. Deliberation in the schools: A way of enhancing civic engagement? Paper presented at the General Conference of the European Consortium for Political Research, Pisa, Italy. http://cdd.stanford.edu/research/papers/2007/civic-education.pdf. September 19, 2008.

Macedo, Stephen. 2005. *Democracy at risk: How political choices undermine citizen participation and what we can do about it.* Washington, DC: Brookings Institution Press.

MacKuen, Michael, Jennifer Wolak, Luke Keele, and George E. Marcus. 2010. Civic engagements: Resolute partisanship or reflective deliberation. *American Journal of Political Science* 54: 440–458.

Macpherson, Crawford B. 1977. *The life and times of liberal democracy*. Oxford: Oxford University Press.

Mamdani, Mahmood. 2002. *When victims become killers: Colonialism, nativism, and the genocide in Rwanda*. Princeton: Princeton University Press.

Manin, Bernard, Elly Stein, and Jane Mansbridge. 1987. On legitimacy and political deliberation. *Political Theory* 15(3): 338–368.

Mann, Bonnie, and William Barnes. 2010. *Municipal officials' views on public engagement city hall, the public, the media and community groups*. Washington, DC: National League of Cities.

Mann, Bonnie, and Matt Leighninger. 2011. *Planning for stronger local democracy*. Washington, DC: National League of Cities.

Mansbridge, Jane. 1983. *Beyond adversary democracy*. Chicago: University of Chicago Press.

Mansbridge, Jane. 1995. Does participation make better citizens? Paper presented at the February Conference on Citizen Competence and the Design of Democratic Institutions, Committee on the Political Economy of the Good Society. http://www.bsos.umd.edu/pegs/mansbrid.html.

Mansbridge, Jane. 1996. Using power/fighting power: The polity. In *Democracy and difference: Contesting the boundaries of the political*, ed. Seyla Benhabib, 46–67. Princeton: Princeton University Press

Mansbridge, Jane. 1999a. Everyday talk in the deliberative system. In *Deliberative politics*, ed. Stephen Macedo, 211–239. New York: Oxford Press.

Mansbridge, Jane. 1999b. On the idea that participation makes better citizens. In *Citizen competence and democratic institutions*, ed. Stephen L. Elkin and Karol E. Soltan, 291–325. University Park: Pennsylvania State University Press.

Mansbridge, Jane. 1999c. Should blacks represent blacks and women represent women? A contingent yes. *Journal of Politics* 61(3): 628–657.

Mansbridge, Jane. 2003. Practice-thought-practice. In *Deepening democracy*, ed. Archon Fung and Erik O. Wright, 175–199. London: Verso.

Mansbridge, Jane. 2004. Deliberation's darker side: Six questions for Iris Marion Young and Jane Mansbridge, interviewed by A. Fung. *National Civic Review* Winter: 47–54.

Mansbridge, Jane. 2005. Quota problems: Combating the dangers of essentialism. *Politics and Gender* 4 (2005): 622–38.

Mansbridge, Jane. 2008. What does the ideal of deliberative democracy demand? In *Political theory workshop*. Stanford University. http://fsi.stanford.edu/events/what_does_the_ideal_of_deliberative_democracy_demand.

Mansbridge, Jane. 2010. Deliberative polling as the gold standard. *The Good Society* 19: 55–62.

Mansbridge, Jane, Janette Hartz-Karp, Matthew Amengual, and John Gastil. 2006. Norms of deliberation: An inductive study. *Journal of Public Deliberation* 2(1): Article 7.

Mansbridge, Jane, James Bohman, Simone Chambers, David Estlund, Andreas Follesdal, Archon Fung, Cristina Lafont, Bernard Manin, and Jose Luis Marti. 2010. The place of self-interest and the role of power in deliberative democracy. *Journal of Political Philosophy* 18(1): 64–100.

Marois, Deb, and Terry Amsler. 2008. Public involvement in budgeting: Options for local officials. *Western City*, November. http://www.westerncity.com/Western-City/November-2008/Public-Involvement-in-Budgeting-Options-for-Local-Officials/.

Marquetti, Adalmir. 2002. Democracia, eqüidade e eficiência: O caso do orçamento participativo em Porto Alegre. In *Construindo um novo mundo: Avaliação da experiênciado orçamento participativo em Porto Alegre, Brasil*, ed. João Verlse and Luciano Brunet. Porto Alegre: Gravi.

Marston, Sally A. 1993. Citizen action programs and participatory politics in Tucson. In *Public policy for democracy*, ed. Helen M. Ingram and Steven Rathgeb Smith, 119–135. Washington, DC: Brookings Institution Press.

Martin, Ileana. 2006. *Collective decision making around the world*. Dayton, OH: Kettering Foundation Press.

Mathews, David. 1994. Community change through true public action. *National Civic Review* 83(4): 400–404.

Mathews, David. 1997. *Is there a public for public schools?* Dayton, OH: Kettering Foundation Press.

Mathews, David, and Noelle McAfee. 2003. *Making choices together: The power of public deliberation*. Dayton, OH: Kettering Foundation.

McAdam, Doug. 1986. Recruitment to high-risk activism: The case of freedom summer. *American Journal of Sociology* 92: 64–90.

McAfee, Noelle. 2004. Three models of deliberation. *Journal of Speculative Philosophy* 18(1): 44–59.

McBride, Cillian. 2005. Deliberative democracy and the politics of recognition. *Political Studies* 53: 497–515.

McCall, Cathal, and Arthur Williamson. 2001. Governance and democracy in Northern Ireland: The role of the voluntary and community sector after the agreement. *Governance: An International Journal of Policy and Administration* 14(3): 363–383.

McCarthy, Thomas. 2002. Vergangenheitsbewaltigung in the USA: On the politics of the memory of slavery. *Political Theory* 30: 623–648.

McCarthy, Thomas. 2004. Coming to terms with our past, part II: On the morality and politics of reparations for slavery. *Political Theory* 32: 750–772.

McCombs, Maxwell, and Amy Reynolds, eds. 1999. *The poll with a human face: The National Issues Convention experiment in political communication*. Mahwah, NJ: Lawrence Erlbaum.

McCoy, Martha L., and Patrick L. Scully. 2002. Deliberative dialogue to expand civic engagement: What kind of talk does democracy need? *National Civic Review* 91(2): 117–135.

McCubbins, Mathew D., and Daniel B. Rodriguez. 2006. When does deliberating improve decisionmaking? Legal Studies Research Paper Series, University of San Diego School of Law No. 07-47: 61.

McGee, Rosemary, and John Gaventa. 2010. Review of impact and effectiveness of transparency and accountability initiatives. http://www.ids.ac.uk/index.cfm?objectid=7E5D1074-969C-58FC-7B586DE3994C885C.

McLeod, Jack M., Dietram A. Scheufele, Patricia Moy, Edward M. Horowitz, R. Lance Holbert, Weiwu Zhang, Stephen Zubric, and Jessica Zubric. 1999. Understanding deliberation: The effects of discussion networks on participation in a public forum. *Communication Research* 26: 743–774.

Melville, Keith, Taylor L. Willingham, and John R. Dedrick. 2005. National Issues Forums: A network of communities promoting public deliberation. In *The deliberative democracy handbook: Strategies for effective civic engagement in the 21st century*, ed. John Gastil and Peter Levine, 37–58. San Francisco: Jossey-Bass.

Mendelberg, Tali. 2002. The deliberative citizen: Theory and evidence. In *Political decision making, deliberation and participation*, ed. Michael X. Delli Carpini, Leonie Huddy, and Robert Y. Shapiro, 151–193. Amsterdam: JAI.

Mendelberg, Tali, and John Oleske. 2000. Race and public deliberation. *Political Communication* 17(2): 169–191.

Mettler, Suzanne, and Joe Soss. 2004. The consequences of public policy for democratic citizenship: Bridging policy studies and mass politics. *Perspectives on Politics* 2: 55–73.

Michels, Ank M. B., and Laurens J. de Graaf. 2010. Examining citizen participation: Local participatory policy making and democracy. *Local Government Studies* 36(4): 477–491.

Michinov, Nicolas, and Corine Primois. 2005. Improving productivity and creativity in online groups through social comparison process: New evidence for asynchronous electronic brainstorming. *Computers in Human Behavior* 21: 11–28.

Mill, John Stuart. [1862] 1962. *Considerations on representative government*. Introduction by F.A. Hayek. South Bend, IN: Gateway Editions.

Min, Seong-Jae. 2007. Online vs. face-to-face deliberation: Effects on civic engagement. *Journal of Computer Mediated Communication* 12: 1369–1387.

Min, Seong-Jae. 2009. Deliberation, East meets West: Exploring the cultural dimension of citizen deliberation. *Acta Politica* 44: 439–458.

Morehouse, Diane L. 2009. *Horizons sustained effects: A report on continuing leadership and poverty reduction activities and outcomes in Horizons alumni communities*. Minneapolis, MN: Northwest Area Foundation.

Morone, James. 1992. *The democratic wish*. New York: Basic Books.

Morrell, Michael. 1999. Citizens' evaluations of participatory democratic procedures. *Political Research Quarterly* 52: 293–322.

Morrell, Michael E. 2003. Survey and experimental evidence for a reliable and valid measure of internal political efficacy. *Public Opinion Quarterly* 67: 589–602.

Morrell, Michael E. 2005. Deliberation, democratic decision-making and internal political efficacy. *Political Behavior* 27(1): 49–70.

Morrell, M. E. 2007. Empathy and democratic education. *Public Affairs Quarterly* 21(4): 381–402.

Morrell, Michael E. 2010. *Empathy and democracy: Feeling, thinking, and deliberation*. University Park: Pennsylvania State University Press.

Moscovici, Serge. 1976. *Social influence and social change*. New York: Academic Press.

Moscovici, Serge. 1980. Toward a theory of conversion behavior. *Advances in Experimental Social Psychology* 13: 209–239.

Mouffe, Chantal. 2000. *The democratic paradox*. London: Verso.

Mouffe, Chantal. 2005. *The return of the political*. New York: Verso.

Mueller, John. E. 1999. *Capitalism, democracy, and Ralph's pretty good grocery store*. Princeton: Princeton University Press.

Muhlberger, Peter. 2003. Political values, political attitudes, and attitude polarization in internet political discussion: Political transformation or politics as usual? *Communications* 28: 107–133.

Muhlberger, Peter. 2005a. The Virtual Agora Project: A research design for studying democratic deliberation. *Journal of Public Deliberation* 1(1): Article 5.

Muhlberger, Peter. 2005b. Attitude change in face-to-face and online political deliberation: Conformity, information, or perspective taking? Paper presented at the annual meeting of the American Political Science Association, Washington, DC, September 1. http://www.allacademic.com/meta/p41612_index.html.

Muhlberger, Peter. 2006. Report to the deliberative democracy consortium: Building a deliberation measurement toolbox. http://www.geocities.com/pmuhl78/abstracts.html#VirtualAgoraReport.

Muhlberger, Peter. 2007. Pro-social reasoning in deliberative policy choices. *International Journal of Public Participation* 1: 1–18.

Muhlberger, Peter, and Jennifer Stromer-Galley. 2009. Automated and hand-coded measurement of deliberative quality in online policy discussions. In *Proceedings of the 10th International Digital Government Research Conference*, ed. Soon Ae Chun, Rodrigo Sandoval, and Priscilla Regan, 35–41. Digital Government Society of North America, Puebla, Mexico, May 17–21.

Muhlberger, Peter, and Lori M. Weber. 2006. Lessons from the virtual agora project: The effects of agency, identity, information, and deliberation on political knowledge. *Journal of Public Deliberation* 2(1): Article 13.

Musso, Juliet, Christopher Weare, Thomas A. Bryer, and Terry L. Cooper. 2011. Toward "strong democracy" in global cities? Social capital building, action research, and the Los Angeles Neighborhood Council experience. *Public Administration Review* 71(1): 102–111.

Mutz, Diana C. 2002a. Cross-cutting social networks. *American Political Science Review* 96: 295–309.

Mutz, Diana C. 2002b. The consequences of cross-cutting networks for political participation. *American Journal of Political Science* 46: 838–855.

Mutz, Diana C. 2006. *Hearing the other side: Deliberative versus participatory democracy*. New York: Cambridge University Press.

Mutz, Diana C. 2008. Is deliberative democracy a falsifiable theory? *Annual Review of Political Science* 11: 521–538.

Myers, David G. 2008. *Social psychology*. 9th ed. San Francisco: McGraw-Hill.

Nabatchi, Tina. 2007. Deliberative democracy: The effects of participation in political efficacy. PhD diss., School of Public and Environmental Affairs, Indiana University.

Nabatchi, Tina. 2010a. Addressing the citizenship and democratic deficits: The potential of deliberative democracy for public administration. *American Review of Public Administration* 40(4): 376–399.

Nabatchi, Tina. 2010b. Deliberative democracy and citizenship: In search of the efficacy effect. *Journal of Public Deliberation* 6(2): Article 8.

Nabatchi, Tina. 2011. Thinking about design: Participatory systems and processes. *Public Administration Review* 71(1): 6–15.

Nabatchi, Tina. 2012a. *A Manager's Guide to Evaluating Citizen Participation*. Washington, D.C.: IBM Center for the Business of Government.

Nabatchi, Tina. 2012b. Putting the "public" back in public values research: Designing public participation to identify and respond to public values. *Public Administration Review* doi: 10.1111/j.1540-6210.2011.02544.x.

Nabatchi, Tina, and Cynthia Farrar. 2011. *Bridging the gap between the public and public officials: What do public officials want and need to know about public deliberation?* Washington, DC: Deliberative Democracy Consortium.

Nabatchi, Tina, and Dragan Stanisevski. 2008. Social inclusion: Building political efficacy with deliberative democracy. Paper presented at the Midwest Political Science Association Conference, Chicago, IL, April. http://citation.allacademic.com/meta/p_mla_apa_research_citation/2/6/6/5/6/pages266566/p266566-1.php. August 05, 2011.

Nass, Clifford, and Laurie Mason. 1990. On the study of technology and task: A variable-based approach. In *Organizations and communication technology*, ed. Janet Fulk and Charles W. Steinfeld, 46–67. Newbury Park, CA: Sage.

National Coalition for Dialogue and Deliberation (NCDD). 2008. Engagement Streams Framework. http://ncdd.org/rc/wp-content/uploads/2010/08/full-streams-hi-res.pdf.

National Coalition for Dialogue and Deliberation (NCDD). 2010. Resource Guide on Public Engagement. http://www.ncdd.org/files/NCDD2010_Resource_Guide.pdf.

National Conference on Citizenship. 2008. Civic health of the nation: Election energizing and engaging Americans, but many are frustrated. http://www.civicyouth.org/PopUps/08_pr_civic_index.pdf.

National League of Cities. 2008. *Governing economies in the 21st century*. Washington, DC: National League of Cities.

Neblo, Michael. 2005. Thinking through democracy: Between the theory and practice of deliberative politics. *Acta Politica* 40: 169–181.

Neblo, Michael. 2007. Family disputes: Diversity in defining and measuring deliberation. *Swiss Political Science Review* 13(4): 527–557.

Neblo, Michael. 2010. Change for the better? Linking the mechanisms of deliberative opinion change to normative theory. Working paper, Department of Political Science, Ohio State University.

Neblo, Michael A., Kevin M. Esterling, Ryan P. Kennedy, David M. J. Lazer, and Anand E. Sokhey. 2010. Who wants to deliberate—and why? *American Political Science Review* 104(3): 566–583.

Nemeth, Charlan J. 1986. Differential contributions of majority and minority influence. *Psychology Review* 93: 23–32.

Nemeth, Charlan J., Jeffrey Endicott, and Joel Wachtler. 1976. From the '50s to the '70s: Women in jury deliberations. *Sociometry* 39(4): 293–304.

Nemeth, Charlan J., and Julianne Kwan. 1985. Originality of word associations as a function of majority and minority influence. *Social Psychology Quarterly* 48: 277–282.

Newman, Anne. 2009. All together now? Some egalitarian concerns about deliberation and education policy-making. *Theory and Research in Education* 7: 65–87.

Nie, Norman H., Jane Junn, and Kenneth Stehlik-Barry. 1996. *Education and democratic citizenship in America*. Chicago: University of Chicago Press.

Niemi, Richard G., Stephen C. Craig, and Franco Mattei. 1991. Measuring internal political efficacy in the 1988 national election study. *American Political Science Review* 85: 1407–1413.

Nye, Joseph S., Philip Zelikow, and David C. King, eds. 1997. *Why people don't trust government*. Cambridge: Harvard University Press.

OECD (Organisation for Economic Co-operation and Development). 2009. *Evaluating public participation in policy making.* Paris: OECD.

O' Flynn, Ian. 2007. Review article: Divided societies and deliberative democracy. *British Journal of Political Science* 37: 731–751.

O'Flynn, Ian. 2010. Deliberative democracy, the public interest, and the consociational model. *Political Studies* 58(3): 572–589.

O'Leary, Brendan. 1999. The nature of the British-Irish Agreement. *New Left Review* 233: 66–96.

O'Leary, Kevin. 2006. *Saving democracy: A plan for real representation in America.* Palo Alto: Stanford University Press.

Ohlin, Tomas. 1971. Local democracy in the telecommunications age. *Svenska Dagbladet* (August 8): 1.

Olson, Mancur. 1965. *The logic of collective action: Public goods and the theory of groups.* Cambridge: Harvard University Press.

Orlitzky, Mark, and Randy Y. Hirokawa. 2001. To err is human, to correct for it divine: A meta-analysis of research testing the functional theory of group decision-making effectiveness. *Small Group Research* 32: 313–341.

Osborn, Alex F. 1957. *Applied imagination.* 2nd ed. New York: Charles Scribner's Sons.

Page, Benjamin I., and Lawrence R. Jacobs. 2010. Understanding public opinion on deficits and social security. Working Paper No. 2, Roosevelt Institute.

Pammett, Jon. 2009. Participation and the good citizen. In *Activating the citizen: Dilemmas of participation in Europe and Canada,* ed. J. DeBardeleben and J. Pammett. London: Palgrave Macmillan.

Parkinson, John. 2003. Legitimacy problems in deliberative democracy. *Political Studies* 51: 180–196.

Pateman, Carole. 1970. *Participation and democratic theory.* Cambridge: Cambridge University Press.

Patterson, Thomas E. 2002. *The vanishing voter.* New York: Knopf.

Patton, Michael Quinn. 1994. Developmental evaluation. *Evaluation Practice* 15: 311–319.

Pearce, W. Barnett, and Stephen W. Littlejohn. 1997. *Moral conflict: When social worlds collide.* Thousand Oaks, CA: Sage.

Pearce, W. Barnett, and Kim Pearce. 2010. *Aligning the work of government to strengthen the work of citizens: A study of public administrators in local and regional government.* Dayton, OH: Kettering Foundation. http://publicpolicy.pepperdine.edu/davenport-institute/content/Aligning_the_Work_of_Government.pdf.

Pellizzoni, Luigi. 2001. The myth of the best argument: Power, deliberation, and reason. *British Journal of Sociology* 52: 59–86.

Peterson, Pete. 2009. Kauai, Hawaii: Local merchants make waves. *Everyday Democracy,* July 20. http://www.everyday-democracy.org/en/Article.1006.aspx.

Phillips, Anne. 1995. *The politics of presence.* Oxford: Oxford University Press.

Pierce, Jason L., Grant Neeley, and Jeffrey Budziak. 2008. Can deliberative democracy work in hierarchical organizations? *Journal of Public Deliberation* 4(1): Article 14.

Pincock, Heather. 2011. Does deliberation make better citizens? Examining the case of community conflict mediation. PhD diss., Maxwell School of Citizenship and Public Affairs, Syracuse University.

Pincus-Roth, Zachary. 2006. *Avenue Q.* New York: Hyperion.

Plein, L. Christopher, Kenneth E. Green, and David G. Williams. 1998. Organic planning: A new approach to public participation in local governance. *Social Science Journal* 35(4): 509–523.

Polletta, Francesca. 2006. *It was like a fever: Storytelling in protest and politics.* Chicago: University of Chicago Press.

Polletta, Francesca. 2008. Just talk: Public deliberation after 9/11. *Journal of Public Deliberation* 4(1): Article 2.

Polletta, Francesca, Pang Ching Bobby Chen, and Christopher Anderson. 2009. Is information good for deliberation? Link-posting in an online forum. *Journal of Public Deliberation* 5(1): Article 2.

Polletta, Francesca, and John Lee. 2006. Is storytelling good for democracy? Rhetoric in public deliberation after 9/11. *American Sociological Review* 71: 699–723.

Poor, Nathaniel. 2005. Mechanisms of an online public sphere: The website slashdot. *Journal of Computer-Mediated Communication* 10(2): Article 4.

Posner, Richard. 2003. *Law, pragmatism, and democracy*. Cambridge, MA: Harvard University Press.

Posner, Richard. 2004. Smooth sailing. *Legal Affairs* January/February: 41–42.

Price, Vincent. 2009. Citizens deliberating online: Theory and some evidence. In *Online deliberation: Design, research, and practice*, ed. Todd Davies and Seeta Peña Gangadharan, 37–58. Stanford, CA: CSLI Publications.

Price, Vincent, and Joseph N. Cappella. 2002. Online deliberation and its influence: The Electronic Dialogue Project in Campaign 2000. *IT and Society* 1(1): 303–328.

Price, Vincent, Danna Goldthwaite, and Joseph N. Capella. 2002. Online deliberation, civic engagement, and social trust. Paper presented at the 2002 Annual Conference of the International Communication Association, Seoul, Korea.

Przeworski, Adam. 1998. Deliberation and ideological domination. In *Deliberative democracy*, ed. Jon Elster, 140–160. Cambridge: Cambridge University Press.

Przeworski, Adam. 1999. Minimalist conception of democracy: A defense. In *Democracy's value*, ed. Ian Shapiro and Casiano Hacker-Cordón, 23–55. Cambridge: Cambridge University Press.

Putnam, Robert D. 1995. Bowling alone: America's declining social capital. *Journal of Democracy* 6(1): 65–78.

Putnam, Robert D. 2000. *Bowling alone: The collapse and revival of American community*. New York: Simon and Schuster.

Rai, Shirin. 2007. Deliberative democracy and the politics of redistribution: The case of the Indian Panchayats. *Hypatia* 22(4): 64–80.

Ratner, Robert S. 2005. The B. C. Citizen's Assembly: The Public Hearings and Deliberations Stage. *Canadian Parliamentary Review* 28: 24–33.

Rawls, John. 1971. *A theory of justice*. Cambridge: Harvard University Press.

Rawls, John. 1993. *Political liberalism*. New York: Columbia University Press.

Resnick, Paul, Neophytos Iacovou, Mitesh Suchak, Peter Bergstrom, and John Riedl. 1994. GroupLens: An open architecture for collaborative filtering of netnews. In *Proceedings of ACM 1994 Conference on Computer Supported Cooperative Work*, chaired by John B. Smith, F. Don Smith, and Thomas W. Malone, 175–186. New York: ACM.

Rhee, June W., and Eun-mee Kim. 2009. Deliberation on the net: Lessons from a field experiment. In *Online deliberation: Design, research, and practice*, ed. Todd Davies and Seeta Peña Gangadharan, 223–232. Stanford, CA: CSLI Publications.

Ridgeway, Cecilia L. 1981. Non-conformity, competence, and influence in groups: A test of two theories. *American Sociological Review* 46: 333–347.

Ridgeway, Cecilia L. 1987. Nonverbal behavior, dominance, and the basis of status in task groups. *American Sociological Review* 52: 683–694.

Riggle, Ellen D., Victor Ottati, Robert S. Wyer, James Kuklinski, and Nobert Schwarz. 1992. Bases of political judgments: The role of stereotypic and nonstereotypic information. *Political Behavior* 14(1): 67–87.

Riker, William. 1982. *Liberalism against populism*. San Francisco: W. H. Freeman.

Rivera, Krisela, Nancy J. Cooke, and Jeff A. Bauhs. 1996. The effects of emotional icons on remote communication. In *CHI '96 Conference companion on human factors in computing systems: Common ground*, ed. Michael J. Tauber, 99–100. New York: ACM.

Roberts, Nancy. 2004. Public deliberation in an age of direct citizen participation. *American Review of Public Administration* 34(4): 315–353.

Roberts, Nancy C., ed. 2008. *The age of direct citizen participation*. Armonk, NY: M. E. Sharpe.

Roberts and Kay, Inc. 2000. *Toward competent communities: Best practices for producing community-wide study circles*. Lexington, KY: Topsfield Foundation.

Robinson, Laura. 2005. Debating the events of September 11th: Discursive and interactional dynamics in three online fora. *Journal of Computer-Mediated Communication* 10. http://jcmc.indiana.edu/vol10/issue4/robinson.html.

Roch, Sylvia G., and Roya Ayman. 2005. Group decision making and perceived decision success: The role of communication medium. *Group Dynamics: Theory, Research, and Practice* 9: 15–31.

Rocha Menocal, Alina, and Bhavna Sharma. 2008. *Joint evaluation of citizens' voice and accountability: Synthesis report.* London: Department for International Development.

Rose, Jonathon. 2009. Institutionalizing participation through citizens' assemblies. In *Activating the citizen: Dilemmas of participation in Europe and Canada*, ed. Joan DeBardeleben and Jon Pammett, 214–231. London: Palgrave Macmillan.

Rose, Jeremy, and Øystein Sæbø. 2010. Designing deliberation systems. *The Information Society* 26: 228–240.

Rosenberg, Shawn W., ed. 2007a. *Democracy, deliberation and participation: Can the people decide?* London: Palgrave Macmillan.

Rosenberg, Shawn W. 2007b. Types of discourse and the democracy of deliberation. In *Democracy, deliberation and participation: Can the people decide?* ed. Shawn W. Rosenberg, 130–158. London: Palgrave Macmillan.

Rosenstone, Steven J., and John M. Hansen. 1993. *Mobilization, participation, and democracy in America.* New York: Macmillan.

Rossi, Peter H., Mark W. Lipsey, and Howard E. Freeman. 2004. *Evaluation: A systematic approach.* 7th ed. Thousand Oaks, CA: Sage.

Rotolo, Thomas. 2000. A time to join, a time to quit: The influence of life cycle transitions on voluntary association membership. *Social Forces* 78: 1133–1161.

Rowe, Gene, and Lynn J Frewer. 2000. Public participation methods: A framework for evaluation. *Science, Technology and Human Values* 25(1): 3–29.

Rowe, Gene, and Lynn J. Frewer. 2004. Evaluating public-participation exercises: A research agenda. *Science, Technology and Human Values* 29: 512–556.

Rowe, Gene, and Lynn J. Frewer. 2005. A typology of public engagement mechanisms. *Science, Technology & Human Values* 30(2): 251–290.

Rushdon, Beth. 2007. Status and participation: A study of process design in Cambodian committees. *International Journal of Public Participation* 1: 1–21.

Rydin, Yvonne, and Mark Pennington. 2000. Public participation and local environmental planning: The collective action problem and the potential of social capital. *Local Environment* 5: 153–169.

Ryfe, David M. 2002. The practice of deliberative democracy: A study of 16 deliberative organizations. *Political Communication* 19: 359–377.

Ryfe, David M. 2005. Does deliberative democracy work? *Annual Review of Political Science* 8: 49–71.

Ryfe, David M. 2006. Narrative and deliberation in small group forums. *Journal of Applied Communication Research* 34: 72–93.

Ryfe, David M. 2007. Toward a sociology of deliberation. *Journal of Public Deliberation* 3(1): Article 3.

Sack, Warren, John Kelly, and Michael Dale. 2009. Searching the net for differences of opinion. In *Online deliberation: Design, research, and practice*, ed. Todd Davies and Seeta Peña Gangadharan, 95–104. Stanford, CA: CSLI Publications.

Saegert, Susan. 2006. Building civic capacity in urban neighborhoods: An empirically grounded anatomy. *Journal of Urban Affairs* 28(3): 275–294.

Salustri, Filippo A. 2005. Brainstorming. http://deed.ryerson.ca/~fil/t/brainstorm.html.

Sanders, Lynn M. 1997. Against deliberation. *Political Theory* 25: 347–376.

Schaap, Andrew. 2004. Political reconciliation as struggles for recognition. *Social and Legal Studies* 13: 523–540.

Schaap, Andrew. 2005. *Political reconciliation.* New York: Routledge.

Schkade, David, Cass R. Sunstein, and Reid Hastie. 2006. What happened on deliberation day? Working Paper No. 298, John M. Olin Law and Economics Research Series. Working Paper No. 06-19, AEI Brookings Joint Center for Regulatory Studies.

Schlosberg, David, Steve Zavestoski, and Stuart Shulman. 2009. Deliberation in e-rulemaking? The problem of mass participation. In *Online deliberation: Design, research, and practice*, ed. Todd Davies and Seeta Peña Gangadharan, 133–148. Stanford, CA: CSLI Publications.

Schlozman, Kay L., Sidney Verba, and Henry E. Brady. 1994. Participation's not a paradox: The view from American activists. *British Journal of Political Science* 25: 1–36.

Schneider, Steven M. 1997. Expanding the public sphere through computer-mediated communication: Political discussion about abortion in a usenet newsgroup. PhD diss., Department of Political Science, Massachusetts Institute of Technology.

Schober, Michael F., and Herbert H. Clark. 1989. Understanding by addressees and overhearers. *Cognitive Psychology* 21(April): 211–232.

Schuessler, Alexander A. 2000. *A logic of expressive choice*. Princeton: Princeton University Press.

Schuler, Douglas. 2009. Online civic deliberation with e-liberate. In *Online deliberation: Design, research, and practice*, ed. Todd Davies and Seeta Peña Gangadharan, 293–302. Stanford, CA: CSLI Publications.

Schumpeter, Joseph A. 1942. *Capitalism, socialism and democracy*. 1st ed. New York: Harper and Row.

Schumpeter, Joseph A. 1950. *Capitalism, socialism, and democracy*. 3rd ed. New York: Harper and Row.

Scully, Patrick L., and Martha L. McCoy. 2005. Study circles: Local deliberation as the cornerstone of deliberative democracy. In *The deliberative democracy handbook: Strategies for effective civic engagement in the 21st century*, ed. John Gastil and Peter Levine, 199–212. San Francisco: Jossey-Bass.

Searing, Donald D., Frederick Solt, Pamela Johnston Conover, and Ivor Crewe. 2007. Public discussion in the deliberative system: Does it make better citizens? *British Journal of Political Science* 37: 587–618.

Sen, Amartya. 1999. Democracy as a universal value. *Journal of Democracy* 10(3): 3–17

Serageldin, Mona, John Driscoll, Liz Meléndez San Miguel, Luis Valenzuela, Consuelo Bravo, Elda Solloso, Clara Solá-Morales, and Thomas Watkin. 2003. *Assessment of participatory budgeting in Brazil*. Washington, DC: Inter-American Development Bank.

Shapiro, Ian. 1999. Enough of deliberation: Politics is about interests and power. In *Deliberative Politics*, ed. S. Macedo, 28–38. New York: Oxford Press.

Shapiro, Ian. 2002. Optimal deliberation. *Journal of Political Philosophy* 10(2): 196–211.

Shapiro, Ian. 2010. *Political representation*. Cambridge: Cambridge University Press.

Simmons, Erin, and Joel Mills, eds. 2010. *Bridgeport, CT: Sustainability Design Action Team report*. Washington, DC: American Institute of Architects.

Sirianni, Carmen, and Lew Friedland. 2001. *Civic innovation in America: Community empowerment, public policy, and the movement for civic renewal*. Berkeley: University of California Press.

Siu, Alice. 2008. The moderation effect of argument quality on polarization in deliberative polls. Paper presented at the annual meeting of the American Political Science Association Annual Meeting, Boston, MA, August.

Siu, Alice. 2009. Look who's talking: Examining social influence, opinion change, and argument quality in deliberation. PhD diss., Department of Communication, Stanford University.

Skidmore, Paul, and Kirsten Bound. 2008. *The everyday democracy index*. London: Demos.

Skocpol, Theda, and Morris P. Fiorina, eds. 1999. *Civic engagement in American democracy*. Washington, DC: Brookings Institution.

Smith, David H. 1994. Determinants of voluntary association participation and volunteering. *Nonprofit and Voluntary Sector Quarterly* 23: 243–263.

Smith, Tom W. 1999. The delegates' experience. In *The poll with a human face: The National Issues Convention experiment in political communication*, ed. Maxwell McCombs and Amy Reynolds, 39–58. Mahwah, NJ: Lawrence Erlbaum.

Smock, Kristina. 2004. *Democracy in action: Community organizing and urban change*. New York: Columbia University Press.

Sniderman, Paul M., Richard A. Brody, and Phillip E. Tetlock. 1991. *Reasoning and choice: Explorations in political psychology*. New York: Cambridge University Press.

Spink, Peter K., Naomi Hossain, and Nina J. Best. 2009. Hybrid public action. *Institute of Development Studies Bulletin* 40(6): 128.

Stanisevski, Dragan M. 2006. Multicultural discourse: A comparative case study of government practices in facilitation of multicultural public discourse in South Florida. PhD diss., Florida Atlantic University.

Stanisevski, Dragan M. 2008. In the shadows of nationalisms: Social inclusion and public recognition of Roma and Egyptian identities in Macedonia. *Administrative Theory & Praxis* 30(4): 476–495.

Stanisevski, Dragan M. 2010. Anti-essentialism in multicultural societies: Facilitating multicultural discourse through tolerance of cultural pluralism. *International Journal of Organization Theory and Behavior* 13(1): 60–87.

Stanisevski, Dragan M., and Hugh T. Miller. 2009. The role of government in managing intercultural relations: Multicultural discourse and the politics of culture recognition in Macedonia. *Administration & Society* 41(5): 551–575.

Stanley, J. Woody, Christopher Weare, and Juliet Musso. 2004. Participation, deliberative democracy, and the internet: Lessons from a national forum on commercial vehicle safety. In *Democracy online: The prospects for political renewal through the internet*, ed. Peter M. Shane, 167–179. New York: Routledge.

Stasavage, David. 2004. *Public versus private deliberation in a representative democracy.* http://www.polarizationandconflict.org/oslopub/Stasavage-private8.pdf.

Steenbergen, Marco R., André Bächtiger, Markus Spörndli, and Jürg Steiner. 2003. Measuring political deliberation: A discourse quality index. *Comparative European Politics* 1: 21–48.

Steiner, Jürg. 2012. *The foundations of deliberative democracy: Empirical research and normative implications.* Cambridge: Cambridge University Press.

Steiner, Jürg, Andre Bächtiger, Markus Spörndli, and Marco R. Steenbergen. 2004. *Deliberative politics in action: Analyzing parliamentary discourse.* Cambridge: Cambridge University Press.

Stone, Clarence N. 2001. Civic capacity and urban education. *Urban Affairs Review* 36: 595–619.

Strodtbeck, Fred. L., and Richard D. Mann. 1956. Sex role differentiation in jury deliberations. *Sociometry* 19(1): 3–11.

Strodtbeck, Fred. L., Rita M. James, and Charles Hawkins. 1957. Social status in jury deliberations. *American Sociological Review* 22(6): 713–319.

Stromer-Galley, Jennifer. 2007. Measuring deliberation's content: A coding scheme. *Journal of Public Deliberation* 3(1): Article 12.

Stromer-Galley, Jennifer, and Peter Muhlberger. 2009. Agreement and disagreement in group deliberation: Effects on deliberation, satisfaction, future engagement, and decision legitimacy. *Political Communication* 26(2): 173–192.

Stromer-Galley, Jennifer, and Alexis Wichowski. 2010. Political discussion online. In *The handbook of internet studies*, eds. Mia Consalvo, Robert Burnett, and Charles Ess, 168–187. Chichester, UK: Blackwell.

Sturgis, Patrick, Caroline Roberts, and Nick Allum. 2005. A different take on the deliberative poll: Information, deliberation, and attitude constraint. *Public Opinion Quarterly* 69(1): 30–65.

Suchman, Lucy, Jeannette Blomberg, Julian E. Orr, and Randall Trigg. 1999. Reconstructing technologies as social practice. *American Behavioral Scientist* 43: 392–408.

Sulkin, Tracy, and Adam F. Simon. 2001. Habermas in the lab: A study of deliberation in an experimental setting. *Political Psychology* 22(4): 809–826.

Sundeen, Richard D. 1992. Differences in personal goals and attitudes among volunteers. *Nonprofit and Voluntary Sector Quarterly* 21: 271–291.

Sunstein, Cass R. 2002. The law of group polarization. *Journal of Political Philosophy* 10(2): 175–195.

Sunstein, Cass R. 2003. The law of group polarization. In *Debating deliberative democracy*, ed. J. S. Fishkin and P. Laslett, 80–101. Oxford: Blackwell.

Sunstein, Cass R. 2006. *Infotopia: How many minds produce knowledge.* New York: Oxford University Press.

Sunstein, Cass R. 2009. *Going to extremes: How like minds unite and divide.* Oxford: Oxford University Press.

Susskind, Larry. 2009. How should you respond to the noisy health reform critics? *The Consensus Building Approach.* August 11. http://theconsensusbuildingapproach. blogspot. com/2009/08/how-should-you-respond-to-noisy-health.html.

Sutherland, Keith. 2008. *A people's parliament: A revised blueprint for a very English revolution.* Exeter: Imprint Academic.

Sutton, Robert I., and Andrew Hargadon. 1996. Brainstorming groups in context: Effectiveness in a product design firm. *Administrative Science Quarterly* 41 (December): 685–718.

Svensson, Jakob. 2008. Expressive rationality: A different approach for understanding participation in municipal deliberative practices. *Communication, Culture and Critique* 1: 203–221.

Talisse, Robert B. 2005. Deliberative democracy defended: A response to Posner's political realism. *Res Publica* 11: 185–199.

Tannen, Deborah. 1994. *Talking from 9 to 5: How women's and men's conversational styles affect who gets heard, who gets credit and what gets done at work.* London: Virago.

Taylor, Charles. 1994. The politics of recognition. In *Multiculturalism: Examining the politics of recognition,* ed. Amy Gutmann, 25–75. Princeton, NJ: Princeton University Press.

Teixeira, Ana C., Jorge Kayano, and Luciana Tatagiba. 2007. Saúde, controle social e política pública. *Observatório de Direitos do Cidadão, Caderno do Observatório dos Direitos do Cidadão* 29.

Teske, Nathan. 1997. *Political activists in America: The identity construction model of political participation.* New York: Cambridge University Press.

Thomas, Nancy L., and Matt Leighninger. 2010. *No better time: A 2010 report on opportunities and challenges for deliberative democracy.* The Democracy Imperative and the Deliberative Democracy Consortium. http://www.unh.edu/democracy/pdf/NBTReport_1.pdf.

Thomassen, Lasse. 2010. The politics of iterability: Benhabib, the hijab, and democratic iterations. *Polity* 43(1): 128–149.

Thompson, Dennis. 2008. Deliberative democratic theory and empirical political science. *Annual Review of Political Science* 11: 497–520.

Thompson, Simon, and Paul Hoggett. 2001. The emotional dynamics of deliberative democracy. *Policy and Politics* 23(3): 351–364.

de Tocqueville, Alexis. [1835/1840] 2000. *Democracy in America.* Trans. Harvey C. Mansfield and Delba Winthrop. Chicago: University of Chicago Press.

Toker, Caitlin Wills. 2005. The deliberative ideal and co-optation in the Georgia Ports Authority's stakeholder evaluation group. *Environmental Communication Yearbook* 2: 19–48.

Townsend, Rebecca. 2009. Town meeting as a communication event: Democracy's act sequence. *Research on Language and Social Interaction* 42(1): 68–89.

Traynor, Ian. 2007. Switzerland reeling as radicals create havoc at rightwing political rally. *The Guardian* October 8.

Traynor, William. 2002. *Reflections on community organizing and resident engagement in the rebuilding communities initiative.* Baltimore, MD: Annie E. Casey Foundation.

Trénel, Matthias. 2004. *Measuring the quality of online deliberation. Coding scheme 2.4.* Berlin: Social Science Research Center.

Trénel, Matthias. 2009. Facilitation and inclusive deliberation. In *Online deliberation: Design, research, and practice,* ed. Todd Davies and Seeta Peña Gangadharan, 253–257. Stanford, CA: CSLI Publications.

Tucey, Cindy Boyles. 2010. Online vs. face-to-face deliberation on the global warming and stem cell issues. Paper presented at the Annual Meeting of the Western Political Science Association, San Francisco, April.

Turner, John C. 1991. *Social influence.* Pacific Grove, CA: Brooks/Cole.

Tyler, Tom R., and E. Allan Lind. 2001. Procedural justice. In *Handbook of justice research in law,* ed. Joseph Sanders and V. Lee Hamilton, 65–92. New York: Springer.

Uhr, John. 1998. *Deliberative democracy in Australia: The changing place of parliament.* Cambridge: Cambridge University Press.

Ulbig, Stacy G., and Carolyn L. Funk. 1999. Conflict avoidance and political participation. *Political Behavior* 21: 265–282.

Urbinati, Nadia. 2006. *Representative democracy: Principles and genealogy.* Chicago: University of Chicago Press.

Vecchione, Michele, and Gian V. Caprara. 2009. Personality determinants of political participation: The contribution of traits and self-efficacy beliefs. *Personality and Individual Differences* 46: 487–492.

Verba, Sidney, and Norman H. Nie. 1972. *Participation in America: Political democracy and social equality.* New York: Harper and Row.

Verba, Sidney, Kay L. Schlozman, and Henry E. Brady. 1995. *Voice and equality: Civic voluntarism in American politics.* Cambridge: Harvard University Press.

Vidmar, Neil, and Valerie P. Hans. 2007. *American juries: The verdict.* Amherst, NY: Prometheus.

Wagle, Swamim, and Parmesh Shah. 2003. *Case study 2—Porto Alegre, Brazil: Participatory approaches in budgeting and public expenditure management.* Social Development Notes Note No. 71. Washington, DC: World Bank. http://siteresources.worldbank.org/INTP-CENG/1143372-1116506093229/20511036/sdn71.pdf.

Walmsley, Heather L. 2009. Mad scientists bend the frame of biobank governance in British Columbia. *Journal of Public Deliberation* 5(1): Article 6.

Walsh, Katherine Cramer. 2003. The democratic potential of civic dialogue on race. Paper presented at the Annual Meeting of the Midwest Political Science Association, Chicago.

Walsh, Katherine Cramer. 2004. *Talking about politics: Informal groups and social identity in American life.* Chicago: University of Chicago Press.

Walsh, Katherine Cramer. 2007. *Talking about race: Community dialogues and the politics of disagreement.* Chicago: University of Chicago Press.

Walzer, Michael. 1997. *On toleration.* New Haven, CT: Yale University Press.

Wampler, Brian. 2007. A guide to participatory budgeting. In *Participatory budgeting,* ed. Anwar Shah, 21–54. Washington, DC: World Bank.

Wampler, Brian. 2009. *Participatory budgeting in Brazil: Contestation, cooperation, and accountability.* University Park: Pennsylvania State University Press.

Wampler, Brian, and Leonardo Avritzer. 2004. Públicos participativos: Sociedade civil e novas instituições no Brasil democrático. In *Participação e deliberação: Teoria democrática e experiências institucionais no Brasil contemporâneo,* ed. Vera S. Coelho and Marcos Nobre. São Paulo: 34 Letras.

Wang, Xiaohu. 2001. Assessing public participation in US cities. *Public Performance and Management Review* 24(4): 322–336.

Warren, Mark E. 1992. Democratic theory and self-transformation. *American Political Science Review* 86: 8–23.

Warren, Mark E. 1996. What should we expect from more democracy? Radically democratic responses to politics. *Political Theory* 241: 270.

Warren, Mark E. 2001. *Democracy and association.* Princeton: Princeton University Press.

Warren, Mark E. 2009. Citizen participation and democratic deficits: Considerations from the perspective of democratic theory. In *Activating the citizen,* ed. Joan P. DeBardeleben and Jon Pammett, 17–40. Chippenham and Eastbourne, UK: Palgrave MacMillan.

Warren, Mark E., and Hilary Pearse, eds. 2008. *Designing deliberative democracy: The British Columbia Citizens' Assembly.* Cambridge: Cambridge University Press.

Webler, Thomas, and Ortwin Renn. 1995. A brief primer on participation: Philosophy and practice. In *Fairness and competence in citizen participation: Evaluating models for environmental discourse,* ed. Ortwin Renn, Thomas Webler, and Peter Wiedemann, 17–33. Boston: Kluwer Academic.

Webler, Thomas, and Seth Tuler. 2000. Fairness and competence in citizen participation: Theoretical reflections from a case study. *Administration and Society* 32: 566–595.

Weiksner, G. Michael. 2005. e-thePeople.org: Large-scale, ongoing deliberation. In *The delibera-tive democracy handbook: Strategies for effective civic engagement in the 21st century*, ed. John Gastil and Peter Levine, 213–227. San Francisco: Jossey-Bass.

Weiss, Carol H. 1998. *Evaluation*. 2nd ed. Upper Saddle River, NJ: Prentice Hall.

Whyte, Glen. 1993. Escalating commitment in individual and group decision making: A prospect theory approach. *Organizational Behavior and Human Decision Processes* 54: 430–455.

Whyte, Glen, and Ariel S. Levi. 1994. The origins and function of the reference point in risky group decision making: The case of the Cuban missile crisis. *Journal of Behavioral Decision Making* 7(4): 243–260.

Wilhelm, Anthony G. 1999. Virtual sounding boards: How deliberative is online political discus-sion? In *Digital democracy: Discourse and decision making in the information age*, ed. Barry N. Hague and Brian Loader, 153–178. New York: Routledge.

Wilson, John, and Thomas Janoski. 1995. The contribution of religion to volunteer work. *Sociology of Religion* 56: 137–152.

Wilson, John, and Marc Musick. 1997. Work and volunteering: The long arm of the job. *Social Forces* 76: 251–272.

Wilson, John, and Marc Musick. 1998. The contribution of social resources to volunteering. *Social Science Quarterly* 79: 799–814.

Wojcieszak, Magdalena E., Young Min Baek, and Michael X. Delli Carpini. 2010. Delibera-tive and participatory democracy? Ideological strength and the processes leading from deliberation to political engagement. *International Journal of Public Opinion Research* 22: 154–180.

Woodard, Michael D. 1987. Voluntary association membership among Black Americans: The post-civil rights era. *Sociological Quarterly* 28: 285–301.

World Bank. 2008. *Brazil: Toward a more inclusive and effective participatory budget in Porto Alegre*. Washington, DC: World Bank.

Wright, Scott. 2009. The role of the moderator: Problems and possibilities for government-run online discussion forums. In *Online deliberation: Design, research, and practice*, ed. Todd Dav-ies and Seeta Peña Gangadharan, 233–242. Stanford, CA: CSLI Publications.

Wright, Scott, and John Street. 2007. Democracy, deliberation, and design: The case of online discussion forums. *New Media & Society* 9: 849–869.

Wyatt, Robert O., Elihu Katz, and Joohan Kim. 2000. Bridging the spheres: Political and personal conversation in public and private spaces. *Journal of Communication* 50: 71–92.

Yamada, Ryota, Hiroshi Nakajima, Jong-Eun Roselyn Lee, Scott B. Brave, Heidy Maldonado, Clifford Nass, and Yasunori Morishima. 2008. The design and implementation of socially-intelligent agents providing emotional support and cognitive support. *Journal of Japan Society for Fuzzy Theory and Intelligent Informatics* 20(4): 473–486.

Yankelovich, Daniel, and Will Friedman. 2011a. *Dialogue, deliberation and public judgment: Making democracy work in a complex world*. Nashville, TN: Vanderbilt University Press.

Yankelovich, Daniel, and Friedman, Will. 2011b. *Toward wiser public judgment*. Nashville, TN: Van-derbilt University Press.

York, Erin, and Benjamin Cornwell. 2006. Status on trial: Social characteristics and influence in the jury room. *Social Forces* 85(1): 455–477.

Young, Iris Marion. 1996. Communication and the other: Beyond deliberative democracy. In *De-mocracy and difference: Contesting the Boundaries of the Political*, ed. Seyla Benhabib, 120–135. Princeton: Princeton University Press.

Young, Iris Marion. 1999. Justice, inclusion, and deliberative democracy. In *Deliberative politics*, ed. Stephen Macedo. New York: Oxford Press.

Young, Iris Marion. 2000. *Inclusion and democracy*. New York: Oxford University Press.

Young, Iris Marion. 2001. Activist challenges to deliberative democracy. *Political Theory* 29(5): 670–690.

Young, Iris Marion. 2003. Activist challenges to deliberative democracy. In *Debating deliberative democracy*, ed. James S. Fishkin and Peter Laslett, 102–121. London: Blackwell.

Young, Iris Marion. 2004. Deliberation's darker side: Six questions for Iris Marion Young and Jane Mansbridge, interviewed by Archon Fung. *National Civic Review* Winter: 47–54.

Zhang, Weiyu. 2005. Are online discussions deliberate? A case study of a Chinese online discussion board. In *III International Conference on Communication and Reality. Digital Utopia in the Media: From Discourses to Facts. A Balance,* ed. Pere Masip and Josep Rom. Barcelona: Blanquerna Tecnologia i Serveis. http://www.weebly.com/uploads/2/2/2/7/222747/cicr_2005.pdf.

Zwicky, Fritz. 1967. The mophological approach to discovery, invention, research and construction. In *New methods of thought and procedure,* ed. Fritz Zwicky and Albert G. Wilson, 273–297. New York: Springer-Verlag.

INDEX

DATE DUE

ILL Due 6/12/13
10398488/

DEC 2 2 2015

DEC 1 0 2014

DEC 2 2 2015

BRODART, CO.   Cat. No. 23-221